10/13 11ᵒ
c 2002

Planning for Retirement Distributions

Tax, Financial, and Personal Aspects

Second Edition

AF876334

Planning for Retirement Distributions

Tax, Financial, and Personal Aspects

Second Edition

Eric Donner

Victor M. Finmann

A Panel Publication

Aspen Publishers, Inc.

This publication is designed to provide accurate and authoritative information in regard to the subject matter covered. It is sold with the understanding that the publisher is not engaged in rendering legal, accounting, or other professional services. If legal advice or other professional assistance is required, the services of a competent professional person should be sought.

—From a Declaration of Principles jointly adopted by
a Committee of the American Bar Association and
a Committee of Publishers and Associations

Copyright © 2002 by Panel Publishers
A Division of Aspen Publishers, Inc.
A Wolters Kluwer Company
www.panelpublishers.com

All rights reserved. No part of this publication may be reproduced or transmitted in any form or by any means, electronic or mechanical, including photocopy, recording, or any information storage and retrieval system, without permission in writing from the publisher. Requests for permission to make copies of any part of this publication should be mailed to:

Permissions
Panel Publishers
1185 Avenue of the Americas
New York, NY 10036

ISBN: 0-156-07232-7

Printed in the United States of America

1 2 3 4 5 6 7 8 9 0

About Panel Publishers

Panel Publishers—including the former Prentice Hall Law & Business, Little, Brown and Company's Professional Division, and Wiley Law Publications—is a leading publisher of authoritative and timely treatises, practice manuals, information services, and journals written by specialists to assist attorneys, financial and tax advisors, and other business professionals. Our mission is to provide practical, solution-based how-to information keyed to the latest legislative, judicial, and regulatory developments. We offer publications in the areas of compensation and benefits, pensions, payroll, employment, civil rights, taxation, financial planning, estate planning, and elder law.

Other Panel products on related topics include:

Books and Manuals

Individual Retirement Account Answer Book
Roth IRA Answer Book
Nonqualified Deferred Compensation Answer Book
Financial Planner's Guide to Qualified Retirement Plans
Retirement Financial Management for Clients Approaching and In Retirement
401(k) Answer Book
The Pension Answer Book
Pension Distribution Answer Book
Pension Investment Handbook
Executive Compensation Answer Book

Electronic Titles and Periodicals

Financial Planner's Library on CD-ROM
Panel Pension Library on CD-ROM
Journal of Deferred Compensation
Journal of Pension Planning and Compliance
401(k) Advisor
Journal of Pension Benefits

PANEL PUBLISHERS
A Division of Aspen Publishers, Inc.
Practical Solutions for Legal and Business Professionals
www.panelpublishers.com

SUBSCRIPTION NOTICE

This Panel product is updated on a periodic basis with supplements to reflect important changes in the subject matter. If you purchased this product directly from Panel, we have already recorded your subscription for the update service.

If, however, you purchased this product from a bookstore and wish to receive future updates and revised or related volumes billed separately with a 30-day examination review, please contact our Customer Service Department at 1-800-234-1660, or send your name, company name (if applicable), address, and the title of the product to:

PANEL PUBLISHERS
A Division of Aspen Publishers, Inc.
7201 McKinney Circle
Frederick, MD 21704

*This book is dedicated to my mother and father,
Nancy and Julius Donner.*

ABOUT THE AUTHORS

Eric Donner, CLU, ChFC

Eric Donner has worked in the estate and retirement planning industry since 1985. He obtained his Chartered Financial Consultant and Chartered Life Underwriter designations from the American College in 1993. Having in-depth knowledge of retirement distribution and IRA planning concepts and tax laws, Mr. Donner successfully developed a financial planning practice with an emphasis on estate planning for clients with large retirement assets. Subsequently, as President and CEO of Retirement Distribution Strategies (RDS), Mr. Donner trained and developed financial advisors in the emerging area of retirement distribution planning. During a period of two and a half years, Mr. Donner and his team of experts trained over 750 financial advisors as retirement distribution specialists. Currently, Mr. Donner is part of a consulting firm that works with select financial institutions to improve the quality of training and marketing related to retirement distribution planning and IRA rollovers.

Mr. Donner has been seen on CNNfn and CNN's "Your Money" and is a frequent speaker at industry trade shows and meetings throughout the financial services industry. Additionally, Mr. Donner has been interviewed by various magazines, including *Investment News, Bloomberg Wealth Manager, BusinessWeek,* and many others. He has also written numerous articles for trade magazines, including *National Underwriter, American Banker,* and *Journal of Financial Planning.*

Victor M. Finmann, Esq.

Victor M. Finmann is a tax, estate planning, and elder law attorney with a concentration in employee benefit plans and retirement distribution planning. He received his J.D. from Brooklyn Law School. Mr. Finmann has written several treatises and practice guides for the American Institute of Certified Public Accountants, Inc. (AICPA) and the National Business Institute, Inc. Throughout the past 26 years, Mr. Finmann has amassed extensive teaching credentials, having taught paralegal, undergraduate, graduate, and continuing education tax and employee benefits courses at Adelphi University, C.W. Post, Hofstra University, Long Island University, and Queens College. Mr. Finmann is also one of the founders of Retirement Distribution Academy, Inc. (RDA), a national educational organization which trains financial advisors and other professionals in the area of retirement distribution planning and which provides consulting services to financial institutions on their IRA forms, documents, and administration procedures. He has been quoted in the *Augusta Chronicle*, *Bloomberg Wealth Manager*, *BusinessWeek*, *Financial Planning Magazine*, *IRA Junction.Com*; *Kiplinger's Retirement Report*, *Newsday*, *The Practical Accountant,* and *Ed Slott's IRA Advisor*, and has appeared on radio and television, where he has discussed a variety of retirement distribution planning issues.

On June 1, 2001, Mr. Finmann testified in Washington, D.C. at hearings held by the Internal Revenue Service and United States Treasury Department on the revised proposed regulations, issued January 17, 2001, on the Required Minimum Distribution rules governing qualified plans and IRAs.

ACKNOWLEDGMENTS

Many of the experiences and concepts expressed in this book come from conversations, meetings, and case studies with clients and advisors in search of a comprehensive retirement distribution strategy. My appreciation goes out to each and every one of them for helping me find my way into this exciting area of planning.

I would like to thank my co-author, Victor Finmann, for his dedication and determination in seeing this book to its completion. A special thanks goes to Michael McCarthy for his degree of commitment and his assistance in formatting the book and its many charts and graphs.

Eric Donner

I would first like to thank my secretary, Carol A. Biedrzycki, for her able assistance in typing multiple drafts of the text of both the 2000 and 2001 editions, and for otherwise making sense of what was all too often a jumble of notes and dictations. I would next like to thank my associate, Mark D. Trucios, Esq., for assisting in many aspects of the production of the 2001 edition and, most importantly, for successfully dealing with the day-to-day demands of my practice, thereby affording me the considerable amount of time needed to devote to this task.

I would also like to thank my dear children, Sara and Adam, for their love and support. Their own personal successes and accomplishments have both motivated and inspired me. Last, I would like to express my deepest gratitude to my wife, Roni, for her infinite patience, her loving and caring concern, and her total and unqualified backing of each of my endeavors, including the undertaking which was this book. Without her support, none of my efforts could ever have been realized.

Victor M. Finmann

PREFACE

In the United States there is a huge lack of knowledge and understanding among advisors and their clients regarding the effects of the distribution rules pertaining to retirement assets. If clients receive the proper planning advice, they can preserve the tax-deferred accumulation of their retirement assets to create a legacy for their children and grandchildren. If they fail to plan properly, their retirement wealth will be subject to enormous income and estate tax erosion upon death. With the information contained in *Planning for Retirement Distributions, Second Edition*, financial advisors can help their clients to understand the impact that the minimum distribution tax law will have on their retirement wealth.

Demographics of the U.S. population illustrate that more and more people are rapidly moving closer to their mandatory distribution age. The members of the aging "baby boomer" population continue to accumulate significant amounts of retirement wealth as they move closer to their Required Beginning Date. This unprecedented demographic phenomenon has created an urgent need for retirement distribution specialists.

The authors' intention in writing this book is simple: to help educate advisors on how to develop a retirement distribution strategy for clients who desperately need help in solving major retirement distribution concerns. Advisors need to realize that clients may be completely unaware of the need for this type of planning. A client's retirement distribution concerns typically surface as a result of tax issues derived from the minimum distribution tax laws. Their concerns erupt when they face the financial and personal impact the tax law has on their retirement wealth. Retirement distribution planning actually goes far beyond the issue of retirement assets and reaches deep into even the personal aspects of our clients' lives.

In *Planning for Retirement Distributions, Second Edition*, you will learn how to:

- Lay out the context of the problem carefully.
- Remain sensitive to the emotions clients attach to their retirement assets.
- Follow clients when they lead you off the track to other planning areas that concern them.

- Lead clients to those other areas when they don't make their own connections.
- Master all the technical information to get clients through the retirement maze successfully.

When you master these steps, you will undoubtedly deepen the value clients perceive in your advice and expand your range of influence in their decision-making. The bottom line for advisors is that stepping up to this problem proactively and thoroughly will not only resolve the issues but will make you the advisor clients call on first. *Planning for Retirement Distributions, Second Edition* not only addresses the technical aspects of tax law and planning strategies but also focuses on how to communicate the full impact of the problem and the value of the solutions to the client.

To become a retirement distribution specialist, you must first understand that retirement assets are different from all other assets and therefore must be treated differently. The book covers technical, legal, and personal aspects of retirement distribution planning, including the following:

- Important aspects of the minimum distribution rules
- Various retirement distribution strategies
- Tax law
- Legal documentation required to implement a strategy
- The effect of a specific retirement distribution strategy on financial and estate planning issues
- The effect of a specific retirement distribution strategy on the beneficiaries
- Emotional and psychological issues that clients will face during the planning process

We will take a journey together through the tax maze of irrevocable life expectancy elections and minimum distribution rules. There is a new Introduction that analyzes the effects of the 2001 Proposed Regulations concerning Required Minimum Distributions and of the Economic Growth and Tax Revenue Reconciliation Act of 2001. (In addition, each chapter is cross-referenced to this analysis.) You will learn the effect that recalculating life expectancy will have on the distribution of retirement assets. Will the hybrid method provide additional tax benefits—and what's the risk? You will learn how the lifting of the Minimum Distribution Incidental Benefits (MDIB) rule allows for the multigenerational tax deferral of pre-tax money. The book will also discuss applicable income and estate taxes, Generation-Skipping Transfer tax, the Unified Credit and Marital Deduction, and the income in respect of a decedent (IRD) tax deduction and the need to carry its tax benefit forward into future generations. Also included are revenue rulings and private letter rulings related to re-tirement distribution planning.

This book will expose you to advanced estate planning strategies that relate to retirement assets, including the best way to work with the following:

- IRAs
- Pension plans
- Profit-sharing plans
- 401(k) plans
- Multigeneration IRAs

We will explore together the common beneficiary designations such as spouse, children, and grandchildren, as well as more intricate beneficiaries such as trusts and charities. This leads us to a very important planning document that is becoming a standard with the IRA planning industry: the Retirement Asset Will. It is a comprehensive beneficiary designation and election document that reflects the tax, financial, and personal and tax philosophies and decisions of the IRA owner. The Retirement Asset Will enforces the multigeneration strategies, allowing the IRA to perpetuate for up to three generations.

Certain financial tools are quite appropriate for retirement distribution planning strategies. Life insurance and investment products, when integrated with the multigeneration IRAs, provide clients with significant income and estate tax leverage. Advanced planning techniques using life insurance with irrevocable trusts, split dollar agreements, and gifting strategies provide an even higher degree of tax leverage. Because life insurance can be confusing in its own right, the book includes a review and comparison of the primary forms of life insurance as they relate to retirement distribution planning.

Once clients begin to realize that their beloved retirement assets have a much longer time horizon, they begin to experience a transition in their investment philosophies. The book explores the reasons for the client's change in investment attitude and discusses various investment strategies that are suitable for multigeneration investing. It also illustrates the differences in investment philosophies that apply to each layer of multigeneration beneficiaries.

The rules of retirement distribution are extremely complicated, and there is a growing demand for qualified advice. As a trusted professional or financial advisor, you need to be prepared to meet the challenges presented through the new retirement distribution planning industry. If you accept the challenge, it can become a profitable venture. Right now, very few attorneys, accountants, financial planners, investment advisors, or insurance advisors can claim that title. Even those who focus their practice on retirement planning take the knowledge only as far as assuring that their clients will have large enough retirement assets to meet their lifestyle goals after their careers are over. When clients reach the age when the law dictates that they have to take action, almost none of these advisors is ready with answers. The knowledge and tools you will receive from this book can pave the way for a successful career as a retirement distribution specialist or can be used on an as-needed basis with clients. In either case, we wish you good luck.

Eric Donner
Victor M. Finmann

INTRODUCTION

In 2001, one regulatory and one legislative development occurred that will have dramatic consequences for the field of planning for retirement distributions. First, on January 17, 2001, the Internal Revenue Service (IRS) published in the Federal Register revised proposed regulations under Internal Revenue Code (IRC) §§ 401(a)(9), 403(b), 408, and 4974 on the Required Minimum Distribution rules. The IRS designed these regulations to replace and supersede virtually all of the rules contained in the initial proposed regulations issued in this area by the IRS on July 27, 1987, and also to replace and supersede the revised proposed regulations issued by the IRS on December 30, 1997 (which had dealt with the issue of the use of trusts as "Designated Beneficiaries"). Second, on June 7, 2001, President Bush signed into law the Economic Growth and Tax Relief Reconciliation Act of 2001 (EGTRRA). Although primarily concerned with income tax and estate tax issues, EGTRRA also contains numerous provisions in the area of qualified plans and IRAs.

The New Proposed Regulations on Required Minimum Distributions

Effective Date. The new proposed regulations are generally effective for years beginning after December 31, 2001. However, the IRS has indicated that IRA owners, and their beneficiaries following their death, will be permitted to choose to have these new rules apply for 2001, although the IRS has not specified exactly how this decision is to be made or documented. Participants in qualified plans, and their bene-ficiaries following their death, will be covered under the new rules for 2001, provided that the plan sponsor of the qualified plan has adopted the Model Amendment set forth in the revised proposed regulations. In fact, and under some circumstances, these new rules can be made to apply retroactively to January 1, 2001.

On June 1, 2001 the IRS held public hearings on the revised rules in Washington, D. C. Victor M. Finmann was afforded the privilege of being one of the few individuals who testified at that hearing. Prior to that date, numerous individuals had taken advantage of their right under the regulatory process to submit written comments to the IRS in connection with the new proposed rules. It is expected that the new proposed rules will become final sometime during the end of 2001, or early into 2002, with a final effective date of January 1, 2002. However, certain of the new proposed rules—most notably the new proposed reporting requirements by IRA Custodians of the yearly Required Minimum Distribution amounts—will probably not be effective until some later date.

Although the new proposed rules will in all likelihood become the final rules effective as of January 1, 2002 (with respect to most of the new rules), and with perhaps very few changes being made to the proposed rules, practitioners in this area should be aware that one of the basic premises underlying most of the rules contained in the revised proposed regulations were severely undermined by an extremely important, but largely overlooked, provision of EGTRRA, which was signed into law on June 7, 2001. That provision of the new law requires the IRS to:

> modify the life expectancy tables under the regulations relating to minimum distribution requirements under § 401(a)(9), § 408(a)(6) and (b)(3), § 403(b)(10), and § 457(d)(2) of the Internal Revenue Code *to reflect current life expectancy*. [emphasis added]

In issuing the new proposed regulations, the IRS had declined to update the life expectancy tables that are required to be used in connection with the Required Minimum Distribution rules, even though the IRS noted that it had received numerous requests in the past to do so. Those life expectancy tables date back to 1986. In issuing the new proposed rules, the IRS took the position that by liberalizing many of the distribution rules—most notably by allowing most individuals to assume that their beneficiary is ten years younger than they are, whether such is the case or not—the new proposed rules greatly extend the payout period for most employees and beneficiaries and lengthen that period more for many individuals than would an update (of the life expectancy tables) to reflect increases in longevity. The IRS and Treasury believe that this lengthening of the distribution period for most employees provides further justification for retaining the existing life expectancy tables at this time.

Therefore, the question becomes: What will the IRS do in light of this new legal mandate that it update the life expectancy tables to reflect current life expectancy? Will it finalize the new proposed rules without making *any* significant changes thereto, while concurrently adopting the updated, and consequently longer, life expectancy tables? Will it decide that individuals in the future should not enjoy the benefits of both more liberal distributions rules and more liberal life expectancy tables? Accordingly, will the IRS backtrack significantly on many of the more liberal distribution rules contained in the new proposed rules, while only then allowing individuals the right to use the updated and longer life expectancy tables required by law? It has even been suggested by at least one knowledgeable IRS representative (although perhaps in jest) that the IRS might adopt a bifurcated approach, with individuals given the choice of either using the new life expectancy tables with the prior Required Minimum Distribution rules (i.e., those rules in effect prior to the issuance of the revised proposed regulations of January 17, 2001) or using the prior life expectancy tables with the January 17, 2001 version of the IRS proposed regulations.

As another possible approach to this issue, the IRS could finalize the proposed regulations later in 2001 or early in 2002, largely in their current form, and then significantly change those rules when the updated life expectancy tables are issued sometime thereafter. The smart money at this time has the IRS finalizing the revised proposed regulations later in 2001 or early in 2002, largely in their current form, with the new life expectancy tables being issued sometime thereafter and with the then-final regulations not being further changed by the IRS at that time. However, it remains to be seen which one of these approaches will be adopted by the IRS. Practitioners will, therefore, have to continue to pay strict attention to subsequent developments in Washington, D.C., to see which way this important issue is finally resolved.

The following discussion explains some of the new features of the revised proposed regulations of January 17, 2001. The Third Edition of *Planning for Retirement Distributions* will incorporate into the body of the text the substance of those regulations, to the extent that those regulations have then become final. However, the body of the text of this Second Edition continues to use and apply the provisions of the two prior sets of proposed regulations in this area (i.e., the proposed regulations of July 27, 1987 and of December 30, 1997). Throughout the Second Edition, where a rule described in the text may have been modified by the revised proposed regulations of January 17, 2001, you will find references to this Introduction. Also, you should note that there are a number of potential problem areas either created by or left unresolved by the issuance of the revised proposed regulations of January 17, 2001. These are presented in Chapter 16 of the Second Edition.

Uniform Distribution Period Table. The new proposed regulations allow individuals at their Required Beginning Date to use a life expectancy table known as the "Uniform Distribution Period Table" in computing the Required Minimum Distribution amounts that are due while they are alive. The table is not a new table, but is in fact the MDIB Table (Minimum Distribution Incidental Benefit Table), which was originally contained in the proposed regulations of July 27, 1987. Practitioners have been using this table for years in computing Required Minimum Distribution amounts in those cases where the plan participant or IRA owner had selected a non-spouse beneficiary who was more than ten years junior to the participant. Built into that table is the assumption that the individual has selected a two-life expectancy payout for retirement benefits, based on the life expectancy of the individual and his or her beneficiary, with the beneficiary assumed to be ten years younger than the individual, whether or not such was the case.

Under the new proposed regulations, this life expectancy table, the Uniform Distribution Period Table, is to be used, regardless of whether or not the individual has a beneficiary at the time, and regardless of whether or not their actual beneficiary at the time qualifies as a Designated Beneficiary, (i.e., one that has a life expectancy under the IRS Required Minimum Distribution rules). The only exception to this rule occurs when an individual has designated his or her spouse as the beneficiary and where the spouse is more than ten years younger than the individual. In that case, the actual joint life expectancy of the individual and spouse can be used, with the life expectancy factor taken from the IRS joint life expectancy tables, which are found in IRC regulation Section 1.72-9.

The effect of using the Uniform Distribution Period Table can be significant. Under the prior rules, an individual who arrived at his or her Required Beginning Date with no beneficiary or no Designated Beneficiary in place had a life expectancy of only 16 years. Under the new proposed regulations, and with the use of the Uniform Distribution Period Table, that life expectancy has increased to 26.2 years. In the typical case of an individual at his or her Required Beginning Date who has designated the spouse as beneficiary, where the spouse was the same age as the individual, their combined life expectancy under the prior rules was 20.6 years. Under the new proposed regulations, that life expectancy has now increased to 26.2 years. This change has the effect of reducing the first year's Required Minimum Distribution amount from a slightly less than 5 percent distribution (1/ 20.6 = 4.85437%) to a slightly less than 4 percent distribution (1/ 26.2 = 3.81679%). While this difference may not at first seem all that significant, over time the difference can be staggering. An example will illustrate the dramatic effect of this one change.

> **Example.** Assume that an IRA owner is age 70, that his wife beneficiary is also age 70, and that there is currently $1,000,000 in the husband's IRA. Under the prior set of IRS rules, their benefits would have been required to be paid out over a period initially determined to be 20.6 years. Under the new rules, that period has now been extended to 26.2 years. The difference in Required Minimum Distributions each year and the remaining amounts on deposit in the IRA under the prior rules and under the new rules are as follows:

	Yearly Required Minimum Distributions		**Remaining Amount in IRA at Year End**	
	Prior Rules	*New Rules*	*Prior Rules*	*New Rules*
Year 1	$48,544	$38,168	$992,775	$1,003,151
Year 5	$68,911	$49,563	$1,075,015	$1,165,530
Year 10	$101,253	$71,602	$1,073,283	$1,351,270
Year 15	$148,774	$100,456	$833,135	$1,472,687

As shown above, this apparent small change can produce dramatic results over time, with yearly Required Minimum Distribution amounts *reduced* by 32.477 percent by year 15, and with retirement asset accumulations *increased* by 76.765 percent by that time.

In the year *following* the year of the death of the individual who had died after the Required Beginning Date, the Uniform Distribution Period Table is abandoned, and subsequent Required Minimum Distributions are based on the remaining life expectancy of the beneficiary. This, too, represents a substantial liberalization of the prior rules. Under the prior rules, once the retirement asset owner had died, the life expectancy to be used for Required Minimum Distribution purposes (assuming a Recalculation/Term Certain payout had been in effect) was the single life expectancy of the beneficiary, determined in the year in which the retirement asset owner had reached age 70½, with that life expectancy factor then reduced by one for each year that had passed. Under the new rules, the beneficiary's life expectancy is to be determined in the calendar year immediately *following* the calendar year of the individual's death, with that life expectancy reduced by one for each year that has passed. In other words, under the new rules every year that the retirement asset owner lives past his or her Required Beginning Date is another year in which the beneficiary's life expectancy is allowed to continue to increase.

Where an individual has died after his or her Required Beginning Date with no Designated Beneficiary, under the new rules the remaining payouts are to be based on the remaining single life expectancy of the individual, determined in the year of his or her death and then reduced by one for each year that elapses. An individual could die without a Designated Beneficiary where there was either no individual named to receive the benefits after the individual had died, or where an estate, charity, or Trust that did not qualify as a Designated Beneficiary had been named as the beneficiary of the retirement assets. Under the new rules, gone are the days when after an individual dies, his or her entire IRA is required to be paid out in full by December 31 of the calendar year immediately following the calendar year of death. This situation frequently occurred where the individual had previously elected a single life expectancy pay-out for benefits on a Recalculation Basis, or where the individual had elected a joint life expectancy payout with a spouse beneficiary who had previously died, and where *each* life expectancy was computed based on the Recalculation Method. In each case under the prior rules, all amounts in the IRA were required to be paid out of the IRA by December 31 of the calendar year immediately following the calendar year of the individual's death. The new rules in either of those cases now allow the remaining benefits to be paid out based on the remaining life expectancy of the IRA owner, determined as of the year of the IRA owner's death, with the life expectancy factor then reduced by one for each year that has passed.

No Irrevocable Elections Due at the Required Beginning Date. Under the prior IRS rules on Required Minimum Distributions, individuals who were interested in performing effective retirement distribution planning needed to make three elections by their Required Beginning Date. The Required Beginning Date is generally April 1 of the calendar year immediately following the calendar year in which the individual attains age 70½. The first election was the individual's choice of beneficiary. The next election was for either a one-life expectancy or a two-life expectancy payout of their benefits. The third election concerned whether benefits were to be paid out based on the Term Certain or Recalculation Method for the individual's life expectancy and, in those cases in which the spouse had been named as beneficiary, whether a Term Certain or Recalculation election was to be made with respect to the life expectancy of the spouse. Each of these elections was irrevocable, in that once the individual had reached his or her Required Beginning Date, the elections could either not be changed, or could be changed only to the *detriment* of the individual.

Under the prior rules, the election of a one-life expectancy or two-life expectancy payout was one of the elections that could *not* be altered after the individual's Required Beginning Date, nor was it possible to alter the election of either the Term Certain or Recalculation Method on the individual or on the spouse's life. Although the choice of beneficiary could usually be changed by the individual after his or her Required Beginning Date, no change in beneficiary designation made after that date could be used to increase the life expectancies that were required to be used to compute subsequent Required Minimum Distributions. If the individual, after his or her Required Beginning Date, had changed his or her beneficiary to one with a shorter life expectancy in the year immediately following the year of the change, the life expectancy of the new beneficiary was required to be used. However, where the individual had changed the beneficiary after his or her Required Beginning Date to one with a longer life expectancy, the life expectancy of that beneficiary could not be used in any subsequent year to compute Required Minimum Distribution amounts. In addition, not only were these elections irrevocable at the individual's Required Beginning Date, with respect to all subsequent Required Minimum Distributions that would be due during the remainder of the individual's life, but those irrevocable elections (absent a subsequent spousal rollover) also governed the payout of those benefits to the individual's beneficiaries following the individual's death.

Under the prior rules, many individuals who had reached or passed their Required Beginning Date were completely unaware of the importance of making the three elections by that date. These individuals were then relegated to having their retirement benefits paid out during the balance of their lifetimes, and after their death to their beneficiaries, based on the operative default provisions contained in the qualified plan document or IRA Custodial Agreement. Often, those default provisions precluded the payout of the retirement assets on a multigenerational basis, and, in some cases, required the payout of all retirement assets within a relatively short amount of time after an individual's death. A retirement distribution specialist whom an individual might have consulted *after* their Required Beginning Date was usually powerless to put the retirement distribution plan back on track, due to the irrevocable nature of the three default elections in effect.

The new proposed rules change all of that. Gone are all of the elections that were irrevocable at the Required Beginning Date. Under the new rules everyone is allowed to use the Uniform Distribution

Period Table, regardless of who their beneficiary is, and even if there is no beneficiary. The one exception to this new rule occurs when a spouse beneficiary is more than ten years younger than the individual. The Uniform Distribution Period Table, as noted above, assumes that the beneficiary is ten years younger than the retirement asset owner, whether or not such is the case. The Uni-form Distribution Period Table also assumes a two-life expectancy payout, and a payout based on the recalculation of the life expectancy of both the individual and the beneficiary.

Under the new rules, individuals are free to select any beneficiary they want without fear that their choice of beneficiary will adversely impact on their requirement to take yearly Required Minimum Distribution amounts. Under the new rules, beneficiaries can be changed any number of times after the Required Beginning Date, with no impact on the yearly Required Minimum Distribution amounts. In the past, individuals who had named their children as beneficiaries of their retirement assets may have wanted to name their spouse as beneficiary, but did not do so because that would have *increased* the amount that they would have had to withdraw from their retirement assets each year. Those individuals are free, under the new rules, to choose the beneficiaries of their choice, including their spouse, without increasing their yearly Required Minimum Distribution amounts.

This one change obviously eliminates a major time pressure that in the past had motivated individuals to complete their retirement distribution planning by their Required Beginning Date. However, from the perspective of the retirement distribution specialist, although this strong motivational factor has now been lost, what has been gained is their ability to perform complete, comprehensive, and effective retirement distribution planning for those individuals who have *passed* their Required Beginning Date. Under the new rules, their potential client base has increased exponentially. No longer must the retirement distribution specialist be the bearer of the bad news that the client's retirement distribution plan (and perhaps even their entire estate plan) does not work and, to make matters still worse, cannot be fixed, even though the previous planning errors have been brought to light, and competent professionals are now addressing each of these important issues. Under the new rules, virtually all prior errors in the retirement distribution plan can be corrected, regardless of the individual's age, provided that the correction occurs *before* the individual's death. In fact, under the new rules, as will be explained in the next section, many errors in the retirement distribution plan can even be corrected up to as late as December 31 of the calendar year immediately following the calendar year of the individual's death. In short, the new rules offer a virtual bonanza of new planning and marketing opportunities to those advisors who have taken the time to master the new rules.

Beneficiary Determined by December 31 of the Year Following the Year of the Individual's Death. One of the most innovative changes brought about by the new proposed regulations is the rule that fixes the individual's Designated Beneficiary as of December 31 of the calendar year immediately following the calendar year of the individual's death. The individual or entity who is the beneficiary *at that time* is the individual or entity whose life expectancy is then taken into account for Required Minimum Distribution purposes. This new rule is applicable whether the individual had died before or after the Required Beginning Date. This new rule, when coupled with the Separate Share Rule discussed below, creates huge opportunities for post mortem planning, in those cases in which the retirement distribution plan had not been properly configured prior to the individual's death. An example will help to illustrate this point.

> **Example.** Louis Biederman names his favorite church as the beneficiary for $100,000 of his $1,000,000 IRA assets, with his three daughters—Jane, Dorothy, and Carol—as the three equal beneficiaries for the balance of the IRA. Louis dies on June 25, 2001. Under the old rules, because the charity has no life expectancy, had Louis died *before* his Required Beginning Date, all amounts in the IRA would have been required to be paid out in full by December 31, 2006, which is the December 31 of the calendar year containing the fifth anniversary of his death. Had he died *after* his Required Beginning Date, under the prior rules, if he had previously elected the Recalculation Method for his life expectancy, all amounts in the IRA would be required to be paid out in full by December 31, 2002 (which is the December 31 of the calendar year imme-

> diately *following* the calendar year of his death). Had he died after his Required Beginning Date under the prior rules, having previously elected a Term Certain payout for his benefits, his beneficiaries would be required to receive minimum distributions each year based on his remaining life expectancy, determined in the year in which he had attained 70½, and reduced by one for each year that has since passed.
>
> However, under the new rules, if the charity is paid out in full by December 31, 2002 (which is the December 31 of the calendar year immediately following the calendar year of his death), the only beneficiaries left on board at that time would be Louis's three daughters. Accordingly, under the new rules, Required Minimum Distribution amounts due for the year 2002, and for all years thereafter, would be based on the life expectancy of the oldest of his three daughters. Under the new rules, by "cashing out" the charity by December 31 of the calendar year immediately following the calendar year of his death, the family removed a beneficiary that had no life expectancy. This allowed the remaining IRA benefits to be paid out to Louis's three daughters based on the life expectancy of the oldest of the three.

Under the new rules, the above result can be made even more advantageous through the use of separate shares for each beneficiary, where those separate shares have been established by December 31, 2002. In the above case, had the charity either been paid out in full by December 31, 2002, or had its share been segregated into a separate IRA by that date, the charity's entitlement to any IRA benefits would no longer have any negative impact on the Required Minimum Distribution amounts, which would then be due to any of Louis's three daughters. In addition, had the three daughters segregated their portions of the IRA by December 31, 2002 into separate Inherited IRAs for each different share, each daughter would be able to base subsequent Required Minimum Distribution amounts from each of the Inherited IRAs on her own remaining life expectancy. Where the age disparity between the beneficiaries is not that great, the ability to take advantage of the "Separate Share Rule" may not appear especially beneficial. However, where the age differential between the several beneficiaries is great (for instance, where there are beneficiaries of different generations), this planning device can result in significant additional retirement accumulations for the younger beneficiaries.

This new planning device is also extremely helpful in those cases involving disclaimers. Under the prior rules, where a Primary Beneficiary had disclaimed retirement assets in favor of a Contingent Beneficiary, the Primary Beneficiary's life expectancy still had to be taken into account for Required Minimum Distribution purposes, where the Primary Beneficiary was *older* than the Contingent Beneficiary and where the individual had died *after* his or her Required Beginning Date. This scenario frequently presented itself where the individual had designated his or her spouse as the beneficiary of the retirement assets and where the spouse had disclaimed that inheritance. The Contingent Beneficiaries under those circumstances, who were usually the children, were then required to continue to use their surviving parent's remaining life expectancy to compute subsequent Required Minimum Distribution amounts. However, under the new rules, this is no longer the case. Under the new rules, as long as the surviving spouse had disclaimed his or her interest by December 31 of the calendar year immediately fol-lowing the calendar year of the individual's death, the life expectancies of the children, and not that of the surviving parent, may be used to compute subsequent Required Minimum Distribution amounts. In addition, if the children by that date had divided the IRA into separate shares for each of their portions, then each child could base subsequent Required Minimum Distributions from each separate Inherited IRA on his or her own remaining life expectancy.

This new planning device can also be extremely helpful in those cases in which a portion of the retirement asset will have to be used to pay estate taxes, funeral expenses, or estate administration expenses, or where the retirement assets are payable into a trust, and where the trust may have to pay some or all of those expense items, and/or may have to pay certain trust administrative expenses. Under the prior rules, the payment of any of those items, either directly or indirectly from the retirement asset, could have been construed by the IRS as the payment to a beneficiary that had no life expectancy. Under the prior rules, such payments could have spelled the end of any possible multigenerational IRA payout. However, under the new rules, as long as each of these items have been paid in full by December 31 of the calendar year immediately following the calendar year of the individual's death, those payments (and consequently those potential additional "beneficiaries") can be ignored for purposes of determining all subsequent Required Minimum Distributions due from the retirement asset.

IRA Custodian Reporting of the Required Minimum Distribution Amounts. The last significant proposed change in the Required Minimum Distribution rules brought about by the IRS revised proposed regulations of January 17, 2001 is the proposal to require IRA Custodians to report the Required Minimum Distribution amounts that are due from each IRA each year. Under existing law, qualified plans and tax-sheltered annuities (403(b) plans) are required to pay out to participants (and to their beneficiaries following their death) the Required Minimum Distribution amounts that are due each year. IRA Custodians, on the other hand, currently have no such requirement. Instead, under existing rules, it is the IRA owner himself or herself who determines the yearly Required Minimum Distribution amount and who is then responsible to ensure that said amount is paid out of the IRA each year. Under the proposed regulations of January 17, 2001, the yearly Required Minimum Distribution amount will be required to be reported each year by the IRA Custodian to both the IRA owner (and, presumably, to his or her beneficiaries following the IRA owner's death), and to the IRS. The obvious intent of this proposal is to make it far easier for the IRS to determine which individuals failed to take their Required Minimum Distributions in any given year or years, with the IRS then having all of the information that it would need to assess the 50 percent excise tax under IRC § 4974, in those cases in which the full Required Minimum Distribution amount was not taken.

At the hearings which were held in Washington, D.C. on June 1, 2001 on the revised proposed regulations, each of the speakers who addressed this issue indicated that they did *not* feel that the IRA Custodians should have to be put in the position of being the "policemen" for the IRS. They each indicated that the IRA Custodians that they represented currently have a difficult enough time in obtaining the IRA owner's date of birth. Under the proposed rule, the IRA

Custodians would be required to obtain and retain updated and accurate information on the spouses of the IRA owners as well, where the spouse had been named as beneficiary and where the spouse was more than ten years younger than the IRA owner. Where the IRA owner had died, the IRA Custodians would need to know that fact, and would then be required to correctly identify each of the individual's beneficiaries and their dates of birth and would also need to know whether any change in beneficiary designations (e.g., through the death or disclaimer of a beneficiary) had occurred during the period beginning with the date of the individual's death and ending with December 31 of the calendar year immediately following the year of death. Where a trust was the beneficiary, the IRA Custodians would also need to know whether the trust qualified as a Designated Beneficiary, and which life expectancies of the different trust beneficiaries would be required to be used for Required Minimum Distribution purposes. They each felt that these kinds of determinations were, to a certain extent, conclusions of law, which, as financial institutions, they should not be required to express an opinion on.

Each of the speakers indicated that it would be impossible for their organizations to accurately report the yearly Required Minimum Distribution amounts based on the remaining complexity of the Required Minimum Distribution rules, and despite the recent IRS attempts at simplification. They indicated that their organizations could be the victims of lawsuits should they erroneously underreport or overreport the yearly Required Minimum Distribution amount. Should they erroneously underreport the yearly Required Minimum Distribution amount, they could be sued by the IRA owner (or by the beneficiary following the IRS owner's death) for the amount of the 50 percent excise tax under IRC Section 4974, in those cases in which the IRS had previously assessed that penalty. Should they erroneously overreport the Required Minimum Distribution amount, they could be sued by the IRA owner (or by their beneficiary following the IRA owner's death) for the extra income tax the IRA owner (or beneficiary following the IRA owner's death) was then required to pay, *and* for the amount of the total retirement benefits lost as a result of having withdrawn more from the IRA, than was required under the law. In other words, in being required to report the yearly Required Minimum Distribution amounts, but without being provided with accurate information, the IRA Custodians fear that they will be put in a position where they cannot win no matter what they do. It remains to be seen to what extent these concerns of the IRA Custodians will be reflected in the final regulations when they are finally published.

What the Revised Proposed Regulations Have Not Changed. Although the revised proposed regulations of January 17, 2001 have changed many of the specific rules governing Required Minimum Distributions from qualified plans and IRAs, they have changed very few of the overall planning theories and strategies that practitioners use in the area of Retirement Distribution Planning. Under the new rules, it is still usually a good idea for individuals during their retirement years to live off of their other assets and not off their retirement assets and to accumulate the retirement assets to the greatest extent possible. In fact, under the new rules, this strategy is even more beneficial because of the reduced yearly Required Minimum Distributions that are generally due under the new rules. Under the new rules, it is still usually a good idea to single out the individual's retirement assets as one of the best assets to use to create a legacy for succeeding generations. In addition, under the new rules, it is usually still essential to fully integrate the individual's Retirement Distribution Plan with the individual's Estate Plan. In fact, under the new rules, because the retirement assets at the individual's death may be far larger and may represent a far larger percentage of the individual's net worth, it is even more important to integrate these two planning disciplines.

Under the new rules, it is still rarely a good idea to name one's estate as the beneficiary of the retirement assets, because an estate has no life expectancy for Required Minimum Distribution purposes. In addition, the new rules have not changed the requirements imposed on trusts for those trusts to qualify as Designated Beneficiaries (other than a change in the documentation requirement, which provides that, in most cases, a copy of the trust document need no longer be given to the plan administrator or IRA Custodian during the individual's lifetime and that, instead, a copy of the trust document generally need not be provided until December 31 of the calendar year immediately following the calendar year of the individual's death). In addition, the new rules have not changed the fact that there is still a 50 percent excise tax imposed under IRC Section 4974 for the failure to have taken the Required Minimum Distribution amount in any given year.

In short, the new rules have not substantially changed most of the general theories and strategies which retirement distribution specialists have evolved over the years, to assist their clients in planning for retirement distributions.

Economic Growth and Tax Relief Reconciliation Act of 2001

The Third Edition of *Planning for Retirement Distributions* will discuss each of these changes in detail, to the extent that they impact on retirement distribution planning. However, the following discussion will touch on a few of those key changes affecting retirement distribution planning.

The portions of EGTRRA that deal with qualified plans and IRAs were derived, for the most part, from the provisions of the Retirement Security and Savings Act of 2000, which had passed the House of Representatives on July 19, 2000 by a vote of 401 for, with only 25 votes against. However due to a threatened veto by then–President Clinton, that bill was not passed in identical form by the Senate and consequently was never sent to Clinton for signature. Accordingly, that bill was never signed into law, despite its obvious broad-based bipartisan support. The main thrust of that bill (and consequently the main thrust of the qualified plan and IRA provisions of EGTRRA), is to once again actively promote savings by companies and by individuals in both qualified plans and IRAs. To that end, EGTRRA contains numerous provisions that increase the contribution limitations and deduction limitations applicable to qualified plans, traditional IRAs, and Roth IRAs, although many of these provisions do not become effective immediately, but are phased in over a number of years. Furthermore, many of the hyper-technical rules and restrictions which had bedeviled employee benefit attorneys, actuaries, and other professionals, and which had worked in the past to substantially reduce contributions and deductions to qualified plans for highly paid individuals, have either been entirely eliminated or have been made far simpler as a result of the passage of EGTRRA. Over the next five to ten years, these provisions of EGTRRA should produce dramatic yearly increases in contributions and accumulations in qualified plans, especially defined benefit plans, as well as significant increases in contributions to traditional and Roth IRAs. This should especially be the case in latter years, as some of the more favorable provisions of the law become effective.

In order to comply with the provisions of the Congressional Budget Act of 1974, virtually all of the provisions of EGTRRA "sunset" after December 31, 2010. This means that those provisions of the law cease being in effect, with the prior provisions of the law (i.e., those provisions that were effective prior to the passage of EGTRRA) once again becoming operative. These sunset provisions, as well as the many different phase in effective dates applicable under the new law, will make it extremely difficult for practitioners to effectuate any type of long-range permanent tax planning for their clients without having to regularly monitor both the client's situation and the status of the Federal tax laws to determine to what extent those plans will have to be modified or changed. Because Republicans and Democrats alike intend to make significant changes to EGTRRA *before* the sunset date of December 31, 2010 arrives, it is virtually a foregone conclusion that, sometime before the December 31, 2010 date, significant changes to the new law will be enacted. Tax planners will have to be ever attentive to the changing moods and political climate in Washington, D.C. Accordingly, until final changes in the tax law are enacted that are *not* scheduled to sunset by a certain date, practitioners will have to build a significant amount of flexibility into their tax planning—including retirement distribution planning.

Despite the confusion created by EGTRRA, it can be said with a fair degree of certainty that, as qualified plan and IRA contributions and accumulations increase in future years under the new law, the importance of proper retirement distribution planning for those increased retirement assets will also increase. This trend, when coupled with the aging of the Baby Boomer generation and the natural tendency for an individual's retirement assets to increase as one gets older, should spell dramatically increased planning opportunities for the retirement distribution specialist in both the near and distant future.

Changes in the Federal Estate Tax Credit Shelter Amount and in the Federal Estate Tax Rates. EGTRRA increases the amount in an individual's estate that is exempt from the Federal estate tax. That amount, formerly known as the "Credit Shelter Amount" but which the new law refers to as the "Applicable Exclusion Amount," is scheduled to increase in the future to the following amounts and for the following years:

Year	*Amount*
2002	$1,000,000
2004	$1,500,000
2006	$2,000,000
2009	$3,500,000

EGTRRA provides that the Federal estate tax is entirely eliminated for individuals dying on or after January 1, 2010. However, under the sunset provisions of EGTRRA, the Federal estate tax returns for individuals dying on or after January 1, 2011, with the Applicable Exclusion Amount then set at $1,000,000 for that year and for all subsequent years. EGTRRA also increases the amount of an individual's estate that is exempt from the generation skipping transfer (GST) tax for assets that will pass to grandchildren or to later generations. Under current law, the GST exemption amount is currently $1,060,000. Under EGTRRA, the amount of the exemption is equal to the amount of the Federal Applicable Exclusion Amount for the year. Accordingly, the GST exemption amount in-creases to $1,500,000 in 2004, to $2,000,000 in 2006, and to $3,500,000 in 2009. The GST tax is entirely eliminated for individuals dying on or after January 1, 2010. However, the GST exemption amount returns to its 2001 level as of January 1, 2011, and is indexed by inflation for each year after 2001.

EGTRRA also reduces the maximum Federal estate tax rates from the current maximum 55 percent rate (with a 60 percent marginal Federal estate tax rate applicable to the extent that the taxable estate is valued between $10,000,000 and $17,184,000) to a maximum 50 percent rate effective for individuals dying on or after January 1, 2002. For each year thereafter, EGTRRA reduces the maximum Federal estate tax rate by 1 percent each year until January 1, 2007, when the maximum Federal estate tax rate is re-duced to 45 percent. The maximum Federal estate tax rate of 45 percent continues until the

Federal estate tax is entirely repealed on January 1, 2010, only to return again on January 1, 2011, when the maximum Federal estate tax rate is once again 55 percent (or 60 percent for certain estates).

The increase in the Federal Estate Tax Applicable Exclusion Amount, the increase in the GST exemption amount, and the reduction in the maximum Federal estate tax rates will make it easier for individuals in the future to pass on a greater percentage of their net worth to succeeding generations, especially in those cases in which a significant portion of the family wealth consists of retirement assets. However, to the extent that on the death of the retirement asset owner or surviving spouse there will still be or would otherwise still be an estate tax, the retirement distribution plan will still have to be carefully integrated with the couple's estate plan to ensure that the smallest possible percentage of the couple's net worth is subject to the Federal estate tax. This planning will usually entail the use of a full Applicable Exclusion Amount in the estate of both husband and wife.

Where the retirement assets constitute a significant portion of the couple's net worth, more and more couples will find that they must fund at least one of the Credit Shelter Trusts with those retirement assets. This will require them to retain the services of competent retirement distribution specialists, who will coordinate their efforts with the clients' estate tax advisors and attorneys to ensure that the couple's Wills and trusts have been designed to use the retirement assets for this purpose and that the couple's qualified plan and IRA Beneficiary Designation forms and Retirement Asset Wills have been properly prepared to accomplish this objective, while allowing those retirement assets to remain in the shelter of those retirement vehicles, continuing to grow on a tax-deferred basis each year. In short, until such time, if ever, that the Federal estate tax is either entirely repealed or is set at a level that allows the estates of most individuals, regardless of how configured, to be entirely exempt from that tax, the services of a retirement distribution specialist will be in ever-increasing demand, to assist the client and their other advisors in structuring estate tax planning and retirement distribution planning, in order to avoid, to the greatest extent possible, the imposition of what then remains of the Federal estate tax law.

Increased Rollover Opportunities. Under the rules that existed before the passage of EGTRRA, distributions from qualified plans, tax-sheltered annuities (403(b) plans), and IRAs could generally be rolled over into IRAs, where the individual could then usually implement a multigenerational IRA payout. Despite this general rollover right under the prior rules, after-tax amounts in qualified plans or in tax-sheltered annuities could *not* be rolled over into an IRA, nor could distributions from either a qualified plan, tax-sheltered annuity, or IRA, to the extent that the distribution had consisted of a Required Minimum Distribution amount. Under the prior rules, distributions from qualified plans could also be rolled over into another qualified plan, but could *not* be rolled over into a tax-sheltered annuity. Similarly, under the prior rules, distributions from tax-sheltered annuities could also be rolled over into another tax-sheltered annuity, but could *not* be rolled over into a qualified plan. Under the prior rules, distributions from IRAs could *not* be rolled over into either a qualified plan or tax-sheltered annuity unless the IRA distribution consisted *entirely* of assets derived from either a qualified plan (where the rollover was being made to a qualified plan) or from a tax-sheltered annuity (where the rollover was being made to a tax-sheltered annuity) *and* to which no regular IRA contribution had ever been made. Under the prior rules, distributions from 457 plans could be rolled over *only* into another 457 plan, and could *not* be rolled over into a qualified plan, tax-sheltered annuity, or IRA. A 457 plan is an eligible deferred compensation plan of a State or local government or tax-exempt employer that meets certain requirements.

These restrictions on rollover rights made it extremely difficult for many individuals to consolidate all of their retirement assets into one place, and under the control of one plan sponsor, one annuity provider, or one IRA Custodian. Under the prior rules, individuals frequently had to create multiple retirement distribution planning documents in order to properly dispose of all of their retirement assets. In addition, with their retirement assets in different places, many individuals often found it difficult or impossible to effectuate an integrated and efficient overall financial plan for the investment of their retirement assets.

EGTRRA changes all of this by permitting rollover rights to exist for the first time as between and among qualified plans, tax-sheltered annuities, IRAs, and government-sponsored 457 plans (but not 457 plans sponsored by non-governmental tax exempt entities). Now under EGTRRA, and starting as of January 1, 2002, distributions from any one or more of these four types of retirement vehicles will generally be eligible to be rolled over into any one or more of the four types of retirement vehicles (except that distributions which are part of a Required Minimum Distribution amount are still not eligible to be rolled over). In addition, under the new rules, although nondeductible after-tax contributions made to IRAs still cannot be rolled over (unless rolled over to another IRA), after-tax amounts in qualified plans can either be rolled over into an IRA or can be transferred directly to another qualified plan by the new law permitting a direct Trustee-to-Trustee transfer of those amounts directly from one qualified plan to another. It should be noted that in no case does the new law require the potential recipient qualified plan, tax-sheltered annuity, 457 plan, or IRA to accept the rollover. Instead, the new law simply allows those rollovers to occur, provided that the potential recipient retirement vehicle has agreed to accept the rollover amount.

The new liberalized rollover rules under EGTRRA should greatly facilitate the use of multigenerational planning for all retirement assets, regardless of whether those assets had originated in a qualified plan, tax-sheltered annuity, 457 plan, or IRA. In addition, investment advisors under these new rollover rules will, for the first time, be able to afford their clients the full range of investment options and choices available with respect to those retirement assets, once their clients have rolled over each of those retirement assets into an IRA, which will then be under the exclusive investment control of the client.

Qualified Retirement Planning Services. EGTRRA adds a new section to the IRC (§ 132(a)(7)) which excludes from an employee's income the value of any "qualified retirement planning services" provided by the employer. The new provision is effective as of January 1, 2002.

The Committee Reports which accompanied the new law indicate that

> employers sponsoring retirement plans should be encouraged to provide retirement planning services for their employees in order to assist them in preparing for their retirement.

The Committee Reports also indicate that the advice which the employer should be providing to its employees in this regard should *not* be limited to information regarding the employer's qualified plan alone, but should also include

> advice and information regarding retirement income planning for an individual and his or her spouse and how the employer's plan fits into the individual's overall retirement income plan.

In other words, by statute, Congress is now officially endorsing the hiring and use of retirement distribution specialists to assist employees when they are faced with the many issues they must address as they plan for and receive their employer-provided retirement benefits. The employer's provision of this planning service, if done within the rules set forth in the new IRC § 132(a)(7), will be considered a nontaxable fringe benefit (i.e., not taxable to the employee).

Under EGTRRA, it should be a simple matter for retirement distribution specialists, armed with this new statute, to convince a number of companies to hire them to render retirement distribution planning advice to their employees. One can see how this captive group of potential clients could readily form the nucleus of a substantial retirement distribution planning practice, with the retirement distribution specialist providing ongoing consulting services to those now-retired employees on a yearly basis for the remainder of their retirement years, and with planning services continuing for the lifetime of the employee's children and grandchildren following the employee's death.

Conclusion

As was the case with the IRS revised proposed regulations of January 17, 2001, the provisions of EGTRRA, while limiting some prior planning opportunities that had existed in the past, on balance provide a wealth of new and more significant planning opportunities for those individuals who are willing to master the several new rules which are now applicable in the area of retirement distribution planning. Moreover, with so much media attention having been focused in recent months on some of the better-known provisions of EGTRRA, advisors should find numerous prospective clients and their advisors waiting for the right individual to come along to unravel, explain, and implement their retirement distribution plan within the context of this latest change in the Federal tax law. The authors wish you, our readers, the very best of luck in your future planning and marketing efforts.

October 1, 2001
Eric Donner
Victor M. Finmann

SUMMARY OF CONTENTS

CONTENTS

CHAPTER 1
CULTURE AND EMOTIONS IN RETIREMENT DISTRIBUTION PLANNING

CONTENTS

1 CULTURE AND EMOTIONS IN RETIREMENT DISTRIBUTION PLANNING

While the psychological factors at work in wealth creation and distribution, discussed later in this chapter, hold the highest place in decision-making, many cultural forces are at work as well. Advisors need to take the time to understand and then to explain this context to clients who seem receptive to it.

When advisors make the effort to broaden their clients' understanding, the clients develop a greater sense of trust in the advisors' experience and ability. By remaining aloof and technical, advisors may create barriers between themselves and their clients.

The Concept of Retirement

Retirement is a modern concept. In an agrarian economy, wealth comes from the ownership of land. Landowners do not worry about money for old age, because they do not retire from anything. Traditional landowners did not work. They inherited the land, made some improvements, and enjoyed their aristocratic prerogatives.

Tenants would farm until their vitality gave out, and then their families would provide for them. The less skilled worked for board in the homes of the rich. When they got old, their masters would likely provide a living of some kind, or they would rely on their families. The more highly skilled workers, such as lawyers, doctors, and artisans, provided services for fees. Guilds would provide for their members' needs when the members could no longer perform services and earn fees.

In the United States, the early professions and trades never developed into the type of rigid organization they did in Europe. Individual investment planning became more important for tradesmen, artisans,

---

Note: Readers should refer to the Introduction for a discussion of issues and concepts covered in Chapter 1—particularly the Federal estate tax amounts and rates—that may be affected by the passage of EGTRRA 2001.

and professionals. When trade produced tangible goods, it could be liquidated or passed along to the next generation, providing funds or care for old age. When the assets produced were services, fees were generally higher and extra money could be put into land that could later be sold to provide a living.

Eventually, business as it is known today boomed, requiring manufacturing processes that relied on human workers. The next waves of immigration to America were motivated not by the promise of land, but by jobs. These jobs, however, did not pay well enough for a worker to save for retirement. In addition, the extended family support system that had existed in the old country had been disrupted by emigration. An entirely new economic class was created. Workers eventually organized themselves to protect their rights and their long-term security. Their influence was bolstered by a wave of reform thinkers whose eloquence and efforts ensured that the worker's problems would be addressed by society at large.

Not until the late 1800s to the early 1900s did most people even entertain the idea that society as a whole should bear some of the responsibility for the economic protection of its members. Germany under Otto von Bismarck established the first social insurance programs for sickness, disability, and old-age protection funded by contributions from employers, workers, and the government. The United States was late in moving into the arena of social security. It was not until the Great Depression overpowered even the staunchest resistance to the need for remedial legislation that the Social Security Act of 1935 was passed.

The New Deal was a powerful expression of the government's potential to use tax-related legislation to effect social change. No one in government—conservative or liberal—has seriously attempted to halt the flow since. On the contrary, social-driven tax legislation has emerged as a nearly annual event.

Retirement Planning Vehicles

The social legislation of the New Deal era nurtured a contradictory cultural view of retirement independence—apart from government support. Now an independent and secure retirement ranks among the highest financial priorities for most people. This independence is now based on three retirement planning vehicles—Social Security, employer-sponsored pension plans, and private savings and investments.

Social Security

The future of Social Security is often a battleground in which tax-based legislation attempts to drive social change. Because this issue is of such importance to most Americans, the press has an opportunity to inflame both sides until it has a dramatic story to report. The most fundamental debate currently is how to continue to fund Social Security. Under the pay-as-you-go system of payroll tax, an increase in the ratio of beneficiaries to workers will inevitably cause an increase in payroll taxes. That might strain the already regressive system beyond the limits of lower paid workers. Is the answer to dip into other tax revenues? If the government takes from income tax revenue, will Social Security then gain dominance over other social programs? Or should the government sever welfare functions from Social Security, and leave it as a forced savings program based on each individual's earnings? The aging of the "baby boomer" population, and its threat to bankrupt the system, will virtually assure a recurrent debate over this issue.

Why would anyone with substantial retirement assets be concerned about any of this? Social Security for these people is what it was intended to be—a rarely used safety net against poverty for the elderly. Nevertheless, retirement thinking is tied to beliefs about Social Security. Even affluent clients are counting on that net to be there for them—especially clients who were around at the birth of the Social Security program. They view it as part of their heritage. They helped build it and feel entitled to it. Advisors should not presume that this issue is not significant to someone sitting on millions of dollars of retirement wealth.

By the 1950s it was taken as a fact of corporate life that generous retirement benefits would be provided by the large corporations to their workers, and that most Americans would be working for the same large corporation for their entire working life. But in the next two decades it became apparent that small businesses were becoming just as successful as big business in employing large numbers of workers, and many people were shut out of the rich pension environment provided by the mega-corporations. That is what gave birth to

IRAs and Keogh plans. In both environments, big business and small business, the government had focused over the years on retirement planning—sometimes expanding planning opportunities and sometimes shutting them down when it perceived that one segment was gaining more than a fair share.

Today, while company pension plans are still treated as the real foundation of retirement planning, they are not nearly as prevalent as they used to be. The era of rich defined benefit plans has ended. The era of the 401(k) plan is firmly established. This means that the responsibility to fund retirement benefits has shifted from corporations to individuals, with the corporation merely providing the savings vehicle and, in some instances, slightly sweetening the deal with its own contributions.

The most recent legislative environment has also resulted in severe limits on contributions to tax-qualified plans for the highly compensated. Executives, business owners, and other highly paid employees are relying more heavily on personal savings or on nonqualified retirement plans. These executive benefit plans are finally making their way down from the big public corporations into the mid-sized privately held companies to provide excellent deferral opportunities for executives. The trade-off for freedom from the complicated ERISA tax law qualification ruling is often the executives' loss of security and the companies' loss of a current income tax deduction. With some creative and sophisticated planning techniques, however, knowledgeable advisors can minimize the executive's security risk and can restore the value of the deduction very effectively.

Meanwhile, the ability of small business owners to use their companies as private tax-shelter havens was drastically curtailed in the 1980s. Opportunities do still exist to use corporate tax advantages to pursue personal wealth accumulation strategies for those fortunate enough to have created their own companies. However, even these successful business owners must have knowledgeable and creative advisors to help them through what is often a complex maze of tax rules.

Employee Savings Plans

For those who have fully utilized company-sponsored, tax-deferred vehicles, and who have treated their investment gains as long-term growth, the future will be richer than they know. Outside of the few truly mathematical minds among us, virtually no one understands the power of large numbers and exponential growth. In a remarkable book titled *The Universe and the Teacup: The Mathematics of Truth and Beauty*, K. C. Cole offers many examples of our brains' incapacity to grasp these concepts. She writes the following:

> One of the main reasons that large numbers grow so explosively is that multiplication is a powerful engine for growth—even when the only number you happen to be multiplying is significantly puny, like the number two. There's an old legend about the mathematician who invented chess that illustrates this very well. The king liked the game so well, the story goes, that he offered the mathematician any prize that she wanted. She asked only for two grains of wheat to be placed on the first square of the chessboard, four on the second, eight on the third . . . and so forth, doubling the number of grains of wheat for each of the sixty-four squares on the chessboard. How much grain did she win? More than human beings had produced in the entire history of the world. That is the power of doubling.

Financial planners frequently use the Rule of 72 to help their clients understand compounded growth. Take an assumed annual rate of growth and divide it into the number 72. That will give you the number of years it will take for your money to double. Sophisticated professional advisors are well aware of this rule; this device has all the appeal of a child's magic trick. But to clients the magic is real. They need to understand the full extent of the power behind compound interest, how it has worked for them in the past, and how it can continue to work for them in the future. Known as the Eighth Wonder of the World, the phenomenon of compound interest can often mean the difference between a difficult retirement, in which many financial sacrifices will have to be made, and a comfortable retirement, in which the individual's pre-retirement standard of living can be easily maintained.

The IRA

In the past few years many individuals who have been investing in company pension plans and in the stock market have achieved impressive growth rates. Even allowing for corrections, their money has doubled much faster than they previously might have believed—$1,000 earning 10 percent simple interest for 10 years yields $11,000. That we can believe. $1,000 earning 10 percent compound interest for 100 years yields more than $13 million. Anyone who can comprehend this will immediately appreciate the beauty of the lowly IRA.

IRAs and Keogh plans were introduced to provide a vehicle for those who were frozen out of the participation in retirement plans of large companies—essentially those employed in small companies and the self-employed. However, nearly anyone could establish an IRA. At the time of their inception, the contribution limits were adequate for the social purpose that they were designed to achieve. However, since then, the contribution limit has become relatively meaningless except for those with no other retirement vehicle available to them.

The ability to defer substantially more money into 401(k) plans with employer matching contributions makes the IRA the neglected child of the tax-deductible investment family. The fact is that the IRAs of the past have lost their appeal. Financial institutions do not aggressively promote IRAs as they used to. End-of-the-year tax planning articles featuring the tax advantages of IRAs are not now as prominent. Mass market financial planning books make a defense of them at best. But take rollovers of huge accumulations in pension plans, and where else would anyone put them? The rollover IRA extends tax deferral and provides investment flexibility better than any other alternative.

As a vehicle to salt away several thousand dollars a year, IRAs are not popular among the wealthy. But as a place to park substantial sums of accumulated retirement wealth, the IRA is extremely attractive. In fact, with more than $9 trillion presently in IRAs and retirement plans, IRAs will soon become the vehicle of choice in the future, as more and more assets pay out of retirement plans into IRAs.

IRAs—as opposed to a company-sponsored retirement plan—provide significant flexibility to the owner. This flexibility will prevail as clients begin facing the tax problems they will inevitably encounter when planning for the distribution of these retirement assets. The real problem now for the affluent is no longer creating wealth; their problem is distributing the wealth effectively in their own lifetime and preserving it for their heirs.

Personal Savings and Investments

As long as Americans habitually favor consumption over savings, personal savings will continue to be the weakest of the three retirement savings vehicles for most people. But the long bull market has offered enormous potential for those with investment resources and has proven to be a retirement savings boon. People in their 60s, who have been planning for retirement for the past ten years, have had their retirement accumulation anxieties significantly reduced as a result of the recent growth in the stock market, and despite recent setbacks in the market. The question for these individuals is whether the additional earnings realized will be used for current or future lifestyle choices.

Estate Planning

Estate planning, unlike retirement planning, is not a modern concern. However, in the past, estate planning affected only a small percentage of the population. Taxation of the transfer of property from one generation to another historically has never been viewed as a significant revenue source for governments. Its purpose has always been to prevent wealth from becoming ominously controlled by too few people—especially when those people were all related. In past eras, when land was the source of most wealth, and only very few people owned most of the land, estate taxation was an obscure high-stakes game between the government and the very rich.

While the concept was originally applied to the aristocrats of Europe, it was ideally suited to American cultural values, in which the self-made man is idealized. As a society, Americans are absolutely convinced that it is possible for anyone to get rich. All it takes, in the view of most Americans, is one great idea, hard work, perseverance, and good luck combined in the right proportions.

Although inherited wealth is not generally respected in this country, inherited wealth is the way most of the truly wealthy in America became so. Look at a list of the great corporate names and trace their history. Many of them are the family names of the entrepreneurial, self-made founders of several generations back. Those individuals are cultural role models, but their history has been largely forgotten.

Dupont escaped the effects of the French Revolution, emigrated to America and produced a high-quality gunpowder favored by our military. Dow Chemical was founded by Herbert Henry Dow in 1897. His research in extractions from brine led him to more than 100 patents, along with a multitude of consumer and industrial products. Henry Ford was a machinist and racing enthusiast who realized that "the way to build automobiles is . . . to make them all alike."

While Americans admire the founders of great companies, many feel that the family inheritors, over generations, have become unambitious, eccentric, profligate, or megalomaniacal, and no longer deserve their wealth. All this inherited wealth smacks of aristocracy. Americans as a whole want to distance themselves from their class- conscious European origins. Today, this aristocratic by-product of wealth, or indirect control of wealth, concentrated in the hands of so few, seems undemocratic—if not a social crime. Many Americans seem to believe that the government has a responsibility to break up large family fortunes in order to create equal opportunity for others.

Thus, gift and estate taxes, first established in 1916, were finally given teeth in 1935. While the general public may feel confident that democratic principles were and still are being upheld, advisors understand that gift and estate taxes have hardly ever made a dent in large family fortunes. Every new tax initiative invariably meets with new tax strategies that can effectively move the wealth or manipulate the wealth around these tax obstacles—as long as the client is willing to invest in the kind of advisory services that can execute the appropriate tax avoidance strategies.

What is far different today, however, is that many more Americans—though still a very small percentage of the total population—will be subject to estate taxes. The issue is no longer an obscure battle between the government and the few privileged descendants of legendary entrepreneurs.

Clients who need advice about retirement distribution planning today typically have earned their wealth by their own efforts. They may not even feel rich; they are just currently successful. They have achieved the American Dream. That dream was never about palaces hung with tapestries; it was about personal fulfillment and financial freedom. They don't feel like aristocrats, so why, they wonder, is the government trying to take away their family's money and, therefore, the family's financial freedom? Naturally, they feel that the fruit of their labors should benefit their families first.

To gauge the depth of this indignation about estate taxation among these entrepreneurial wealthy, try presenting these individuals with a basic estate-planning question: If your wealth can go to only three places when you die—your family, the government, and charity—which is the most important place for your wealth to go?

The answer will be *family* in nearly every case. Charity would be the second choice, and the government the last choice.

Then ask your client the following question: If you had the freedom to decide how much of the assets remaining in your estate would be received by each of these three when you die—a freedom you do have, by the way—what amount would you assign to each?

The answer for family will be, *Almost all of it.* Most people tend to set a dollar figure or a percentage to go to charity, perhaps psychologically based on the tithing principle that may still permeate social consciousness. When people are resistant to leaving significant assets to charity, it is often because they assume that the charitable share will reduce the family's share, not the government's. When they consider an appropriate share to leave to the government, they will invariably assign the same figure: *nothing*. And they will mean it.

What few clients realize is that when they have large retirement assets locked in IRAs to preserve tax deferral, they do not have the freedom to choose where those assets will go—unless they had previously done the proper estate and retirement distribution planning. Instead, when they die—or when their spouse dies after them—they will often pass large tax bills on to their family members, typically in the year following the year of their death.

This set of circumstances is certainly not what our society intended when it went about attempting to break up massive inherited wealth for the common good. What looms on the horizon for financially successful clients who fail to plan properly is the breakup of their family's financial freedom. It is, therefore, up to their advisors to first help them understand how they became the targets of these tax rules, and to then help them get out of the line of fire.

Emotions of Retirement Planning

The technical components of decision-making will often take a back seat to the many emotional components. Although tax-driven decisions always seem logical and businesslike, clients will follow through on those decisions, however correct they might be, only if the decisions *feel* right. Whenever clients let their reason overrule their intuition, they inevitably harbor doubts that can surface later on, to unravel the retirement distribution plan at the first hint that any of their doubts have been confirmed. These emotional reactions may end up being the foundation of any decision-making process. The most careful and creative tax-driven planning will go nowhere if it fails to adequately address the personal and emotional needs of the client.

Tax Indignation

For many people, indignation is the emotion that finally compels them to do retirement distribution planning. Some people feel mildly indignant. For them, paying taxes is a regrettable and painful, but necessary, trade-off to sustaining the quality of life available in this country. Others feel that the government will never get it right, and, for them, paying taxes is like watching their hard-earned money being blown out to sea. Their level of indignation is high. Most people currently facing the retirement distribution maze are on the high-indignation end of the tax acceptance spectrum.

Retirement plan assets can especially exacerbate these feelings of indignation because, while they are tax-deferred, they are also *double-taxed.* Of course, there are additional tax consequences to retirement plan assets. For example, distributions from retirement assets are subject to a 50 percent penalty tax if the Required Minimum Distribution amounts are not taken by the Required Beginning Date. And, unlike other assets that receive a step-up in cost basis when the owner dies, retirement assets do not. In addition, when retirement plan assets are paid out, they are generally taxed at ordinary income tax rates, rather than at capital gains rates, as similar investments would be. In short, retirement assets are treated completely differently from any other assets when it comes to their tax consequences.

Actually, the Required Minimum Distribution rules can cause a more substantial evil than double taxation, but you generally won't encounter much strong client emotion over that issue. The Required Minimum Distribution rules are technical and difficult to reason through. However, for most people, the deadline for making their retirement distribution decisions are sufficiently far ahead into the future, and their ignorance of the various issues involved is so significant that these retirement issues can go largely unaddressed until it is too late.

Fear of Not Having Enough

One other issue that can cause a deep emotional reaction in the client and must be dealt with by the competent retirement distribution specialist is the client's retirement income needs. Most clients feel they will not have enough money to retire on. The dread that they will not have enough is nearly universal. It doesn't matter how much they have. The same fear that hangs over the head of an elderly widow living off a modest fixed pension in a modest retirement community hangs over the heads of multimillionaires. Never underestimate the emotional power of this fear. *Will my retirement savings last my lifetime? If I give some of my money away to my children now, will I be humiliated by some day having to ask for it back?*

In fact, people *should* be concerned that their money might run out, not for the reasons that they might think, but for reasons they are largely unaware of. Consider the common wisdom about retirement income planning. Read any of the consumer advice books about the subject. Look at the pictures in retirement planning brochures—happy, silver-haired couples surrounded by two generations of loving family members on a woodsy picnic day, swinging expensive seven irons toward the 15th hole in some sunbelt oasis, or enjoying the luxury of an island-hopping cruise. The American concept of retirement seems to be all about the fulfillment of long-delayed desires, the excitement of travel, and the indulging of grandchildren.

The articles and brochures all serve to emphasize that underlying fear: Will the money run out? They focus on basic planning strategies. Project future needs. Define the work time horizon. Determine the best investment strategy to make sure the money will be there. No one—particularly the affluent, who are already living this lifestyle—wants to miss out on that retirement picture. So it is better to overprepare.

The problem with this retirement picture is that it represents only one scene of a three-scene reality. There are two other stages common to the experience of those who are retired. Everyone looks forward to Stage One, depicted in the brochures. If wealthy Americans are over-prepared for that picture, so much the better. Their reserves assure them that they can deal with the other two stages.

Stage Two is the deterioration of health followed by a prolonged serious illness. Eighty percent of all deaths are preceded by a prolonged serious illness, according to the Statistical Abstract of the United States. Prolonged illness is likely to have a high cost.

In Stage Three one partner dies, and the survivor may be left in a threatened position. As health deteriorates, without a partner to help, life can become very expensive indeed.

For those who have accumulated multimillion-dollar pension plans and IRAs, even the worst-case scenarios for Stage Two and Stage Three can usually be dealt with financially. The retirement distribution specialist can help clients get past the fear that they will be unprepared for these later stages, should they develop. The specialist should point the clients through these stages to the tax, financial, and personal consequences of retirement distribution planning that the clients and their heirs will face. That planning, if done correctly, can alleviate much of the financial distress typically experienced in these latter stages.

The Tendency to Procrastinate

Advisors who work on estate planning issues know how easy it is for clients to procrastinate resolving these issues. You will not find many people who want to talk about their own mortality. Later seems the best time to deal with these issues.

When people do get around to completing their planning—especially after their health has been threatened and mortality no longer seems an abstract event—they may undergo unexpected psychological reversals.

They may abandon decades-old beliefs because they suddenly see life from a new perspective. The retirement distribution specialist should be alert to this phenomenon, and ready to listen when it happens. Probe into the clients' underlying beliefs, but be flexible enough to respond to sudden changes in thinking, particularly when health and longevity questions arise.

Do you honor the old maxim that claims that the customer is always right? Or do you feel a moral responsibility to see to it that the client does the right thing despite his or her initial inclination to do something else? The pressure is on the retirement distribution specialist to become a more effective communicator and facilitator. The challenge is to explain in layman's terms what is admittedly complex, incomplete, and often confusing tax rules. Be sure the clients understand what their problems are from an estate and income tax point of view, and how problems in one area can compound tax problems in others. Without understanding why things are as they are, clients will never have confidence in their decisions. You will want to draw other family members of the clients into the process, especially in cases in which multigenerational planning is to be considered. As baby boomers move into their 50s, 60s, and 70s, and face retirement distribution planning, certain aspects of their emotional makeup will surface that may have been barely evident up to now. In addition, these baby boomer families are more likely to have two spouses equally participating in income production and financial decisions. Demographic complications more prevalent in this generation, such as second marriages and combined families, will become even more common in the future. Advisors in the future dealing with these issues will need to become more adept in effectively communicating with their clients.

CHAPTER 2
THE ROLE OF THE RETIREMENT DISTRIBUTION SPECIALIST

CONTENTS

2 THE ROLE OF THE RETIREMENT DISTRIBUTION SPECIALIST

At present, tens of thousands of advisors are serving millions of clients who face substantial retirement distribution planning issues. For the most part, these clients are only vaguely aware of the problems that loom before them. In general, these advisors lack the knowledge and training needed to help their clients understand the many issues involved and to construct appropriate solutions. Advisors to the affluent should be encouraged to investigate the tax code and to take pre-emptive action to alert their clients to the many problems associated with the distribution of their retirement funds. If not, many clients will not even know that these problems exist until it is too late.

Beyond that, a reasonable percentage of these same advisors should assume the role of the retirement distribution specialist, on behalf of both their clients and their colleagues. The title Retirement Distribution Specialist implies a number of characteristics. These specialists should possess the following traits:

- Sufficient knowledge to ask the retirement distribution questions that no one else is asking
- The technical expertise necessary to fully interpret the client's financial and emotional data
- The professional competence to be able to design and implement effective solutions
- The relationship skills needed to develop trust and confidence on the part of the client and the client's family members, and to track and adjust the retirement distribution plan far into the future

Who Makes a Good Retirement Distribution Specialist?

Accountants

There are several entry points in which the topic of retirement distribution planning can be broached with clients. The most common one is age. When the client reaches age 70½—the Required Beginning Date—significant events concerning retirement are about to occur. The advisor most effectively positioned at this age-based entry point is the client's accountant, in part because an annual planning mindset has been established between accountant and client, driven by the need to prepare tax returns each year.

In addition, the accountant in all probability has had access over the years to the necessary data concerning the client's retirement plans and IRAs. Each year, changes in the client's potential retirement distribution situation should be well known to the accountant. Most important, when the client first gets a glimmer of the significance of the Required Beginning Date, the accountant is the person the client is most likely to call to help address these issues.

Attorneys

Attorneys may be the ones who are best positioned to serve as retirement distribution specialists. Most affluent people would point to their attorney as the advisor who handles their estate planning needs. After all, it is the attorney who drafted the documents that are the tangible manifestations of the planning process.

The problem with the attorney as retirement distribution specialist is that the law in this area is so complex, and law practices are now so specialized, that gaps in the planning process can appear, even in instances involving the most prestigious law firms. Trust and estate attorneys typically view retirement distribution rules as the domain of ERISA attorneys. ERISA attorneys, on the other hand, seldom have access to the estate planning client, nor do they proactively market their expertise to estate planning attorneys, even within their own firms. Besides, most of their knowledge is focused on creating and maintaining qualified retirement plans, not on efficiently distributing the assets therefrom. The unfortunate result is that all too often no attorney in the firm is assigned the responsibility for creating, implementing, and coordinating a comprehensive retirement distribution plan.

Estate Planners

While the accountant commands the most obvious entry point, the next most likely candidate to be a retirement distribution specialist is the advisor who handles the client's estate planning process. In many instances, that person is the individual's accountant or attorney. However, the estate planning specialist may be a *third* type of advisor who is neither the accountant nor attorney.

In the past, the estate planning process has largely disregarded retirement assets. It was assumed that retirement assets would be distributed and entirely consumed before death and, therefore, were not a material factor in designing the typical estate plan. However, such is no longer the case. In fact, the opposite should be assumed because, among affluent executives, professionals, and business owners, the long bull market has dramatically increased the value of the retirement assets far beyond the client's ability to consume those assets during the retirement years. Retirement assets are now a major part of many estates. In fact, they may be the largest single asset owned by clients, representing in many instances more than half the value of their estate. Those assets, in all likelihood, will *not* be entirely spent before death. Moreover, the total lifetime distribution and depletion of those assets should, in most instances, be avoided.

Typically, the worst thing to do with retirement assets is to lump them into the estate and treat them as just another estate asset. The retirement distribution specialist's role is to separate the retirement assets from the general estate plan and to subject them to a separate planning process. Once the retirement distribution plan is in place, the advisor must then bring the retirement assets back into the overall estate planning process, to integrate the two sets of solutions into one coherent integrated plan. Estate planning should never be a discrete event. Clients whose wealth is significant enough to warrant creative estate planning solutions are likely to think that once the estate plan has been developed, the planning process is complete and the plan can remain unchanged until they die.

The truth is that estate plans completed more than several years earlier may run the risk of being significantly out of date. Tax laws change frequently. Family circumstances, desires, and goals may also change. Finances change. Insurance product suitability and insurance company performance may change dramatically within the span of just a few years. An annual review of the estate plan is, therefore, essential. So, too, is the retirement distribution plan.

The annual review is an entry point to retirement distribution planning and a time to make sure that nothing has been overlooked. The conscientious estate planner who also serves as retirement distribution specialist will, therefore, have natural entry points annually. Additional entry points may arise as the client's facts and circumstances change, and the estate plan is therefore thrown off track.

One potential drawback to this entry point approach is that, in many cases, comprehensive retirement distribution planning occurs so near the age 70½ date that the luxury of a well-considered, comprehensive, and carefully tested planning process does not exist. Another obvious drawback to this approach is that the client may die before reaching age 70½ and, accordingly, may not have implemented the proper retirement distribution strategy. (See Chapter 12 for a more detailed discussion of this topic.) Another problem is that very few professional advisors from any of the traditional estate planning fields actually perform annual or regularly scheduled reviews. Advisors typically wait for their clients to inform them of some significant change that might affect their estate plan. However, clients are not necessarily sufficiently aware of retirement distribution issues to know when such an issue may have arisen. As a result, opportunities for effective retirement distribution planning are frequently missed.

Insurance Planners

Another choice for the role of the retirement distribution specialist is the insurance planner. The insurance planner may frequently possess an in-depth knowledge of the intricacies of the client's estate plan and is often more willing than the attorney or accountant to undertake the annual review obligation with energy and commitment. The insurance planner may very well be the ideal candidate for the role of the retirement distribution specialist. There is, however, one drawback—the need to overcome advisor and client biases over his or her presumed self-interest. Life insurance is a commission-based product rather than a fee-based service. This fact, which is well known to the client and to the client's other advisors, often operates to preclude a life insurance advisor from sitting on the client's side of the table. Insurance professionals who have succeeded with wealthy clients have invariably earned their client's respect by their scrupulous attention to providing quality services over the years, and by their willingness to become effective team players with the other decision-making advisors that their clients have come to rely on. Accordingly, their credentials for the role of retirement distribution specialist can be as strong as anyone else's.

Pension Consultants

Having designed and administered the very qualified plans responsible for such large retirement assets, pension consultants have a natural market advantage. Their mission has been defined in terms of retirement asset accumulation. Accumulation, however, eventually leads into distribution.

Of all the professionals who may be involved in this area, pension specialists should have the least trouble with the rules of retirement distribution, because they have been living with these same rules in the insulated world of pension and profit sharing plans. When these advisors realize that, in focusing on retirement accumulation exclusively, they have completed only half the job, it should be a fairly simple positioning shift for them to go back to their clients to complete the second half of the job, namely the retirement distribution phase.

Investment Advisors

Another choice for the role of the retirement distribution specialist is the investment advisor. The magnitude of the client's retirement distribution problem is often directly attributable to the success of the client's investment advisors and their investment management strategies. Affluent clients frequently possess a wide range of investment knowledge, and often have great confidence in their various investment advisors. Some clients want direct and complete control over their investment decision-making, while others turn control over these decisions to a trusted financial decision-maker. Neither end of the spectrum is necessarily better, and many clients find themselves somewhere in an undefined middle. Most clients want their advisors to take the time to inform them of their various investment options. However, they also frequently want someone whom they trust implicitly to handle their accounts, without having to go over every last detail and investment choice with them.

Wherever clients may fall on the spectrum, however, the investment advice which they are typically getting does not include detailed advice on retirement distribution strategies, even in those instances in which retirement assets may be the bulk of their investment resources.

An investment advisor should realize that minimizing a client's Required Minimum Distributions each year will maximize the amount of the client's retirement assets left to be managed. Moreover, because investment goals and strategies typically change in the context of multigenerational planning, there is usually tremendous opportunity in this arena to increase the added-value of the investment specialist's advisory services. Additionally, investment advisors typically have the most direct connection to the retirement asset itself. Since the advisors already have, in all likelihood, large measures of the client's trust, they owe it to themselves and their clients to complete the financial planning task entrusted to them. After all, their job is to assist the client in the efficient use and investment of the client's assets. In performing retirement distribution planning for their clients, they are merely extending this role.

Stockbrokers

Is it likely that a stockbroker will become a retirement distribution specialist? The role does not appear to fit the stereotyped idea of stockbrokers as transaction-oriented rather than planning-based. While quality stockbrokers are often experts in their field and trusted by their clients, they tend to be the advisory professionals who are least informed about retirement distribution rules.

Nevertheless, stockbrokers certainly have the capacity to fill that role if they are willing to learn and to expand the context of their client relationships. In fact, many stockbrokers have already fulfilled that role successfully. In addition, as the financial services industry wakes up to the incredible revenue opportunity associated with retirement distribution planning—advisory fees, product sales, assets under management—based on a proven ability to package planning solutions under their brand names, the national brokerage institutions may well be positioned in the future to be *leaders* in the retirement distribution field.

In summary, every advisor on the client's team is potentially qualified for the role of the retirement distribution specialist. All it takes on the part of the advisor is the necessary commitment to this new specialty.

CHAPTER 3
THE ANALYSIS, DESIGN, AND IMPLEMENTATION OF THE RETIREMENT PLAN

CONTENTS

3 THE ANALYSIS, DESIGN, AND IMPLEMENTATION OF THE RETIREMENT PLAN

It takes only one of the client's advisors to alert the client to the urgent need for comprehensive retirement distribution planning. However, the responsibility to make that wake-up call should not be limited to the retirement distribution specialist, as no advisor can entirely avoid the responsibility of making the client aware of this need and introducing the client to planning process. Once the client has been alerted to the problem, the advisor can then either act as the retirement distribution specialist, working directly with the client to solve various retirement distribution issues, or assist the client in finding another qualified professional to help resolve those issues.

From that point on, the real work of the retirement distribution specialist involves three stages—the analysis, the design, and implementation. Within each of these stages, the retirement distribution specialist serves in the capacity of both technician and facilitator.

The success of the technician role depends on an in-depth knowledge of the rules and regulations of the tax code and the mechanics of the planning strategies available within the tax law's framework. The facilitator role has two parts of its own. In one part, the retirement distribution specialist calls on ideas that integrate all the disciplines involved in retirement distribution planning into one coordinated planning effort. The other part requires that the specialist possess the skill and willingness to enter the emotional minefield that may lie hidden within the client's circumstances.

Analyzing the Needs of the Client

The first stage in which to apply these two roles is the analysis stage. Initially, the retirement distribution specialist serves as a technician. His or her first responsibility is to quantify that need for the client. To do that, the retirement distribution specialist must gather the relevant data. Such data can be found in the following areas:

- The retirement plan
- The investment plan
- The estate plan

With business-owner clients, the business plan—particularly the pension, continuity, and succession components—provides an additional layer of data.

The Role of Technician

Acquiring access to all of the necessary data is ordinarily extremely difficult, but approaching the client in the role of technician will help. When affluent clients are approached by advisors and planners, they tend to resist, wary of a potential sales pitch—for products or services, commissions or fees. They would, of course, far prefer being advised in a professional way about their problems and then being offered objective recommendations for solutions. The more data a planner requests, the more this resistance can build. The client may feel that the more data the planner sees, the greater the chances that a sales opportunity will present itself. Only when planners have taken the time to establish sufficient credibility and trust will clients let go of that resistance and release the data. On the other hand, there is a natural assumption that a technician is objectively performing his or her job. There is much less resistance, and credibility is established fairly readily. The fact that another of the client's trusted advisors may well have recommended the technician to perform this work enhances the technician's credibility.

The role of facilitator requires an even greater investment in time spent building trust with the client, in order to produce the soft data necessary to complement the hard data. The hard data is very likely to reveal incomplete or erroneous work performed in the past by other long-term advisors whom the client must still trust. In many instances, these problems have been caused by a lack of information; rarely were they willful. As a technician you can only alert the client to these problems. However, in your role as facilitator, you should be able to gain the client's confidence and then be able to help resolve the issues.

The Role of Facilitator

While the technician's role may be most evident initially, the facilitator's role should quickly become dominant. A facilitator should move the analysis ahead by showing a broad understanding of the many planning issues involved and the process needed to resolve them. In the facilitator role, you need to prove that you have the client's best interests in mind, while endeavoring to support the basic position of the client's other advisors, given the information that they were working with. Your objective is to fix, as best you can, the client's retirement distribution planning problems, as well as any other related planning issues that might arise, rather than to assign any blame to any of the client's other advisors.

In retirement distribution planning, you have to be a team player—playing on the client's team, not on your own. In the rare instances when your efforts reveal someone else's negligence or fraud, make the facts known to the client judiciously—usually by working first through their other advisors to reach consensus on the conclusions. This will prove that you are all on the same side in attempting to protect the client's interests. The most effective way to earn a high level of commitment from your client is to communicate openly with the other advisors, rather than working alone.

Progress Reports

As the data-gathering and analysis move forward, send a series of progress reports with preliminary conclusions and recommendations to the client and to the other members of the advisory team. These reports can flag potential problems as well as complement areas in which the planning seems to be exactly correct and on track. If there is any danger that the progress report implies an indictment of previous work, write the report as a joint memo to the client from the whole decision team, so that the client will enjoy a sense of security that the whole team is in agreement with the conclusions cited in the report. The report can end with a few questions intended to propel the client on to the next step in your investigation of the data.

The importance of these questions cannot be overstated. One of the goals of the relationship-building effort is to have clients realize that you, as the retirement distribution specialist, are asking questions that no other team member had ever asked before. In fact, some of your questions have probably been asked many times before. However, the client may never have grasped the significance of the question or understood the question in the right context. These kinds of questions can work to establish the bridge between the technician role and the facilitator role, by demonstrating the two kinds of expertise the retirement distribution specialist possesses—a precise grasp of the relevant technical details of the tax law and a broad understanding of the planning issues and the processes necessary to resolve them.

The questions can be used to stimulate creative problem-solving with the other advisors on the client's decision team and can reduce the threat of the work being second-guessed later on. Much depends on how the questions are presented. The advisor should always avoid raising non-productive doubts. However, most advisors value opportunities to enhance their work, and they accept rhetorical challenges willingly. Make sure that the messages your reports convey are non-judgmental ones.

Building Trust

At the beginning of the planning process, you are endeavoring to build trust with clients, so that they feel comfortable disclosing to you both their financial data and their emotional concerns. Building trust begins with the assumption that you are there to protect the client against possible problems and to assist the client in locating possible opportunities. You are not there to explain your latest proposed planning solution. That is how the facilitator role supports the technician role. In other words, clients are initially more interested in knowing that you are aware of and sympathetic to their concerns than in hearing your proposed solutions. They want to know that you are willing to take ownership of their problems and to assure them that an acceptable solution can and will be found

The actions that tend to weigh the most in earning the client's trust are often the little ones that for the unskilled advisor may go largely unnoticed. For example, in the course of a meeting—such as the initial meeting to obtain the data necessary to design the retirement distribution plan—there are four steps to establishing trust:

1. Participate in the rituals of social contracts.
2. Search for common bonds.
3. Set the agenda of the meeting.
4. Ascertain the client's true objectives and concerns.

Step 1: Participate in the Rituals of Social Contracts

The first step involves the rituals of social contracts. If you do not succeed at the ritual contracts level, you cannot possibly progress to the other high levels. Rituals include all the little interactions of introduction—handshakes, offers of refreshment, seating, and exchange of business cards. Clients unconsciously look for behaviors and expressions that demonstrate a compatible relationship style and an understanding of business manners. While these nuances can often be hidden below the surface, these unconscious perceptions can be made visible by our actions and conduct. For example, you may want to decline an offer of coffee, perhaps because of a reluctance to be the cause of extra effort or because of a desire to get right down to business. However, coffee drinking can form part of an important social contract. By ignoring this, you may not only pass up a chance to make and keep a contract, but you may also be unwittingly signaling a desire to plunge ahead on your personal agenda without taking adequate time to let the clients express theirs.

Step 2: Search for Common Bonds

The second step in trust-building is the search for common bonds—people, places, experiences, and beliefs shared by both parties. Out of those common bonds can emerge data about circumstances and lifestyle choices. A discussion of the common shared weather can turn into a discussion of abnormal weather experiences shared. Suddenly a perfunctory exchange on the weather can lead to a more profound shared experience about weather disasters you have both encountered and the lessons learned from them. A discussion of sports can be transformed into a mutual appreciation of athletic ability and aspirations of excellence. These discussions, if successful, can lead to favorable judgments. If unsuccessful, they can lead the client to a vague sense of uncertainty and a lack of confidence in the advisor.

Mutual acquaintances can serve as even more powerful trust magnets. This is especially so where co-workers are the subject of discussion. The quality of the people you work with will often directly reflect on you. However, there are pitfalls here too. You do not want to be perceived as a name-dropper or as someone who is willing to violate a prior confidential communication. There is also the risk that the client has had a negative relationship with a mutual acquaintance.

Even if you are dealing with an existing client whom you know well, these first two steps can be important in re-establishing an atmosphere of trust and disclosure. These steps, if handled correctly, will remind the client why he or she values the relationship with the advisor, and should continue to be used by the advisor in subsequent meetings with the client, to further solidify the relationship.

Step 3: Set the Agenda of the Meeting

With completion of the common bond search, state the goals for the discussion and give the client an idea of what questions to expect. Clients will agree to most proposed meeting agendas because they may be reluctant to volunteer information spontaneously. Agreeing to a limited agenda is a way to appear open while hedging on full disclosure. The client will most likely want to wait to discuss the emotional issues that can profoundly affect retirement distribution planning until your relationship is more established.

During this phase of the planning process, your approach should be to ask questions that challenge the intellect, not the emotions. Questions about the future are safe territory, since people do not generally feel they can be held accountable for what has not yet occurred. The same is true for subjects that are hypothetical or idea-oriented. Past actions and decisions are generally low-risk questions, because clients will tend to rationalize away the questionable outcomes of past decisions. If you take this data gleaned during the early stages of the planning process as gospel, you may be surprised later to find that the client's underlying emotions have surfaced, changing the nature of their responses to these same questions.

Step 4: Ascertain What the Clients Feel

If you do not reach this step, the data you get will always be suspect. One way to ascertain whether the client's intellectual and emotional decisions coincide is to explore the subjects discussed in the fact-finding phase from an emotional perspective. For example, if a client gave a perfectly reasonable response in a hypothetical decision area, test it by asking what actual decisions made in the past followed the hypothetical model. To further explore this area, create a comparison between the ideal world and the real world. Also, test the client's stated view of the future against present decisions and test past decisions against present ones.

If you find inconsistencies, the discrepancy can be gently pointed out. When clients realize that these disparities may be indicators of problems, their true emotional issues often emerge. That is why clients frequently say, "Nobody ever asked me that question before." What they are really saying is that nobody had ever broken through their defenses before in such a positive way to expose their true underlying feelings.

Gathering Data

Once you have progressed through these trust-building stages, you are ready to use the Confidential Retirement Distribution Questionnaire and Retirement Distribution Planning Checklist provided on the disk that accompanies this book. These forms are designed to sup-port your interview technique and procedures from the viewpoints of both technician and facilitator. When acting as a technician, take careful notes as a way of demonstrating your acute listening skills. The use of the questionnaire and checklists will demonstrate a sense of organization, focus, and competence that can inspire the client's confidence. On the other hand, when acting as facilitator, push away the paperwork to demonstrate your empathy and concern for the client. Listen for the emotional issues that lie behind the hard facts being presented.

Because retirement distribution planning draws from several disciplines and can raise emotional issues that involve family members, a standardized objective approach to this subject supports both roles. Clients need to see that there is a default standard to the planning process—the non-emotional and objective technician side—into which they can fit their emotion-laden family situations.

Generally, the data-gathering process will not be successful if both spouses are not involved. However, it is common in the generation now reaching age 70 to find some husbands still sheltering their wives from the "burden" of having to make financial decisions. When this is the case, you may find that you have no choice in the initial stages of data-gathering but to deal with the husband alone—sometimes even when the wife is present at the meeting. Do not hesitate, however, to challenge that situation and offer your own data-gathering default standard. That standard should acknowledge the need for input from the other advisors as well as family members.

The questionnaire and the checklists provide an agenda for the meeting. They reveal the client's tax, financial, and personal philosophies and circumstances. The discussion should answer the following questions:

- What is the size and disposition of the retirement assets?
- What is the size of the retirement assets relative to the client's other assets?
- What are the retirement income needs of the husband and wife?
- How much excess capital is in the retirement assets?
- What are the income and estate tax implications for that excess capital?
- Should the tax-deferred growth of the retirement assets be preserved? How?
- Should the children and grandchildren inherit the tax-deferred growth in order to enjoy a lifetime income stream? How?
- How should the beneficiaries of the excess capital in the retirement assets meet their estate tax liabilities?
- What are the appropriate investment strategies for multigenerational retirement assets?
- How should the advisory team undertake the tasks of multigenerational retirement distribution planning?

Determining the Size and Disposition of Retirement Assets

The data-gathering process begins by identifying the type of retirement assets and their ownership—husband's and wife's considered separately. It is important to understand the types of retirement plans in which the assets are held, since each type may contain its own restrictions and offers its own unique notions. It is also necessary to know who is the trustee of each retirement plan, and to understand what influence the client may have in amending a qualified plan, if amending the plan may create a more favorable environment for multigenerational planning purposes.

Of course, it is necessary to examine beneficiary designation documents—first, to ascertain whether they have been set up correctly to achieve the client's goals. For example, it is very common for clients to have neglected designating contingent beneficiaries. In many instances, the election forms provided by an IRA Custodian may not have made clear whether contingent beneficiary designations are even possible. The client's surprise that so elementary an issue has been overlooked may prove to be a watershed event, opening the client's mind to the value of more sophisticated retirement distribution planning.

Second—and perhaps more important—the advisor needs to probe the reasoning behind the client's goals and the designations that have resulted. At this point, clients are likely to want to discuss their what-if-the-money-runs-out scenarios. Take the time and make the effort to show the client that you understand his or her concern, that it is a common concern in retirement accumulation planning and retirement distribution planning, that these concerns will be adequately addressed, and that the proposed retirement distribution plan does make sense from a personal and emotional point of view.

When you listen effectively to the reasoning of the client, ask challenging questions, but always show support for the answers you receive. In this way, you will earn the right to proceed to the next phase in the planning process—the examination of the client's financial documents. The client will be able to accept your need to verify whether their emotional reaction to this issue matches the financial reality of the situation. Generally, the first document to look at is the financial statement. Drawing up investment statements for all of the retirement assets is the next step. The client, however, may be reluctant to release these statements to you, wary that you are interested in them only to, say, promote your own investment services. The client may be quite satisfied with his or her recent investment results and might not be willing to entertain investment alternatives. That is why it is so important to take a client down the logical pathway outlined above, demonstrating why it is necessary for the advisor to analyze investment statements. For example, an advisor is likely to want to analyze the investment results in order to verify whether or not there may be excess capital in the retirement assets—in other words, whether there will be tax problems associated with the current retirement distribution plan. The second reason is to find out who are the trustees or custodians of IRA and other plan assets, in order to discover the various IRA and plan document default provisions, and whether those provisions will accommodate multigenerational planning strategies. The investment strategy, if the advisor is interested in that aspect of the client relationship, becomes an issue only much further down the line in the implementation phase of the retirement distribution plan.

Remember that retirement income needs for the client will always be more of an emotional issue than a financial issue. Most people have developed an income expectation and a comfort level associated with the income level they were receiving just before their retirement. They are used to seeing a certain set amount on a periodic check. Ignoring all other factors, the clients will probably initially choose to distribute a similar amount from their retirement assets each period to maintain that same income stream.

The fact that during their working years that amount covered *both* expenses *and* savings does not change the emotional importance of receiving the same amount during retirement. Therefore, distributing pre-tax retirement assets in the same periodic amount as they had previously been receiving, then paying income tax on that amount, and then finally investing the after-tax excess income again in taxable investments, probably will not strike them as an inefficient use of their retirement assets. The emotional fixation on a set monthly or annual income figure blurs the otherwise obvious financial inefficiency involved in this approach.

Asking the clients directly if they think they will need that much income during their retirement years to live on will probably result in a response such as, "We're not sure, but let's not take any chances." Accept that response at its face value and as a sensible defensive position, but also question whether—if you were to discover excess pre-tax capital in their retirement assets—they would be interested in continuing the compounded growth of their retirement assets each year, minimizing income taxes on yearly distributions, and thereby avoiding the unnecessary loss of capital in their retirement assets.

Analyzing the Need and Sources for Retirement Income

In order to discover if the opportunity to preserve income tax savings exists, you need to analyze the retirement income needs of the client. Presumably, an income needs analysis has already been performed by one of the advisors, and a formal planning document summarizing those results is in existence. If there is no such formalized plan, and if retirement has already commenced, verify retirement income planning informally and measure that plan against current experience. It is seldom effective to press for precise figures on income needs. It is usually a mistake to refer to retirement income as a "budget." Affluent clients may take offense at the concept of living on a budget. Finally, explore the plans that are in place for each spouse based on whether the husband or wife survives the other.

In addressing each of these issues, emphasize that your questions are not meant to replace any planning that has already taken place. Rather, your questions are intended to help you get a clearer picture of the planning decisions that were previously made and how they affect retirement distribution planning.

It is also appropriate at this point to identify other family members who might figure into the retirement distribution equation—namely, children and grandchildren. Clients may hesitate before including grandchildren in this equation, not wanting to presume what is best for them. In your role of technician, you can respond to that concern by explaining how achieving the goal of extended tax deferral is often based on a multigenerational view, and that the use of the grandchildren's ages can dramatically expand the planning opportunities associated with the use of retirement assets. The personal and emotional considerations involved in providing long-term income to children and grandchildren are separate issues that typically will be addressed at a later stage in the planning process. In your role as facilitator, you can nevertheless elect to explore these issues at this point, or you can wait until the client is more comfortable discussing them later on in the planning process.

Setting the Assumptions for the Plan

All of these questions naturally tie in with the tax and interest rate assumptions to be used in the illustration of the retirement distribution plan. Now that you have established the client's income needs and investment concerns, the client can determine whether his or her past and current tax and investment situations should be used for future projections, or whether adjustments should be made. For example, some clients envision a move to another state—perhaps one with a more moderate climate—in their later retirement years. This change of state residency may have a substantial impact on their future income tax liability and, therefore, should be factored into their retirement assumptions.

Since assumptions tend to blend the real with the hypothetical, a discussion of assumptions provides an excellent framework for exploring alternative possibilities without pressure. Using *if . . . then* scenarios and *A vs. B* choices, you can uncover tax, financial, and personal philosophies that the clients may not have been able to articulate directly. You may also be able to identify inconsistencies between their stated goals and their prior actions that need to be further explored and, if possible, resolved.

Reviewing Estate Planning Documents

The client may react with hesitation and confusion when you reach the next step: asking to review the estate planning documents. Clients typically do not want another advisor probing into areas already taken care of by other trusted advisors. They may feel protective of those advisor relationships and fear that issues may be raised that they are not prepared to address. They may fear that their estate plan will be dissected, leading to unexpected—and perhaps undesirable—changes. Why shouldn't the client feel resistance to this process?

Just as the questionnaire is not designed to address retirement income needs specifically, it was not designed to directly address traditional estate planning issues. It is primarily designed to isolate the retirement asset from the other assets that make up the estate. This will enable the advisor to focus on achieving the retirement distribution goals. At the end of the process, the two planning segments will be coordinated.

The advisor should approach that goal as a technician. You will need to establish the estate tax attributable to the retirement asset. Remember, retirement assets (when computing income in respect of a decedent deductions) are assumed to be taxed in the highest marginal Federal estate tax bracket and, accordingly, will be subject to estate taxes at the highest level in the client's estate. To establish that level, you will need to quantify the client's taxable estate. However, the client will likely allow you to perform that analysis *only* if there are opportunities to use the retirement distribution planning in furtherance of the estate planning goals. Conflicts will arise between the estate plan and the retirement distribution plan if the initial estate plan had assumed that the retirement assets would be depleted by the time of the death of the client and spouse.

Estate planning documents that should be reviewed should include not only the wills of both husband and wife, but also both of their powers of attorney. You will need to determine how these documents will affect retirement distribution planning, particularly with respect to the irrevocable life expectancy elections to be made at age $70^1/_2$. Other documents to be reviewed include the following:

- Revocable trusts
- Irrevocable trusts
- Family partnership agreements
- Foundations
- Charitable trusts
- Life insurance policies and beneficiary designations
- Life insurance policy summaries, projections, and ledgers
- Estate plan summary documents outlining the goals and objectives

Look specifically at the strategic objectives behind these documents. Here are two questions to ask:

1. Are the Unified Credit Amount and annual gifting opportunities being used effectively?
2. If life insurance is being used as a tool for estate tax funding, is it structured to remain outside of the estate itself and, therefore, not subject to estate tax?

If trusts are involved, find out who the trustees and beneficiaries are. You may find inconsistencies between the trustees and beneficiaries for the estate planning purposes and the trustees and beneficiaries for the retirement distribution planning purposes. This shows why separate planning, followed by integrated planning, is necessary to prevent the estate planning distribution goals from conflicting with the retirement distribution goals.

Reviewing Life Insurance Policies

The request for life insurance policies is likely to be another sensitive issue for clients for reasons that are examined in the life insurance chapter (see Chapter 10). No client wants to endure another life insurance sales pitch. Make it clear that you want to see those policies in order to identify existing coverage and then to determine whether retirement distribution planning, as formulated, produces any shortfall in coverage. To the extent that there is a shortfall, quantify the shortfall and determine whether any additional policies will be needed. If the retirement distribution plan results in an estate tax liability for retirement assets, life insurance is likely to be the most efficient way to fund the liability. Repositioning existing policies may create even greater efficiencies. The life insurance beneficiary designations may also provide valuable information within the retirement distribution planning context. Another reason for reviewing life insurance policies is to discover whether they are or were part of any qualified plan asset. If so, there may be an opportunity to recover PS-58 costs and avoid double income taxation on the distribution of the policy to the plan participant. See Chapter 16 for a fuller discussion of this topic.

In each of these areas, there is the technician's need for the factual data and the facilitator's need for the underlying emotional considerations that explain why certain decisions had been made and certain planning strategies adopted. In shifting from the analysis phase to the design phase, you will need to understand both of these components, so that your recommendations can be reconciled with any existing estate planning documents or decisions that are not to be altered.

Identifying Planning Gaps

In many instances, you will uncover significant planning gaps. Some of these gaps may be the result of incomplete planning. In the years before retirement, some people procrastinate or even avoid the planning process entirely. In some cases, the advisors may not have taken a proactive role in directing the planning efforts, or they may have simply acquiesced to their clients' unwillingness to assist in the coordination of the advisory team or in the resolution of certain issues. Sometimes plans are flawed due to misinformation or incorrect assumptions. Sometimes the estate plan is simply out of date, due to changes in circumstances. In rare cases, the estate plan is inadequate because the advisors were incompetent or even disreputable.

As the retirement distribution specialist, you should not be distracted by the client's other planning needs, except as they relate to the retirement distribution issues. However, once the retirement distribution plan has been formulated, independent of other planning needs, it should be integrated with the overall estate plan and other investment strategies. That is the time to deal with these planning gaps—after the client has seen you finish the job you were engaged to complete.

Helping Clients Articulate Their Personal Philosophies

Rounding out the analysis stage are two more areas that need to be explored with the client. Each of these areas will probably require you to abandon your technician's role altogether, and may prove to be the most emotionally sensitive issue involved in the process—the personal philosophy of the client as it relates to family wealth, and the personal feelings of the client as they relate to their individual family members. All the data gathering about tax and financial issues, retirement income needs, and estate plans may prove entirely fruitless and misguided if these important personal issues are not fully understood and addressed. It is essential that you discover the client's philosophy—or emotions—about his or her children and grandchildren inheriting wealth. Some of those thoughts and feelings may be identifiable from past estate planning decisions. However, often one finds that those decisions are out of date or, perhaps, had never been made in a truly informed manner. Past decisions may have to be acknowledged and challenged before they can be applied to the retirement distribution planning process.

Naturally, most affluent clients prefer keeping wealth in the family rather than letting the government appropriate it. However, the very factors that initially enabled the client to achieve wealth often contribute to interpersonal tensions. Successful people frequently earned their success at the expense of family involvement. They may have used money over the years as a substitute for emotionally supporting their other family members. These habits may have led some family members into character weaknesses, dependencies, or defiant and profligate behavior. Even if the client and his or her other family members had at one time shared strong beliefs concerning wealth and family stewardship, family relationships over time may have disintegrated into belligerence or isolation.

Every family history contains elements that must be dealt with in the retirement planning process. One minor incident may cause the client to withhold or alter the relevant data. You may find yourself concluding the analysis stage, proceeding to the design stage, and formulating a perfect retirement distribution plan—except for one thing. And that one thing may keep the client from implementing any of your recommendations.

One way to avoid this problem, and still obtain the vital information that you need, is to offer a model family decision framework as it relates to retirement distribution planning. Describe a typical decision track—though not necessarily the one you expect the client to follow—in which the involvement of other family members plays a critical role in developing the plan. If the client is unwilling to go down that track, you can ask for his or her model. If the present alternative, in your experience, is likely to lead to problems, you can ask the client for an explanation and can gently probe until the client is comfortable revealing the true reasons behind his or her reluctance to accept your model. Another possible approach is the issue of the stewardship of the family wealth in terms of controls, both during and after the client's life. Give the client hypothetical examples of control mechanisms and ask for his or her opinion. The first response may still be on the hypothetical level, but with a few judicious inquiries, you may be able to locate the practical and emotional sources of these underlying opinions. Ultimately, this can lead to a plan to include family members in the planning process—or at least to communicate the plan to family members once it has been decided upon.

Identify the Roles of Advisory Team Members

Another potentially sensitive issue in the analysis stage is the respective roles of the other members of the client's advisory team. Whether or not family members play an active role in this process, the client must accept that his or her professional advisors have to. Legal, accounting, pension, trust, custodial, investment, and insurance personnel should all have design input, and each will have certain implementation tasks to perform.

Many affluent clients tend to keep their advisors isolated from each other, possibly in an attempt to avoid any conflicts or perhaps because varying degrees of trust are associated with each different relationship. As a result, planning efforts may remain disjointed, incomplete, and uncoordinated. To remedy this situation, suggest a default model under which you will all work. If the client balks at this, he or she should be made to offer an alternative model—and justify it—or reveal why he or she does not trust the advisors to work together effectively. Let the client see examples of how working relationships have been managed effectively in other instances to the benefit of a particular client. This may even include providing prototype communication pieces and scripting the initial client-advisor interactions. In the end, you should have earned the right to use your model, particularly if you have successfully communicated the need for a spirit of cooperation among the members of the client's advisory team.

Whether this analysis stage has extended over two meetings or even half a dozen, if you treat data-gathering procedures as a part of the process of establishing credibility and building a high-level working relationship, you are more than halfway home. What remains are the mechanical steps involved in developing the solutions that will meet the client's specific goals and your commitment to implement the retirement distribution plan and to assist in monitoring the plan each year to ensure that it continues to be appropriate for the client's changing circumstances.

Designing a Retirement Distribution Plan

The process now moves from the analysis phase to the design phase. It is time to decide what to do with all the data that has been collected and analyzed. This is the stage in which the retirement distribution specialist will negotiate the tax maze on behalf of the client. For the competent retirement distribution specialist, this stage is easier to work in than the analysis stage, because the advisor knows all the twists, all the turns, all the false pathways, all the dead ends, and all the hidden routes.

The Engagement Agreement

The transition from the first stage to the second can be accomplished effectively with the use of an engagement agreement. Engagement agreements, common in consultation projects, can be invaluable in setting the working agenda and the expectations of both client and advisor. The creation of the engagement agreement may precede the data-gathering work.

The engagement agreement is an absolute necessity in successful retirement distribution planning. From the client's point of view, the engagement letter provides the safety of a contract, spelling out the obligations—short-term and long-term—of the retirement distribution specialist, as well as the expected outcome of the project—again, short-term and long-term. The term *engagement* implies that the client has an obligation to participate actively in the decision-making process. From the retirement distribution specialist's perspective, the engagement agreement justifies the fee obligation which the client has undertaken and offers the standards by which the work will be completed and judged. Because other advisors can play such an important role in the analysis and design stages of the planning process, the engagement letter helps create a decision team mentality in the mind of the client and discourages the client from either isolating or favoring particular advisors to the detriment of others, or to the detriment of the project as a whole.

The advantage of using the engagement agreement after, rather than before, the analysis phase is that the client by that time will have developed a relationship with you and will have gained a sense of your work-product standards. The agreement will simply formalize what the client has already been experiencing. Of course, for existing clients, you will already have proven the value of your approach. In either case, the engagement agreement can provide a powerful way to focus the client on the goals, cost-benefit, and timeframe of the work.

A critical aspect of the design stage is to begin with clearly articulated client goals that truly reflect his or her tax, financial, and personal philosophies. The advisor should not lose sight of these philosophies in the complexities of designing the retirement distribution plan. Too often, professional advisors, with their wealth of technical knowledge and strategic creativity, can get lost in the intricacies of their solutions, forgetting that the client was not prepared to follow them down that path. The specific client goals should be the starting and ending point of all design efforts.

The methodology employed in the design phase is always to review all the data that was gathered and separate the issues associated with retirement distribution planning from all other planning issues—retirement accumulation issues, estate planning issues, and so forth. The various options should then be examined purely from a retirement distribution planning perspective, following these steps:

1. Identify problems, and convert them into goals that reflect the client's tax, financial, and personal philosophies.
2. Develop solution options to achieve those goals.
3. Integrate the retirement distribution plan with the client's estate plan, investment strategies and any other tax and financial planning that the client has already implemented.

The design stage will involve at least two meetings with the clients, once the data-gathering stage has been completed. To the extent that other family members are encouraged to participate, and do participate, in the plan design phase, additional meetings are likely and may prove to be valuable.

Clients often claim they want their financial, tax, and legal advisors to tell them what to do, because so many of the decisions to be made are painful or difficult, or involve obscure concepts and jargon-laden language. What clients usually mean when they say that, however, is that they want to be able to fully understand their options and be given expert and professional guidance as to which option they should choose. They will then choose the best options themselves.

Discussing the various planning techniques in the abstract can sometimes be helpful, but retirement distribution tax law and strategies may be too difficult to follow, until clients see their own particular circumstances and opportunities quantified on paper. The design work should be directed toward the completion of a written report on alternatives, to be presented in an informal decision-making environment. The final recommendations should be based on the client's reaction to the various alternatives proposed. Typically, the decisions are made at the informal meeting, and a final sign-off occurs at a later, formal meeting. Practically speaking, the decision-making process may involve a series of meetings, as new data emerges.

The Informal Report

Your informal report should focus on three major decisions:

1. How to allocate the retirement assets among various beneficiaries to achieve the client's tax, financial, and personal goals.
2. How to distribute the retirement assets and how to pay income taxes on these assets during the client's lifetime.
3. How to arrange the disposition and control of the retirement assets and how to pay income and estate taxes after the client's death.

The informal report need not bring into the picture all the implications of these options on the client's existing estate plan. Few clients can deal effectively with such complexity. The informal reports should, however, offer a menu of planning alternatives and should show how each one works in either advancing or retreating from the client's overall planning objectives.

However, the informal report may provide a comfortable vehicle in which to engage other family members in the planning process. Some preliminary or tentative decisions can be based on the informal report. This could be a good time to test both the client's true objectives and the long-term impact of those decision alternatives on the client's intended beneficiaries. With the family members' input, the various planning alternatives can be converted into a more formal and finalized design plan.

The Formal Report

The formal report takes the client's informal decisions and isolates the most effective strategies to achieve the retirement distribution planning goals. From the report and the oral presentation the client should be able to make relatively simple decisions of the yes-no or A-B type. Some clients will want to have the freedom to decide. Others may want to first hear what the advisory team recommends. The formal report should, therefore, be adopted to the decision-making style of the client.

This is also the time when the impact of these decisions on other planning issues should be evaluated, anticipating the integration of the retirement distribution plan into the overall estate plan. Life insurance and investment product alternatives will likely make up another component of the formal report.

This is the point at which the advisor will have to decide on the optimum number of meetings required to communicate the report. How much information can the client absorb in one dose? If decisions to be made are not first broken down into smaller, self-contained issues, the client may feel overwhelmed. The obvious defense against that feeling is to put off making any decisions at all. Once that over-load button has been pushed, it is frequently difficult to get the client back on the decision track.

On the other hand, if the decision-making process is too incremental, the client may become discouraged over the length of the process and lose interest in completing the project.

One advantage the retirement distribution specialist has over the estate planning specialist in bringing clients to a decision is the government-imposed deadline of the Required Beginning Date. Emotionally, clients often feel that death is far enough away to allow for procrastination. It may take the death of a friend or someone in circumstances similar to their own to shake clients out of that sense of complacency. But age 70½ cannot be evaded. The downside of this advantage is that waiting until age 70½ can create intense pressure to implement a decision.

This final stage of the design process involves a mastery of the consultation process. Complicated decision information will have to be presented after an equally involved client education effort had just been completed. The advisor may have to hold back on asking the client to make another set of decisions, so as not to unduly complicate or obscure the decisions that must be made first. Finally, just as the client begins to feel the satisfaction of having completed the retirement distribution plan, you may have to reveal the fact that the plan requires that a retrofit be performed on other estate or financial plans already in place.

The pressure to effectively communicate applies not only to the oral communication of the alternatives and recommendations, but also the written documentation. Your clients have doubtlessly never seen a written retirement distribution plan before, because retirement distribution planning has emerged only recently as a separate discipline.

The retirement distribution specialist is forced into unexplored territory. However, because the field is so new, the retirement distribution specialist is unlikely to be hindered by entrenched decisions. Before 1997, the advice the client usually received with respect to the retirement assets was simple: consume the retirement assets or they will eventually be triple-taxed. Today, the message is different: preserve as much tax deferral as you can for as long as you can. For most

Americans, consuming has traditionally been easier than preserving. Preserving usually entails a long-term perspective and a well-documented plan, that clients can go back to and understand years after they had made their initial decisions.

Here are the basic documents you will need in order to effectively communicate the results of the design stage:

- A simple summary document that shows in broad terms the goals of the plan and the various strategies involved.
- A one-page summary for each IRA in the multigenerational strategy, describing the beneficiary designations and life expectancy elections, as well as the time horizon for the Required Beginning Date and the initial Required Minimum Distribution amounts.
- Documentation of the beneficiary, trust, and charitable strategies incorporated into the retirement distribution plan for each IRA.

Implementing the Retirement Distribution Plan

The next stage, implementation, usually begins in earnest at the second design meeting, when the multi-plan integration issues have first surfaced and the retirement distribution planning process becomes a truly multi-discipline process. Each advisor on the client's decision team may have implementation tasks to perform, as the retirement distribution plan is integrated with the overall estate plan and investment strategy.

The Retirement Asset Will

The implementation of a retirement distribution plan always calls for the completion of a beneficiary designation. The client may have previously been provided with a line or even a page on a plan or IRA designation form, possibly even with a couple of boxes to check, that they feel might qualify as a meaningful menu of their possible beneficiary choices. Clients often fail to realize the significant impact their choice of beneficiary will have on their tax, financial, and personal goals.

A separate document should often be used for beneficiary designation and method of payment election purposes. This document is the *Retirement Asset Will*—a beneficiary designation and election document that directs the transfer of retirement wealth and provides the documentation for the irrevocable elections required to be made by the client at the Required Beginning Date. The Retirement Asset Will should be used in most estate plans in which there is significant retirement wealth, even in those instances in which the client is not yet approaching age 70½. This document can be viewed as a parallel document to a client's will—disposing of those retirement assets under a methodology parallel to but separate from that of the other estate probate assets. The method of payment choices in the Retirement Asset Will can be used as a vehicle to distribute the retirement wealth consistent with the goals and philosophies represented in the client's Will.

A Retirement Asset Will is so important because, in order to do proper retirement distribution planning, individuals must have made the proper elections prior to the earlier of their date of death or their Required Beginning Date. The forms they are asked to execute by the IRA Custodian typically do not address each of the issues that must be raised. To the extent that the issues remain unaddressed, payouts from the IRA either after the client's death or beginning at age 70½ will be based on the default provisions contained in the IRA Custodial Agreement. Because these default provisions are generally worded in a way that can conflict with the client's desire to use a multigenerational payout of their retirement assets, many individuals will find their retirement distribution strategies thwarted by the application of the unduly restrictive default provisions contained in these IRA Custodial Agreements. IRA Custodial Agreements are discussed in greater detail in Chapter 14.

Many professional advisors are of the belief that a properly drawn trust and/or Will can contain all of the appropriate provisions to fully preserve retirement assets and accommodate retirement distribution planning. They often fail to recognize that the terms of the Will or trust will only affect retirement assets once the retirement assets have been paid into the Will or trust. Until the retirement asset has been paid into the Will or trust, the disposition of the retirement asset will be determined by the operative provisions of the Adoption Agreement/Designation of Beneficiary and Method of Payment Election

Form completed by the client, and on the default provisions contained in the IRA Custodial Agreement, unless superseded by a Retirement Asset Will. It is of no avail for a Will or trust to contain detailed and comprehensive provisions providing for the payout of retirement assets, when those provisions do not affect the payout of these assets until after the assets have been paid out of the retirement asset. An improperly drawn Adoption Agreement/Beneficiary Designation form or Retirement Asset Will can require the immediate payment of the entire retirement asset into the Will or trust after the individual's death. This will thereby unnecessarily accelerate income tax liability for the beneficiaries of that retirement asset, and will kill all future income tax deferral and severely hamper subsequent wealth accumulation.

In addition to beneficiary choices, life expectancy for the family unit, and minimum distribution issues, the Retirement Asset Will should include provisions addressing other important planning issues, including the following:

- Presumption of death
- Prior or subsequent death of a primary or contingent beneficiary
- Disclaimers
- Fractional interests
- Beneficiary withdrawal, investment and transfer rights
- Custodial issues

A properly drafted Retirement Asset Will can tie together all of the loose ends of the retirement distribution planning process. It can also be an extremely effective communication tool in presenting your recommendations to the clients.

The Implementation Team

Prepare the client for this stage, so that it does not come as a surprise at the end of the design stage. Early in the analysis stage, make it clear to the client that because the client's other advisors and family members will feel the impact of retirement distribution planning, they should be brought into the planning process. Clients may agree to that ideal model conceptually, but may not take the initiative to act on it. The retirement distribution specialist has a responsibility to bring the planning team together and to handle the communication between the players. The players on the professional advisor side should include, at a minimum, the following individuals:

- Estate planning attorney
- Accountant
- Pension consultant
- Insurance advisor
- Investment advisor

On the family side, the participants will include the client, and may include the following other individuals:

- Spouse
- Children
- Grandchildren

Other people who may have an impact or insight into the planning process could include other personal, business, and charitable advisors, spouses of children or grandchildren, and even former spouses.

Based on the client's tax, financial, and personal circumstances and philosophies, suggest which of these team members should attend certain meetings. Discuss what level of input the client should ask of each of them. You can supply the client with copies of memos and letters to appropriate advisors and family members to help reassure the client that the goals of the meeting and the need for their participation are being effectively communicated to the appropriate individuals.

There are both constructive and defensive reasons for these steps. On the constructive side, generally the more input the better. The more commitment and energy devoted to the planning process, generally the more comprehensive the resulting plan. Also, the last thing you want is to keep someone out of the loop, only to have to struggle with their late or destructive input that may arise from lack of knowledge or misplaced self-protective measures.

One more important consideration is the need for an attorney who is well versed in retirement distribution planning. The attorney will be needed to draft any Retirement Asset Will or trust documents to be used in the plan. An attorney who lacks precise knowledge of the tax law applicable to these documents can put the entire retirement distribution plan at risk. It is not worth the risk of using an inexperienced attorney in this area, even for the sake of trying to preserve an existing client-attorney relationship.

It will probably fall to the retirement distribution specialist to sell to the client and his or her current attorney the idea of bringing in an experienced attorney in this area to write those documents.

Once roles have been clearly defined and agreed to among the professional advisor members of the team, compensation issues should be addressed. Each profession has its own compensation standards, with fees generally negotiable in the overall best interests of the client. Whenever professional work is performed, fees should be paid. However, compensation for time spent on the project may not be the most effective basis for compensation. Instead, if insurance and investment product decisions are involved, the sale of those products will typically generate commissions. These commissions can be factored into the fee of the retirement distribution specialist, whether or not the retirement distribution specialist sells those products.

The Components of Implementation

Once the team is in place, there are four components to the implementation stage of the retirement distribution planning:

1. Tax planning;
2. Investment planning;
3. Insurance planning;
4. Personal planning;

Tax planning includes the drafting of all legal documents involved in the plan—primarily a beneficiary designation and method of payment and election document, also known as the Retirement Asset Will (see Chapter 14). In addition to the beneficiary document, there may also be trusts, powers of attorney, and other legal documents to be prepared.

These documents must all be drafted by a qualified attorney—either the client's attorney, perhaps aided by specimen documents, or by an attorney specialist with whom the retirement distribution specialist has already established a relationship. Both options have advantages and disadvantages. Using the client's existing attorney may carry a risk of inaccuracy if the attorney is not fully familiar with all of the tax issues involved in retirement distribution planning. The use of such an attorney will require more oversight on the part of the retirement distribution specialist. On the other hand, using an outside attorney who is fully knowledgeable in this area will reduce the risk of diminished quality. What will be lost, though, is an opportunity to bring added-value resources to the local attorney, who can work with the retirement distribution specialist now and in the future.

Investment planning means more than investment strategy and investment selection. It encompasses all of the custodial functions of the IRAs used in the plan. The IRA Custodian's policies and procedures must be compatible with the needs of the retirement distribution plan. An officer of the IRA Custodian company should sign and accept the Retirement Asset Will drafted by the attorney, so that the client's choices and elections will be honored by the IRA Custodian following the client's death. Again, a choice must be made about using the client's existing IRA Custodian or bringing in a new IRA Custodian in the event that the advisor tests the policies, procedures, and systems of the client's IRA Custodian and finds them lacking.

The IRA Custodian and legal resources must be carefully coordinated. The attorney drafting the Retirement Asset Will should note the name of the IRA Custodian and account numbers on each Retirement Asset Will for each separate IRA and should include in the document all of the provisions for achieving the goals of the retirement distribution plan. This implementation step is so fundamental that the retirement distribution specialist should oversee it from start to finish.

Another significant step is the development and implementation of the investment strategy. There may be several advisors on the team capable of handling this aspect of the plan—for example, a stockbroker or other investment advisor. Accountants are increasingly including investment advisory services within their practices, as are many insurance advisors. Although clients may have existing professional relationships which they may prefer to leave intact, they may be receptive to explore other options at this juncture and may seek guidance from the retirement distribution specialist in this area. (If you offer to fill this role yourself, your objectivity in this aspect may appear compromised, and you will have to find a way to continue to communicate with the client so as to keep yourself on the advisor's side of the table.)

The investment component of the plan involves two key issues:

1. Where will the assets be invested?
2. How will the investments be structured for each separate IRA?

The answer to those questions may change as the client's investment philosophy changes through his or her use of a multigenerational approach to retirement distribution planning (see Chapter 6). However, once those investment decisions have been made, they must be implemented by the investment advisor and IRA Custodian for long-term management purposes.

Life insurance planning is crucial to this process, regardless of whether existing life insurance policies can be used or new policies are required. The life insurance specialist plays a critical role in the implementation of the life insurance planning component of the retirement distribution plan. Unlike the investment component of the plan, the life insurance component does not require any coordination with the IRA Custodian. Instead, the need to create a life insurance trust brings together the estate planning attorney and the insurance advisor. An improperly drafted trust could result in the life insurance proceeds being included in the estate. This result would severely undermine the goals and much of the work of the retirement distribution plan, not to mention raising professional liability issues that the heirs might feel obligated to pursue.

The insurance advisor may already have taken responsibility for the analysis and design of the insurance component of the plan. This work typically includes a thorough evaluation of existing policies and a comparison with new policy alternatives, so that both the suitability and pricing factors meet the current needs of the client and the plan. As part of the implementation process, the insurance advisor must now take responsibility for the underwriting phase of the process, so that the policies are timely implemented in conjunction with the other components of the retirement distribution plan.

In addition to oversight responsibilities in each of these planning components, the retirement distribution specialist should also become involved in determining the amount and the timing of the payment of the first Required Minimum Distribution. This is important because the first distribution, which can be taken by either the Required Beginning Date or earlier in the prior year when the client attained age $70^1/_2$. Waiting until the Required Beginning Date to take the first year's Required Minimum Distribution forces the client to take two distributions in that same calendar year, as the second distribution will be due by December 31 of that same year. That means two income tax hits during the same year. Therefore, this approach, which contains certain obvious drawbacks, must be thought through carefully.

Personal planning is often the component of the plan in which the retirement distribution specialist emerges as the key player.

You initiated the relationship by alerting the client to a specific problem/opportunity. To get the client to understand the problem/opportunity, you had to lead him or her through a maze of tax, financial, and personal issues. You spent time and effort creating an environment of trust that allowed the client to disclose to you a considerable amount of very confidential information and private feelings. You next assembled and coordinated an advisory team to help the client through the decision-making process. That was the analysis phase.

During the design phase, you tailored a multigenerational solution to the retirement distribution problem that assured retirement security for the client and the client's spouse, and that maximized tax-deferred growth of the retirement asset to provide an income stream throughout the lifetimes of the client's children and grandchildren.

Implementation so far has involved drafting a Retirement Asset Will and making beneficiary designations and life expectancy elections, as well as drafting appropriate trusts for the multigeneration IRAs. You next integrated the retirement distribution plan with the estate plan, making necessary adjustments to minimize overall estate tax liability. You then arranged for life insurance funding to cover that portion of that liability as it related to the retirement assets. You next coordinated your efforts with the IRA Custodian of multigeneration IRAs to assure that the decisions made as part of the retirement distribution plan would be implemented through the IRA Custodian's administrative systems. You then helped the client to design an investment strategy to achieve his or her goals and those of his or her heirs, and you may have also arranged for the investment advisory resources to manage the assets over time.

Finally, you documented all aspects of the retirement distribution plan in summary form, so that the client understands how he or she got through the maze and has some reasonable expectation of the twists and turns that remain ahead. This last step required that you communicate the retirement distribution plan not only to the client but to other family members as well.

Now the plan is in place, and the first distributions after age $70^1/_2$ must be made. Here is where the long-term commitment to the client relationship becomes tangible for the client. The plan structure is in place, and now the plan mechanics begin to kick in. The client gets to see the conceptual process actually working.

It is up to the retirement distribution specialist at this stage to make sure that the plan is working correctly and that the client understands it is working correctly. The most obvious result of the retirement distribution plan is the yearly distribution of retirement assets—the first two of which were calculated based on a known quantity, the account balances at the end of the previous year. The tax, financial, and personal decisions about the timing of those first two distributions and the income tax ramifications of those decisions were all calculated, analyzed, and decided upon far in advance.

The client can then watch this process unfold each year and gauge whether the yearly payout of the retirement assets follows the plan or not.

Annual Plan Review

Your administration system should be able to illustrate this process and then produce written reports that confirm what was illustrated. Along with the confirmation of the predictable actions, the administration system should project future distributions based on income needs assumptions, investment assumptions, tax assumptions, and other factors relevant to the client's situation. Each year the client should receive this report and should participate in an annual plan review, in which results are monitored and then compared with the projections.

The assumptions should then be reexamined and adjusted, with new projections performed as needed. As a result of this review process, each year's distribution becomes a decision event—taking into account the tax, financial, and personal issues that may have changed from the previous year. All of this works to cement your relationship with the client and adds both real and perceived value to your advisory services.

From the client's perspective, the review is more than just a report on how the plan mechanism has performed and is expected to perform in the future. The annual review also reinforces all of the potential emotional aspects of the plan—either positively or negatively. For example, suppose that the client feared that the spouse's financial security was still in doubt. Even though the plan had adequately addressed this issue, it may take the annual review meeting to prove to the client and spouse that the plan will in fact more than adequately provide for the spouse's security, while at the same time achieving substantial long-term value for the other contingent beneficiaries who will be receiving yearly payments of retirement assets long after the spouse has died.

If the plan is performing better than projected (i.e., the investment returns are up), the annual review will be a decision event as well as a validation of the plan. Running above projected performance means that there is excess growth in the IRAs, and something has to be done with that excess growth. Here are some options:

- Distribute more retirement assets currently and expand lifestyle choices.
- Distribute more retirement assets currently and use the extra money to maximize gifting or charitable strategies.
- Leave the excess growth in the IRA because this year the client is in a higher income tax bracket.
- Leave the excess growth in the IRA to increase the effect of tax-deferred compounding in future years.

If the investment growth is below projections, another decision has to be made about the future distribution of the retirement asset. Whatever the actual investment results to date, new Required Minimum Distribution amounts have to be computed by the retirement distribution specialist each year as part of their yearly implementation commitment.

This personal planning aspect of the implementation function is performed at least annually until death occurs. At that time, a transition takes the implementation function to a new level. Until this time, the multigenerational aspect of the retirement distribution plan has been in a maintenance phase with the client. Now that the client is dead, the plan transforms into the multigenerational phase. After all the work of analysis and design, after all the creative concepts and good intentions of all the parties involved, should the implementation fail at this point, the IRAs may be subject to immediate and complete distribution with potentially dire tax consequences. In other words, the entire effort would be largely wasted. It is the retirement distribution specialist's responsibility to ensure that the next phase in the retirement distribution plan is executed flawlessly.

For spousal beneficiaries, this transition usually entails an IRA rollover. This will mean new beneficiary designations, new life expectancy elections, and very likely a new multigeneration IRA approach: analysis, design, and then integration with a *new* set of tax, financial, and personal circumstances and philosophies.

For children and grandchildren beneficiaries, this transition requires a retitling of the IRA in the deceased owner's name, for the benefit of the beneficiaries. If the IRA Custodian is not instructed properly, a mistake could wipe out much of the value of the multigeneration IRA through immediate income taxation. The retirement distribution specialist must ensure that the IRA Custodian strictly adheres to the terms and provisions of the client's previously executed Retirement Asset Will.

To mitigate any risk, take a spreadsheet approach to the administration system. Have the spreadsheet track all the IRAs, all the beneficiary designations, all the life expectancy elections, and all the IRA Custodian default provisions, as well as all the estate plan integration strategies, trusts, insurance policies, investment strategies, and performance history. The spreadsheet data should all be updated each year as part of the annual review. With this spreadsheet approach, you will be offering your client two additional security measures.

First, if anything happens to you, as the retirement distribution specialist, the plan will continue passing on all relevant data to your successor, whoever that may be.

Second, upon the death of your client, the transition of the plan to the client's spouse, children, grandchildren, or other beneficiaries will be seamless, as all relevant information is automatically carried over and applied to the next set of beneficiaries.

In the analysis and design stages, your facilitator role probably already made you a de facto advisor to other members of the client's family. However, once the client's death occurs, your advisory position formally transitions to the second and third generations. Yearly Required Minimum Distributions must then be tracked and projected for each beneficiary using the same annual review procedures you had established for your initial effort. At the death of the parent-client or the death of the spouse-client, the estate tax process must be implemented. IRD deductions for income tax purposes must be calculated and then recovered each year as IRA distributions are made (see Chapter 11 for a discussion of the Income in Respect of a Decedent (IRD) deduction).

In short, the strength of your client relationship goes far beyond that of other professional advisors in terms of both content and longevity. Your yearly ongoing administrative advisory services to the client and to other family members should assure your role as a trusted family advisor for years to come.

CHAPTER 4
REQUIRED MINIMUM DISTRIBUTIONS

CONTENTS

4 REQUIRED MINIMUM DISTRIBUTIONS

Americans are encouraged by the government to save for their retirement. The government allows them to defer taxes on the contributions to and the accumulations on their tax-qualified plans. However, it is the intention of Congress for retirees to deplete those qualified retirement plan and IRA assets during the course of their retirement years, rather than pass these assets on to their beneficiaries, who can continue the tax deferral of those assets to still another generation. In other words, the government wants its tax revenue back. It, therefore, encourages—actually, attempts to force—people to entirely consume their retirement assets during their lifetimes.

April 1 following an individual's 70th birthday is generally the final date at which the distributions must begin. This rule applies regardless of whether the individual needs the retirement assets or not. Congress presumes that people will withdraw the assets from their retirement vehicles at such a rate that the bottom of the retirement pot and death will magically converge at the same instant. The assumption is that everyone will thereby have a comfortable retirement and the government will fully recover the deferred tax revenue.

This premise is the basis of the Required Minimum Distribution rules. At first glance, everybody wins. The retiree has needed retirement income, and the government gets its long-awaited tax revenue For many Americans, these rules may work fairly well. However, some are fortunate enough to have accumulated *more* retirement assets than they actually need to support their retirement lifestyle. For these

---

Note: Readers should refer to the Introduction for a discussion of issues and concepts covered in Chapter 4 that may be affected by IRS's issuance of the Revised Proposed Regulations governing Required Minimum Distributions and by the passage of EGTRRA 2001. These include: the Uniform Distribution Period Table; the elimination of irrevocable elections at the individual's Required Beginning Date; the determination of the designated beneficiary by December 31 of the year following the year of the individual's death; and what rules and strategies the Revised Proposed Regulations have *not* changed.

people, this is not a win-win situation. For them, the loss of the tax shelter of the retirement assets is a big loss. However, if the rules are not met, the loss can get bigger—a 50 percent excise tax is slapped on the undistributed Required Minimum Distribution amounts. If that is not enough, estate taxes will be due in addition to the income taxes which will also be due when the retirement assets are paid to the beneficiaries after the individual dies.

Many people caught in this system are unaware of their current plight. They may happily celebrate their 70th birthdays not thinking ahead six months to the profound tax, financial, and personal implications of turning age $70^1/_2$.

> **Example:** Distinctions, Inc. is a family business that manufactures decorative office items for executive offices throughout the country. Two brothers, Herb and Simon, began the company many years ago. Herb took on the marketing side, while Simon maintained the designs. Herb's wife, Betty, handled the financial management of the company.
>
> Herb and Simon began thinking about their possible retirement and their long-term lifestyle plans. Their immediate goal was to revamp their current buy-sell agreement. The buy-sell agreement analysis opened estate planning and retirement issues, which led to some life insurance implications.
>
> As an advisor talked with the business owners, he uncovered a fact that everyone else had apparently missed: Herb had just reached the magic age of $70^1/_2$. When the advisor briefly explained the Required Minimum Distribution Rules to Herb, he grew very concerned. No one had addressed any of the issues relating to Herb's $2,000,000 or Betty's $1,000,000 in retirement assets. Fortunately, although Herb had already attained age $70^1/_2$ he had not yet reached his Required Beginning Date, so he still had some time to be able to evaluate his options. Herb and Betty met with their advisor several times to discuss their personal goals and philosophies regarding the transfer of wealth and the huge tax problems their children and grandchildren could face

> if their significant retirement assets were not handled correctly.
>
> Herb told his advisor that he had $50,000 in an IRA. The brokerage firm in which the IRA was held earlier that year had automatically issued a minimum distribution check. The internal IRA management system of that IRA Custodial firm tracks the ages of each of the IRA owners. When an IRA owner reaches age 70½, the system automatically provides individuals with their first year's distribution check based on retirement assumptions selected by the IRA Custodian. The system automatically generated Herb's Required Minimum Distribution check—without evaluating any of the implications and without advising Herb of any of his alternatives with respect to the payment of his IRA benefits. Fortunately, this problem concerned only the $50,000 IRA, and not the combined $3,000,000 in retirement plan assets which Herb and Betty owned.

The puzzling aspect of Herb's story is why no one had advised him earlier of the tax and financial impact of the Required Minimum Distribution rules in the tax law. Herb and Betty had worked with a stockbroker. Their accounting firm had given them good advice on the business side and did their tax planning, as well as their corporate and personal tax returns each year. However, the firm never gave them any advice on how to deal with the Required Minimum Distribution rules. The estate planning attorney had no background in the Required Minimum Distribution rules. The issue of retirement distribution planning had simply fallen through the cracks.

CPAs, attorneys, and financial advisors have a responsibility to inform clients of the implications of turning age 70½. The advisors should flag that date and periodically remind the client about it. Advisors should contact clients far enough in advance of the age 70½ date to allow them to engage in some unhurried and comprehensive retirement distribution planning.

Second, advisors should explain to their clients the various options available to them. Here is where things immediately get complicated. The basic tools seem simple: beneficiary designations and the life expectancy elections. However, clients must understand that retirement distribution planning, while highly complex, offers considerable opportunities for creativity from a tax, financial, and personal perspective. In order to advise clients effectively in this area, an advisor needs to become a retirement distribution specialist, one who has mastered all of the rules, strategies, and procedures.

The Rules of Required Minimum Distributions

The rules on Required Minimum Distributions cover all types of tax-deferred retirement plans, including corporate qualified plans, IRAs, Keogh plans, 403(b) annuity plans, and Section 457 plans. The Internal Revenue Code section dealing with Required Minimum Distributions is IRC §401(a)(9), with respect to distributions from qualified plans, including Keogh plans. The Internal Revenue Code section dealing with Required Minimum Distributions from IRAs is IRC §408(a)(6).

These two statutory provisions contain only a bare bones recitation of the Required Minimum Distribution rules, however. The "bible" which most practitioners refer to in this area is the proposed regulations that the IRS issued on July 27, 1987. Those regulations run 43½ double-columned pages, including introductory comments and a comprehensive table of contents. Additional and revised proposed regulations in this area were issued by the IRS on December 30, 1997.

Although lay people will certainly have some difficulty reading the proposed regulations, practitioners in this area may find that, despite the complexity of the subject matter, the proposed regulations have been outlined and organized in such a way as to present each small piece of information in both a readable and comprehensive form.

When an issue arises with respect to retirement distribution planning, an advisor would do well to check the proposed regulations, to see if that situation has been explicitly covered. If the proposed regulations are silent on an issue, practitioners may want to check IRS Private Letter Rulings or Technical Advice Memorandums (TAMs) to determine whether the IRS had ever previously addressed that particular issue.

The problem with research in this area is that the proposed regulations do not have the force and effect of law and do not even have the force and effect of final regulations. In fact, one court has indicated that the legal effect of a proposed regulation is no more than the legal effect of an argument made in a party's legal brief before the court. In other words, it has virtually no legal effect, unless and until favorably ruled upon by a court.

Private Letter Rulings and TAMs similarly cannot be cited as precedent in any court proceeding. However, they are illustrative of current IRS thinking in that area. Accordingly, a practitioner, when faced with a problem for a particular client that is identical to a problem presented in a prior Private Letter Ruling or TAM, may feel reassured if the issue had been resolved in the taxpayer's favor in the Private Letter Ruling or TAM, even though during an audit the practitioner would not be able to cite the Private Letter Ruling or TAM in any court proceeding, as authority for the taxpayer's position. However, at the audit level, most IRS agents will go along with a similar holding contained in an IRS Private Letter Ruling or TAM.

At the time of this writing, the proposed regulations are over 13 years old, with no immediate prospect for becoming finalized. Therefore, for now and for the foreseeable future, practitioners will have to continue to rely on the proposed regulations, Private Letter Rulings, and TAMs for the specific guidance that they may need in strategizing and implementing a client's retirement distribution plan.

The Required Minimum Distribution rules are divided into two categories, covering two completely different situations. The first set of rules applies when an individual dies before his or her Required Beginning Date. The other set of rules applies when the individual dies at or after his or her Required Beginning Date. The focus of this book is on the latter group. The rules governing distributions on death prior to the Required Beginning Date are covered in Chapter 12.

Required Beginning Date Rules

If the individual dies before his or her Required Beginning Date, the rules that are applicable are the death benefit provisions, while if the same individual were to die on or after his or her Required Beginning Date, the set of rules that would be applicable would be the living payout rules. Clients and advisors may assume erroneously that when an individual dies, the death benefit rules automatically are to apply to the payout of the remaining portion of the individual's benefits. They may not appreciate the fact that if death had occurred *after* the Required Beginning Date, the rules applicable to the payout of the remaining portion of the individual's benefits would be determined under a *continuation* of the living payout rules, rather than under the death benefit rules.

Until 1997 and with certain exceptions to be noted below, the tax law set the Required Beginning Date for most individuals as the April 1 in the calendar year *following* the calendar year of the attainment of age $70^1/_2$ for most types of plans. However, the Small Business Job Protection Act of 1996 made certain changes to this rule effective as of January 1, 1997. The reason for the change had largely to do with the complaints many large companies had voiced associated with beginning retirement distributions to individuals who had reached age $70^1/_2$ but who were still employed. Many large department stores, for instance, routinely continue the employment of their sales force and clerks well beyond age $70^1/_2$. For the most part, those employees resented having to begin to receive their retirement benefits while they were still employed. Moreover, the companies objected to the administrative problems presented by that situation as well. Eventually their voices were heard by Congress and the statute was changed.

These changes, however, do *not* affect the Required Beginning Date for IRAs. IRA accounts, as well as qualified retirement plan assets that have been rolled over into IRAs to preserve tax deferral, are still required to begin Required Minimum Distributions by April 1 of the calendar year *following* the calendar year of the attainment of age $70^1/_2$, as before. The rules applicable to tying an individual's Required Beginning Date to the time when an individual has attained age $70^1/_2$ also have an impact on payments from tax-sheltered annuities, also known as 403(b) plans. Tax-sheltered annuities are annuities purchased by public schools, by a state or local government, or by a charitable, religious, or educational organization that is exempt from tax under Internal Revenue Code §501(c)(3). The Required Minimum Distribution rules are applicable to tax-sheltered annuities for years beginning after 1986, but only with respect to earned benefits after December 31, 1986 *and* post-December 31, 1986 earnings on the individual's December 31, 1986 annuity balance. Benefits earned *before* January 1, 1987 are *not* subject to the rules on Required

Minimum Distributions, but instead are subject to the rules that had existed before 1986 with respect to distributions from tax-sheltered annuities.

The new Required Beginning Date for distributions from qualified retirement plans is April 1 of the calendar year following the *later* of the calendar year of attainment of age 70½ or the calendar year in which the employee retires. This rule change might sound promising to business owners who plan to remain active in the business, particularly since the term *small business* figures so prominently in the title of the Act. The new rules, however, do not apply to individuals who have attained age 70½ and who own *more* than 5 percent of a business. Owners of more than 5 percent of a business must begin distributions by April 1 of the calendar year following the calendar year of the attainment of age 70½, even if they continue working after age 70½. In addition, the new rules will *not* apply to any other employees of the plan sponsor, unless the plan sponsor has amended its plan incorporating therein the new liberal distribution rules permitted by the Small Business Job Protection Act of 1996. Practitioners should be aware that in determining the 5 percent ownership threshold, certain ownership attribution rules in IRC § 318 will be applicable. Under these rules, the interests of the business owned by the individual's spouse, children, grandchildren, and parents may be attributed to the participant. Certain other attribution rules may also be applicable.

A final exception to the general rule requiring distributions at a Required Beginning Date is keyed into the time when an individual has attained age 70½. The minimum distribution rules that were in effect prior to the passage of the Tax Equity and Fiscal Responsibility Act of 1982 (TEFRA) allowed certain individuals, including the owners of businesses, to defer commencement of receipt of their benefits from the plan until their actual retirement date, even if that date occurred well past the time at which they had attained age 70½. When the first rules were instituted in 1982, requiring those individuals to begin distributions by age 70½, notwithstanding their continued employment, an exception was made for those individuals who wished to opt out of the new rules and continue their deferrals. Subsequent changes in the law, including the passage of the Tax Reform Act of 1986, continued to recognize these opting-out elections, which have come to be known as the TEFRA § 242(b)(2) Elections or simply the TEFRA Elections and which were required to have been made by December 31, 1983. Individuals with properly drawn TEFRA § 242(b)(2) Elections that have not previously been revoked are, therefore, still allowed to continue to defer the commencement of receipt of all of their benefits from the plan, as long as they continue their employment. This opting-out provision applies not only to benefits accrued prior to 1982 but also applies to all subsequent accruals.

However, there is a price to pay in continuing to maintain a TEFRA §242(b)(2) Election. The price is that once the election has been revoked, typically by the participant's retirement, all distributions that were previously required to have been made but that were not made due to the operation of the TEFRA §242(b)(2) Election must be made up. For instance, an individual who had timely executed a TEFRA §242(b)(2) Election and who continued employment until age 80 would find that, usually, in the year following the year of termination of employment, he would be required to make up all of the distributions that were missed for the years in which he had turned age 70½, 71, 72, 73, 74, 75, 76, 77, 78, 79, and 80. Those 11 years of distributions would be required to be all made and all taxed in one year and would *not* be eligible for rollover treatment. It is for this reason that advisors in this area should inquire as to whether a client has a TEFRA §242(b)(2) Election in effect and should proceed quite cautiously before canceling any such election.

The Small Business Job Protection Act of 1996, by making the event of retiring a potential trigger for Required Minimum Distributions but in offering no clear definition of retirement, created more gray areas and confusion in this area. How many hours of work or how much compensation earned will disqualify an individual from being considered as "retired"? Can an employee retire, then rejoin the company later, postponing minimum distributions during the subsequent employment period? If an employee retires from one employer but undertakes employment with another or with an acquiring company, must minimum distributions begin from the retirement plan of the first company plan, but not from the plan of the second company?

These new rules now present a potential planning advantage to highly compensated executives and professionals who:

- Do *not* own more than 5 percent of the business or partnership.
- Continue working but would prefer to defer income taxes as long as possible.

- Delay minimum distributions until after retirement to shift distribution income into a lower income tax bracket after earned income has stopped.

For everyone else, particularly for business owners and people who retired before age 70½, the 1996 changes in the Required Beginning Date rules are irrelevant. For them, the effect of the Required Beginning Date is as follows:

- Participants who are greater than 5 percent owners who attain age 70 prior to July 1 of any calendar year and who will be 70½ by December 31 must receive their first distribution by April 1 of the following calendar year, whether or not they are still employed.
- Participants who are greater than 5 percent owners and who attain age 70 on or after July 1 of any calendar year and will be 70½ in the *following* calendar year must receive their first distribution by April 1 of the calendar year *following* the calendar year in which they attained age 70½, whether or not they are still employed.

First-Year Distribution Calculation

Once the Required Beginning Date has been established, the next step is determining the first year's Required Minimum Distributions. As noted earlier, the first year's Required Minimum Distributions can be deferred until as late as April 1 of the calendar year following the calendar year in which the individual attains age 70½. To compute the Required Minimum Distribution amount due for the first year, the year-end account value in the year *prior* to the first distribution year is determined. That value is then divided by the life expectancy factor applicable to the participant or the life expectancy factor applicable to the participant and beneficiary, if joint life expectancy has been chosen. For those whose birthday falls before July 1, the applicable account balance would be the account balance at the end of the year before the year in which they had attained age 70½. For those whose 70th birth-day occurs on or after July 1, the applicable account balance would be the account balance at the end of the year in which they turn 70½.

In determining year-end values, for plans that have a plan year end-ing on December 31 and for all IRAs that automatically have a year ending on December 31, the account balance to be used is the account balance as of the December 31 of the calendar year *prior* to the calendar year in which the individual had attained age 70½. The rule becomes somewhat more complicated when the plan's year-end is not on a December 31. In those instances, the account balance is measured as of the plan's Valuation Date in the calendar year immediately *preceding* the calendar year for which the Required Minimum Distribution amount is to be determined.

For instance, with a plan year ending on October 31, the applicable account balance for purposes of measuring the individual's Required Minimum Distribution due for 1999 would be the individual's account balance in the plan as of October 31, 1998, with certain adjustments. All employer contributions and forfeitures allocated to the participant's account *after* the October 31 Valuation Date but *before* the January 1 of the following year are added back and used to increase the individual's account balance before computing the Required Minimum Distribution amounts. Similarly, distributions from the plan made *after* the October 31 Valuation Date, but *before* the January 1 of the succeeding year are subtracted out, before computing the Required Minimum Distribution amounts.

For plans that are defined contribution plans in which yearly statements are routinely provided that indicate the individual's account balance as of the applicable Valuation Date in any given year, the computation, with adjustments, can be done relatively simply. However, in plans that are defined benefit plans, the services of an actuary may be necessary in order to compute the lump sum value of the individual's accrued benefit earned in the plan up to that point in time. Once that amount has been determined, however, and the necessary adjustments made, the computation proceeds along the lines outlined above, assuming, of course, that the plan does, in fact, permit the lump sum payment of a Participant's benefits.

The first distribution can be delayed until the Required Beginning Date—April 1 of the following calendar year—or it can be taken before the end of the calendar year immediately preceding the April 1 Required Beginning Date. The second distribution will be due by December 31 of the *same* year as the April 1 Required Beginning Date. Therefore, for those who postponed the first distribution until some time between January 1 and April 1, there will be two Required Minimum Distribution amounts due in that calendar year. Because many individuals do not even hear about the Required Beginning Date 70½, they are often forced into taking their first and second Required Minimum Distributions in the same calendar year. Many individuals do not want to avail themselves of the right to double up on their first two years' Required Minimum Distributions. They reason that by delaying the distribution required for the first year into the second year, they will be doubling up on their tax liability for that second year. Often that will be the case, with a resulting higher income tax liability. However, a careful analysis of the client's income tax brackets for both the year in which the individual attained age 70½ and for the following year should be performed, and the individual's anticipated allowable deductions for those two years should be analyzed. Also taken into account should be the monetary benefit of deferring the payment of the tax due on the first year's Required Minimum Distribution, by paying that distribution in the calendar year *after* the calendar year in which the individual attained age 70½.

In addition, a client opting to defer the first year's distribution into the second year should remember that, when computing Required Minimum Distributions for the *second* year, an adjustment should be made. The adjustment allows the individual to subtract out from the prior year's account balance the Required Minimum Distribution amount that was required for that first year but was deferred until the second year.

> **Example:** Grace, who attained age 70½ in 1999, has an IRA worth $100,000 as of December 31, 1998. She elected to defer the first year's distribution until April 1 of the year 2000. She is using a term certain method of payment and is using her life expectancy alone for purposes of computing Required Minimum Distribution amounts. For 1999 her Required Minimum Distribution amount would be $6,250 ($100,000 ÷ 16).
>
> If her IRA balance as of December 31, 1999 is $106,000 before computing her year 2000 Required Minimum Distribution, she would subtract from her December 31, 1999 balance the $6,250 Required Minimum Distribution amount she had received on April 1, 2000.

Accordingly, her Required Minimum Distribution amount for the year 2000 would be \$6,650 (\$106,000 – \$6,350 = \$99, 750 ÷ 15 = \$6,650).

One trick that several estate planning or elder-law attorneys have used in planning for distributions for the first distribution year is to time the first year's distribution into a year in which high medical expenses might arise. Although it may not be known in advance in what year high medical expenses will be incurred, in some situations that fact may be established relatively accurately. For instance, an individual who suffered a stroke on October 1 of a particular year will in all likelihood be immediately hospitalized, with the hospitalization stay being paid by Medicare. If the discharge from the hospital is expected shortly, with a long, expensive stay in a nursing home anticipated for the following year, a clever retirement distribution advisor would have the individual's first distribution from the plan or IRA, assuming that the individual had turned age 70½ in that year, deferred until the next year, when the high deductible medical expenses anticipated for that second year could be used to offset the taxable income generated by the distribution from the qualified plan or IRA.

Several IRA Custodians have automated systems that send a Required Minimum Distribution check to individuals by the end of the year in which they attained age 70½. Take great pains to ensure that such automated systems are *not* in place for your clients. The automated systems for the most part are not sufficiently sophisticated to have accurately analyzed the client's situation and to have selected for the client the Required Minimum Distribution strategy *best* suited to the needs of that individual.

In many instances, the representatives of the IRA Custodian have not even met with the IRA owner or the advisors to the IRA owner to determine what Required Minimum Distribution elections should have been made. However, often the entire retirement distribution planning process has been triggered by clients who had suddenly received in the mail one of those automated distribution checks from their IRA Custodian. If no planning had been done prior to the receipt of that check, you may find that there is still sufficient time to do proper retirement distribution planning, because frequently these checks are sent in the year in which the individual attained age 70½ and are not deferred until the following year. That generally leaves the client with January, February, and March of the *following* year to implement the proper retirement distribution planning strategy.

Calculation of the Required Minimum Distribution Amount

Calculation of the Required Minimum Distribution amount involves dividing the value of the retirement account by the applicable life expectancy divisor. At this point, review with your clients the fact that division involves two terms—*dividend* and *divisor*. The dividend is the number to be divided—in this case, the account value. The divisor is the number by which the dividend is to be divided—in this case the life expectancy factor. If the planning goal is to end up with the smallest possible Required Minimum Distribution amount and thereby retain income tax deferral for the longest possible time, the goal is to create *the largest possible divisor.*

$$\frac{\text{Account Value: } \$1{,}000{,}000}{\text{Life Expectancy: } 16 \text{ years}} = \$62{,}500 \text{ Required Minimum Distribution}$$

The strategies that create the largest possible divisor—in other words, those which produce the highest life expectancy factor—begin with the designation of the proper beneficiaries. This decision often involves weighing complicated tax, financial, and personal considerations, all of which are covered in the next chapter. Assuming that the proper beneficiary designations have been chosen, you should focus on the different mathematical implications of the various life expectancy elections available.

Life Expectancy Calculation

Clients must understand that life expectancy elections are mandatory, and in certain instances irrevocable. Upon reaching the Required Beginning Date, the client must make an irrevocable life expectancy election. This rule was designed to prevent people from manipulating changes in their circumstances that affect life expectancy in an effort to evade income taxation on Required Minimum Distributions.

Life expectancy election is not one choice. The election requires three separate sets of choices:

- Who is to be the beneficiary?
- Should single life expectancy or joint life expectancy be used?
- Should one or both of the chosen life expectancies be recalculated?

Beneficiary Designation

An individual who owns an IRA will naturally want to designate a beneficiary who will receive his or her retirement benefits in the event of death. Beneficiaries typically chosen include the individual's spouse, children, and grandchildren. As will be explained in greater detail later, when beneficiaries who are individuals (in other words, living human beings) have been designated, the life expectancies of those individuals can be used along with that of the IRA owner for purposes of computing the Required Minimum Distribution amounts due each year. In this way, two life expectancies instead of one can be used.

However when an individual has selected a non-person, such as an estate, a trust (with certain exceptions), or a charitable organization as a beneficiary, those entities are considered as having *no* life expectancies. Accordingly, an individual who has made any of those choices will be limited to using only his or her own life expectancy for purposes of computing the Required Minimum Distribution amounts due each year. It is especially important for clients to understand this distinction early in the planning process because, armed with this knowledge, they may decide *not* to designate estates, trusts, or charities as their beneficiaries.

In addition, as will also be explained in greater detail later on, when an individual fails to designate any beneficiary, the default provisions contained in the IRA Custodial Agreements will fill in the gaps. Many IRA Custodial Agreements provide that the individual's estate is the default beneficiary. This means that unless your clients have elected otherwise, in those instances their retirement benefits would be paid to their estates upon their deaths and without the ability to use their beneficiary's life expectancy for purposes of computing yearly Required Minimum Distributions while they are alive.

The significance of allowing that particular default provision to operate, in the event that the individual has died *before* his or her Required Beginning Date, is that not only will their estate be paid the benefits after their death, but all of the benefits would be required to be paid out of the IRA by December 31 of the calendar year containing the fifth anniversary of the individual's death. That means that a severe penalty will be imposed upon the client's family for the client's failure to designate an individual as his or her retirement beneficiary. This can raise significant liability issues for advisors when such events occur.

Single Life Expectancy vs. Joint Life Expectancy

The choice is simple. The plan participant or IRA owner chooses whether to use his or her own life expectancy alone or the joint life expectancy of himself or herself and the beneficiary. The results of this decision determine which life expectancy table in IRC §1.72-9 will be used—Table V for single life expectancy or Table VI for joint life expectancy.

The default provisions contained in most IRA Custodial Agreements permit the use of the second life expectancy *without* requiring that the IRA owners have also affirmatively elected to use the second life expectancy. In other words, an IRA owner through the mere act of designating individuals as the retirement beneficiaries, under the terms of most IRA Custodial Agreements, would be permitted to use those life expectancies for purposes of computing Required Minimum Distribution amounts payable each year. At least three Private Letter Rulings (199915063, 199951053, and 200018057) have authorized this practice, even instances in which the IRA Custodial Agreement does not specifically address.

In some IRA Custodian Agreements, however, the default provisions *require* that an affirmative election be made if the life expectancies of those beneficiaries are to be used. Individuals whose retirement assets were in an IRA sponsored by a Custodian whose IRA Custodial Agreement contained that requirement would find that the payouts during their lifetime would be limited to the period measured by their life expectancy alone and that after their death, in certain instances, all IRA benefits would be required to be paid out in full by the December 31 of the calendar year following the calendar year of death. The only safeguard in that situation is for the individual, in addition to having named beneficiaries, to have also affirmatively elected to use the life expectancies of those beneficiaries in determining Required Minimum Distribution amounts payable each year. In that way, the problematic default provisions contained in the IRA Custodial Agreement would not be operative.

Recalculation of Life Expectancy

Whether to recalculate life expectancy each year or to apply a fixed life expectancy term is a complex issue. If joint life expectancy is chosen, the decision-making process goes to another layer—not simply whether to recalculate or *not*, but whether to recalculate *both* life expectancies, to recalculate *either* life expectancy, or to recalculate one life expectancy but not the other—a combination approach. These separate sets of election alternatives can have far-reaching tax, financial, and personal implications to the client that must be carefully evaluated.

The default provisions in most IRA Custodial Agreements require that *both* the life expectancy of the individual and the life expectancy of the individual's spouse (if selected as beneficiary) are required to be recalculated each year, unless the IRA owner had elected that recalculation was not to apply. As will be demonstrated later, there are virtually no instances in which the optimum retirement distribution strategy for an individual would have him or her recalculating his or her own life expectancy, as well as the life expectancy of their spouse. Yet this is the result that would automatically apply in those instances in which the IRA Custodial Agreement had mandated the dual recalculation, unless the IRA owner had elected otherwise. Under those circumstances, the IRA owner should affirmatively elect whether one (and which one) or both of the life expectancies are *not* to be recalculated, in order to circumvent the otherwise automatic application of that default provision.

Fixed Term Method

The fixed term method—often referred to as the *term certain method, the period certain method, the subtract one method,* or *the non-recalculation method*—initially sets the life expectancy according to 70½ electing single life expectancy, the life expectancy from the tables is 16 years. The individual's life expectancy divisor for that first year is 16, and his first year's Required Minimum Distribution amount is 1/16 of the account balance. The second year it will be $^{1}/_{15}$ and so on, each year until year 16, when the life expectancy divisor is one, and the entire prior year's IRA balance is distributed. The following year both the dividend and the divisor are zero and any residual small amounts in the IRA must all be paid out. And then you die, theoretically. As you can see, the term certain method forces the complete distribution of retirement assets by the end of the term, thereby assuring full taxation of the IRA benefit by the end of the period certain.

Recalculation

The recalculation method for the same single life begins with the same 16-year initial life expectancy and $^{1}/_{16}$ of the prior year's IRA account balance as the first year's Required Minimum Distribution amount. However, according to the actuarial assumptions built into the IRS tables, life expectancy one year later is reduced by *less* than one year. Rather than only a 15-year life expectancy in year two, life expectancy is 15.3 years because the recalculation method is being used, the *actual* remaining life expectancy of the individual is utiof a 71-year-old, according to the IRS tables, is 15.3 years. Therefore, recalculation produces a higher divisor and a lower Required Minimum Distribution from the second year onward.

Table 4-1

Impact on Death: Joint Life Expectancy - Term Certain Election for Both Participant & Spouse

Year	*Death of Participant*		*Death of Spouse*		*Simultaneous Death*	
1	20.6		20.6		20.6	
Year of Death						
2	19.6	*Spouse can continue joint life benefit or rollover to their IRA*	19.6	*Participant can continue joint life benefit*	19.6	*Contingent Beneficiary can continue joint life benefit*
3	18.6		18.6		18.6	
4	17.6		17.6		17.6	
5	16.6		16.6		16.6	
6	15.6		15.6		15.6	
7	14.6		14.6		14.6	
8	13.6		13.6		13.6	
9	12.6		12.6		12.6	
10	11.6		11.6		11.6	
11	10.6		10.6		10.6	
12	9.6		9.6		9.6	

Table 4-1, *Cont.*

Impact on Death: Joint Life Expectancy - Term Certain Election for Both Participant & Spouse

Year	*Death of Participant*	*Death of Spouse*	*Simultaneous Death*
13	8.6	8.6	8.6
14	7.6	7.6	7.6
15	6.6	6.6	6.6
16	5.6	5.6	5.6
17	4.6	4.6	4.6
18	3.6	3.6	3.6
19	2.6	2.6	2.6
20	1.6	1.6	1.6

Fixed Term vs. Recalculation

At first glance, therefore, the recalculation method would seem to offer a significant advantage because the divisor to be used each year after the initial year will be larger. But the relative advantages and disadvantages of each of these two methods must also consider the tax treatment of the retirement account balance at the IRA owner's death.

Table 4-2

Single Life Expectancy Divisors: Terms Certain vs. Recaluclation

Year	Single Life Expectancy *Term Certain*	Single Life Expectancy *Recalculation*
1	16	16
2	15	15.3
3	14	14.6
4	13	13.9
5	12	13.2
6	11	12.5
7	10	11.9
8	9	11.2
9	8	10.6
10	7	10.0
11	6	9.5
12	5	8.9
13	4	8.4
14	3	7.9
15	2	7.4
16	1	6.9

If an IRA owner whose benefits are being paid under the fixed term method dies prior to the 16th year, the beneficiary may elect to continue fixed term distributions, thus spreading out the impact of income taxes over the remaining portion of the 16-year period left. However, under the recalculation method, once the life used for recalculation has ended in the *following* year there is no life expectancy remaining. Accordingly, under the recalculation method, where only one life expectancy is being used, the entire IRA balance must be paid to the beneficiary by December 31 of the calendar year following the calendar year of death. That means the entire income tax recapture takes place in one year.

Table 4-3

Joint Life Expectancy Divisors: Term Certain vs. Recalculation

Year	Joint Life Expectancy Term Certain/ Term Certain	Joint Life Expectancy Recalculation/ Recalculation
1	20.6	20.6
2	19.6	19.8
3	18.6	18.9
4	17.6	18.1
5	16.6	17.3
6	15.6	16.5
7	14.6	15.7
8	13.6	15.0
9	12.6	14.2
10	11.6	13.5
11	10.6	12.8
12	9.6	12.1
13	8.6	11.5
14	7.6	10.8
15	6.6	10.2
16	5.69	9.6
17	4.6	9.1
18	3.6	8.5
19	2.6	8.0
20	1.6	7.5
21	1	7.1

Table 4-4

Impact on Death of Participant: Joint Life - Recalculate Both Life Expectancies

Joint Life Expectancy	*Conversion from Joint to Single Life Expectancy At Death*	
20.6	20.6	*Death of Participant*
19.8	*15.3*	*Single Life/Recalc.*
18.9	14.6	
18.1	13.9	
17.3	13.2	
16.5	12.5	

Table 4-5

Impact on Death: Joint Life Expectancy - Recalculation Election for Both Participant & Spouse

Year	*Death of Participant*		*Death of Spouse*		*Simultaneous Death*	
1	20.6		20.6		20.6	
Year of Death						
2	15.3	*Spouse must switch to single life recalculate or roll over an IRA*	15.3	*Participant must switch to single life recalculation*	0	*Contingent Beneficiary must receive 100% pay-out of remaining balance by Dec. 31 in the year after death*
3	14.6		14.6			
4	13.9		13.9			
5	13.2		13.2			
6	12.5		12.5			
7	11.9		11.9			
8	11.2		11.2			
9	10.6		10.6			
10	10.0		10.0			
11	9.5		9.5			
12	8.9		8.9			
13	8.4		8.4			
14	7.9		7.9			
15	7.4		7.4			
16	6.9		6.9			
17	6.5		6.5			
18	6.1		6.1			
19			5.7		5.7	

The government gives, and the government takes away. Some people shy away from adopting the fixed term method because they connect the idea of the entire IRA account balance being required to be entirely distributed by a fixed point in time with the instinctive fear of running out of money before they die. This can be a misleading assumption, since most people who do not need their full retirement income each year will deposit the post-tax distributions in a separate account, which separate account will grow each year with new contributions and post-tax earnings. After their IRA has run out, they will still have the assets remaining in the separate account. The big negative is that they lose the benefit of tax-deferred compound interest in the IRA.

For joint lives—participant and beneficiary—the fixed term method works much the same way. Life expectancy for a couple, ages 70½, is 20.6 years, using *both* actual ages in the IRA joint life expectancy tables. Using joint life expectancies produces a larger life expectancy divisor and, therefore, smaller yearly Required Minimum Distributions. Like in the single life, fixed term example above, the second-year divisor is one less than the divisor from the year before or, in this case, 19.6 (20.6 minus one), with one year subtracted each year there-after until the 20th year, when the divisor has been reduced to .6 years and the entire prior year's account balance must be distributed. If the IRA owner dies prior to the end of the fixed term, the surviving beneficiary can elect to receive the remaining benefits. If the beneficiary dies first, the IRA owner can continue the payout method over the balance of the period left as elected over the remaining period. If the IRA owner and the beneficiary both die, the beneficiary can elect to continue to receive the benefits in the same manner.

An additional planning opportunity may arise by virtue of the use of a joint life expectancy when compared with that of a single life expectancy. At the death of the IRA owner prior to the end of the term, the spouse as beneficiary can either continue payments based on the number of years left to the fixed period or roll the retirement assets into a new IRA and base the subsequent distributions on joint life expectancy of the surviving spouse and a new beneficiary. This opportunity is especially valuable to a surviving spouse beneficiary who is beyond age 70½. It is a one-time opportunity for the spouse to make new elections on a deceased IRA owner's retirement account and to lock in new life expectancy factors.

Suppose a couple elects to use the recalculation method for *both* life expectancies. For the first year the life expectancy divisor is still 20.6 years if both are age 70½. But in the second year, actuarially speaking, the couple's life expectancy is not one year less. Instead of the 19.6-year life expectancy factor that would have been applicable under the fixed term method, under the recalculation method, and based on the joint life expectancy tables the applicable joint life expectancy factor is 19.8 years. This increased divisor reduces the yearly Required Minimum Distribution amount.

There is a tradeoff, however, for the higher divisor should the individual whose life is being recalculated die. In the year *following* the year of death, the survivor must switch from the joint life expect-

Table 4-6

Joint Life Expectancy Divisors: Term Certain vs. Recalculation vs. HYBRID

Year	Joint Life Expectancy *Term Certain/ Term Certain*	Joint Life Expectancy *Recalculation/ Recalculation*	Joint Life Expectancy *Recalculation/ Term Certain*
1	20.6	20.6	20.6
2	19.6	19.8	19.4
3	18.6	18.9	18.5
4	17.6	18.1	17.3
5	16.6	17.2	16.5
6	15.6	16.5	15.4
7	14.6	15.7	14.7
8	13.6	15.0	13.7
9	12.6	14.2	12.7
10	11.6	13.5	11.8
11	10.6	12.8	10.8
12	9.6	12.1	10.1
13	8.6	11.5	9.2
14	7.6	10.8	8.4
15	6.6	10.2	7.6
16	5.69	9.6	7.0
17	4.6	9.1	6.5
18	3.6	8.5	6.1
19	2.6	8.0	5.7
20	1.6	7.5	5.3
21	1	7.1	5.0

ancy tables to the single life expectancy table. In the second year, for example, the 19.8-year joint life expectancy would drop to only 15.3 years, based on the single life table, had one of the two individuals died in the prior year.

For a surviving spouse beneficiary, there is still the option to roll the benefits into a new IRA and base distributions from that IRA on the joint life expectancy of the surviving spouse and a new designated beneficiary. And as with single life recalculation, the death of *both* spouses results in the beneficiary being required to receive the entire remaining balance in the IRA by December 31 of the calendar year *following* the calendar year of death. This result, needless to say, can be devastating.

The Hybrid Method

Both life expectancies within the joint life expectancy can be handled differently with respect to the recalculation of life expectancy. One life can use a fixed term while the other uses the recalculation method. When only one life expectancy is being recalculated, the methodology for calculating life expectancy is more complicated. This is known as the Hybrid Method for calculating Required Minimum Distributions.

Table 4-7

Impact on Death: Joint Life Expectancy - Hybrid Method - Recalculation Participant/Term Certain Spouse

Year	Death of Participant		Death of Spouse		Simultaneous Death	
1	20.6		20.6		20.6	
	Year of Death					
2	15	*Spouse must switch to single life term certain or roll over to an IRA*	19.4	*There is no effect on the participant's distributions*	15	*Contingent Beneficiary can receive distributions based on the spouse's remaining term certain single life expectancy*
3	14		18.5		14	
4	13		17.3		13	
5	12		16.5		12	
6	11		15.4		11	
7	10		14.7		10	
8	9		13.7		10	
9	8		12.7		8	
10	7		11.8		7	
11	6		10.8		6	

Table 4-7, *Cont.*

Impact on Death: Joint Life Expectancy - Hybrid Method - Recalculation Participant/Term Certain Spouse

Year	*Death of Participant*	*Death of Spouse*	*Simultaneous Death*
12	5	10.1	5
13	4	9.2	4
14	3	8.4	3
15	2	7.6	2
16	1	7.0	1
17		6.5	
18		6.1	
19		5.7	

Both the participant and spouse beneficiary are permitted to use the recalculation method. However, a beneficiary who is *not* the participant's spouse is *not* permitted to use the recalculation method. Accordingly, in the case of non-spousal beneficiaries, the only way in which the hybrid method can be used is if the participant's life is to be recalculated, but that of the non-spouse beneficiary is not.

The public as a whole is almost entirely ignorant of the availability of the Hybrid Method and is equally unaware of the many possible benefits associated with its use. One of the reasons for the extreme lack of knowledge and information in this area is that there are no IRS tables or charts that specifically illustrate the Hybrid Method. The Hybrid Method was developed in the proposed regulations issued by the IRS on July 27, 1987 and can be found in Question E-8(b). Those proposed regulations are the *only* source of reference with respect to the use of the Hybrid Method. Because there are no IRS charts which illustrate the use of the Hybrid Method, the life expectancy factors to be used each year under the Hybrid Method must be extrapolated by the practitioner from other IRS life expectancy tables. In spite of the extra effort needed to develop the numbers to be used in the Hybrid Method, its benefits may far outweigh the added difficulties associated with it.

In the case of a married couple, if the IRA owner and beneficiary spouse are in good health, recalculating the IRA owner's life expectacy and not the spouse's life generally makes sense. The first year's life expectancy computation remains the same as if both lives are being recalculated. However, for the second year, life expectancy is calculated using the actual age of the person whose life is being recalculated—in this case the IRA owner—as of the last day of the second distribution year and the "adjusted age" of the other person—in this case the spouse.

Adjusted Age

To find the "adjusted age" of a person, first establish his or her age at the end of the first distribution year. Then find his or her single life expectancy factor for that year under the IRS single life expectancy

Table 4-8

Impact of Death On Life Expectancy Divisors: Single Life vs. Joint Life with Spouse vs. Joint Life with Child (MDIB)

Year	Term Certain *Single Life Expectancy*		Term Certain *Joint Life Expectancy*		Term Certain *Joint MDIB(*) Life Expectancy*	
1	20.6		20.6		26.2	
2	15	***Death of***	19.6	***Death of***	25.3	
3	14	***Participant***	18.6	***Participant***	14.4	
4	13		17.6		38.5	*Child's*
5	12		16.6		37.5	*remaining term certain*
6	11		15.6		36.5	*life*
7	10		14.6		35.5	*expectancy*
8	9		13.6		34.5	
9	8		12.6		33.5	
10	7		11.6		32.5	
11	6		10.6		31.5	
12	5		9.6		30.5	
13	4		8.6		29.5	
14	3		7.6		28.5	
15	2		6.6		27.5	
16	1		5.6		26.5	
17			4.6		25.5	
18			3.6		24.5	
19			2.6		23.5	
20			1.6		22.5	
21			1		21.5	

*Assumes joint life expectancy with a 41-year-old child.

table. Then remove one year from the life expectancy for each subsequent distribution year. For instance, suppose the spouse is age $70^1/_2$ at the end of the first distribution year. According to the IRS single life expectancy table, her life expectancy is 16 years. To calculate her "adjusted age" in year two, reduce 16 by 1 and find the matching age on the IRS single life expectancy table. Age 72 has a life expectancy of 14.6, while age 71 has a life expectancy of 15.3. When the computed life expectancy falls between two numbers on the table, the proposed regulations require you to use the life expectancy factor applicable to the higher age, which in this case is 72.

Accordingly, in year two, the life expectancy would be calculated as follows. The husband's life expectancy is recalculated based on his actual age in year two of 71, and with his spouse's life expectancy adjusted to age 72. The result of the combined age 71/ age 72 joint life expectancy factor is a joint life expectancy factor of 19.4. The required rounding up to determine the "adjusted age" is likely to produce a slightly higher Required Minimum Distribution amount in the early years than might otherwise be applicable where *both* lives are being recalculated each year. It may even produce a slightly higher Required Minimum Distribution amount for one or more years than might otherwise be applicable where *neither* life is being recalculated. Certainly the calculation under the Hybrid Method are more complicated than under the other two methods available. However, the trade-off may be worth it. With the Hybrid Method, when the IRA owner dies, his life expectancy is recalculated as zero in the year *following* the year of death. At that point his surviving spouse beneficiary will simply switch to remaining single life expectancy, calculated as of the first distribution year and reduced by one for each succeeding distribution year. Remember that a surviving spouse as beneficiary can still always roll over the assets into a rollover IRA. If the spouse whose life is *not* being recalculated dies first, that death has no impact on the Required Minimum Distribution amount each year because the life that died was not a life that was being recalculated. This is unlike the switch to single life expectancy, which is required when one of the lives which was being recalculated dies. With the Hybrid Method, the IRA owner is assured that distributions will continue at a predetermined minimum distribution rate for as long as he lives, even if he should live well beyond his initially calculated life expectancy. On the other hand, the prior death of his spouse will *not* cause the acceleration of any Required Minimum Distribution amounts, because his spouse's life expectancy had been based on a term certain methodology, not a recalculation basis.

Minimum Distribution Incidental Benefit

If the spouse is not the beneficiary, but a non-spouse—such as a child or grandchild—is used instead, then only the participant's life expectancy can be recalculated, while the life expectancy of the beneficiary must be based on a term certain basis. However, at this point another rule crops up, called the Minimum Distribution Incidental Benefit, or MDIB Rule.

Large age differences between the participant and a much younger child or grandchild beneficiary *without* the application of the MDIB Rule would dramatically reduce yearly Required Minimum Distributions amounts and extend tax deferral far into the future. However, the government intends for tax deferral to produce adequate retirement income, not abundant estate accumulation. Always intending to stay ahead in these tax-vs.-deferral skirmishes, the government came up with a rule to cover situations in which the designated beneficiaries are much younger than the participant.

The MDIB Rule states that if a non-spouse beneficiary is more than 10 years younger than the participant, a predetermined life expectancy divisor is substituted for the actual life expectancy divisor that would otherwise result from the use of the actual ages of the participant and beneficiary. The MDIB life expectancy divisor is taken from a table in IRC Proposed Regulations §1.401(a)(9)-2.

According to the MDIB rules, a non-spouse beneficiary who is more than 10 years younger than the participant will be deemed to be 60 years old when the participant is 70½ for minimum distribution calculation purposes. For the participant who is 70½ with a non-spouse beneficiary more than 10 years younger, life expectancy is 26.2 in the first year, 25.3 in the second year, and 24.4 in the third year, no matter what the age of the younger beneficiary actually is.

It is important, however, to note that the MDIB Rule does *not* apply to spousal beneficiaries. Thus an individual whose spouse is 20, 30, 40 or more years his or her junior, will find that by using the actual life expectancy of that spouse, Required Minimum Distributions can be reduced each year to a very small number, thereby dramatically increasing tax deferral and wealth enhancement for the next generation. The use of the spouse's *actual* age, regardless of how young the spouse actually is, can play an especially important role in retirement distribution planning for individuals who have second or third marriages. Frequently the age disparity between the marital partners in those cases is *greater* than in the case of first marriages.

Despite the limitations imposed by the MDIB Rule, the participant can still benefit from a strategy in which a non-spouse is named as beneficiary. First, even with the limitation of the 10-year spread, the applicable life expectancy divisor is significantly larger than it would be if the participant were using single life expectancy only or joint life expectancy with a spouse who is near the participant's age. Even more important in terms of extending tax deferral, when the participant dies, the MDIB rule drops out and is eliminated from the formula, thereby allowing the younger beneficiary's actual age to be used.

A common mistake in this area involves beneficiary forms which are written in such a way that the MDIB Rule is *not* automatically eliminated at the participant's death. Under that scenario, Required Minimum Distributions after the participant had died would still be required to be made pursuant to the more restrictive MDIB Rule, not-withstanding the fact that at that point IRS rules would not require the MDIB Rule to still apply.

In the year following the year of the participant's death, the MDIB Rule drops out and the MDIB limited life expectancy factor is replaced by the beneficiary's actual remaining life expectancy, calculated as of the first distribution year and reduced by one for each subsequent distribution years. For example, a 70½ year old participant could name a 41-year-old child as his primary beneficiary upon reaching the Required Beginning Date. If the death of the participant occurs during the third year of distributions, the calculation to reflect the elimination of the MDIB rule is as follows: in the year following the year of death of the participant, the beneficiary, who is now age 44, must look back to the single life expectancy based on their attained age (41) as of December 31 of the year in which the participant turned age 70½. For each year a distribution was due, the beneficiary must subtract one term certain year from the original age

41.5 year term certain life expectancy determined at age 41. Since three distribution years have now passed, the beneficiary's remaining life expectancy for the fourth distribution year is 38.5 (41.5 years minus 3 years). If the beneficiary subsequently dies, the death has no impact on the Required Minimum Distribution calculation, since the life expectancy of the beneficiary was not being recalculated. Benefits in that case could still be paid over the remaining portion of the 38.5 period certain left. Using the life expectancies of children and grandchildren as part of the retirement distribution strategy can, therefore, add significant leverage to the continuation of tax deferral on retirement accounts.

Other Planning Aspects of Turning 70½

Experience has shown that clients will have no emotional attachment to any of these alternative life expectancy choices. Planning remains just an exercise. Without seeing the year-by-year details of the comparisons of the different Required Minimum Distribution amounts and remaining IRA balances, clients are not likely to get excited over whether the life expectancy divisor is 19.4 or 19.8. Life expectancy is only simple mathematics made tediously complicated. However, when clients realize that these mathematical calculations can be manipulated to achieve their tax, financial, and personal goals, something else happens. Clients see the money they earned over their lifetime and saved for these later retirement years either protected from tax erosion or decimated by it. In other words, they see it in their own grasp and then in the hands of their loved ones, or they see it slipping through.

This discussion leads to another planning aspect of turning 70½. The participant must designate primary and contingent beneficiaries. Most people will have already designated a beneficiary for their retirement assets, but often the decision is made with only the recipient in mind. The client's decision must be consistent with their broader planning goals, including personal and financial philosophies. Upon reaching the Required Beginning Date, the client's beneficiary choice becomes irrevocable for the purposes of calculating Required Minimum Distribution amounts.

Beneficiary designations are not final in the sense that after the Required Beginning Date an IRA owner is precluded from changing his or her beneficiary choices. Those choices are always available to the participant. What is meant by the use of the words *irrevocable* or *final* is that any such changes *after* the Required Beginning Date may have adverse consequences.

When a change in beneficiary designation which a participant has made after the Required Beginning Date would result in *larger* Required Minimum Distributions due for all years starting with the year following the year of the change, those larger Required Minimum Distributions would be required to be made. When the changes that the participant has made after the Required Beginning Date would otherwise result in *smaller* Required Minimum Distributions due each year, the effect of that change is ignored, and the original *higher* Required Minimum Distributions are still required to be paid. In other words, at the individual's Required Beginning Date, the various choices made are locked in like a ratchet. Subsequent changes can never be used to *lengthen* the pay-out period and reduce Required Minimum Distributions, but may have the effect of shortening the payout period and increasing Required Minimum Distributions. In either event, the government is never in a worse position and, under certain circumstances, can be in a better position than it otherwise would have been had no changes been made. That means, of course, that the *participant* is never in a better position, and may be in a worse position than if no change in beneficiary had occurred.

The effects of various beneficiary designation choices upon Required Minimum Distributions and the resulting tax consequences can become critical issues. This aspect of retirement distribution planning is covered in detail in Chapter 5.

The Flexibility of an IRA

A client's particular distribution options are always limited and controlled by the terms of the applicable document governing the retirement asset, which may be more restrictive than what the law allows. This one additional factor can have enormous planning consequences. The retirement distribution specialist may, therefore, have to analyze the plan and determine what planning limitations exist within the plan document and what steps can be taken, if necessary, to expand the planning possibilities. Most qualified plans and 403(b) plans limit the individual's distribution choices to only a select number of options. These options might include life annuities, period certain annuities, and lump sum distributions. If you were to ask your clients what their plan distribution options are, you would be hard-pressed to find one who could give you an informed answer. The only way to effectively advise these individuals may be for you to obtain the plan document and read the provisions relating to the various distribution options. Not all plans allow all options. The Required Minimum Distribution rules themselves provide substantial flexibility in determining the Required Minimum Distribution, amount due each year.

Any strategy which involves paying out retirement benefits on a multigenerational basis will require that the retirement assets remain in the shelter of a tax-deferred vehicle for many years into the future. When retirement assets have already been placed into an IRA, the guaranteed perpetual life of the IRA Custodian as a financial institution is assured and multigenerational retirement distribution planning can easily occur. However, when retirement assets have not yet been rolled over into an IRA but are still in the shelter of a qualified plan, certain additional issues may present themselves. A client who is the sole proprietor of a business or a partner in a partnership that sponsors the plan should be advised that upon their death, the entity sponsoring the plan may suddenly come to an end. The end may either be required under state law or may come about due to economic circumstances or other family issues unrelated to retirement distribution planning.

If the plan sponsor company that has adopted the qualified plan comes to an end, the qualified plan itself must then come to an end. This means that at that time, all of the assets accumulated in the retirement plan must be paid out. Such horrific results can be mitigated when the beneficiary of the retirement assets is the individual's spouse, because surviving spouse beneficiary is always afforded the right to roll over distributions into his or her own IRAs.

Once the surviving spouse has rolled over those assets into his or her own IRA, the continued tax deferral and tax-sheltered growth can continue for many decades into the future. However, in those instances in which the beneficiary of the retirement assets is not the spouse, or in those instances in which the spouse had previously died, no rollover option is available, and often all retirement assets must be paid out of the shelter of the qualified plan within a brief period of time after the individual's death.

Example: Bill Pitt was an attorney and the owner of 100 percent of the stock of a professional corporation (professional association) in which his law practice operated. The professional corporation sponsored a Keogh plan. Bill's wife had died several years before Bill, and he had designated his two children equally as the beneficiaries of his Keogh plan. He had previously elected to have the plan benefits paid out to his two children after his death, over a period measured by the life expectancy of his oldest child. Bill died at age 68. Under the requirements of the estate law of the state in which Bill lives, his professional corporation must come to an end within six months after the date of his death. By that date, if benefits have not been fully paid out of the plan, the plan may become disqualified, insofar as it will no longer be sponsored by a viable company. Bill's children would, therefore, be forced to receive 100 percent of the retirement benefits in the six-month period *before* the professional corporation had come to an end and would be required to pay income tax on the full amount of the distribution. They would *not* be allowed to roll those assets over into their own IRAs, nor would they be permitted to pay those benefits out over their life expectancy, as Bill had planned.

When retirement assets have been accumulated in a qualified plan, often the strategy of choice is to have those benefits paid out of the shelter of the qualified plan into an IRA, so that the above problem will not arise. One possible way to save the situation in the above example would present itself if one of Bill's children were an attorney and was made the successor owner of Bill's professional corporation. In that way, the business could continue into the future and continued tax deferrals could be achieved. However, planning solutions like that may not always present themselves.

The provisions of many qualified plans do not permit in-service distributions. Accordingly, if a client is still working for the company at the time that retirement distribution planning is taking place, the advisor may find that the plan document does *not* permit any current payout of such benefits, so as to permit a rollover to an IRA. However, in those instances in which the business is either owned entirely by the client or substantially controlled by the client, it may not be difficult to amend the plan document to permit such in-service distributions. Therefore, clients wishing to maximize retirement distribution planning options should consider rolling over their benefits into an IRA if the lump sum form of payment is available. The greatest flexibility in retirement distribution planning can generally be found in IRAs, notwithstanding certain IRA custodial issues that may have to be addressed, which are discussed in Chapter 14.

When one contemplates all the planning areas that are affected by the simple act of the client's turning $70^1/_2$, all the potential irrevocable mistakes that can be made, and all the planning that needs to be completed in a very compressed period if the client is to achieve maximum planning advantage, one can readily understand why becoming a retirement distribution specialist can prove so important a development to one's professional practice.

CHAPTER 5
BENEFICIARY DESIGNATION

CONTENTS

5 BENEFICIARY DESIGNATION

Once you have effectively carried out the analysis and design phases of a comprehensive retirement distribution plan, your clients should be receptive to listening to your specific planning recommendations. That willingness will in all likelihood be premised on your appreciation of their underlying core beliefs, which are:

- They do not need all of their retirement assets to live on.
- If one of them dies, the other is to be well provided for.
- Everything left over is as good as lost to taxes after the second death.

It is now time to discuss with the client his or her first and foremost important planning tool—beneficiary designation. In nearly every pension plan and IRA in which the participant has a spouse, he or she will designate the spouse as beneficiary.

You will need to point out to the client the fact that, if the client wants to alleviate many of the tax problems associated with the ownership of retirement assets, one of the most effective strategies is to bypass the spouse for a portion or all of the retirement assets, and instead designate the children or grandchildren as beneficiaries. This strategy naturally will be employed only when it can be demonstrated that the spouse will not need the retirement assets to live on. In performing this analysis for the client, the "What-if-the-spouse-needs-the-money-after-all?" objection should be specifically addressed. The advisor will no doubt have to revisit the retirement income needs and distribution analysis to alleviate

---

Note: Readers should refer to the Introduction for a discussion of issues and concepts covered in Chapter 5 that may be affected by the IRS's issuance of the Revised Regulations governing Required Minimum Distributions and by the passage of EGTRRA 2001. These include: the Uniform Distribution Period Table; the elimination of irrevocable elections at the individual's Required Beginning Date: the determination of the designated beneficiary by December 31 of the calendar year following the calendar year of the individual's death; the Federal estate tax amounts and rates; and what rules and strategies have *not* been changed by the Revised Proposed Regulations.

these clients' concerns. The advisor will have to thoroughly explain the safeguard mechanisms that can be built into the retirement distribution plan. Those safeguard mechanisms will be discussed shortly.

Another question which should probably be discussed at this point, although it will doubtless surface later on, is: Should the children and grandchildren inherit all of this wealth? There are several important emotional issues, and several significant tax considerations which will have to be addressed.

By the time they have attained age 70½, most parents may feel that they have a good handle on how their children will deal with inherited wealth.

The children after all by that time are already adults, and possibly even middle-aged adults, with perhaps adult children of their own. Young grandchildren, on the other hand, are still a largely unknown quantity. It is impossible to predict what a grandchild currently in preschool might do if given access to several hundred thousand dollars at, say, age 18. (For more information on preparing heirs for their inheritance, see Chapter 7.) Designating grandchildren as beneficiaries of retirement assets can extend the tax-deferred growth of these assets for many decades, and can offer the grandchildren a legacy that might otherwise have gone in taxes to the government. Because the benefits of this type of multigenerational retirement distribution planning can be so significant, any problems associated with a grandchild inheriting too much wealth should be effectively dealt with, so as not to pose an obstacle to this proposed retirement distribution strategy.

Whenever grandchildren have been designated as beneficiaries of retirement assets, the possibility of the imposition of the generation-skipping transfer taxes must also be addressed. There is no point in minimizing one type of tax only to incur another.

Generation-Skipping Transfer Tax

The way the current estate tax system is configured, no estate taxes are generally due upon the death of the first to die of the husband and wife. This is so because the bulk of the assets of the first to die are typically transferred to the surviving spouse. The surviving spouse is then afforded an unlimited estate tax marital deduction, which entirely offsets any estate taxes which might otherwise have been due. However, upon the death of the surviving spouse, estate taxes are due without any offsetting estate tax marital deduction. After the couple's wealth has transferred to the next generation, their children find themselves in the same position as their parents with respect to their inherited assets. Generally, no estate taxes are due on the death of the first to die of the child and the child's spouse, due to the operation of the unlimited estate tax marital deduction, with the estate tax due when assets are transferred from that child and spouse to their children following their death.

The system is designed in such a way that the Internal Revenue Service (IRS) can be expected to levy estate taxes at least once in every generation. Wealthy people in the past have tried to circumvent this system by skipping or bypassing intervening generations. This typically is accomplished by making a distribution to a trust, which provides an income-only interest to children, with a remainder interest to grandchildren. However, in more extreme cases, the planning, usually accomplished through trusts, can involve income interests payable to more than one generation, with the ultimate remainder interests payable to individuals several generations beyond that of the creator of the trust. Whenever any such strategy is implemented, the IRS will have been bypassed.

The IRS, over time, developed certain defenses to these strategies. Congress enacted these defenses into law as the Generation Skipping Transfer Tax (GST). Briefly stated, the GST tax rules impose an additional estate tax on the transfer of wealth in those instances in which an intervening generation has been skipped. The additional estate tax is imposed at the highest bracket—currently 55 percent—and is imposed in addition to the regular estate tax assessed of that asset.

Fortunately, there is a significant dollar exemption below which the GST will not be imposed. The exemption allows for the transfer per donor of $1,000,000 to the generation beyond the skipped generation, before the GST is imposed (increased by cost of living in 2000 to $1,030,000). Accordingly, a couple wishing to avail themselves of the maximum exemption amounts could together transfer $2,060,000 in 2000 to their grandchildren without the imposition of any GST. In many instances, the use of either one $1,000,000 GST exemption or two $1,000,000 GST exemptions is more than adequate to allow for a significant portion of the couple's retirement assets to be passed directly to their grandchildren, without the imposition of any GST.

At this point and not later, the advisor should make every attempt to bring the client's children into the planning process. The sons and daughters of the client will no doubt have a strong opinion on the effect of large sums of money being inherited by their children. They should have an opportunity in the planning process to make those opinions known. You may discover that many of the children of your clients are adamantly opposed to your clients' designating their grandchildren as beneficiaries. They may feel that it is morally wrong for them to be passed over as the beneficiaries of those assets. It is your responsibility in suggesting and implementing this type of retirement distribution strategy to deal with any such emotional issues that may arise at either the client level or at the level of the client's children.

Beneficiary Designation Alternatives

At age 70½, the client's choice of the beneficiary takes on added personal, financial, and tax significance. At the Required Beginning Date, the individual designated as beneficiary becomes a person whose age can be used to calculate the Required Minimum Distribution amounts payable each year. Although the beneficiary may be changed in later years, the life expectancy election remains irrevocably locked into the life expectancy of the beneficiary designated as of the Required Beginning Date—except when changed in the government's favor.

Here are some commonly asked questions about this issue.

1. *What happens if there is more than one beneficiary?*

The tax rules require that the age of the oldest beneficiary be used in determining the Required Minimum Distributions. In other words, the benefits of the younger ages of several of the beneficiaries and the possibility of lower Required Minimum Distributions are lost.

2. *What happens if there is no designated beneficiary?*

The plan document or IRA Custodial Agreement typically contains certain default provisions that often assume the beneficiary to be the estate of the participant. However, many plan documents and IRA Custodial Agreements list the surviving spouse as the default beneficiary, if no beneficiary has been named by the individual. The next default beneficiary listed is often either the individual's estate or the individual's children, followed by the estate. If these choices are not in keeping with an integrated retirement distribution plan, in each instance, the default provisions should be superseded by actual written elections made by the participant in a timely fashion.

3. *What happens if the estate is the designated beneficiary?*

In that case, when the participant dies, the assets become part of the estate of the deceased. This means that the assets are payable to the individual's estate.

The client may intend to pass the retirement asset by Will as part of his or her overall estate plan. In the Will someone is designated as the ultimate beneficiary. However, naming the estate as a beneficiary is not the way to accomplish this objective. The retirement asset is immediately subject to estate taxes and, in many instances, will be subject to accelerated income tax liability. This will occur, for instance, if the individual had died before his or her Required Beginning Date. The IRS does not accept the estate as a "Designated Beneficiary" for purpose of calculating the Required Minimum Distributions. After all, an estate has no life expectancy. Therefore, even if the individual should survive until his or her Required Beginning Date, there can be no joint life expectancy strategy at that time to reduce the Required Minimum Distributions payable thereafter and thereby extend tax deferral.

If the estate has been named as the beneficiary and the individual has died before his or her Required Beginning Date, all amounts accumulated in the qualified plan or IRA must be paid out to the estate by December 31 of the calendar year containing the fifth anniversary of the individual's death, thereby destroying continued tax deferral and wealth accumulation.

If the estate has been named as the beneficiary and the participant has survived to his or her Required Beginning Date, all distributions made to the participant while the participant was alive would be required to be based on the use of the participant's single life expectancy alone. If that life expectancy were being recalculated, all amounts accumulated in the qualified plan or IRA on the individual's death would be required to be paid out to his or her estate by December 31 of the calendar year *following* the calendar year of the participant's death. If at the individual's Required Beginning Date, benefits were to be paid over a term certain method of payment measured by the participant's life expectancy alone, at the participant's death, benefits could be paid to the individual's estate over the balance of the term certain period remaining.

> **Example:** Adam has reached his Required Beginning Date and has designated his estate as beneficiary. He has elected that benefits are to be paid over his life expectancy alone without recalculation, which according to IRS tables is 16 years. If Adam were to die five years into the payout stream (i.e., at age 75), the balance of the amount in the IRA could be paid out to his estate in yearly increments over the remaining 11 years (16 years - 5 years = 11 years).

In short, it is difficult to justify having no designated beneficiary and equally difficult to justify naming the estate as the designated beneficiary.

4. *What happens if the spouse is named as the designated beneficiary?*

This is the most common occurrence and no doubt represents our society's ideal for how retirement income best supports the family structure. This distribution scenario had been based on the tradition of the husband as the family's primary provider. By the time of the husband's retirement, the children have in all probability established their own adult lives. Mom and Dad live comfortably, enjoying the fruits of their efforts. They pay income tax on the portion of their retirement asset which is distributed to them each year from the IRA into which Dad had rolled the retirement plan benefits which he had received when he retired from the company. Now Dad is age $70^{1}/_{2}$ and has to begin to receive his Required Minimum Distributions.

The money, as it develops, is sufficient for retirement. Dad finally gets to play all the golf he wants. He then dies peacefully. If Dad had elected non-recalculating life expectancy (i.e., term certain), either single life or joint life, Mom can continue to receive distributions for the remaining portion of the period elected. If Dad had elected joint life recalculation on each life, in the year following Dad's death, Mom is required to switch from joint life expectancy to single life expectancy, resulting in suddenly much larger Required Minimum Distributions. When she dies, the next beneficiaries, presumably the children, must receive the entire remaining benefit by December 31 of the calendar year following the year of her death. They must then pay the full income tax and estate tax due on the value of the IRA. This unfortunate pay-out scenario could have been avoided had Dad made the proper elections at his Required Beginning Date.

The Traditional Strategy

In the Traditional Strategy, the spouse is the primary beneficiary. In the one life expectancy calculation scenario, Mom is going to have to depend on her money management skills or pay for investment advice to make the remains of the now-paid-out IRA last the rest of her life. When she dies, the government gets its deferred estate taxes at last. The children will then pay estate taxes on what is still left of the former retirement asset, an asset the government never intended the children to inherit in the first place.

The Spousal Deferral Strategy

Under the One-Year Rule, beneficiaries, including spousal beneficiaries, are allowed to pay out the retirement benefits over the beneficiary's life expectancy, with the first payment due by December 31 of the calendar year following the calendar year of the individual's death, assuming that the individual had died before his or her Required Beginning Date, and the proper payment options had been elected.

As noted above, this rule applies to all individuals designated as beneficiaries, including the individual's spouse and other individuals designated as beneficiaries. However, the spouse as beneficiary has an additional right not afforded to any other beneficiary. That right allows the spouse to retain the IRA in the name of the deceased participant, and to defer the commencement of receipt of benefits until December 31 of the calendar year in which the participant would have reached age $70^1/_2$. For a spouse who is interested in deferring retirement distributions as long as possible and taking as little or no retirement income currently, this can be an extremely valuable planning device.

> **Example:** Brad and Sara are married and are both age 60. Brad had designated Sara as his sole beneficiary. Brad then dies. By leaving the IRA in the name of Brad, Sara can defer commencement of the first distribution from Brad's

> IRA until December 31 of the calendar year in which Brad would have reached age $70^1/_2$. In this case, the deferral is ten years. At that point, Sara would be required to begin receiving Required Minimum Distributions from the IRA, based on her life expectancy determined at that time.

In this example, if Sara had been Brad's sister and not his wife, Sara would have been required to have commenced receipt of Brad's benefits by December 31 of the calendar year *following* the calendar year of his death. She would not have been able to enjoy the benefits of the possible ten-year deferral. However, in electing to continue the IRA in Brad's name, Sara had opted not to exercise her right to make a spousal rollover. The spousal rollover would have enabled Sara to designate her own new beneficiaries and method of payment selection with respect to benefits in her rollover IRA.

Under certain circumstances, the use of the spousal deferral option may carry disadvantages. This could prove especially true if the surviving spouse were to die prior to implementing a spousal rollover. Accordingly, all of the advantages and disadvantages of this approach must be thoroughly explored and discussed with the client before a retirement planning strategy is implemented. In addition to these two distributions, continuing the optional income stream established by the participant, or employing the spousal deferral rule, the government affords Mom still another retirement distribution payout. This last alternative is extremely attractive, in that it allows for the payout of the retirement assets over the longest period of time. That third alternative is known as the "Spousal Rollover Strategy."

The Spousal Rollover Strategy

With this strategy, when Dad dies, regardless of how life expectancy was being calculated, Mom receives Dad's entire retirement benefit and then uses her spousal rollover privileges. With the rollover she establishes her own IRA with her own Required Beginning Date. By naming her own new beneficiaries, presumably the children, she can use joint life expectancy, thereby reducing subsequent Required Minimum Distributions and further extending the tax deferral on the retirement asset.

Until several years ago, it was not known whether the spousal rollover device was available in those instances in which the participant prior to his or her death had reached or passed his or her Required Beginning Date; nor was it known whether or not the device was available in a case in which a surviving spouse had similarly reached or passed his or her Required Beginning Date. Several Private Letter Rulings issued within the last few years, however, have made it abundantly clear that the spousal rollover technique is available regardless of whether or not the participant and/or surviving spouse have reached or have passed their Required Beginning Date.

> **Example:** Jim and Grace are married and are now both 80 years old. At Jim's Required Beginning Date, he had elected that benefits in this IRA be payable over the term certain joint life expectancy of himself and Grace that, computed at that time, provided for a payout of 20.6 years. At age 80, Jim dies, leaving Grace as the sole beneficiary of the IRA. At that time, Grace can elect a spousal rollover and can transfer the assets from Jim's IRA into a new IRA established in her own name. In the new IRA, Grace can designate her own beneficiaries and her own method of payment options. Under Grace's IRA, benefits would be required to commence by December 31 of the calendar year following the calendar year of the rollover. If at that time Grace was age 81 and she had designated her children as her beneficiaries, benefits would begin to be paid out under that joint life expectancy method. Taking into account the effects of the MDIB rule, this would call for a payout of at least 16.8 years. Contrast this with the 9.6 year payout (20.6 years - 11 years = 9.6 years) that would have remained, had Grace continued the payout strategy in Jim's IRA and had not elected spousal roll-over treatment.

With the rollover strategy, the retirement asset can be distributed slowly, thereby allowing the bulk of the asset to continue to grow on a tax-deferred basis, and thereby also avoiding a dramatically accelerated income tax bite.

This strategy works well, except in one situation: the case where Mom did not need the money in the first place. In that case, there is likely to be a substantial amount of retirement assets left over upon Mom's death and correspondingly more assets in her estate that will be subject to estate tax. If Mom really did not need the money, then perhaps she should not have been designated initially as the beneficiary. Had the children and grandchildren been designated as beneficiaries, non-retirement assets could have been used instead to fund Mom's retirement lifestyle and later used to pay estate taxes, with income tax deferral on the retirement assets extended decades longer.

In other words, if Mom truly did not need the money—it having been predetermined that under no likely scenario would she have had a need for the retirement assets—then a multigenerational approach should probably have been employed. Multigenerational strategies will be covered in the next chapter.

5. *What happens if a trust is the beneficiary?*

Five rules govern the use of a trust as the designated beneficiary of retirement assets. If each of the rules is satisfied, the trust beneficiary can then be treated as the designated beneficiary of the retirement assets, and the life expectancy of the trust beneficiary can be used with that of the participant's at the participant's Required Beginning Date, to determine the Required Minimum Distributions. If the trust has more than one beneficiary, the oldest beneficiary's age is required to be used to determine life expectancy and Required Minimum Distributions.

Simply stated, when each of the applicable trust rules is followed, the trust is in effect ignored and the measuring lives are deemed to be the measuring lives of the beneficiaries of the trust, as if payments are being made directly to the beneficiaries and not indirectly to them through the trust vehicle.

When the applicable requisite trust rules are not followed, the life expectancies of the beneficiaries of the trust cannot be used, and the trust is deemed to be an unacceptable designated beneficiary. Accordingly, under those circumstances, it is considered as if the individual had designated *no* beneficiary, and the consequences discussed above in the context of naming an estate as beneficiary would be applicable.

Rule #1: The first rule applicable to the use of trusts as Designated Beneficiaries is that the trust must either be irrevocable from inception or must become irrevocable upon the death of the participant. Initially, the IRS proposed regulations published in 1987 did not contain this precise requirement. The initial rule required a trust to be either initially irrevocable or to become irrevocable by the participant's death or the participant's attainment of the Required Beginning Date, whichever was earlier.

This initial rule proved somewhat problematic in those instances in which the client's estate plan was to be effectuated largely through the use of a revocable trust. A revocable trust typically will provide that it can be amended or changed at any time up until the date of the individual's death, at which time the trust becomes irrevocable. An individual who had designated a revocable trust as beneficiary and who had died prior to the Required Beginning Date would have complied with the first trust rule. That trust, upon the individual's death, would have become irrevocable prior to the individual's Required Beginning Date. However, were that same individual to have died after reaching his or her Required Beginning Date, the trust would have remained revocable at and beyond the individual's Required Beginning Date. In fact, it would have remained revocable up until the date of the individual's death. Accordingly, in that case the first trust rule would have been violated.

Over the years, the IRS had received numerous comments criticizing the effect of the application of what seemed to many practitioners to be an unduly harsh rule. On December 30, 1997, the IRS responded to this criticism and issued revised proposed regulations. The revised proposed regulations changed the irrevocable requirement by eliminating the requirement that the trust become irrevocable by the individual's Required Beginning Date. Accordingly, trusts that are now revocable can be used as beneficiaries of retirement assets in full compliance with the requisite trust rules, even though the individual may survive well past age 70½ and the trust may not become irrevocable until the individual has died, which death may occur sometime well past the individual's Required Beginning Date.

The question has arisen as to whether or not a trust contained in a Will can be named as a designated beneficiary, according to the requisite trust rules. A trust named in a Will is known as a "testamentary trust." An argument against the use of a testamentary trust to serve this purpose is that, until an individual dies, a trust contained in a Will is not a binding and legally enforceable document.

Practitioners who had looked with anticipation to the terms of the December 30, 1997 revised proposed regulations for guidance on this particular issue were disappointed to learn that the revised proposed regulations simply did not address this issue at all. However, since December 30,

1997, numerous individuals in the National Office of the IRS have indicated that testamentary trusts can now be used as acceptable designated beneficiaries of retirement assets in full compliance with the trust rules, notwithstanding the fact that testamentary trusts, until the individual has died, are by their very nature revocable and not actually in being.

This liberalized rule is extremely beneficial for advisors. One of the obstacles to implementing a comprehensive retirement distribution plan is the cost for the preparation of the underlying legal documents. When clients have already spent a considerable amount of money in the preparation of appropriate Wills and trusts, they are often reluctant to spend any more money creating new trusts and adding additional layers of complexity to the estate planning process, in order to integrate the Required Minimum Distribution rules into their overall estate plan. However, where *inter vivos* trusts or testamentary trusts have already been created, it is now possible to utilize those preexisting trusts as designated beneficiaries, in full compliance with the requisite trust rules, thereby saving the client the additional cost of having to retain counsel to prepare additional legal documents. However, the advisor should review the existing documents with the client's attorney to determine whether those documents, as currently worded, are 100 percent appropriate for immediate use by the client for this purpose without some minor adjustment.

One final note: Many advisors in this area assume that if a testamentary trust can serve as an acceptable designated beneficiary, the way to fund the testamentary trust is to word the beneficiary designation form so that the beneficiary named is the "estate." The advisor may reason that, if the estate is named as beneficiary, the retirement assets will be paid into the Will, which in turn will direct its distribution into the various trusts contained within the Will document.

That simplified application of the retirement distribution rules, however, does not work. The IRS would view such a designation as if the participant had no designated beneficiary, notwithstanding the fact that the retirement assets would be paid into the Will and eventually would be paid into the trusts established in the Will for the benefit of the individual's beneficiaries.

The IRS's reasoning is that although a trust can be used as a conduit for the payment of retirement benefits—while retaining the right to use the life expectancy of the individual trust beneficiaries—an estate cannot be similarly used. Accordingly, if, for example, Peter Smith wished to designate a particular trust in his Will as the beneficiary of his retirement assets, he should list the beneficiary as "John Smith, as the initially designated Trustee, under the Peter Smith Trust established in Article Fifth of the Last Will and Testament of Peter Smith dated July 1, 1999." Under such a designation, and assuming that each of the other trust rules was complied with, the life expectancies of the individual beneficiaries of the Peter Smith Trust would be able to be used for purposes of computing Required Minimum Distribution amounts payable each year.

Rule #2: The second rule which must be followed in order for a trust to qualify as a "Designated Beneficiary" of retirement assets is that the trust beneficiaries must be individuals, and not corporations, estates, or charities. Otherwise there can be no life expectancy to be used to calculate Required Minimum Distributions—from the IRS's side—and therefore no tax deferral advantage—from the participant's side. As noted earlier, when there are multiple beneficiaries, the IRS requires that the life expectancy of each beneficiary must be considered, with the ultimate life expectancy to be used based on the life expectancy of the oldest beneficiary. A problem arises when both individuals and non-individuals have been named as beneficiaries in one trust. Because neither of those entities has any life expectancy, none of the life expectancies of the individual beneficiaries can be used for purposes of the Required Minimum Distribution rules.

Accordingly, when there are to be multiple beneficiaries—some individuals and some entities—a better practice would be to first divide up the retirement asset into separate accounts. In this way the life expectancies of the individuals can be used for the one retirement asset in which they alone have been designated as beneficiaries, while not precluding the use of those life expectancies by mixing those retirement assets with the retirement assets that are to be paid to the beneficiaries who are not individuals—estates, charities, or other entities.

Remember, beneficiary designation at the Required Beginning Date is the government's way of drawing a boundary around the issue of life expectancy. Within that boundary the government creates the greatest likelihood that the retirement asset will be completely distributed during the life of the participant and individual beneficiary, and that, therefore, within that time frame the government will recover its deferred tax revenues. The government does not care if the beneficiary is changed later, as long as the substitution of a new beneficiary cannot be used for the purpose of increasing the life expectancy divisor.

Rule #3: The beneficiaries must be identifiable from the trust instrument. The requirement of identifiable beneficiaries is the government's safeguard against the participant slipping in a younger beneficiary within a poorly worded class at his or her discretion, and then using that new younger beneficiary's longer life expectancy. The oldest member of the class has to be identifiable, even if he or she is not mentioned by specific name.

The proposed regulations recognize that it may not be possible at the time that a beneficiary designation form or trust is written to identify, by specific name, each of the members of a class who are to be benefited. Specifically, the proposed regulations permit such designations as "to my children" without having to mention each particular child by name. At the time the beneficiary designation form is signed, the individual may have had only two children, while at the time of his or her death, there may then be three. Under IRS rules, each of those three children would receive a third of the retirement asset upon the individual's death, had the individual defined the class of beneficiaries as "my children." During the lifetime of the participant, benefits would be payable beginning at the participant's Required Beginning Date, based on the joint life expectancy of the individual and the oldest of the children (either of the initial two children, or of the later three). Similarly if the participant were to die prior to his or her Required Beginning Date, under the One-Year Rule, all benefits would be payable over the life expectancy of the oldest child. (However, see Chapter 12 for an exception to that rule.)

Rule #4: A copy of the trust instrument is to be provided to the plan administrator, or a list of all of the beneficiaries of the trust (including contingent and remainder beneficiaries) is provided to the plan administrator along with a description of their entitlements. If the trust is revocable, the individual must also provide the plan administrator with a copy of each trust amendment within a reasonable period of time after an amendment has been made. For IRAs, the documentation described above must be provided to the IRA Custodian, IRA Trustee, or Individual Retirement Annuity provider. This filing requirement must be completed by the later of the individual's Required Beginning Date, or the date on which the trust has been named as beneficiary.

Rule #5: The trust must be valid under State law. This last requirement has to do with a State's rule that a trust, in order to be valid under State law, be in writing, signed by the trust creator, and either notarized or witnessed by one or more witnesses.

The failure to meet any of these five rules will mean that, although the retirement benefits will be payable to the trust at the participant's death, during the participant's lifetime, only the participant's life expectancy can be used to determine the Required Minimum Distributions that are due each year, without the right to use the life expectancies of the trust beneficiaries.

The common misconception is that, at the death of the participant, the IRA itself becomes an asset of the trust. That is what typically happens with life insurance policies and proceeds, and perhaps with other estate assets, but that is not what happens with retirement assets. If that were to occur, the transfer of the assets in IRA to the trust would be deemed a distribution of the entire IRA, and income taxes would be immediately due on the full value of the retirement asset. The IRA in that case would essentially die with the participant.

The better practice would be to retain all of the assets in the IRA, while paying out of the IRA into the trust each year only the Required Minimum Distribution amounts. The amount paid out of the IRA each year would then be deposited into the trust, for accumulation or eventual payout to the trust beneficiary or beneficiaries, while the bulk of the IRA assets would remain intact in the shelter of the IRA. In this way, the assets remaining in the IRA each year can continue to enjoy tax-deferred growth and wealth accumulation.

Trusts designated as beneficiaries of any retirement assets need to be drafted or at least reviewed by attorneys that specialize in this area and are familiar with all the legal and tax issues surrounding retirement assets—which assets, because of their built-in income tax liability and Required Minimum Distribution rules, are different from all other estate assets. It does not matter what kind of trust is involved—a Credit Shelter Trust, Qualified Terminal Interest Property (Q-TIP) Trust, standard caretaker trust for children or grandchildren, or any other type of trust. In each case, the IRA should remain intact in the name of the participant, deceased, after his or her death, for the benefit of the trust as beneficiary. The Trust and Retirement Asset will then control the IRA principal from a distance, rather than from within the trust itself. The income stream—the yearly Required Minimum Distributions amounts—is then paid from the IRA to the trust each year and, based on the specific trust distribution provisions, is then distributed out of the trust to the trust's ultimate beneficiaries.

Example: Joshua used different IRAs in designating benefits for each of his six grandchildren. However, instead of each grandchild individually being named as the beneficiary of each IRA, a separate trust established for the benefit of each grandchild was named as IRA beneficiary. The six IRAs totaled the value of Joshua's Unified Credit Amount of $675,000 in 2000. This will allow him to avoid any estate taxes due on those assets upon his death. The trust documents will have to be carefully drafted in order to assure that upon Joshua's death the IRAs are preserved intact, preventing the loss of the continued tax deferral. Upon his death, the IRAs will continue to be owned by him, deceased, for the benefit of each trust established for each individual grandchild. In that way, Joshua can achieve his three-part goal of extending tax deferrals, eliminating estate tax on the transfer of his retirement asset, while at the same time creating some Trustee discretion over the retirement asset while the grandchildren are still minors.

6. *What happens if a charity is named as beneficiary?*

If a client intends to leave some assets to children while leaving other assets directly to a charity, there is an advantage in selecting retirement benefits as the asset to go to the charity. Charities and Charitable Remainder Trusts are exempt from income tax. Charities designated as heirs of retirement assets will not have to pay any income taxes upon receipt of those assets. However, when family members are bypassed as the beneficiaries of the retirement assets, they lose the extended tax deferral that can be achieved through the multigenerational approaches to retirement distribution planning. They would therefore be sacrificing potential tax-favored growth over the course of the payout of the Required Minimum Distribution amount each year, which payouts could have produced decades of both an income stream and tax-deferred investment return for them. For a more detailed discussion of charitable giving strategies using retirement assets, see Chapter 8.

7. *What happens if a change in beneficiary designation takes place?*

If a designated beneficiary dies after the participant's Required Beginning Date, the effect on the life expectancy calculation and, therefore, on Required Minimum Distributions, follow the patterns outlined earlier in the life expectancy discussion. The death of a beneficiary at that time is not generally considered a change of beneficiary. The contingent beneficiaries previously designated by the participant move into first place and will be entitled to the benefits upon the participant's death. Future Required Minimum Distributions continue to be based on the effects of the original elections made by the participant at the Required Beginning Date. In that sense, nothing changes.

The one exception to this rule would occur in the event that life expectancy at Required Beginning Date was being measured by the individual's life and that of his or her spouse, with the spouse's life expectancy being recalculated each year. If the spouse beneficiary were to die subsequent to that date, in the year following the year of death of the spouse beneficiary the spouse's life expectancy would drop to zero, and all subsequent Required Minimum Distribution payments would be based on the remaining life expectancy of the participant alone.

These considerations deal only with a change of beneficiary due to the death of a prior beneficiary. The proposed regulations are quite clear that the life expectancy of a contingent designated beneficiary need not be taken into account, when the contingency that must arise in order for the contingent beneficiary to be paid any retirement benefits is the death of a prior beneficiary.

There is, of course, another way in which beneficiaries can be substituted—namely by the actual redesignation by the participant of a new beneficiary. In the typical case in which X designates A as primary beneficiary and B as contingent beneficiary, if X were to die, the life expectancy of B need not be taken into account in determining Required Minimum Distributions payable to A, as long as A is still alive. If X reaches his or her Required Beginning Date, A's life expectancy will be used for purposes of computing Required Minimum Distribution amounts payable each year. If A then subsequently dies, A's life expectancy will continue to be used, notwithstanding the fact that B has now, in effect, moved up to become the primary beneficiary following A's death.

The proposed regulations indicate that if the contingency that must occur in order for B to receive benefits is a contingency other than A's death, then B's life expectancy must be taken into account initially. For instance, X may designate A as the primary beneficiary, with B as contingent beneficiary to take precedence over A, were A to marry out of his or her faith.

Because the contingency that must arise for benefits to be paid to B is a contingency other than A's death, B's life expectancy would be required to be taken into account for purposes of computing the Required Minimum Distribution amounts payable to X each year, notwithstanding the fact that A is still alive. If B were older than A, the addition of B's life expectancy would shorten the payout period and increase Required Minimum Distributions payouts each year, at least after X's death and perhaps after the MDIB rules were no longer applicable. However, if B were younger than A, the addition of the consideration of B's life expectancy would have no effect on either the pay-out period, or on the amount of yearly Required Minimum Distribution payable either before or after X's death.

The bottom line is that, if for some reason—divorce being a common reason, but other relationship changes can easily be contemplated—the participant chooses to change beneficiaries, the tax rules prevent such a change from subsequently altering life expectancy computations favorably for the participant, meaning that the rules prevent any reduction in the Required Minimum Distribution amounts which might otherwise be due each year. In other words, the government has assured itself that no change in beneficiary designation can adversely impact on the elections which the participant had made at the Required Beginning Date from the government's perspective. Whether the benefits go to one beneficiary or to another is of no concern to the government, as long as the government continues to receive its deferred tax revenues each year, according to the participant's original elections made at the time of the Required Beginning Date.

8. *What about the arrival of additional children or grandchildren?*

What can be done to equalize distributions to these new family members? Since Required Minimum Distributions are determined by the life expectancy of the primary beneficiary (or by the life expectancy of the oldest of all of the primary beneficiaries), the beneficiaries must all be identifiable at the time the life expectancy elections are made. If additional children or grandchildren arrive after the Required Beginning Date, their individual ages and life expectancies cannot be used for purposes of calculating Required Minimum Distributions. The new arrivals, however, can be included in a multigenerational retirement distribution strategy, by being permitted to share in any retirement asset income stream based on Required Minimum Distributions calculated with reference to another beneficiary's life expectancy.

The question from a practical point of view is how subsequently born children or grandchildren can be brought into the mix. One way is through the use of a trust as the beneficiary of the retirement asset. Under this methodology, the individual establishes a trust in which the various beneficiaries of the trust are not identified with specificity until the oldest member of the class reaches age 21. At that point, the individuals in the class are identified, and separate shares are established in each of their names.

> **Example:** Robin names one testamentary trust as beneficiary of her IRA. The trust is established collectively for each of her grandchildren. When Robin dies, she has four grandchildren, but by the time the eldest of her grandchildren has reached age 21, she has six grandchildren. According to the terms of the trust, at the time the oldest grandchild is age 21, the trust is divided into six subtrusts, with each subtrust then administered for the exclusive benefit of each of the six grandchildren.

One problem inherent in this approach is that the life expectancies to be used will be tied into that of the oldest grandchild. Often there is a large age disparity among the client's children and an even larger age disparity among the client's grandchildren. One way to maximize the deferral periods and not have the life expectancies of all of the grandchildren tied into the age of the oldest grandchild is to first divide the individual's retirement asset into separate shares, each for the benefit of the family of each particular child.

> **Example:** Jules has three children. He divides his IRA into three separate IRAs, each for the benefit of his grandchildren collectively from a common parent (the children of his three children, A, B, and C) and each payable through a trust established collectively for the benefit of the children of that particular one of his children. When Jules dies, he is survived by four grandchildren, two from child A, one from child B, and one from child C. Each of the three trusts—the trust for the children of child A, the trust for the children of child B, and the trust for the children of child

> C—provides that the class of beneficiaries in each trust is to be left open until Jules's oldest grandchild has attained age 21. When that date arrives, there are six grandchildren: two from child A, two from child B, and two from child C. Each of those grandchildren is then made a one-half beneficiary of the respective trust established by Jules for their benefit, and for the benefit of their siblings.

So far, it would appear that there is no difference between the results of this example and the results of the prior example. However, in this last example, the life expectancies of each of the beneficiaries of each trust were not measured by the life expectancy of the oldest of the six grandchildren, but instead were measured by the life expectancy of the oldest grandchild beneficiary of each trust. In other words, with respect to the trust established for the benefit of the children of child A, benefits would be paid out over the life expectancy of the eldest of A's children. With respect to the trust established for the benefit of the children of child B, benefits would be payable over the life expectancy of the eldest of B's children, and with respect to the trust established for the benefit of the children of child C, benefits would be payable over the life expectancy of the eldest of C's children. In this way, additional deferrals can be accomplished. Moreover, a perhaps more important objective will have also been accomplished. With the dividing of the IRAs into three separate IRAs along each of the three family lines (Child A line, Child B line, and Child C line), each of the three children could then be given the right, as Trustees of the trust established for the benefit of each of their children, to manage their children's retirement assets, free from the supervision and control of their other siblings. In this way, the children can retain some measure of control over the assets of the trust established for the benefit of their own children until their own children have sufficiently matured.

CHAPTER 6
THE MULTIGENERATION APPROACH TO MAXIMIZING TAX DEFERRAL

CONTENTS

6 THE MULTIGENERATION APPROACH TO MAXIMIZING TAX DEFERRAL

Each of the following three strategies for the multigeneration IRA increases the tax deferral potential: Multigeneration Traditional Approach, Multigeneration Spousal Rollover Approach, Multigeneration Participant Direct Approach.

The Multigeneration Traditional Approach provides the least tax deferral potential of the three methods, while the Multigeneration Participation Direct Approach provides the greatest.

Multigeneration Traditional Approach

In the Multigeneration Traditional Approach, the spouse is designated as primary beneficiary, with the children and/or grandchildren named as contingent beneficiaries, all within one IRA. This approach, which by far is the most prevalent strategy in use today, assumes that the spouse will survive the participant and will then roll over the IRA assets to a new IRA—naming the children and grandchildren at that time as the primary beneficiaries of the new spousal IRA. One limitation associated with this strategy is that only the life expectancy of the oldest individual child or grandchild can then be used to extend Required Minimum Distributions after the surviving spouse dies. Assuming two children and four grandchildren, with the oldest child age 45 and the youngest grandchild age 2, under this method all of the beneficiaries would be deemed

Note: Readers should refer to the Introduction for a discussion of issues and concepts covered in Chapter 6 that may be affected by the IRS's issuance of the Revised Proposed Regulations governing Required Minimum Distributions and by the passage of EGTRRA 2001. These include: the Uniform Distribution Period Table; the elimination of irrevocable elections at the individual's Required Beginning Date; the determination of the designated beneficiary by December 31 of the year following the year of the individual's death; the Federal estate tax amounts and rates; and what rules and strategies have *not* been changed by the Revised Proposed Regulations.

Figure 6-1

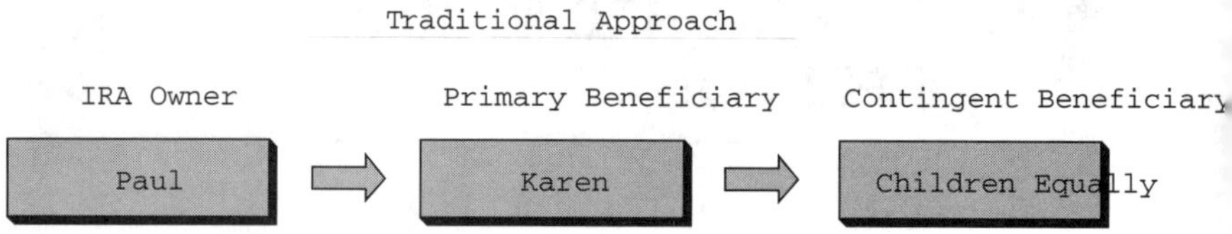

to be age 45 for purposes of determining life expectancies and tax deferral time horizons. Another obvious drawback to this strategy is the fact that it relies entirely on the spouse of the IRA owner surviving the IRA owner. If the spouse should predecease the IRA owner, the Multigeneration Traditional Approach cannot be used.

Multigeneration Spousal Rollover Approach

The Multigeneration Spousal Rollover Approach employs a strategy which allows the spouse to control the retirement assets after the IRA owner's death, while using the specific life expectancies of each child and/or grandchild to reduce Required Minimum Distributions. Under this approach, the spouse is named the primary beneficiary of the IRA. At the participant's death, the spouse rolls over the IRA into multiple IRAs, with a separate child or grandchild named as the primary beneficiary of each separate IRA. Each IRA uses the age of the specific designated child or grandchild, subject to the Minimum Distribution Incidental Benefit (MDIB) Rule and the ten-year age spread limitation, to determine life expectancy and Required Minimum Distributions. When the spouse dies, the MDIB Rule is eliminated, and the actual remaining age of each beneficiary becomes the basis for life expectancy computations for that particular IRA. This technique of using the longer life expectancies of each individual child and grandchild allows each child or grandchild to defer income taxes on the IRA assets for decades. However, the IRA owner must be the first spouse to die in order for the Spousal Rollover Approach to be available. If the spouse predeceases the IRA owner after the IRA owner has reached the Required Beginning Date, the minimum distribution amounts and time horizon will be based, at best, on the remaining joint life expectancy of the IRA owner and deceased spouse, rather than on the remaining life expectancies of the children or grandchildren. This is the risk clients must carefully assess before naming their spouse as primary beneficiary.

The rules governing spousal rollovers are essentially the same as those that apply to a participant in a retirement plan. The most important difference is that, while a participant may roll over assets from one qualified plan into another plan or into an IRA, the spouse may roll over death benefits from a participant's qualified plan only into an IRA. In addition, if a Required Minimum Distribution amount is due to be distributed in the year of the rollover, that Required Minimum Distribution must be distributed and cannot be rolled over.

In addition, IRS rules do not permit the rollover of payments that are one of a series of substantially equal payments made over the life expectancy of the participant, the joint life expectancy of the participant and designated beneficiary, or that are payable over any period of time equal to ten years or more. A rollover can be made with the participant's total account balance in the plan or with the participant's partial balance in the plan, except if a partial distribution is considered part of a series of substantially equal payments.

Remember that the spousal rollover can occur regardless of the age of the participant or spouse as of the date of death, and regard-

Figure 6-2

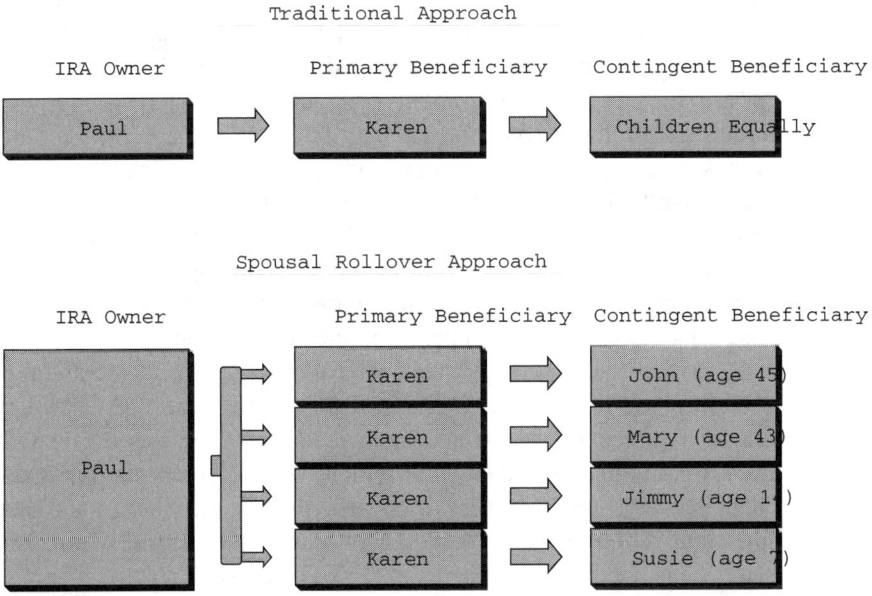

less of whether or not either the participant or spouse had reached or passed their respective Required Beginning Dates.

Accordingly, the rollover of benefits from the participant's qualified plan or IRA into the spouse's IRA can occur after the participant has reached his or her own Required Beginning Date and or after the spouse has reached the Required Beginning Date. However, once the benefits are actually distributed directly to the spouse, they must be rolled over into the IRA within 60 days or the rollover privilege is lost.

Instead of making a distribution out of the retirement account to a spouse who then rolls the assets back into an IRA, the spouse can effect a trustee-to-trustee transfer, in which case assets are transferred directly from the qualified plan of the deceased spouse or directly from the IRA Custodian of the deceased spouse's IRA to the Custodian of the spousal rollover IRA. In this way, no assets are ever received by the spouse beneficiary, and accordingly no possibility of income taxation can arise in any year. In addition, there is no limitation on the number of trustee-to-trustee transfers that can occur in any given year. This is different from the regular IRA distribution rules, which permit only one rollover per year of IRA funds.

Nevertheless, the longer the spouse waits to complete the rollover, the more advantages can be lost. For one thing, Required Minimum Distributions—and, therefore, income taxation—continue at the higher rate until the rollover change is completed, and subsequent Required Minimum Distributions are thereby reduced. If fact, if the surviving spouse dies before the rollover has been completed, subsequent Required Minimum Distributions may have to be made on the basis of a single life expectancy alone, thereby causing Required Minimum Distributions to potentially become quite high. If the participant and spouse's life expectancy were both being recalculated, in the year following the year of death of the surviving spouse, without the spousal rollover, all amounts in the retirement asset would have to be paid out—thus entirely ending all future tax deferrals.

Both the traditional and spousal rollover approaches are fairly straightforward and offer the advantage of providing the maximum financial protection to the spouse who is designated as the beneficiary of all the individual's retirement assets. Accordingly, under either scenario, the spouse need not fear that she or he may not have sufficient retirement assets to live on. Each scenario also provides some considerable potential to extend tax deferral.

Multigeneration Participant Direct Approach

If, upon careful analysis, it is determined that the surviving spouse will not need the retirement income, perhaps the spouse should not initially have been named as the primary beneficiary for that asset,

Figure 6-3

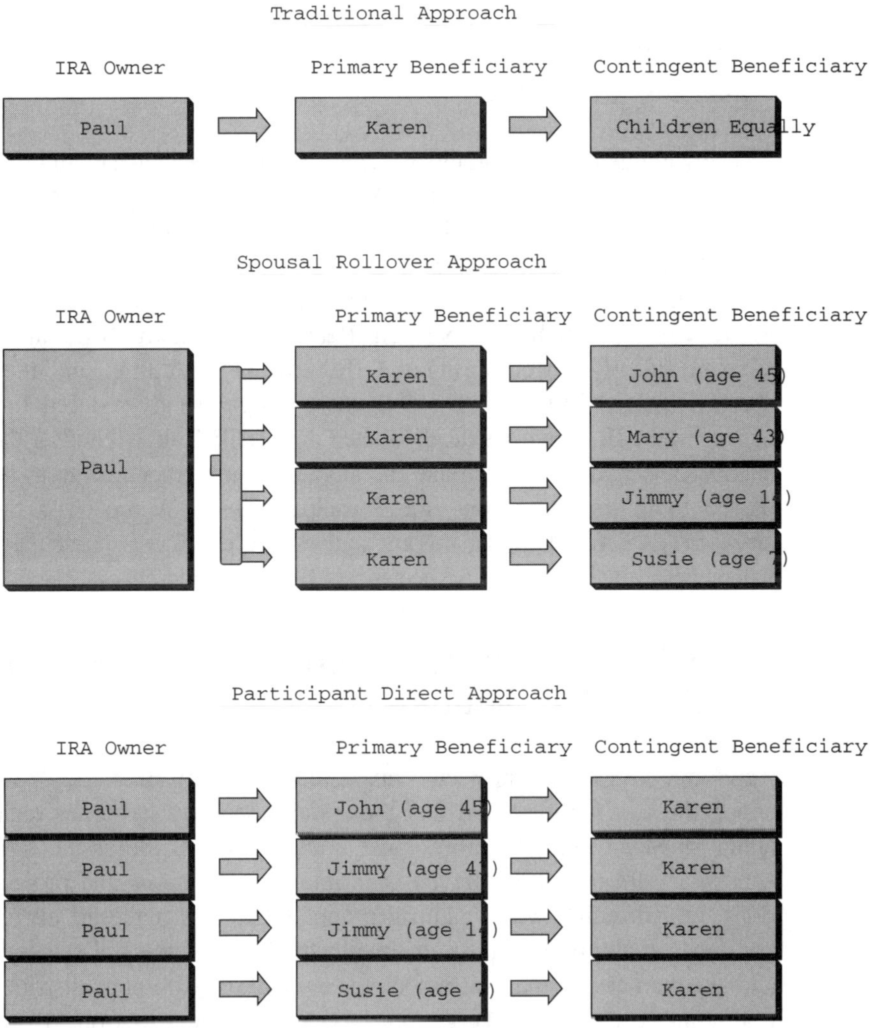

especially because of the irrevocable nature of the various Required Beginning Date elections. If it is safe to skip or bypass the spouse for this asset, tax deferrals can be significantly enhanced through the use of the Multigeneration Participant Direct Approach.

The most likely candidates for the Multigeneration Participant Direct Approach are clients with the following three characteristics:

1. They have a significant amount of wealth.
2. They dislike paying taxes.
3. They have reasonably good relationships with their children and/or grandchildren.

The Multigeneration Participant Direct Approach entails splitting the retirement asset into separate IRAs, with different children and/or grandchildren designated as the primary beneficiaries of each separate IRA. This approach offers the most favorable life expectancy factors, despite the initial limitations as imposed by the application of the MDIB Rule. Through this approach, Required Minimum Distributions are significantly lower during the IRA owner's lifetime, and then yearly Required Minimum Distributions are significantly reduced further upon the IRA owner's death—when the MDIB Rule is lifted. If the client's objective is to maximize the amount of retirement assets to be passed to future generations, the Participant Direct Approach is the answer. Tax deferrals under this method can be enormous, particularly when using the longer life expectancies of grandchildren.

Resurfacing Concerns about the Security of the Surviving Spouse

As compelling as this projected tax deferral strategy may appear on paper, the advisor may find that the spousal security issue has once again surfaced, and therefore must once again be addressed. Clients' fears are not often allayed by printed presentations and projections, all brimming with beautiful graphics that can make art out of columns of numbers. The more intellectually convincing the theory and the numerical analysis associated with this retirement distribution strategy, the more likely it may be for the client to wonder one more time: *Are you sure my spouse won't need the money?*

When clients are advised on estate planning matters, they typically receive advice from their professional advisors designed to reduce their taxable estates by gifting away assets while they are alive to their children and/or grandchildren, and/or to charities. In this way they can avoid the imposition of estate taxes on those assets, at rates equaling 50 percent or higher. They are also typically advised that, along with these gifting strategies, they should not sacrifice control over their assets. When faced with these two conflicting goals—gift assets away to save estate taxes or maintain control and grow assets to increase legacies—most individuals opt to continue to maintain control over their assets. Most older Americans, over the years, have disciplined themselves to live within their means and to thereby continue to accumulate assets, all the while continuing their control over those assets. While such reasoning may seem fine to the client in the estate planning area, it may not ring as true to them in the context of retirement distribution planning, because retirement assets and estate assets are treated differently in the client's mind. For most people with large estates, there is an understanding—both logical and emotional—that the purpose of accumulating wealth in the estate is multigenerational. Assets in the estate represent a legacy to be passed on from one generation to the next, to be used by succeeding generations of family members in satisfaction of their specific needs in the future. In fact, just the opposite is true. However, clients over the years have been convinced that their retirement assets—their reward for years of hard work—exist solely to fulfill their retirement income needs and should be spent in their entirety prior to their death.

The advisor may, therefore, have to spend a considerable amount of time refocusing the client's perspective from one in which the retirement assets are to be consumed and spent down, to one in which, to the greatest extent possible, the retirement assets are to be saved for future generations. In performing this refocusing task, however, the advisor should take extra precaution with clients to make sure that a contingency plan is in place for a surviving spouse, and that the retirement distribution plan can be implemented in such a way that the surviving spouse is not put at risk, or made to rely on other family members for his or her financial needs after the IRA owner has died. No matter how viable a retirement distribution plan may look on paper, life may present unexpected circumstances that could result in the spouse needing far greater assets than was originally projected.

Yet, despite these contingency plans, the spouse may still have concerns about being bypassed and having all of the retirement assets pass directly to the children and grandchildren. If that issue is still a major concern to the spouse, the goal of increasing tax deferrals on the retirement assets should take second place to the goal of increasing financial security for the spouse. The solution in that case may be to use a multigeneration combination approach.

Multigeneration Combination Approach

In the Multigeneration Combination Approach, an individual establishes their retirement assets in multiple IRAs, some for the benefit of children and/or grandchildren and one or more in which the spouse has been named as the primary beneficiary. When the IRA owner dies, the spouse adopts the Spousal Rollover Approach for those IRAs in which the spouse has been named as primary beneficiary. This strategy will provide the spouse with financial peace of mind gained from having control over that retirement asset. The spouse will know that he or she will receive a portion of the nest egg to be used during retirement. At the same time, maximum tax deferral can be achieved with the balance of the IRA assets in which the children and grandchildren are named primary beneficiaries.

When the owner dies, the IRAs in which the children and grandchildren have been named as primary beneficiaries are then retitled as Inherited IRAs for the benefit of the children and grandchildren beneficiaries, and their actual remaining ages are used for purposes of the calculation of all future Required Minimum Distribution amounts.

When the surviving spouse dies, the spousal Rollover IRA is payable to the children and grandchildren whom the spouse has named as primary beneficiaries. Accordingly, after both spouses have died, the children and grandchildren are left as the primary beneficiaries of two sets of IRAs—those established for their benefit by the original IRA owner, and those established for their benefit by the IRA owner's spouse. Both sets of IRAs are then payable to the children and grandchildren over their remaining life expectancies.

Disproportionate Distribution Strategy

There is yet another way in which the parents can exercise control over their IRA assets during their lifetime. Although the law requires the Required Minimum Distribution amount to be computed separately for each IRA, the IRS does not require that the total Required Minimum Distribution amounts for *all* IRAs be paid from each separate IRA on an exact proportionate basis. Instead, the IRS allows the total Required Minimum Distribution amount from all IRAs to be taken from any one of the IRAs, or from any combination of the IRAs, in any proportion or amount as long as the total Required Minimum Distribution for all IRAs has been taken for that year. In the following example, a couple decided to take disproportionate distributions from their several IRAs established for the benefit of each of their children. The children were also made to understand the value of the tax deferral potential of the grandchildren's IRAs, and were willing to support their parents' tax deferral strategy.

> **Example:** Richard and Lisa have three children. Richard had $1 million in an IRA that he then divided up into four IRAs: one for each of his three children in the amount of $200,000 each, with the balance of the $400,000 in IRA assets listing Lisa as the primary beneficiary. In this way, on Richard's death, the children will receive IRA assets worth $600,000, roughly the total of the current federal Unified Credit Amount, with the balance of the assets payable to Lisa, who will be eligible for the federal estate tax marital deduction. Each year amounts are required to be distributed from the four IRAs based on the life expectancy of each individual IRA beneficiary. If in any given year Richard decides he is having difficulty with his daughter, Melissa, he may decide to implement a disproportionate distribution strategy, in which each of the Required Minimum Distribution amounts due from the four IRAs in the aggregate will be taken 100 percent from the IRA allocable to Melissa. In this way, the balance in the IRA allocable to Melissa will be substantially reduced, thereby giving Richard greater control over the distribution of wealth to

> Melissa, and appropriately penalizing Melissa for wayward behavior.
>
> Alternatively, assume that Richard still wishes to benefit each of his children equally, but due to a successful investment strategy, each of the IRAs for each child has now grown to $230,000 or $690,000 in the aggregate between the three IRAs. If Richard were to die with the IRAs for the three children aggregating $690,000, there would be a small federal estate tax due in his estate, insofar as the $690,000 amount exceeds the current federal Unified Credit Amount of $675,000 by $15,000. Richard can rectify the situation by taking the Required Minimum Distribution amounts due for each of the four IRAs only from the three IRAs allocable to his children, and in that way eliminate the $15,000 excess, so that on his death, the total of those three IRAs does not exceed the $675,000 amount.

The amount of the Required Minimum Distribution which will be due each year, where children and/or grandchildren have been named as the IRA beneficiary, is typically a small number, representing, in the early years, usually less than 4 to 6 percent of the value of the IRAs. What if the adjustment that an individual wants to make between IRAs requires a bigger adjustment? The answer is to implement a trustee-to-trustee transfer. Individuals with multiple IRAs can effectuate the transfer of assets from one IRA to another by trustee-to-trustee transfers. There is no limit on the number of trustee-to-trustee transfers that an individual can make in any given year.

In the prior example, we discussed a situation in which an individual allocated roughly the Federal Unified Credit Amount to three IRAs established for the benefit of each of his three children. If the investment strategy that the individual had pursued had grown each of the IRAs from $200,000 to $300,000, with the result that the total amounts in these IRAs for the benefit of the children when aggregated together was now $900,000, that amount would be $225,000 more than the current Federal Unified Credit Amount of $675,000 applicable for 2000 and 2001. The overage could certainly be rectified by a distribution of $225,000 to the individual, but the excess distribution would result in additional income taxes being due, and the amount distributed (the $225,000) would be far and above the amounts required to be distributed that year under the Required Minimum Distribution rules.

An individual in this situation should take the Required Minimum Distribution amount due for that year from the three IRAs proportionately, but should then effectuate a trustee-to-trustee transfer in which the balance of the IRA assets allocable to the children, and over and above the $675,000 amount, is removed from the IRAs allocable to the three children and placed into the IRA allocable to the spouse. Since the assets in the IRA allocable to the spouse will be eligible for the marital deduction, no estate tax would then be due on the individual's death.

If a participant finds that certain family relationships have deteriorated over time, one strategy is to use the disproportionate IRA distribution method to cause the realignment of the IRA assets among beneficiaries that the IRA owner still favors. This would leave a larger, and, therefore, more secure, share of the total assets in IRAs allocable to individuals the participant still wants to benefit. There is complete flexibility available to take totally proportionate IRA distributions in one year, and totally disproportionate the next. In fact, the participant can take 100 percent of the Required Minimum Distributions from one IRA—even depleting it completely, while receiving no distributions at all from any of the other IRAs—as long as two *total* Required Minimum Distribution amounts due from all IRAs for that year have been taken.

These disproportionate rules apply only to IRAs and to 403(b) plans. The IRS allows the Required Minimum Distribution amounts from all IRAs to be aggregated and taken in disproportionate percentages from which one or more of the IRAs the individual chooses. Similarly, the IRS allows all 403(b) plans that the individual participates in to be aggregated, with disproportionate distributions taken from one or more of the 403(b) plans as the individual chooses. However, IRAs and 403(b) plans cannot be aggregated together for purposes of these rules, but instead, must each be considered separately. In addition, if the retirement asset is still in one or more qualified plan, the participant must calculate and receive Required Minimum Distributions from each plan separately, and cannot aggregate the Required Minimum Distribution amounts due from each plan, and then take disproportionate distributions from one or more of the qualified plans.

Therefore, it should be apparent at this point that one of the most beneficial aspects of implementing multigenerational wealth transfer strategies for retirement assets is that the IRA owner retains complete control over the assets while he or she is alive. The assets all the while still remain in the shelter of his or her own IRA. Through creative distribution allocation strategies (either disproportionate distributions or by effecting trustee-to-trustee transfers), the client during his or her lifetime can continue to exercise complete control each year over the IRA accounts. Moreover, through the use of trusts as IRA beneficiaries, the client can continue to maintain control over all of the IRA accounts even after death.

This high degree of flexibility and control can be maintained over those assets if the most important safeguard had been established at the outset—the inclusion of the entire family unit in the retirement distribution planning process.

Family Communication

Very few families are capable of addressing—let alone overcoming—communication obstacles that may have developed over a lifetime. The advisor, however, should not let the family ignore the need for effective communication, especially in the multigenerational retirement distribution planning area. The advisor should strive to establish an ideal planning environment, one in which certain ingrained attitudes may be softened and in which the opinions and feelings of any reserved or taciturn family members are drawn out. The advisors should encourage debate and discussion and should strive to reconcile opposing family views. On occasion, the advisor might even caution the client with their own true "war stories" of families that had engaged in prolonged and heated disputes over retirement and estate planning issues and, because of their particular family dynamics, were never able to resolve those issues—with the resulting loss of substantial planning opportunities and increased estate and income taxes due.

In the absence of compelling reasons to treat family members otherwise, great efforts should be made to see to it that all family members are treated equally. Even the mere appearance of any form of favoritism should be scrupulously avoided. A significant amount of family ill-will or disputes can be traced to one child feeling that he or she—or his or her child—is being singled out for some unfavorable treatment. Whether or not the client is engaging in any form of unequal treatment, these feelings will have to be adequately addressed if the proposed multigenerational retirement distribution approaches are to be successful.

If the advisor suspects that hidden family issues or agendas will later prevent certain family members from implementing the retirement distribution strategies they had previously agreed to, rest assured that problems will eventually surface. The result may be a family disaster. The advisor should therefore do everything possible—which might be quite substantial, based on the trust the family accords the advisor and their faith in the advisor's expertise and professionalism—to preempt the problems at the outset.

Retitling an IRA

Only a spouse can roll over an Inherited IRA into her or his own IRA. For non-spouse beneficiaries, inheriting an IRA would mean receiving the entire IRA outright and paying income taxes immediately on the entire IRA balance, or receiving a yearly payout from the IRA based on the remaining joint life expectancies of the deceased IRA owner and designated beneficiary. The only way to prevent this is by retitling the IRA properly after the IRA owner's death. The retitling process leaves the IRA in the IRA owner's name as a deceased individual, but with Required Minimum Distribution amounts payable to the designated beneficiary each year based on the beneficiary's life expectancy, depending on the date of the IRA owner's death (either prior to or after the IRA owner's Required Beginning Date) and depending on the prior election the IRA owner had made. It is extremely important to communicate this requirement clearly to clients and to their children and grandchildren.

The proper retitled IRA should read as follows:

> IRA of [name of deceased IRA owner], deceased, for the benefit of [name of beneficiary], grandchild [or other relationship] as beneficiary.

In effect, what is inherited is not the IRA itself, but the future yearly Required Minimum Distribution payments—in other words, the lifetime income stream generated by the IRA. After the IRA owner's death, the IRA beneficiary typically has substantial control over the management and investment distribution of the IRA assets, unless alternative arrangements had previously been made (for instance, a trust established for the benefit of the individual who has been designated as beneficiary). If the client divides the IRAs into multiple IRAs, each separate IRA will have its own separate destiny under the control of the beneficiary of that particular IRA.

If the beneficiary has control over the IRA, he or she can ignore the advantage of tax deferral and distribute all of the assets in the IRA currently. This will result in an income tax bill for the full value of the IRA and the loss of all possible future tax-deferred growth for that particular beneficiary. It is, therefore, important for the children and grandchildren to know the particular value in taking only the Required Minimum Distribution amounts from the IRA each year and in that way maximizing the value of the IRA over decades. The education process begins with the retirement distribution specialist's commitment to educating both parents and children, assuming that the grandchildren at that time are too young to grasp the financial concepts. It continues with the children's commitment to pass on that understanding to their own children when they are of age. The retirement distribution specialist should monitor the results of the retirement distribution plan each year communicating all pertinent information yearly to the appropriate family members.

It may take some searching to find an IRA Custodian who is agreeable and capable of handling the sophisticated arrangements discussed in this chapter. Until financial institutions incorporate these complex multigenerational planning strategies into their administrative policies and procedures, the search for a suitable IRA Custodian may prove to be a significant stumbling block for many advisors. Clients will feel frustrated if their advisors recommend creative and comprehensive retirement distribution plans that cannot be implemented because an acceptable IRA Custodian cannot be located. An effective retirement distribution specialist must be, therefore, an implementor, not only a strategist.

> **Example:** For Stacey Hall, the goal was to mix a measure of control with a measure of freedom. Her IRAs which are to benefit her grandchildren will be retitled at her death as follows: "IRA of Stacey Hall, deceased, for the

benefit of the Bradley Hall, Grandchild Trust as beneficiary." The Required Minimum Distributions after her death will be distributed to each grandchild's trust established for their benefit. The yearly income tax due on each yearly IRA distribution will be paid by each trust, with the remaining amount accumulated in the trust, to be distributed to each of the grandchildren from their respective trusts upon their attainment of certain specified ages, as set forth in the trust. Upon Stacey's death, the beneficiaries' actual remaining life expectancies will be used to determine their yearly Required Minimum Distribution amounts.

If this arrangement were to be established, in the early years after Stacey's death, the resulting divisor for the Required Minimum Distributions could be as large as 50, 60, or even 70 years. The relatively high life expectancy divisors in the early years virtually guarantee a relatively modest level of annual income to the grandchild's trust each year and works to protect the grandchild against any improvident use of the IRA assets while the grandchild is still young. In addition, eventual distributions from the trusts can be set up in to be made on an after-tax basis to the grandchildren.

Stacey arranged for a trust to hold the IRA proceeds until the grandchildren were each 40, with the investment and distribution decisions for the trust—and, therefore, the control of the IRA asset itself—in the hands of the parents as trustees until that time. When a grandchild reaches age 18, the trust provides that all subsequent Required Minimum Distribution amounts are payable from the IRA directly to the grandchild. Each year the Required Minimum Distribution amounts begin to get a little larger. This affords the grandchild a modest escalating income stream that can be used as a basis to determine the grandchild's ability to handle what may prove to be a significant inheritance.

Stacey also decided to give the grandchildren additional access to the amounts in the trust, by making increasing percentages of the principal of the trust—and

> therefore of the net IRA asset itself after taxes—available at certain specified age increments. These percentages can be made to apply to the IRA assets themselves as well as to the trust. For instance, at age 30, the grandchild can be given access to one-third of the trust principal and one-third of the IRA asset, with an additional one-third made available when the grandchild had attained age 35.
>
> At age 40, the trust ends, distributing all of its assets to the grandchild. At that same time, the grandchild gains total direct control over the remaining assets in the IRA.
>
> If tax-deferred growth is not the goal of the grandchild at that time, once the grandchild had attained age 40, he or she would be free to cash out the IRA entirely.

Under this scenario, both the Retirement Asset Will and the trust agreement provide that all assets then in the trust are to be distributed outright to the grandchild. All assets then remaining in the IRA continue to remain in the IRA, with only the Required Minimum Distribution amounts paid out each year. These subsequent yearly payments are then made directly to the grandchild and not to the trust. The grandchild at that point has, therefore, become the absolute outright owner of all of the Required Minimum Distribution amounts that had been payable to the trust each year up until that point.

In addition, the grandchild now is the absolute outright beneficiary of the entire IRA account and, accordingly, can decide each year, on a totally discretionary basis, whether to take only the Required Minimum Distributions from the IRA that year or to accelerate distributions and receive larger IRA distributions. Alternatively, the grandchild at that point could elect to close the IRA entirely and receive a complete distribution of the entire IRA balance.

What then would have been accomplished by the use of this planning device? The answer is that, until each grandchild had reached age 40, the assets were allowed to remain in the IRA to the greatest extent possible and were allowed to continue to accumulate on a tax-deferred basis for their benefit, protected from the psychological and/or fiscal immaturity of each grandchild. Both the principal and income stream during the grandchild's minority and somewhat beyond were protected through the intervening use of the trust. Principal distributions then commenced to each grandchild judiciously once he or she attained certain older ages, with absolute control over the IRA asset deferred until the grandchild reached the fiscally responsible age of 40.

At age 40, the grandchild was then allowed on his or her own to decide whether or not he or she wanted to continue only the minimum distribution payments from the IRA each year. Were the grandchild to elect this option, he or she would continue to enjoy each year maximum tax-sheltered growth during the remaining period of his or her life expectancy. However, should the grandchild decide at that time to close the IRA and receive a distribution of the entire balance in the IRA, the grandchild would be effectuating a distribution plan that would be no different from the distribution plan devised by his or her grandfather for the payment of the other estate assets in the trust, in that all other assets in the trust were payable outright to the grandchild upon attainment of age 40. In this way, and through the intervening use of the grandchild's trust as the beneficiary of the IRA asset (instead of the grandchild being named directly as the IRA beneficiary), maximum flexibility, control, and continued tax-deferred growth can be realized.

CHAPTER 7
PREPARING HEIRS FOR THEIR INHERITANCE

CONTENTS

7 PREPARING HEIRS FOR THEIR INHERITANCE

Passing wealth to the next generations is a tradition perhaps as old as civilization itself, but inherited wealth can be a double-edged sword—as likely a curse as a blessing. Many individuals are aware of stories in which people with money come to no good end—especially ill-gotten gains. Those without great wealth may take comfort in the belief that the transfer of wealth over successive generations inevitably brings on the decline of character and family values, and eventually the loss of the wealth itself. Certainly we have all heard horror stories of trust fund brats who lead frivolous, troubled, and meaningless lives, or of sibling rivalries brought about by great family wealth that inevitably lead to vicious legal battles, imprisonment, or perhaps even the morgue. These cases may not be the norm, but they certainly seem to occur often enough for the danger signs not to be ignored. Whatever the reasons, unearned money may bring its share of trouble.

Retirement distribution specialists will have to understand these psychological factors that are at work in order to protect their clients and other family members from the myriad problems associated with inheriting wealth. The advisor should be able to offer his or her clients the prospect of keeping accumulated wealth within the family, while avoiding its unwanted side effects. Where clients are candid enough to communicate their fears about inherited wealth, advisors should be especially committed to dealing with these issues.

Excellent reference sources on this subject can be obtained from an organization called The Inheritance Project, Inc. The goal of its founders is to document through personal interviews the experiences of heirs, and to transform the various lessons learned into practical applications for integrating the specific wealth transfer strategies into what is often complex emotional framework. The Project typically has dealt with families whose wealth, often accumulated over many generations, consists largely of non-retirement assets. The same psychological effects associated with inherited wealth, however, can be manifest in any type of inherited asset.

When dealing with multigenerational retirement distribution planning, it is often fair to assume that the heirs will be inheriting money that was hard-earned by their parents or grandparents. Retirement assets, after all, represent deferred wages, which, by definition, were based on one's labors. If an inheritance was earned long ago by distant generations of ancestors and has been passed along through a series of stewards to succeeding generations, it is unlikely that any significant portion of the inheritance today consists of retirement assets.

One major concern typically voiced by the generation that had earned the money is that the receipt of the wealth may have an adverse impact on the generation inheriting the wealth. The members of the older generation, which had earned the wealth, may view their heirs with a mixture of protective pride and critical displeasure. They often see in their children and grandchildren too few signs of the values, practices, and philosophies that had helped them earn, accumulate, and then deal with their affluence. Yet, their impulses to protect and to provide for their children and grandchildren are often so strong that their progeny are invariably coddled, causing them to live their formative years at a lifestyle level that can never duplicate the conditions their parents had endured—conditions which fostered the life-coping strengths of the older generation. The members of the younger generation are not likely to understand what the members of the older generation felt when they experienced the following:

- Living without money
- Earning their first dollars
- Using the earned money to meet their basic living expenses
- Watching the money begin to accumulate
- Risking the total loss of the money
- Managing debt
- Seeking and following professional advice

These experiences all play critical roles in creating a money psychology—one that controls how people earn, save, borrow, and spend money throughout their lifetime. It is the strengths and weaknesses in individuals' money psychology which dictates what steps they will be willing to take to earn and then to retain their money. This outlook includes the following:

- How one disciplines oneself to save money, or fails to do so
- How much money one is willing to borrow and how one manages debt repayment
- How one decides which funds are to be spent, and the attachments one forms to material purchases

Children will develop their own relationship with money, and will develop their own earning, savings, borrowing, and spending psychology. One problem with inheritors is that, unlike their ancestors, who had earned the money, they missed the opportunity to learn many practical lessons. Without these valuable lessons and experiences, they may never develop a healthy perspective on money. This means more than the oversimplified notion that money is either earned or not and that if it is not earned, it is somehow bad. Earning and accumulating wealth carry the knowledge, skill, and insight by which a person can successfully manage money.

By the Required Beginning Date, the children of the participant and spouse are very likely fully grown, with their money psychology probably well established. They may still unlearn some bad habits and may still learn some good ones, but usually any such adjustments will be minor. However, with the grandchildren there is usually still time left to mold their psychology of money. How is the ideal attitude toward earned income achieved with the younger generation?

First, because it is the grandparents' money, the grandparents should not abdicate to their own children the process of educating their grandchildren as to the proper money psychology. Besides, communication obstacles may have already been developing between the parents and their children. It may, therefore, be more effective and more emotionally satisfying to the grandparents, if the grandparents—with the advice and consent of the grandchildren's parents—assume the primary instructive role. In previous generations, when family members lived in close proximity to each other, there was an expectation that the grandparents would be the teachers of their grandchildren and the bestowers of wisdom on them. This system for communicating knowledge still seems like a good system from every point of view, and when it can be revived and sustained, the subject of money seems to be a natural topic to be covered.

However, the fact that someone is a grandparent—and has earned and accumulated substantial assets in his or her lifetime—does not automatically mean that he or she has a healthy relationship with money. What needs to be communicated to the grandchildren is the necessary guidance to assist them in discovering on their own a desirable relationship with money. Some grandparents may not be capable of assuming this role because of their own problems in dealing with money. If clients are in this predicament, an advisor can often assist them by covering the following basic issues with the grandchildren.

Work and Income Provide a Purpose in Life

If one were to ask people of modest means why they work, the answer will probably be, "To make money, to earn a living." Ask the same question of someone who has inherited significant wealth, and he or she may not have an answer, since earning a living was never an issue for them.

Inheritors who have successfully thought this issue through are more likely to say that they work so that they have a purpose in life. This is certainly a more satisfying answer than having to work to earn a living. Whether or not work is necessary for financial survival, it is certainly important in maintaining a healthy psychological attitude. Children should be given an understanding of both of these essential components of work as they mature, especially in those instances in which they are going to be provided with a secure lifetime income stream from a multigenerational IRA. It may not be easy to teach these two components to affluent youngsters. Affluent teenagers and young adults may be able to secure jobs on their own , or their parents may have certain business contacts which can be called upon to help their children find fulfilling employment. Ideally, though, these lessons should start earlier.

In many families, it is common to establish some kind of chores-and-allowance system for the children. However, in very affluent families, the institution of this system is often made difficult by the fact that most, if not all, of the responsibility for completing the standard household chores has been turned over to paid domestic workers. While one generation grew up mowing the lawn for a couple of dollars a week, a gardener would have to be laid off if the individuals in the next generation were to begin regularly cutting the grass. In the same way, while one generation may have started a business mowing neighbors' lawns or delivering newspapers, the next generation may live in a neighborhood where all of these jobs are already by paid adult workers. As corrosive an influence as unearned income might be, it may be equally dangerous to teach children that there will always be someone around to do the necessary chores or housework. If children do not pay attention to how the housework is done and how it is paid for, they may come to take too much for granted—as if the completion of household chores is an inscrutable mystery that somehow just gets done.

One possible way to get around this problem is for the grandparents to give an occasional paid day off to the employee who performs certain household tasks, and to have one of their grandchildren perform that task instead. Grandparents can then supervise the grandchildren in the work, compensating them accordingly when the work has been completed. Where the work involves the use of tools or technical expertise, the grandchildren should be encouraged to apprentice themselves for a few hours, or even for a few days—and experience and learn the necessary mechanical and/or technical skills. This strategy may not meet with everyone's approval, but where the relationship between the paid household workers and the children can support it, this strategy may work quite well.

For some clients, the mere idea of their grandchildren performing menial manual labor may not seem like an attractive idea. The advisor may, therefore, want to present another way of addressing this issue. Chores such as lawn-mowing and newspaper delivery may seem like jobs from another era. America is well into a new economic and social order in which many manual labor jobs have been replaced by information or technological jobs. Why not work with these societal and labor trends, and search for or create employment opportunities for the grandhildren that involve imagination, problem-solving, and project management skills?

Why should raking leaves be a paid job for children, while other creative or intellectual accomplishments earn only non-monetary praise? During summer recess or school breaks, the grandchildren can be involved in a series of such projects for which they can earn income. Participation in these projects, created by grandparents, would not only be instructive but also may also more accurately reflect the grandchildren's future employment alternatives.

Here are some ideas to give clients if they want to create jobs for their grandchildren:

- Help a grandchild launch a virtual professional song writing career and act as the virtual music publisher.
- Hire a grandchild to conduct neighborhood sports clinics for younger, less accomplished children.
- Encourage a computer-oriented grandchild to hold computer training and tutoring sessions.
- For a green-thumbed grandchild, provide capital with which the grandchild can rent a garden plot. Invest in garden tools, seeds, seedlings, or whatever else the grandchild may need for this activity.

Any number of similar entrepreneurial opportunities are available that can be used to encourage the grandchildren into converting those talents, energies, and abilities into earning power. The added benefit of this approach is that it provides a foundation for the second intrinsic value of work—work as a means of providing a purpose in life and as a source of self-esteem.

Money Management

In addition to building positive attitudes toward work through compensation, many mechanical and practical aspects of money management should be learned. In their interviews with heirs, The Inheritance Project repeatedly found examples of people who throughout their youth and into their early adulthood had never balanced a checkbook or paid a bill and who therefore felt helpless as adults when first asked to do so. Money was a kind of mystery in their lives. It was just there, like electricity in a wall socket or water in a tap. They never saw where the money had come from, how it had gotten there, or what happened to it after it came out, performed its function, and then disappeared down the proverbial drain, or transformed itself into some other form.

Many advisors in this field recommend that by age 13 or so a child should open a checking account and be given a credit or debit card.

While some banks may provide these services as a way to educate future customers, others may not. However, a bank which does not ordinarily have this policy may make an exception to this rule for an affluent family who is one of the bank's preferred customers. By establishing check and credit transaction limits and by requiring a monthly balance statement or debt payment, a young person not only sees the methodology of money exchanges, but also experiences first hand the range of emotions associated with dealing with money, whether spending, depositing, or withdrawing it.

Another suggestion is to let the child actually write the checks for the family's household bills from the family checking account in order to earn an appreciation of the cost of maintaining the current lifestyle of the family. Most children grow up thinking that electricity, water, and trash collection are services that simply are performed as a fact of life with no costs, fees, or charges associated therewith. The only message that they were ever likely to have received in the past to the contrary was when someone had chided them about wasting water after spending more than 20 minutes in the shower. However, that experience will never match the impact of writing the monthly family budget checks and seeing the actual bite which the monthly expenses can take out of the family checkbook.

If this educational process is followed, the practical process of money management will be openly understood by each member of the family unit. The children will have witnessed, firsthand, the differences in attitudes about earning, saving, borrowing, and spending. If, on the other hand, the family finances are kept hidden from them or are only discussed in vague generalities, problems in dealing with money may often develop later on. Children may develop negative feelings about having money or may develop an irrational need to hide any outward appearance of affluence. No one wants a child to act ostentatiously or to use the outward manifestations of wealth as a means of judging the value of others, but the denial of wealth may indicate a high degree of guilt associated with inherited wealth and may present an even greater problem.

One step beyond the mere education of certain earning and spending issues, and which may be applicable to older grandchildren, is for the grandparents to form a grandchildren's investment club or grandchildren's partnership, funded initially with capital allocated to each individual grandchild-partner. Although this approach could be conducted as a hypothetical exercise, the use of real money will certainly give it much more impact. A collective investment philosophy or risk-return goal should be decided upon to guide the decision-making process. The club could do its own investment analysis and planning or can follow the lead of a financial newsletter or mutual fund. It may even purchase some time from a willing money manager, depending on the grandparents' financial and time commitments to the project. The investment club could even evolve over time into a family bank, making loans to members within the family unit. At a minimum, these efforts should produce a rudimentary understanding of the various financial markets, and at best may produce an extremely sophisticated and comprehensive understanding of investment strategy. An added byproduct of these efforts will be the large measure of self-awareness the grandchildren may develop about their own attitudes toward risk tolerance and rate-of-return expectations.

The Psychology of Money

Most people can accept the concept that money, in the abstract, is simply a resource neither intrinsically good nor bad. Unfortunately, few people can maintain such a reasoned perspective when it comes to their own attitude about money. Money can do strange things to people's minds. The absence of money can cause a huge emotional stress or a constructive driving force in life—again, a positive or a negative. The irony is that an abundance of money can also be a source of stress, or it can serve as a constructive driving force in life—a positive or a negative. Most of us look on inheritors with a mixture of envy and respect. People wonder what it must be like to have the financial freedom not to have to work and the option of doing nothing or anything one chooses with one's time.

From reports that inheritors have given about how unearned money has actually affected their lives the surprising and disturbing news is that feelings of financial freedom and security are *not* the automatic consequence of inheriting wealth. For many, the effect of unearned money has been very much the opposite. Inheritors may feel trapped by their inherited wealth. They may never learn how to work, may never enjoy the self-esteem that comes from being truly productive and may never experience true personal independence.

Common Problems of Inherited Wealth

The work of The Inheritance Project, Inc. has documented the substantial psychological impact that inherited wealth may produce upon the heirs. The fact that the founders of the Project are also inheritors themselves has allowed them to interpret their data from an insider's perspective. Here are some common problems that have been identified as being associated with inherited wealth.

Wealth Is Viewed As Unreal

One common psychological effect of inherited wealth is a feeling in the heirs that money is somehow unreal or is unconnected to them. For one thing, many of the heirs have never actually controlled any significant sums of money, or even seen any significant sums of money until well into their adulthood. In most instances, all significant assets for the heirs' benefit had been held in trust, managed by trustees, and doled out to the heirs in accordance with the benefactors' wishes. Accordingly, the heirs never really feel rich. In fact, they may feel quite the opposite, especially if the income stream they receive each year is relatively modest compared to the overall size of the trust asset itself.

This can lead the heirs to decide to live very restricted lives, with inheritors denying themselves any luxuries or even denying themselves some of life's necessities, simply because they feel that they do not have enough money, and feel uncomfortable or unworthy in asking the trustees for more. They may recognize that money is a tool, but for the most part it can remain a mystery to them. They see themselves as different from other people, who, for the most part, appear to understand how to earn, accumulate, and manage money. They can often experience feelings of isolation, alienation, and insulation. They may feel that they are sitting on the inside, watching as real life goes by. Ironically, all of this can make for a meager and painful existence in the midst of actual abundance.

Wealth Can Foster Feelings of Dependency

The presence of a continuous stream of unearned income can lead to feelings of dependency and lack of empowerment on the part of the heirs. This can be compounded by the fact that many inheritors have grown up with minimal parental contact and an inordinate reliance on servants and nannies. Their situation can create an unreal model for how, in the "real world," things get done and may produce in the heirs a dangerous lack of self-confidence. From these problems can come the stereotypical tendencies of the rich—a tendency toward impulsiveness and excessiveness, and a lack of focus, direction, and follow-through.

Wealth Can Produce Lack of Goals

What about the idea that with so much money people can do anything they want to do? In practice, the heirs seldom learn to put their hearts into any long-term goals. In practice, the fact that they can do anything they want only makes them devalue anything they do. Commitment for most individuals usually entails making sacrifices and overcoming obstacles. To know that sacrifice is totally unnecessary and that obstacles can be eliminated effortlessly through a liberal use of the unearned money can make it difficult for the heirs to take any long-term goals very seriously.

Wealth Can Produce Guilt

Unearned wealth can also produce enormous feelings of guilt. Moreover, sometimes the wealth may have derived from activities of questionable social value—for example, the exploitation of human or natural resources. While such exploitation may or may not have been judged harshly generations ago and over time the exploitation may have evolved into a more benign use of people and materials, still, by today's sensibilities, the original wealth and all of the accretions thereon may still be judged harshly. This treatment might not seem to apply to retirement distribution assets, which are likely to be thought of as derived from an individual's work effort and not produced automatically by some heartless exploitive institution. But what if the company that had funded the pension benefit initially has since been condemned for environmental pollution or some other socially reprehensible activity? Will the taint of that activity carry over to the retirement assets when the grandchildren are to receive them? If substantial guilt is associated with these inheritances, the heirs could wind up spending their lives apologizing for their inheritance, or may instead seek irrational ways in which to spend their inheritance so as to "cleanse the money." Alternatively, the heirs might become compulsive, unhealthy workaholics in order to prove to themselves and to others that they do *not* need and do *not* want the wealth that they have inherited.

Wealth Can Lead to Resentment

Any emotional difficulties may be made even more troubling when inheritors experience resentment—real or perceived—from peers. This experience can happen at any time—childhood, adolescence, or adulthood. For children and teenagers, an abundance of desirable material objects may create or expand friendships initially. However, inevitably, some backlash may arise. Adult inheritors may find their professional accomplishments invalidated in the eyes of others because their work achievements are thought of merely as a form of occupational therapy, or a hobby. With a lifetime of this type of negative external reinforcement—some derived even from other family members—inheritors tend to go to extremes, often unrealistically expecting either too much or too little of themselves.

Wealth Can Bring Fear of Loss

One of the most devastating concerns common to inheritors is a deep dread of what might happen if they were ever to lose all of their wealth. For all the freedom, independence, and the multitude of choices that wealth supposedly offers, if heirs do not have control over their assets and if they do not eventually mature into self-sufficiency, this loss anxiety may overcome them. They may rationalize that if they did not earn the money in the first instance, how could they possibly replace the money if it were ever to be lost? Stories abound about lottery winners who, in short order, fell from relative affluence. How is inherited wealth any different, they ask.

Wealth Brings the Problem of the Transfer of Assets

Other anxieties may arise from the way in which assets are transferred. Traditionally, the most effective way to escape estate taxation was to skip generations. This was done by providing to the children only an income interest from the assets, while leaving the assets themselves to the grandchildren. In many cases, this tax-driven strategy caused intergenerational resentments, which may have been a key factor in irrevocably damaging the relationships between the individuals' children and grandchildren.

One aspect of the problem is the resentment of the second generation toward the members of the first generation. The members of the second generation who have been bypassed in favor of their children may feel that they were passed over because they were somehow viewed by their parents as unworthy. The fact that the first generation had implemented this strategy purely as an estate tax savings measure is not often appreciated. A second aspect of this problem is that grandparents often make the asset transfer decisions to pass wealth *directly* to grandchildren without first consulting the parents of the grandchildren. The grandchildren inherit the money from the IRA, while the parents inherit only the psychological baggage, which may be the one remaining vestige of their relationship with their parents.

When trusts are used to pass assets, restictive trust provisions which can severely limit the heirs' access to those assets send a very clear message to the heirs about their trustworthiness—or lack of it. This message, which is subliminally communicated to the heirs, is passed along with the retirement asset itself as part of the legacy. The intentions of the benefactors may have been laudatory, but the actual effects of these good intentions may prove both hurtful and counter-productive. On the other hand, leaving money outright to emotionally and immature beneficiaries may prove even more disastrous from a psychological perspective. In fact, there may be no way to win this battle between the protection of those assets for the beneficiary's benefit and the protection of the beneficiary's ego from feelings of inadequacy and lack of self-worth.

Lessons Learned

The overriding lesson to be gained from each of these psychological issues is that money should not be passed along to heirs without also passing along to them a corresponding set of coping skills and the proper attitude to support the wealth. For the retirement distribution specialist the lesson is this: No clever tax-driven strategy ever exists in a vacuum. What good is a precise knowledge of the tax code and the ability to creatively exploit certain wealth transfer loopholes if, as a result of those efforts, several generations of heirs are psychologically damaged in the process?

The moral obligations and professional liabilities of retirement distribution planning advisors may arise as much from what the specialists say and do as from what they may fail to say and do. Advisors face compelling moral, ethical, personal, and emotional issues that they must learn to address and master. Retirement distribution specialists have an obligation to warn clients of the many potential non-legal issues inherent in the retirement distribution planning process. The psychological implications of transferring substantial retirement assets, along with the psychological implications of the precise manner in which those assets are transferred, should not be overlooked. With the advisor's assistance, the client should be able to find the most suitable balance to be struck between tax-driven strategies and emotion-driven strategies.

Still, many professional advisors often hesitate before allowing themselves to be drawn into the currents of family relationships. Many advisors may feel that their involvement in these emotional issues may hinder their ability to address the tax and financial problems which they were retained to solve. The argument could be made that clients have to take responsibility solving these emotional issues themselves, and that emotional issues should play no part in the advisor's role. As a practical matter, however, these emotional issues will have to be addressed, because they will inevitably come to the fore, and may then work to derail the entire retirement distribution planning process. To prevent these issues from festering and becoming progressively worse, it may be necessary to point them out to the client and offer constructive advice on possible solutions. If these emotional issues are not addressed, an advisor's vaunted objectivity may actually get in the way of the client's desire to implement the appropriate retirement distribution strategy and ultimately work to undermine the retirement distribution plan itself. Perhaps a little subjectivity should be judiciously but courageously applied. A willingness on the advisor's part to challenge the client's preconceived assumptions or to confront the client's bias, may in the long run be more productive than remaining benignly aloof from these issues. The urge to minister to and nourish the client, to coax him or her along despite his or her insecurities, may in the end prove to be the right and honorable course of action.

The Test of Family Values

The retirement distribution specialist should consider not only the psychological makeup of the individual inheritors, but also that of the family unit as a whole. Clear empirical evidence exists about the causes of certain family breakdowns. If these elements are part of the family dynamics involved in a case, his or her obligation to address these issues can become even more compelling, and under those circumstances, the task becomes even more formidable. If the advisor has not accurately perceived these emotional issues, he or she should, at a minimum, provide the family with a list of those issues which families in general should watch out for under those circumstances.

When dealing with these emotional issues, there are no guarantees of success, nor will there be much comfort should these emotional issues subsequently surface. However, at least in that case, the advisor will have been diligent, thorough, and compassionate, yet still professional.

The problem with assessing family values is that many of the values are only subtly evident. Mothers, fathers, children, and grandparents all profess to want what is right for each other. All concerned sincerely believe that they have the best interests of each other at heart. However, the problems arise when their words and actions create family conflict, sometimes unintentionally. Advisors are not in the business of assigning blame. However, facts, feelings, and mixed messages, communicated by the various family members, may all reveal severe underlying family conflict. The advisor may often find that until many of these emotional issues have been resolved, a creative and proactive retirement distribution strategy may have little chance of being implemented.

Mixed Messages about the Psychology of Money

Enormous psychological stress can be imposed on certain family members by the collective weight of the family psychology of money. This psychology may manifest itself differently in each family member, especially where the children had been given mixed messages about money while they were growing up. Take one common occurrence among the extremely wealthy—the problem of being asset rich yet cash poor. A common result of this phenomenon is a paralyzing and fearful mixed message. Even though the children may live in a mansion, their parents may continually bemoan the high cost of its maintenance or upkeep. A miserly cloud may gather over certain family members who are otherwise surrounded by luxury. Wealthy parents may often want to prove to their children that they are just like anyone else, by shunning any form of ostentatious display. However, in the next instance, the parents may demonstrate to the children that they are different from others by insisting they recognize their obligation to take care of people less fortunate than they are.

Communicating inconsistent or contradictory messages is not a fault unique to affluent parents. Children from every type of socioeconomic background grow up dealing with conflicting parental signals and messages. The crucial difference with the wealthy is that when children have access to large amounts of money, or the expectation of access to large amounts of money, their character development can be put at risk. One way to minimize this risk is for parents to make a concerted effort to examine their own attitudes toward money, and to bring their own words and actions into line with their own true beliefs. Unfortunately, the likelihood is that without proper counseling, most parents will never see this inconsistency. It is, therefore, up to their advisors to point out these discrepancies to them, and to help them find the emotional and psychological resources to resolve these differences. Advisors do not need to judge the clients. However, they do need to anticipate the effects the family's attitude toward wealth will have on the particular retirement distribution strategy being proposed.

Mixed Messages about Work

Another by-product of confused family values over money is the mixed signals parents may send about work. Among the affluent, their attitude toward work may range from a condemnation of idleness on the one hand to a profound disdain for certain kinds of work or a tendency to patronize the career efforts of their children on the other. For example, inheritors often may be drawn toward low-paying jobs. They may throw themselves into such work as a way of resolving their emotional need to somehow give back what they have received. While parents may feel some measure of pride at these efforts, they may unconsciously send a signal to the child that, in effect, they regard the work as not real work, but rather merely as a moderately productive way to stay occupied. This message can often be reinforced by co-workers when the co-workers discover that the inheritor is secretly wealthy and does not need to work.

At the other end of the spectrum, inheritors may become workaholics, driven to create and maintain high-paying careers as a statement to themselves, their parents, and their peers that they can make it to the top of the ladder entirely through their own efforts. While this path may appear to resolve an otherwise ambiguous attitude toward work, it can wreak havoc on certain family relationships, especially in those instances in which a workaholic attitude is frowned on by the individual's parents, or by the individual's children. In other words, for many of the children of the wealthy, there may be no way to win.

One way in which advisors can approach this issue is to ask an adult child, "What do you do?" The advisor should then ask the parents, "What do your children do?" The advisor should then listen for the underlying emotional messages conveyed in the answers and in the tone resonating behind the words. The advisor should observe body language. How wide is the apparent gap between the children's attitude toward what they do and the parents' view of their work? Many affluent second- and third-generation members find that a healthy attitude toward work may be one of the most difficult objectives to achieve. If work is indeed a source of satisfaction to them, one can only imagine the many obstacles that had to be overcome for them to have arrived at that point of view.

The different attitudes about work among family members can become even more pronounced in the context of a family-owned business, especially in those instances in which founder-parents want the children to work with them in the business, while the children really want to strike out on their own. Parents may exacerbate this problem by forcing the children into taking jobs in the family business at experience levels considerably above or below those suited for the children. The parents may then voice disapproval when a child is not performing adequately on the job. The children, on the other hand, may feel a sense of obligation to stay with the family enterprise. The children may, in the short run, actually convince themselves that they are happy working there. However, in the long run, if they are not truly happy with their choice staying with the family business, conflicts will inevitably arise and their performance at the family business will suffer, as will the prospects for the continued success of the family business.

Conflict over Unequal Treatment

Another problem arises when parents have an ideal that all the children should be treated equally. This seemingly laudable goal may lead to conflict because the exactly equal treatment of each child fails to take into account individual differences in personality, abilities, and interests. An additional problem may arise when parents encourage one child's interests in the business while ignoring that of others. This inconsistent treatment may result from differing views of the role of firstborn and later-born children, or from differing views about different roles assigned to male and female children.

Lack of Attention to Home Matters

People do not build fortunes without a strong commitment to their careers. More often than not, this means that time and attention at home is being sacrificed. In addition, founders of successful businesses, high-powered executives, and professionals are seldom individuals with small egos and passive natures. They frequently have a way of igniting fireworks around themselves both at work and at home. Many wealthy families have found a way to successfully manage these time, attention, and ego conflicts. However, most have not.

Children who feel deserted and isolated during their formative years (typically the parent's high earning years) are likely to experience anger and resentment when their parents give them the "we did it all for you" speech. They do not respond favorably when parents remind them of the many advantages and privileges which they enjoy but have never apparently valued. In the context of that family situation, the prospect of an inheritance can become all the more problematic. Some children can come to resent their inherited wealth as the outward manifestation of the lack of affection they received as children. Some may use their inherited wealth in a misguided, wasteful, or even self-destructive way.

Another contributing factor to this problem is the comparison successful parents invariably make between their lives and those of their children. They talk about the many difficulties they had to overcome to achieve their financial success, and bemoan the fact that their children have had everything handed to them. They point out their great respect for high standards of industry and excellence, and their children's apparent disregard for these all-important virtues. They applaud their ambitious nature, and contrast this with their children's inertia and lack of purposeful activity.

Sadly, parents who have struggled to achieve financial success often begrudge their children the very gifts that they had mightily struggled to achieve. They may dismiss the often valiant efforts made by their children to succeed by pointing out that their children did not have to start from scratch, as they did. Even in those instances in which these views are not expressed in so many words to the children, they may nevertheless be communicated by the parents subliminally or through innuendo.

Different Views of Philanthropy

The opposite problem may occur when parents, consciously or unconsciously, pressure their children to becoming the stewards of the family wealth. Many affluent parents who think beyond the self-centered goal of constantly increasing the family fortune may want to instill ideals in their children about using the family wealth to achieve higher moral and social ends. Company founders are typically proud of the fact that their success has created hundreds or perhaps thousands of jobs for many families. Over time, the business ownership may have become separated from the family members, but the wealth remains, along with the family's perceived obligation to continue its good efforts. Unfortunately, while the parents' goal in this regard may be admirable, their behavior toward their children may send a different message. There may be a continuing undercurrent of criticism directed at the children: that they do not take the family name and the responsibility that it entails seriously enough and that they lack the requisite character and temperament to deserve the stewardship of the family wealth.

Mixed Messages about Independence

Finally, parents may outwardly encourage or even exhort their children into achieving independence—financial and psychological—by actively using many of the resources that the family's success can offer. However, in private meetings with their advisors, the parents may develop tax and financial plans that actually seek to manipulate and control the children and undercut their independence by severely limiting their access to the family wealth, or by placing certain restrictions or conditions on their entitlement to their inheritances. Although parents may genuinely want their children to be successful in their own right, they may also want to shield their children from certain of life's risks. This conflicted view of the family's wealth may not even become apparent to the children until their parents' full estate plan has been revealed, which typically is not until some time after the parents have died.

The Role of the Advisor in Family Conflicts

When advisors see signs of these emotional issues building in a family, they should:

- Point out their own personal observations and perhaps challenge family attitudes over certain emotional issues.
- Ensure that the retirement distribution planning process, which often is to be carried out over decades and over generations, does not exacerbate these emotional issues.
- Try to direct the family members to resources that can be used to help them deal with these issues.

- Be willing to listen to all sides of these issues.
- Recommend professional counseling when mixed messages about trust, communication, affection, and personal worth surface and appear incapable of successful resolution.

Taking a hand in the resolution of certain family emotional conflicts is not an easy assignment, or one which an advisor typically relishes. The advisor's efforts may at first appear counterproductive. The advisor may receive criticism from some family members over his or her involvement in this process. However, even when clients are taken aback by an advisor's direct challenge to one or more of their preconceived ideas, or to an outmoded or ingrained way of thinking, this kind of honest and objective evaluation is precisely what many wealthy individuals really seek in their most valued advisors. Many successful people have no peers in whom to confide. Typically, everyone around them either defers to their way of thinking or assumes that a person who is financially successful must be knowledgeable about all other phases of their life. Accordingly, the affluent client may not know who else to turn to for help with these issues. If the retirement distribution specialist perseveres along these lines, he or she may find that he or she has become one of the client's most valued advisors. The advisor's hard-earned reputation for honest, tough, and comprehensive evaluations may, in the end, be the highest measure of his or her true worth as a trust advisor.

CHAPTER 8
CHARITABLE GOALS AND RETIREMENT DISTRIBUTION STRATEGIES

CONTENTS

8 CHARITABLE GOALS AND RETIREMENT DISTRIBUTION STRATEGIES

Charitable activities are not generally driven by tax considerations. The tax code supports what our society takes to be a natural compassionate impulse in human beings. As a society we agree that money may not be the source of happiness, but having enough money is typically viewed as a fortunate state of affairs. We may think of the Puritans, who shaped many of our cultural values, as a dour lot. However, they viewed affluence as one indicator of divine grace and saw generosity as a virtue. Not surprisingly, with or without the tax code, affluent individuals frequently feel a moral and ethical responsibility to reinvest part of their wealth for the benefit of those who are not as fortunate.

The cultural values that support this sense of responsibility can perhaps be traced to even earlier sources. The European aristocratic tradition established an ideal more than a thousand years ago of *noblesse oblige*, the obligation of the nobility to assist the other classes through their moral leadership and, where necessary and appropriate, through material assistance. This spirit continues to survive today as a respected value in our society, even though barely a remnant of nobility survives. The tradition of the tithe, setting aside one-tenth of one's income as an offering to God, has even more ancient roots, probably predating the Christian era. The rules of hospitality throughout the ancient world suggest that

---

Note: Readers should refer to the Introduction for a discussion of issues and concepts covered in Chapter 8 that may be affected by the IRS's issuance of the Revised Proposed Regulations governing Required Minimum Distributions and by the passage of EGTRRA 2001. These include: the Uniform Distribution Period Table; the elimination of irrevocable elections at the individual's Required Beginning Date; the determination of the designated beneficiary by December 31 of the year following the year of the individual's death; the Federal estate tax amounts and rates; and what rules and strategies have *not* been changed by the Revised Proposed Regulations.

human beings have always expected charitable behavior from each other, and that the very foundation of our societal structure may, in fact, depend on it. Our role models of selfless giving—for example, a wealthy philanthropist, such as Andrew Carnegie, or a nun devoting her life to the care of others under a vow of poverty, such as Mother Teresa—are often among the most influential and widely respected people in the world.

The various tax benefits of giving, however, are not lost on wealthy individuals. The government's encouragement of charitable giving through various tax advantages reinforces our belief that the investment in social capital is and always should be an integral component of our economic system.

Yet if these charitable feelings run so deep, and are so universal, then why does charitable gifting not play a more important role in most individual's estate planning? Affluent clients tend to want their surviving family members to realize the full measure of their financial success. If clients are asked how much of their estate they want their family to inherit, the usual and immediate answer is, "As much as possible." In other words, all of it—if that can be accomplished.

A follow-up question to ask clients is, "How much of your estate do you want to leave to the government?" The answer is near uni-0versal and immediate: "As little as possible." In other words, none of it—if that can also be accomplished.

These two ingrained beliefs are without a doubt the two main reasons why affluent clients are willing to subject themselves to the often painful process of estate planning. When asked how much of their estate they are willing to leave to charity, clients will usually have to pause to consider their answer. This third question is not one that clients typically have even thought of, nor do they typically have a knee-jerk response to the question. There is a stereotypical response to this question. That response is: "I'm not sure; maybe 10 percent, or whatever amount my family will not need." Some people may offer a round number, but often the number is based on a quick calculation of 10 percent of their assets. The tithe apparently is still a powerful concept in our collective unconsciousness.

One reason for the hesitation concerning charitable giving is an instinctive understanding that the three shares do not properly add up. If every dollar of wealth is passed to the family, and nothing is to go to the government, a vague 10 percent to go to charity is no longer possible. The 10 percent for charity, the client reasons, therefore has to come from the family share, which otherwise would have gone to the other family members.

Clients have to be shown that working within the framework of these first two goals alone (all to the family and nothing to the government) may not employ enough estate planning tools to reduce their estate tax liability down to zero, thereby enabling them to successfully pass their entire wealth on to their family members after their death. Although clients may fantasize about realizing each of these first two goals, it may not be possible to realize them in the current estate tax environment. The option of paying no estate taxes at all may depend on the client's willingness to bring charitable gifting into the picture. By employing certain charitable gift-giving techniques, it may be possible to reduce estate taxes to zero, or in fact to any number the client chooses. Most of the estate tax savings realized with this approach will be taken from the government's share, while some will come from the shares which otherwise would have gone to the heirs. However, there are certain life insurance strategies which can be used, which fully pay back to the heirs the share that is now payable to the charity.

Retirement Assets as Funds for Charitable Dispositions

What role should the retirement assets play in charitable planning? It is hard to deny the appeal inherent in using the retirement assets to fulfill charitable planning objectives. Because the charitable institution is tax-exempt, there will be no income taxes due on any distributions paid from the retirement asset to the charity. Moreover, a charitable bequest will remove the retirement asset from the estate, thereby generating an estate tax charitable deduction and, consequently, reducing overall estate taxes in the individual's estate. Meanwhile, family members or other estate heirs will not generally have to pay any income tax on the other non-retirement estate assets, which they will then inherit in lieu of the retirement assets. Additionally, these other assets will receive a step-up in income tax basis on the individual's death, so that no capital gains will be due by virtue of either the transfer of those assets to other family members, or upon the subsequent sale of those non-retirement assets by the other family members. Retirement assets, on the other hand, do not receive a step-up in basis on death. Consequently, the family members would have owed income taxes on the assets they received through the retirement vehicle.

Another way to look at the use of retirement assets is to consider the worst-case scenario in leaving those assets outright to family members. The tax erosion is likely to be around 75 to 80 percent, after all income and estate taxes have been paid from those assets. This figure assumes that the family members are in a position to itemize their deductions and can use the income in respect of a decedent (IRD) deduction to reduce the income taxes which would otherwise be due on the payment of those retirement assets to themselves. If the family members are very young or for any reason are unlikely to itemize their income tax deductions, the tax erosion could rise to as high as 90 percent.

Another way to look at this analysis is to say that every dollar provided to a charity does not reduce by a dollar the inheritance which would otherwise have gone to family members. Instead, estate taxes at 55 percent, and income taxes at rates ranging from approximately 15 percent to 40 percent, would have eroded most of the benefits the family members would have received, thereby reducing the loss to the family unit to only approximately 10 percent to 30 percent of the value of the retirement asset passing to the charity.

In other words, a $1 million IRA paid outright to a charity on an individual's death reduces overall family wealth by only $100,000 to $300,000. This represents a relatively cheap expenditure, compared to the $1 million benefit to be realized by the charity.

However, this analysis is somewhat simplistic, in that it ignores the fact that inherited retirement assets are generally not immediately subject to income tax, but in fact can be structured to produce tax-deferred growth and income streams for years into the future. Over time, and depending on the interest rate applied, the tax-deferred growth will in many instances more than offset the loss in estate taxes and income taxes, which otherwise would have been saved, had the retirement asset been paid directly to a charity on the individual's death. In those instances in which proper planning has not been done and the retirement asset is required to be immediately paid out of the shelter of the retirement account upon the individual's death, the comparison is a valid one.

For someone whose charitable commitments are stronger than the commitment to extend tax deferral—or for someone whose family circumstances or prior irrevocable elections limit their current potential to take advantage of certain tax deferral strategies otherwise available when dealing with retirement assets—funding those commitments with retirement assets may certainly make sense.

The Beneficiary Designation

The cornerstone of charitable planning with retirement assets is the properly drafted beneficiary designation form (Retirement Asset Will). Some of the problems associated with designating a charity as beneficiary of retirement assets were covered in the chapter on beneficiary designation (Chapter 5). However, a more specific analysis of that issue as it relates to charitable giving follows.

The primary problem concerning the use of retirement assets to fund charitable bequests stems from the fact that a charity is not considered a "Designated Beneficiary" for the purposes of the Required Minimum Distribution rules. Remember, beneficiaries must be individuals. Charities have no life expectancy; therefore they carry no Minimum Distributions, only maximum distributions.

When a charity has been named as the sole beneficiary of a retirement account, on the individual's death prior to the Required Beginning Date, all benefits are required to be paid to the charity by December 31 of the calendar year containing the fifth anniversary of the individual's date of death.

When a charity has been named as one of many beneficiaries of a retirement assets, the fact that a charity is an entity with no life expectancy will taint the entire retirement asset, and will once again cause all benefits to all beneficiaries to be paid from the retirement asset by December 31st of the calendar year containing the fifth anniversary of the individual's death (where the individual has died before his or her Required Beginning Date). This result will occur even in those instances in which there are other beneficiaries who are individuals (for instance, the spouse, children, or grandchildren of the decedent). In this case, the charity will benefit from the designation and will receive its allocable share of the retirement asset. The charity, because of its tax-exempt status, will owe no income tax liability on the retirement asset it has received. The family members, on the other hand, who have been named as beneficiaries will derive virtually none of the benefits associated with retirement distribution planning. In fact, they will get a sizable tax bill within roughly five years for their allocable share of the retirement asset, with no significant prospect for further tax-deferred growth.

A better policy would have been to divide the retirement asset into separate shares prior to the individual's date of death, with one share allocable to the charity and with the other share allocable to named individuals. In that way, if the individual dies before the Required Beginning Date, although the IRA allocable to the charity would be required to be paid in full by December 31 of the calendar year containing the fifth anniversary of the individual's death, the second IRA allocated to the named individuals could continue to enjoy tax deferred growth by basing subsequent payouts on the life expectancy of the oldest beneficiary of that second IRA. (See Chapter 12 for a fuller discussion of the death benefit rules applicable when someone has died before their Required Beginning Date.)

It is important to understand that naming a charity as primary beneficiary of retirement assets also has a negative effect on Required Minimum Distributions occurring during the individual's lifetime. When calculating the Required Minimum Distribution amounts (because a charity has no life expectancy), the IRA owner at his or her Required Beginning Date must use his or her own single life expectancy, rather than a joint life expectancy with a named beneficiary. As a result, Required Minimum Distributions occurring during the IRA owner's lifetime, beginning at his or her Required Beginning Date, will be significantly higher than they otherwise would have been had named individuals been designated as beneficiaries and had joint life expectancies been used. Moreover, if the individual lives long enough, he or she may outlive his or her projected life expectancy (16 years for a term certain payout), leaving nothing in the IRA at the individual's death and, accordingly, no benefit payable to the charity.

Methods of Benefiting a Charity

There are four ways in which retirement assets can be used to benefit a charity:

1. Leave the retirement assets directly to the charity.

Of the four charitable giving options available with retirement assets, this one presents the fewest problems, leaving the retirement asset directly to the charity on death by having the charity as the beneficiary of the retirement asset. Under this approach, the designated beneficiary is the charity alone. However, this option will apply only in those situations in which the client either has no heirs or has no desire to leave any portion of the retirement assets to the heirs. In such a case, extending tax deferrals after the individual's death is not an objective. As long as there is only one goal—the charitable one—this option should be chosen. If the individual is interested in naming both charitable and non-charitable beneficiaries for the retirement asset, the individual should split a single IRA into two IRAs prior to his or her death, and prior to his or her Required Beginning Date, with separate beneficiary designations for each portion. This will prevent the "tainting" of the portion of the IRA allocatable to the non-charitable beneficiaries.

2. Leave the retirement assets to the surviving spouse, who in turn, will leave the retirement assets to the charity at his or her death.

This second option is similar to the first option in that each has the same end result—the payment of the retirement asset to the charity. However, with this second option, the end result is simply one step removed. Upon the IRA owner's death, the spouse rolls the IRA over into his or her own rollover IRA and now owns that IRA. However, a new goal has been added: to first provide financial support for the surviving spouse for the rest or her or his life before any charity is to be benefited. When the spouse rolled over the decedent's IRA into his or her own IRA, new beneficiary designations and new payment methodologies were created. If the surviving spouse intends to leave the retirement assets to a charity, the charity should be named as the sole designated beneficiary for that asset. On the spouse's death, the entire retirement asset is then paid outright to the charity.

As in the first option, the charity is to receive the residual retirement assets left after the IRA owner's death (in this case, the surviving spouse). However, this strategy, because the spouse's Required Minimum Distribution beginning after the rollover has been completed, does not take advantage of any joint life expectancy payout of benefits. This will naturally diminish the amount available to the charity upon the spouse's death, in that larger Required Minimum Distribution would have been due each year prior to the surviving spouse's date of death. Extending tax deferrals may not have been a primary motivation in such a case, but using the retirement asset to fund the charitable objective inevitably mixes tax deferrals into this equation. Moreover, under this methodology, if the surviving spouse lives to his or her projected life expectancy, by that date all assets will have been paid out of the IRA to the surviving spouse, leaving the charity with no benefits. Accordingly, if other means could have been employed to satisfy the charitable objectives, the retirement asset could have been used as a more powerful tax-deferred engine to produce significant retirement accumulations for the benefit of the surviving spouse, and then for the benefit of children and/or grandchildren after the death of the surviving spouse.

3. Leave the retirement assets to a Qualified Terminable Interest Property (Q-TIP) Trust with the trust principal ultimately going to the charity at the second death.

Q-TIP Trusts are a common technique found in many estate plans of affluent clients. Their effect is to postpone estate taxation until the surviving spouse's death through the use of the unlimited marital deduction, while denying the surviving spouse control over the assets. The purpose of most Q-TIP Trusts is provide lifetime income to a surviving spouse while preserving the trust principal for the benefit of the children of the creator of the trust after the surviving spouse has died. Most often the strategy applies when second marriages have created blended families and the asset owner wants to make sure that the assets after the death of the surviving spouse are payable in the desired manner, to the people the asset owner has selected. They are also used when an individual fears that a surviving spouse might remarry and make significant gifts to a new spouse or to children of a new spouse, thereby severely disrupting the asset owner's testamentary plan. A Q-TIP Trust may also be established if the surviving spouse lacks business acumen, is suffering from diminished capacity, or is a target for requests for loans or gifts from relatives or unscrupulous outsiders—in short, if the surviving spouse cannot be trusted with the management, investment, or distribution of the asset.

On the surface, leaving the retirement to a Q-TIP Trust does not appear to significantly alter the situation discussed above with respect to the second option. The spouse still receives the financial security associated with yearly payments made from the retirement asset to the Q-TIP Trust and from the Q-TIP Trust, in turn, to the surviving spouse. The charity still receives what is left over on the spouse's death. This third option simply adds an intervening trust vehicle to assure the proper control of the retirement asset both during and after the life of the surviving spouse. The issue of assuring the proper control can be crucial where the interests of children, especially children from prior marriages, have to be protected and balanced with the income interests of a second, third, or even fourth spouse. In other words, the very presence of the Q-TIP Trust suggests that more than one motive may lie at the heart of the retirement distribution plan—motivations concerning the achievement not only of charitable goals, but of other family goals as well.

One of the goals sought in designating a charity as beneficiary of a gift is a deduction on the estate tax return of the owner of the retirement asset. In the scenarios discussed in options 1 and 2 above, the charity was to receive an outright bequest immediately following the death of the owner of the retirement asset. Under this third option, however, although the charity is ultimately to receive an outright inheritance, the inheritance is deferred until such time as the intervening trust (in this case, the Q-TIP Trust) has ended.

Current income tax rules deny estate tax deductions for all residual interests passing to a charity through a trust, unless the trust has been properly structured as a Charitable Remainder Trust (CRT) and unless the trust conforms to each of the tax rules applicable to that type of trust. It is possible in option number 3 to configure a Q-TIP Trust as part of a CRT, so that an estate tax marital deduction would be available for the portion of the IRA assets allocable to the Q-TIP Trust share of the trust, with an estate tax charitable deduction secured for the remaining share of the trust which qualifies as a CRT. In this way, 100 percent of the retirement asset will be eligible for an estate tax deduction—either as marital deduction or a charitable deduction.

However, unless both the Q-TIP Trust rules and CRT rules are strictly followed, the result could be the loss of the estate tax marital deduction and/or the loss of the estate tax charitable deduction. Accordingly, great care should always be taken whenever the situation calls for naming a Q-TIP Trust that must qualify for the estate tax marital deduction as beneficiary, or whenever a charity has been named as an ultimate beneficiary of retirement assets through a trust that provides an interim income interest before the interest of the charity is to vest.

4. Leave the retirement assets to a CRT, naming the charity as the remainder beneficiary of the trust.

This option offers the most promise for integrating charitable and family goals. Among affluent clients, CRTs are fairly widely known and frequently used. Many affluent clients have attended numerous seminars on the subject, sponsored by every form of non-profit or not-for-profit organization. Under this approach, the CRT is named as the beneficiary of the retirement assets, with a specific charity or family foundation named as the recipient of the remainder interest in the trust. During the term of the trust, the trust distributes income to the heirs each year until such time as the trust comes to an end. The ending of the trust is usually made to coincide with the end of a fixed period or the death of the trust beneficiaries. At that time the CRT pays the residual interest outright to the named charity. This approach is both practical and desirable. The mechanism of tax deferral preserves and even grows the asset for the benefit of the charity, while providing an income stream for the benefit of the children and/or grandchildren during their lifetimes. Note, however, that with this approach the surviving spouse has been entirely bypassed.

If the CRT has been drafted properly, upon the death of the owner of the retirement asset, an estate tax charitable deduction will be available, based on the present value of the future residuary interest passing to the charity. The precise value of that future interest, and hence of the current estate tax deduction, will depend on the applicable federal interest rate at the time and the period that the charity must wait before its interest ultimately vests.

Obviously, the longer the deferral period, the smaller the present value of the bequest to the charity, and hence the lower the estate tax deduction. Conversely, the shorter the period the charity must wait to have its interest vest, the higher the present value of the benefits ultimately payable to the charity, and hence the higher the current estate tax deduction. Therefore, the longer the deferral period, the *lower* the estate tax deduction. Providing deferrals during the remaining life expectancy of the children will defer the date of vesting of the charitable interest until sometime well into the future. Deferring the vesting date during the lifetime of grandchildren will defer the vesting even further and will reduce the present value of the estate tax deduction to a considerably lower figure. Moreover, under current tax rules, where the charity's residual interest is not worth at least 10 percent of the value of the asset, the trust will not qualify as a CRT and no estate tax deduction will be available. Accordingly, great care should be taken when dealing with CRTs, in those cases in which the interest to go to the charity is not to vest until well into the future. An individual constructing a CRT will often accelerate the otherwise vesting date in order to ensure that the trust can qualify as a CRT and that a charitable deduction will therefore be available.

Rather than paying the entire yearly income stream from the CRT directly to the heirs, a portion of the yearly distributions could be used to purchase a wealth replacement insurance policy on the life of the children, which policy can be owned by an irrevocable life insurance trust. The policy proceeds can then be used to provide an additional inheritance for the grandchildren and/or to the charity, and can effectively be used to replace a portion of the retirement assets lost to estate taxes.

One additional problem associated with the use of the CRT has to do with the measuring lives to be used for purposes of the Required Minimum Distribution rules. When an individual at the Required Beginning Date has designated a CRT as a beneficiary, the individual is deemed to have no designated beneficiary and benefits must be paid out during the individual's remaining lifetime based solely on the individual's life expectancy alone. Typically, at the death of the individual, 100 percent of the assets in the retirement vehicle are paid into the CRT.

Ordinarily, the wholesale payout of retirement assets can pose a substantial problem, in that significant income tax liability is then accelerated. However, in this case, the retirement benefits were payable to a tax-exempt entity. Accordingly, income taxation has been entirely avoided. The CRT then pays yearly income to the children, who continue, in effect, a tax-favored income stream, in that distributions are made to them each year from the CRT, with the children being required to pay income tax *only* on the amounts of income that they actually receive each year from the CRT. Therefore, even though the shelter of the retirement vehicle has been entirely lost, the children have gained the shelter of the CRT in that they are made to pay tax only on the taxable income they receive each year from the CRT.

A similar result is achieved when a CRT has been established to provide an income stream for the benefit of the surviving spouse, with a remainder interest to the charity. Typically all of the assets in the retirement vehicle are immediately paid into the CRT on the IRA owner's death, with the surviving spouse then receiving yearly income payments from the CRT which are taxable (if at all) only as each yearly income payment is received.

Under the Required Minimum Distribution rules it is possible to structure payouts into a trust in which the life expectancies of the individual beneficiaries who are to receive yearly income payments will be used, prior to the time when the interest of the charity will vest. However the instances in which the life expectancies of the individual trust beneficiaries can be used for Required Minimum Distribution purposes before an interest to a charity vests will rarely arise. Instead, advisors will find that the goal of continued tax deferral of the retirement asset may have to be sacrificed to the greater goal of having the charity designated as the remainder trust beneficiary.

As explained above, under the typical CRT scenario, on the death of the owner of the retirement asset, the assets are not usually retained in the shelter of the retirement vehicle, but instead are typically immediately transferred entirely into the CRT. Once that step has been completed, continued tax deferral in the retirement vehicle is not possible. However, such deferral is then unnecessary insofar as the lifetime beneficiary of the CRT then receives additional deferrals through the shelter of the CRT with their yearly income payments from the CRT.

A final benefit associated with the use of CRTs can occur in those instances in which an individual who has passed his or her Required Beginning Date belatedly discovers that the elections that were in place at that time with respect to choice of beneficiaries and/or term certain/recalculation elections are not beneficial to the family unit. As noted previously, once the Required Beginning Date has passed, it is not possible to correct those designations without adverse consequences.

However, an individual faced with that situation could at that time change his or her beneficiary designation, substituting a CRT as their designated beneficiary. Although such a change may cause future Required Minimum Distributions to increase slightly during the remaining lifetime of the retirement asset owner, additional deferrals after the owner's death can be achieved that might otherwise have been lost.

> **Example:** Linda, at her Required Beginning Date, had designated her estate as beneficiary of her IRA benefits and had failed to elect out of the recalculation provisions contained in the IRA Custodial Agreement. Accordingly, by December 31 of the calendar year following the calendar year of her death, all assets would be required to be paid out of the shelter of the retirement vehicle, regardless of who is to eventually receive those retirement assets through her estate.
>
> If Linda instead at age 75 were to substitute a CRT for the estate as designated beneficiary, there would be no change in the Required Minimum Distributions amounts required to be paid to her each year while she was alive, because in each case, her choice of beneficiary (either the estate or the CRT) is a beneficiary without an applicable life expectancy. However upon her death, significant benefits would have been achieved for the

family unit. Even though all of the assets would still be required to be paid out of the shelter of the retirement vehicle by the December 31 of the calendar year immediately following the calendar year of her death, no immediate income taxes would be due. Instead, the CRT would receive the retirement assets at that time free from any income tax and would begin to pay an income stream for the benefit of Linda's heirs, namely her children. Each year the children would receive this income stream, which would be subject to income tax each year (if at all) only as amounts were received by them. In effect, this device replaces the shelter of the retirement vehicle with the shelter of the CRT.

Separating the Goals and the Accounts

One more option is available to clients wishing to benefit charities with assets from qualified plans or IRAs. Under this device, clients divide the retirement assets into separate IRAs; ones that will be used to achieve their family goals and ones that will be used to achieve their charitable goals. The children and grandchildren are then designated as the individual beneficiaries of the separate IRAs that are to be used to achieve family goals, under the Participant Direct Approach. These IRAs preserve tax-deferrals based on the use of joint life expectancy payouts with the IRA owner, subject to MDIB rules, and then based on the beneficiaries' actual life expectancies once the IRA owner has died. Meanwhile, the IRA in which the charity has been named as beneficiary, having no life expectancy beyond the single life expectancy of the IRA owner, receives 100 percent distribution at the IRA owner's death. With such a strategy, the IRA owner's charitable objectives can be fully realized. If a correctly designed transfer of the retirement asset to charity is made, the charity will not pay any income tax on the distribution and the IRA owner's estate will receive an estate tax charitable deduction for the amounts transferred from that IRA to the charity. Moreover, in meeting the client's charitable goals, the family members will also be benefited with a lower estate tax bill, thereby allowing them to keep a higher percentage of the other non-retirement assets received by them through the estate.

CHAPTER 9
HOW TO PAY ESTATE TAXES

CONTENTS

9 HOW TO PAY ESTATE TAXES

Retirement assets cannot be transferred by any of the traditional methods of gifting or estate planning. They cannot be gifted, nor can they be transferred to a trust without losing their character as retirement assets. Moreover, they are transferred by beneficiary designation, and *not* by will bequest. Accordingly, they truly stand alone, unique in the client's inventory of assets. Nevertheless, they are subject to estate taxes, payable nine months from the date of the death of the owner of the retirement asset. By age $70^1/_2$, most people with significant assets will have taken steps to reduce their estate tax liability. For them, the estate tax due on retirement assets just seems like an additional problem associated with these assets. When an advisor explains that estate taxes on retirement assets will be due, clients may question why they had extended tax deferral on their retirement assets, only to saddle their heirs with an immediate estate tax liability on those same assets.

In many instances, the client's estate plan may have entirely omitted the consideration of retirement assets from the planning process. Many planners are guilty of ignoring these assets because they mistakenly believe, based on the social psychology of our culture, that the retirement assets will most likely be exhausted just before or simultaneous with the individual's death. Until the advent of multigenerational retirement distribution planning, it was common to urge clients to spend their retirement assets first of all their disposable assets, precisely because this was the way to avoid the double taxation on those assets (estate tax and income tax)—actually triple taxation in the days of the 15 percent excise tax on excess retirement distributions or excess retirement accumulations. Now it is clear that the wisest course for the client is to first consume their non-retirement assets, reducing Required Minimum Distribution amounts to the lowest possible level each year, preserving tax deferrals, and making adequate provisions for the

Note: Readers should refer to the Introduction for a discussion of issues and concepts covered in Chapter 9—particularly the Federal estate tax amounts and rates—that may be affected by the passage of EGTRRA 2001.

payment of the estate taxes attributable to retirement assets as an integrated part of the client's overall estate plan.

The multigeneration IRA concept preserves income tax deferrals as long as possible, in keeping with the client's objectives. This strategy alone cannot eliminate the estate taxes due on those as-sets. Even under the Spousal Rollover approach for multigeneration IRAs, and utilizing the unlimited marital deduction and the spousal rollover, the estate taxes are not eliminated, but merely deferred until the death of the surviving spouse.

Calculating the Estate Tax

A way to determine the total federal estate tax attributable to the retirement assets is to calculate the tax due on all of the assets includible in the individual's taxable estate, then compute the total federal estate taxes due with the retirement assets removed. The difference in estate taxes equals the amount of federal estate taxes attributable to the retirement assets.

Table 9-1

Taxes with IRA Asset		*Without IRA*
Other Estate Assets:	$3,500,000	$3,500,000
IRA Asset:	1,000,000	0
Total Estate:	4,500,000	$3,500,000
Federal Estate Taxes:	$1,559,650 (A)	$1,116,050 (B)

Taxes with IRA (A)	$1,559,650
Taxes Without IRA (B)	1,116,050
Federal Estate Tax on IRA Asset	$443,600 (44.36%)
State Estate Tax on IRA Asset of	$106,400* (10.64%)
Total Federal and State Estate Tax on IRA Asset	$550,000 (55%)

*Assumes state estate tax is equal to the State Death Tax Credit

This method of calculation causes the retirement assets to be taxed at the highest marginal federal estate tax bracket, relative to the total estate size, and is the method used to compute the IRD deduction, attributable to those retirement assets. (*Note*: See Chapter 11 for a full discussion of the IRD deduction). For many clients, retirement assets at this asset level will have largely lost the benefit of the graduated estate tax rate system.

Explaining Estate Taxes to Clients

Even when clients profess to understand that there is a significant potential estate tax liability assessed against their assets to be transferred upon their death, the devastating impact of the estate tax bite frequently remains under-appreciated.

Advisors can help clients appreciate the dramatic impact which estate taxation will have on their net worth by engaging the client in a simple exercise. Have clients add up all the income they think they have earned over their working years, including profits from investments. Then calculate for them the rough income tax liability that has been paid on that amount over their lifetimes. Deduct the income tax liability from the total earnings figure, to show them what income taxes have done to their wages and earnings over the period of their life-time. They will then readily see that the total of the government's take over their lifetimes has been between one-third to one-half of all that they have earned. It is only then that clients may suddenly grasp the enormity of their potential estate tax liability.

The advisor should then focus on the assets that remain after the payment of income taxes. With what they have left, clients have paid for all of their lifetime ordinary, necessary, and nonrecurring expenses. Deducting all of those costs, clients can see that they still have a substantial legacy left to pass on to their heirs and to the charitable institutions that mean the most to them. They know that this net amount will be taxed again after they die, but the emotional impact of that next loss may seem remote to them, considering that they will be beyond its pain when it is time to actually write the check to the government for the estate taxes due. What clients need to understand is that the government has its own designs for their wealth—involuntary philanthropy.

Table 9-2. Federal Estate Tax Rates

If the amount with respect to which the tentative tax to be computed is:	The tentative tax is:
Not over $10,000	18 percent of such amount
$10,000 but not over $20,000	$1,800 plus 20 percent of the excess of such amount over $10,000
$20,000 but not over $40,000	$3,800 plus 22 percent of the excess of such amount over $20,000
Over $40,000 but not over $60,000	$8,200 plus 24 percent of the excess of such amount over $40,000
Over $60,000 but not over $80,000	$13,000 plus 26 percent of the excess of such amount over $60,000
Over $80,000 but not over $100,000	$18,200 plus 28 percent of the excess of such amount over $80,000
Over $100,000 but not over $150,000	$23,800 plus 30 percent of the excess of such amount over $100,000
Over $150,000 but not over $250,000	$38,800 plus 32 percent of the excess of such amount over $150,000
Over $250,000 but not over $500,000	$70,800 plus 34 percent of the excess of such amount over $250,000
Over $500,000 but not over $750,000	$155,800 plus 37 percent of the excess of such amount over $500,000
Over $750,000 but not over $1,000,000	$248,300 plus 39 percent of the excess of such amount over $750,000
Over $1,000,000 but not over $1,250,000	$345,800 plus 41 percent of the excess of such amount over $1,000,000
Over $1,250,000 but not over $1,500,000	$448,300 plus 43 percent of the excess of such amount over $1,250,000
Over $1,500,000 but not over $2,000,000	$555,800 plus 45 percent of the excess of such amount over $1,500,000
Over $2,000,000 but not over $2,500,000	$780,800 plus 49 percent of the excess of such amount over $2,000,000
Over $2,500,000 but not over $3,000,000	$1,025,800 plus 53 percent of the excess of such amount over $2,500,000
Over $3,000,000	$1,290,800 plus 55 percent of the excess of such amount over $3,000,000

Ask clients how much more of their wealth they would like handed over to the government upon their death. Does another half seem fair? Clients certainly will not think so, yet that is precisely what the government demands and will receive, unless proper planning has been done.

As noted earlier, the Unified Credit Amount (also known as the Credit Shelter Amount, the Exemption Equivalent Amount, or the Applicable Credit Amount) for both 2000 and 2001 is $675,000. Estates with assets of $675,000 or less in 2000 and 2001 are entirely exempt from any federal estate tax. However, you will note from Table 9-2 that an estate with $1 over that amount is subject to estate tax at the 37 percent marginal estate tax bracket, with the tax brackets increasing quickly until the $3 million level is reached, at which point the federal estate tax bracket is 55 percent. You will also note from Table 9-3 that a credit is afforded against the federal tax for estate taxes paid to a state government. However the maximum amount of that credit is 16 percent, thereby offsetting the federal estate tax by at most a maximum offset of 16 percent.

The Estate Tax Process

When death occurs, an individual's assets are either transferred by Will, by beneficiary designation, or by operation of law. All the assets owned by the decedent at death are included in the individual's gross taxable estate—e.g., cash, art, personal property, real estate, trust shares, life insurance, employee benefits, business interests, joint assets, qualified plan assets, and IRAs. Where the precise value of an asset is uncertain, the government can assign a fair market value to the asset, placing the burden of proof, in most instances, on the taxpayer to show that the taxpayer's valuation of the asset, which invariably will show a lower value for that asset is, in fact, the correct valuation.

From the gross value of the decedent's assets, the government allows for the subtraction of the decedent's debts, funeral expenses, administration costs, a marital deduction if available, and charitable donations to take effect at death. Estate taxes are then calculated on the remainder. As noted earlier, after $3 million of net assets, estates are in a marginal maximum federal and state estate tax bracket of 55 percent.

In most instances, the estate taxes are due in full within nine months from the date of the individual's death. Nine months is not generally long enough to find a market for certain relatively illiquid assets, let alone to find a fair market value price as the IRS determines it to be. If the executor of the estate is forced to sell an illiquid asset at a fire sale in order to raise the necessary cash to pay the estate taxes, as far as the government is concerned, it is simply the heirs' tough luck.

When a client sees the possibility of his or her total net worth subjected to this kind of confiscatory process, the emotional impact of estate taxation can become painfully clear.

Methods of Paying Estate Taxes

Clients can choose from the following three alternative methods for paying the estate taxes due on their retirement assets:

Method 1. Using Retirement Assets

A round-numbers example will perhaps best illustrate this method. Suppose the retirement assets to be transferred to beneficiaries at the death of the surviving spouse total $1 million. and that retirement distribution planning has projected a multigeneration IRA distribution income stream to extend tax deferrals on that asset for five or six decades into the future. After all other estate reduction strategies have been implemented, the other estate assets in the estate total $3,500,000, making the total estate value $4,500,000 for estate tax purposes. A total federal estate tax of $1,559,650 will be due to the IRS within nine months of the second spouse's death, with probably another $335,600 due to the state within that same period of time. Of the total $1,895,250 amount ($1,559,650 plus $335,600), $550,000 will be allocable to the retirement asset.

If retirement assets are to be used to pay this allocable portion of the estate tax, $550,000 could be withdrawn from the separate IRAs, either proportionately or disproportionately, to pay that portion of the estate tax bill. However, those distributions would then be taxable to the beneficiaries as income received by them in the tax year in which the distributions took place. So $550,000 will not cover the total tax bill of estate taxes and income taxes.

At a 40 percent marginal federal and state income tax bracket, the taxpayer may find that an additional $220,000 has to be withdrawn from the IRA in order to net the $550,000 amount necessary to pay the federal and state estate taxes due. However, the withdrawal of an additional $220,000 from the IRA at a 40 percent marginal income tax bracket will incur an additional income tax liability of $88,000 to be due, which in turn will require the imposition of additional income taxes ($220,000 x 40%), which in turn will require the withdrawal of additional assets from the IRA to pay these new taxes, which will again cause the imposition of still more income taxes to be due. This computation goes round and round until the taxpayer finds that roughly three-quarters of

Table 9-3. Allowable Credit for State Death Taxes

Taxable Estate Balance*		**Base Credit of**	**Plus %**	**On Amounts Over**
Less Than Or Equal to	$90,000	$0	0.80%	$40,000
"	$140,000	$400	1.60%	$90,000
"	$240,000	$1,200	2.40%	$140,000
"	$440,000	$3,600	3.20%	$240,000
"	$640,000	$10,000	4.00%	$440,000
"	$840,000	$18,000	4.80%	$640,000
"	$1,040,000	$27,600	5.60%	$840,000
"	$1,540,000	$38,800	6.40%	$1,040,000
"	$2,040,000	$70,800	7.20%	$1,540,000
"	$2,540,000	$106,800	8.00%	$2,040,000
"	$3,040,000	$146,800	8.80%	$2,540,000
"	$3,540,000	$190,800	9.60%	$3,040,000
"	$4,040,000	$238,800	10.40%	$3,540,000
"	$5,040,000	$290,800	11.20%	$4,040,000
"	$6,040,000	$402,800	12.00%	$5,040,000
"	$7,040,000	$522,800	12.80%	$6,040,000
"	$8,040,000	$650,800	13.60%	$7,040,000
"	$9,040,000	$786,800	14.40%	$8,040,000
"	$10,040,000	$930,800	15.20%	$9,040,000
Greater Than	$10,040,000	1,082,800	16.00%	$10,040,000

*Note: The Taxable Estate Balance equals the Federal Taxable Estate after $60,000 has been subtracted therefrom.

the entire amount in the IRA has been withdrawn to first pay federal and state estate taxes and federal and state income taxes on the estate taxes, and federal and state income taxes on the federal and state income taxes, and so on.

The above example may be somewhat oversimplified, since it fails to take into account the IRD deduction—an income tax deduction item attributable to the receipt of retirement assets for which federal estate taxes had previously been paid. (The IRD is discussed in detail in Chapter 11.) In fact, after correct IRD deduction had been taken into account, the amount necessary to pay *both* income tax and estate tax amounts due on the retirement asset would be approximately $721,941, depending on the various income tax brackets attributable to the various beneficiaries.

What, therefore, has been given up? In order to pay the estate tax from the retirement asset itself, a dollar of tax required a dollar of the asset, plus an additional 22.256 cents in income tax, assuming a 40 percent marginal income tax bracket and a 44.36 percent IRD deduction.

Table 9-4, based on the prior example, illustrates the basic calculations to determine estate taxes, income taxes, and the total IRA distribution required to pay all federal and state estate and income taxes due on the IRA asset. (Please note that for purposes of the situation, the State Death Tax Credit is assumed to be at a marginal 10.64 percent rate.

Income taxes on the retirement assets will have to be paid eventually, as distributions are made from the IRA each year, but is it prudent to pay so much in income taxes in one year, especially when that year is the first year? After all, a significant portion of the real value of an IRA to its beneficiaries is its ability to produce compounded tax-deferred growth each year and over a long period of time. That same money, if left in the IRA to grow on a tax-deferred basis with only the lowest Required Minimum Distribution amount paid out each year, obviously will far outpace the growth potential of that same asset after it has been paid out of the shelter of the IRA and decimated by immediate estate and income taxes.

Although the operation of the IRD rules and the mechanics for recovering the IRD deduction can be cumbersome, advisors should not lose sight of the tremendous income tax benefit that the recipient of the IRD item will realize, as distributions are made to the beneficiary each year and a significant portion of the amount of each yearly distribution is exempt from federal income taxation. Moreover, most people do not object to paying taxes on assets that are continuing to produce income for them each year, especially where those assets continue to grow in value each year. The real problem arises in those cases where proper retirement distribution planning has not been done, causing all the retirement assets to be included in income in one year. In that case, the retirement assets would be required to be immediately paid out of the shelter of the retirement vehicle in one year, with the IRD deduction immediately used up at that time. The beneficiaries would then be left with only the net residual amount to accumulate for them on an after-tax basis each year thereafter.

Table 9-4

A.	Estate Taxes	
	IRA Asset	$1,000,000
	Federal Estate Tax	($443,600)
	State Death Tax	($106,400)
	Total Estate Taxes	($550,000)
B	IRA Amount Withdrawn to Pay Estate and Income Taxes	$772,560.00
	Income Tax Rate After IRD Deduction	x 22.256%
	Income Taxes	$171,940.95
C.	Total IRA Distribution Required to Pay Estate and Income Taxes	
	Federal and State Estate Taxes	$550,000
	Income Taxes	171,941
	Total Distribution	$721,941

Method 2. Using Non-Retirement Assets

The second alternative for paying estate taxes due on the retirement assets is to use other non-retirement after-tax estate assets to pay the estate taxes due on the *entire* estate, including the estate taxes attributable to the retirement assets. With this method, a dollar of estate tax due requires only a dollar from the estate. Comparing this method with the prior method, rather than paying estate and income taxes totaling $721,941, a reduced amount of only $550,000 is due. The immediate income tax bite of $171,941 has, therefore, been entirely eliminated by using non-retirement assets to pay the estate taxes due on the retirement assets.

However, there are two problems with this approach. The first problem is that the estate may not have sufficient liquid non-retirement assets to pay the estate taxes which are due. In fact, when estates consist largely of illiquid assets—real estate, collectibles, family businesses—there may be little likelihood that sufficient liquidity can be found within the nine-month time frame from the date of death, in which the estate tax bill must be paid. Yet this configuration is how most estates are constituted unless comprehensive estate planning had previously taken place. A comprehensive estate plan will have identified, in advance, which assets on death will have to be sacrificed to pay the estate taxes which are due.

The second problem is that the liquidation plan may look fine on paper, but ultimate success will depend upon market conditions existing at the time of the estate owner's death, applicable to those assets which are to be sacrificed to pay the estate taxes. The heirs have only nine months to convert the hard assets into the necessary liquid cash. That period might be the worst nine-month period in recent memory in which to sell real estate, marketable securities, art, rare coins, or vintage cars. Moreover, few transactions are as complex as the sale of a portion or all of a family business. How can this sales process be compressed into nine months? What if the estate assets consist largely of stock in a closely held company? The sale of that stock could have devastating effects on the company and/or on the heirs, and might not even be permissible under applicable contract law under federal or state regulatory law.

Complicating the picture is the fact that the IRS may try to impose a market value figure for these assets which is significantly higher than the figure assigned to those assets by the client's accountants, appraisers, or estate attorneys—and which figure cannot be realized with an actual sale completed within the nine-month time frame. That means that the dollar-for-dollar assumption is distorted because assets that are taxed based on a certain assumed dollar value may only realize a fraction of that amount upon their sale. In that case, the balance of the shortfall will have to be made up from other sources.

Method 3. Using Life Insurance

For years now, the case for the utilization of life insurance as a vehicle for funding estate tax liabilities has been well established among advisors to the affluent. In fact, this strategy may have already been implemented at least in part by a sizable percentage of their clients. A primary benefit associated with using life insurance as a funding tool is that it possesses significant tax advantages that virtually no other funding vehicle enjoys. The various income tax and potential estate tax advantages of life insurance can be harnessed to provide an efficient way to pay estate taxes with discounted dollars. The ability of life insurance premiums to be leveraged into higher death benefits is the second main reason why life insurance is often the funding vehicle of choice for the payment of estate taxes.

Under a spousal rollover multigeneration IRA strategy, estate taxes will not be due until the death of the second spouse. In a typical case using this approach, the life insurance premiums needed to purchase a policy with a $550,000 death benefit are paid by the IRA owner through gifts made each year directly to the IRA beneficiaries, or to a trust established by the IRA owner for their benefit. In this example, this gifting technique can allow the policy death benefit of $550,000 (the amount of the projected estate tax liability) to be excluded from the taxable estate of the IRA owner. Under this approach, the IRA shrinkage is eliminated, while the cost of paying the estate taxes is significantly lower than the $721,941 needed in the first method for paying estate taxes, and is still substantially lower than the $550,000 needed in the second method. Using the life insurance method, the amount needed to pay the estate taxes has been reduced to the amount of the premiums due on the policy, which, depending on the type of policy purchased and the year of the death, may have cost the IRA owner considerably less than $100,000.

Under the Participant Direct Approach, the spouse is bypassed for a portion or all of the IRA assets, with the IRA assets payable instead to the children and/or grandchildren under a multigenerational payout strategy. This approach may involve an estate tax being due in the estate of the IRA owner, insofar as the IRA assets which pass to the children and grandchildren will not be eligible for the federal estate tax marital deduction. Accordingly, once the value of that benefit has exceeded the Federal Unified Credit Amount applicable for that year ($675,000 for 2000 and 2001), estate taxes will be owed. However, where the client had made prior arrangements for the payment of those estate taxes—for instance, with life insurance—the Participant Direct Approach may still be preferable, in that the estate tax liability will have already been pre-funded through the purchase of the life insurance policy.

In another case, an individual many years ago had funded a $500,000 insurance policy on his life, payable to his children, which policy proceeds will not be includible in his estate because it is also owned by his children. If that individual were to use the Participant Direct Approach with respect to only $675,000 of his IRA assets, the federal estate tax due in his estate would be zero, assuming a death in 2000 or 2001.

However, the Participant Direct Approach could be utilized in this case to a greater extent, by having the individual's children receive IRA assets on his death worth $1,866,110. In that case, a federal and state estate tax liability of $500,000 would have been incurred in his estate. The children could then pay the $500,000 estate tax liability with the proceeds from the insurance policy which is payable to them, and would then be able to continue the multigenerational payout on the more than $1.86 million in IRA assets, free from any subsequent estate taxes due in the estate of either parent.

In order to take advantage of these discounted dollar strategies using life insurance, two things are necessary. First, the client—and/or spouse in some cases—must be insurable. Second, the advisor must be able to find the money somewhere in the client's assets to pay the insurance premiums due each year. Waiting until the client is age 70½ can complicate both requirements, because insurability issues may have arisen by then, with premium costs prohibitively expensive by that time.

The next chapter will look at life insurance in detail as it relates to retirement assets.

CHAPTER 10
THE ROLE OF LIFE INSURANCE IN RETIREMENT DISTRIBUTION AND ESTATE PLANNING

CONTENTS

10 THE ROLE OF LIFE INSURANCE IN RETIREMENT DISTRIBUTION AND ESTATE PLANNING

Chapter 9 addressed the three options available to clients to enable their heirs to meet the estate tax liabilities on inherited retirement assets at their death. The three alternatives are double-taxed dollars (estate and income taxes); single-taxed dollars (estate tax only); and double-discounted dollars (life insurance).

In this chapter, the focus will be on life insurance, the obvious winner among the three choices for paying estate taxes. Instead of the government figuring out when death will occur, life insurance company actuaries assume death and compute the risk. Instead of the client investing his or her assets to get a return large enough to be able to pay the ultimate estate tax bill, life insurance companies invest the money until the client's death. Instead of asking the client's family to pay the full estate tax liability, insurance companies charge annual premiums in advance of the liability being incurred.

Would clients who know that their estates face the future expense of estate taxes which are due all at once be willing to fund that expense up front through an insurance strategy? An indication that they would can perhaps be seen in the similar funding situation found in many college tuition programs today. Baby boomer parents are no longer just saving for their children's college education. Instead, they are using these programs to prepay college tuition expense currently and at a discount.

One reason clients may not use the life insurance option to prefund their estate tax liability is that life insurance is not always available as a choice. There is the issue of health and insurability, which may force premium costs up significantly. Even with favor-

Note: Readers should refer to the Introduction for a discussion of issues and concepts covered in Chapter 10—particularly the Federal estate tax amounts and rates—that may be affected by the passage of EGTRRA 2001.

able health, clients may choose to pay the lower premiums associated with smaller policies, rather than opting to fund the full amount of coverage necessary to meet the *full* projected estate tax liabilities. For many clients, the analysis is simply a cash flow issue.

Another possible reason for clients shunning this option is a lack of a true understanding of life insurance. Few clients understand that life insurance is nothing more than buying future money today at a deep, deep discount. Perhaps no one ever explained it to them in that way. The previous explanations given to them about how life insurance works may have been overly complicated. Or, worse, the explanations may have been so simplistic that the concept appeared to them to be "too good to be true." Worse yet, an unprofessional life insurance representative may have offended the client by engaging in scare tactics designed to frighten the client, spouse, and/or children with horror stories about what can happen to the surviving family members if the "right" amount of life insurance has not been purchased. Many clients have a knee-jerk reaction to the words *life insurance*. Often it is the same knee-jerk reaction associated with the word *taxes*. In short, many clients do not initially view life insurance as their protector against the evils of estate taxation.

Part of the current prejudice against life insurance is perhaps a vestige from another era of financial products and business sensibilities. It was an era of relatively simple and limited investment choices and, regrettably, an era of relatively crude sales methods. In the past, people purchased insurance from agents who represented only one life insurance company. People generally understood that they needed life insurance because it provided protection against certain potential financial catastrophes. Most also understood, however, that beyond the protective aspect of life insurance, the very low internal rates of return within the policy did not make it an especially attractive investment vehicle when compared with virtually any other alternative then existing. They generally did not appreciate life insurance as a potential funding tool. Most people simply bought the insurance protection they needed, which meant that term life insurance was more commonly purchased than cash value life insurance.

Buyers of term insurance had to get used to the idea that premiums would go up each year, due to the fact that term insurance is only a one-year contract, which is renewed each year for a specified period of time. With term coverage, the insurer recalculates the premiums due annually based on current actuarial and cost assumptions, as well as on certain mortality assumptions. Clients who purchased term coverage had to deal with the fact that when the term coverage ended, they might not be able to continue *any* insurance coverage due to health issues which may have subsequently developed.

The problems inherent in term insurance often led clients to rethink the merits of cash value, whole life policies. Cash value policies extend coverage until death, whenever that occurs, instead of merely to the end of a specified term, and level the yearly premium cost each year so that there are no financial surprises as the years of the term of coverage added up. There are other sweeteners in to cash value deal. For example, policyholders can borrow against their cash values at below-market rates. In addition, cash value life insurance carries with it certain tax advantages that no other financial product possesses.

Financial and accounting advisors of past eras were quick to point out to their clients that the true cost of level premiums was higher yearly premiums up front. Furthermore, borrowing against a policy's cash values was usually not as efficient an investment strategy as achieving higher investment return with other assets and then simply cashing in that asset when needed. While the tax advantages associated with insurance ownership were potentially powerful, with low internal rates of return within the policies, the potential power was seldom realized. The prior conventional wisdom was therefore simply this: buy term and invest the difference.

The life insurance industry as a whole excelled in combating that mindset.

The term vs. whole life debate probably never occupied most clients' minds for more than several hours. If one had asked a client in the past to explain the real differences between term and whole life insurance coverage, most would have had little to say. Eventually, however, clients did figure out that when they purchased a whole life policy rather than a term policy, the agent received a higher commission. The insurance agent, seen as biased in this process, was suspect in most people's minds. The truth, however, was that whole life insurance was often in the client's best interest.

Historically, insurance agents were trained to be salespeople, not problem-solvers. The insurance company that employed them kept track of their success based on premium dollars paid, rather than on client satisfaction. In that era, life insurance was not viewed as a service-intensive product. The commitment of the insurance agent to his or her client, it was thought, did not have to extend beyond ensuring that the insurance policy did not lapse. People did not—and still do not—like to face the fact that they need life insurance. It is a reminder to them that sooner or later they are going to die. The better agents were able to overcome this emotional obstacle by emphasizing insurance as a device designed to provide the client with peace of mind and to provide their loved ones with financial security. The less skilled agents simply resorted to their age-old scare tactics.

Life Insurance Today

The life insurance industry today has changed considerably. This is certainly the case among the more experienced and successful insurance practitioners. Today the word *agent* is viewed as a relic left over from the contractual relationship which life insurance advisors had with the insurance company they represented. The term today does not describe an agency/principal relationship in the same way it used to. Successful life insurance advisors today no longer represent a single insurance company. No one insurance company can continue to be competitive in all product areas. No one insurance company can achieve exemplary investment returns with perfect consistency. No one insurance company has the service capacity to fully meet every client's needs. Every successful insurance company today realizes that its most productive agents represent other companies as well, and are content that a sizable portion of the business which these agents write each year is written through their company.

Over the past several years, life insurance companies have begun to successfully crack down on many of the standard misrepresentations that agents in the past had made, ostensibly on the company's behalf. Insurance company compliance officers now comb all documentation to remove any language or illustrations which might prove to be inaccurate or misleading. In the financial services sector today, accurate and full disclosure is the ideal. Individuals who have been found to have violated these new standards are routinely driven out of the industry.

Life insurance products today are among the most sophisticated financial investments available. There is currently a wide array of insurance product types, each of which may be uniquely suited to a particular client's family and financial circumstances. With all these choices, shopping for life insurance can be truly a mind-boggling experience, far removed from the simplistic historic choice between whole life or term coverage.

There is no right insurance product ideally suited to all fact patterns. Similarly, there is no single right insurance product to be used within the narrow parameters of retirement distribution planning. When recommending a particular insurance product, the retirement distribution specialist should provide guidance to clients, taking into consideration every aspect of a client's lifestyle and financial circumstances. The good news is that considerably less life insurance coverage may be needed today than advisors had been used to recommending in years past. This is largely due to the fact that there is no longer a 15 percent excise tax on excess retirement accumulations. Also, through multigenerational distribution planning strategies, the income tax erosion of the asset is not immediate, but instead can be deferred decades into the future, with its overall impact thereby significantly reduced.

Typically, consumers today are still likely to opt for the least expensive insurance alternative, reasoning that if they have made a mistake, at least it won't cost them as much. But for retirement distribution planning specialists, this line of reasoning may lead to costly and perhaps catastrophic results. Unfortunately, many unskilled professional advisors and affluent clients still get caught in the *lowest premium* game.

Term Insurance

If costs are measured by premium dollars, then the lowest insurance cost alternative will always appear to be pure term insurance, when compared with permanent whole life insurance. However, the life insurance which is needed in connection with retirement distribution planning is typically needed on a long-term, permanent basis. While there may not be distribution-specific life insurance products designed exclusively for retirement distribution planning, term insurance is clearly the wrong choice. Term insurance, however, can be the right product for clients who only want to insure against their risk of dying during a definite and finite period of time.

With retirement distribution planning, the problem is reversed. It is not the risk of dying within a certain time frame that can create certain potential financial problems. Death is a certainty. It is the timing of death that causes the problem. Whenever death occurs, insurance must be in place to prevent the financial nightmare from arising—namely, the inability of the surviving family members to pay the estate taxes in full when they are due. The gamble is that insurance coverage may end before death occurs. With term insurance the stakes in that gamble are simply too high. Once the term is over, if death has not occurred, the likelihood of being able to extend the term coverage, or to obtain new insurance coverage at reasonable premium rates or at any cost, might not be that great. Permanent insurance entirely eliminates this risk.

Permanent Insurance

All forms of permanent insurance have a term insurance component built into the policy. The pure cost of term coverage makes up a portion of the yearly premium amount due on all types of insurance policies. Any additional premium amount paid into the policy represents an investment component of the policy, designed to fund the permanent insurance coverage and to allow participation in certain tax advantages which are associated with the use of permanent life insurance, and which can be found in no other form of financial instrument.

The first major tax advantage associated with life insurance is that the death benefit goes to the beneficiaries free of income tax and, if properly structured, can pass entirely free from all estate taxes. The second major advantage associated with life insurance is that the investment component of the policy—the amount of money contributed into the policy over and above the cost of the pure term coverage—grows income-tax-free. Since the tax-free earnings are used to find a portion of the life insurance coverage, in effect the insurance is largely purchased with pre-tax dollars. That gives permanent life insurance an enormous advantage over other methods used to accumulate money and to solve the estate tax problems associated with retirement assets.

Another important factor in this analysis is time. Without the tax advantages associated with the use of life insurance, the owner of the retirement assets may have to increase investment risk in order to achieve the growth necessary to accumulate a certain sum within an uncertain time frame. Yet most individuals do not want to take on additional risk in their retirement years.

There are several types of permanent insurance. In each, the amounts contributed to the policy grow on a tax-deferred basis (with the gains used to pay a portion of the cost of coverage on a pre-tax basis) and with the contributions credited with interest, based on the company's ability to grow the capital. What distinguishes one form of policy from another is the identity of the party that is to take on a portion or all of that investment risk.

Investment Risk

In a traditional whole life policy, premiums remain constant throughout the term of the contract—until such time as the insured dies or the policy matures. The insurance company prices the product accordingly to account for variations in mortality expenses, lapses, and investment results over a long period of time. In this scenario, the life insurance company appears to take on more risk than the policyholder, in that the control over premium payments and premium amounts are in the hands of the policyholder, through level premiums guaranteed for the life of the contract. In fact, however, the insurance company does have a way to control that risk. It can retain pricing flexibility by adjusting the interest rate credited to the policyholder's prior premium payments, and as reflected in the annual dividends credited to the policy.

The traditional whole life contract has given rise to hybrids of whole life in which the control over the basic components have shifted between the insurance company and the policyholder. Here are three such examples of these hybrids:

- **Universal Life:** The insurance company has control over investments, but gives the policyholder some control over premium payments or over death benefits by utilizing investment gains.
- **Variable Life:** The insurance company controls the amount of the death benefit and the level of premium payment, while the policyholder controls the investment choices.
- **Variable Universal Life:** This form of policy shifts to the policyholder control over investment choices, premium payments, and over the amount of the death benefit.

Single or Joint Life Policy?

A policy may be written on an individual basis or on an individual and joint basis. The former is known as a single life policy, although it is not typically referred to in this way, while the latter type of policy is known as a survivorship or second-to-die policy.

Coverage to fund the estate tax liability—using a Participant Direct Approach with a multigeneration IRA, for example—would call for a single individual permanent insurance policy on the life of the IRA owner, since the insurance benefit is needed at the death of the owner to provide the child or grandchild with sufficient funds to pay the estate taxes which are due. However, if a Spousal Rollover Approach is to be used, then a survivorship policy makes sense, since the estate tax liability and the death benefit payment both occur at the time of the death of the second spouse to die.

A traditional retirement distribution strategy—one in which all retirement assets are payable to the surviving spouse—would rely on a second-to-die policy. If there is no spouse, or if the spouse is not named as the beneficiary of the retirement asset, no rollover option would be available. Accordingly, a single life policy on the life of the IRA owner would be most appropriate.

Policy Price

From the client's perspective, determining the most cost-effective type of policy is a function of how many of the pricing factors the client wants to take on and the degree of flexibility the client has in making premium payments within his or her cash flow and budgetary parameters.

From the insurance company's perspective, effective pricing of the different types of permanent insurance depends on actuarial, underwriting, investing, and management factors and skills. As long as all the pricing components can remain reasonably predictable, the company will know that it can remain competitive in the marketplace and still earn a high enough rate of return on its policyholders' capital to meet its current and projected obligations under each insurance contract.

The actual cost of life insurance cannot be definitively determined until the contract has been fully performed—which will occur either at the policyholder's death or at the time of the endowment of the contract. From the 1940s to the 1970s, actual policy performance consistently exceeded the insurance company's projections because all the factors involved in a policy's pricing structure were relatively stable. Therefore, premiums were kept constant. Since the 1970s, however, certain distinctions among the various financial services disciplines have become blurred, creating enough uncertainty to make financial contracts with the typical duration of the average permanent life insurance policy—20, 30, or more years—difficult to price.

Expansion of customer choices has increased the pressure on insurance companies to make less conservative pricing assumptions. A wave of product design creativity emerged in the insurance industry in the 1980s, with the results of that effort being mixed at best. Since then, the bulk of the policies have not performed as illustrated. This was due to factors both within and completely outside the control of the companies issuing the policies.

Policy Illustrations

One current problem in the insurance industry revolves around the use of the words *as illustrated.* In addition to being able to define for clients all the policy type alternatives, advisors need to understand how to evaluate the various policy pricing factors inherent in each illustration, so that one policy can be compared with another in a meaningful way.

Much has been written about the difficulties in understanding, let alone comparing, several different policy illustrations. Several more radical analysts in the past had advised their clients to simply throw out illustrations as being entirely useless. However, a more productive way to make illustrations understandable to both consumers and advisors alike has come about through the efforts of the National Association of Insurance Commissioners (NAIC) in the form of the Life Insurance Illustrations Model Regulation. The guidelines discuss five factors that affect policy illustrations. Advisors should understand each of these factors should and be able to convey the significance to their clients. The five factors are as follows:

1. Guaranteed vs. non-guaranteed elements;
2. Interest rates;
3. Mortality;
4. Expenses;
5. Lapses.

1. Guaranteed vs. Non-Guaranteed Elements

In the states in which the NAIC model has been adopted, agents are required to give clients a basic illustration which follows the guidelines contained in the Model Regulation. Clients are then required to sign a disclaimer acknowledging that they have received a copy of the illustration and understand that the non-guaranteed components shown in the illustration are subject to change.

The basic policy illustration shows the guaranteed components of the policy death benefit and cash surrender values, as well as the premium payments that support them. Non-guaranteed elements can be included in the illustration preceded by the guaranteed elements, and only if clearly labeled. The two components can also be split between basic and supplemental illustrations. The summary will typically show policy values for years 5, 10, and 20, and at age 70, based on premium payments under three different scenarios—guaranteed values, non-guaranteed values, and midpoint values—in order to show the range of performance possibilities.

The validity of each of these illustrated scenarios is bolstered by the NAIC's requirements applicable to the insurance companies themselves. The insurance companies must certify to their State

Insurance Commissioner that each set of assumptions used in producing an insurance illustration was, in fact, based on the company's actual and demonstrable experience. In order to reduce the possibility that too-aggressive assumptions will eventually force the company to increase charges to policyholders, the regulation also requires the company to certify that it will break even on the product within 15 years—even if every policyholder continues to maintain his or her policy until that time.

2. Interest Rates

Comparing and interpreting the interest rates contained in several different policy illustrations can be problematic in that the interest rates shown do not always reflect the same underlying information. A client cannot make an informed decision in this regard if one rate credited to the accumulation component of a policy is a gross rate *before* any expenses are subtracted, while the interest rate quoted in an illustration from another policy is a *net* rate, which includes investment expenses. A third illustration could show a net rate, including investment expenses, profit loads, as well as certain other expensed items.

In participating policies, interest is credited as dividends. For tax purposes, dividends are considered a return of excess premiums paid. Dividends reflect the fact that the company earned *higher* returns or experienced *lower* expenses than it had projected, with the insurance company then passing some of the gain to its mutual policyholders. Dividend interest rates are usually net of interest expense. However, non-participating policies and other product types may use interest rates net of *both* investment and company expenses and of profit loads.

Another difference in the way interest rates are calculated lies in the method of crediting used by the insurance company. There are two distinct methods of interest allocation—the Portfolio Method, and the New Money Method.

Portfolio Method: The Portfolio Method determines the total investment return on the total portfolio held by the insurance company. All policies are then credited with the same interest rate, whether the policies had been purchased recently or years before in previous interest environments. This approach results in more stable rates of return over time, but with one group of policyholders effectively subsidizing another, depending on the interest rates in effect at the time of insurance purchase.

New Money Method: The New Money Method, or Investment Year Method, separates each block of policies based on the calendar year of purchase and separately tracks the assets and investment income applicable to each block. This approach is perhaps more equitable from an individual policyholder's point of view, but has the effect of causing more significant shifts up or down.

For policies which remain in force over a long period of time, an equalizing effect takes place which brings the interest rates produced by the two allocation methods together. Although the choice of interest allocation method is not critical to policy performance, it does play a critical role when initially comparing one policy to another. If different interest rate allocation methods are used, one policy may illustrate considerably better than another, depending on the current interest environment, although ultimately this illustrated advantage may prove to be illusory. If the illustrated interest rate is not supported by current experience, or if it is supported by a portfolio rate that is different from current new money rates, a future change in interest rates should be expected, even in the absence of a change in new money market rates.

3. Mortality

Mortality is the third factor influencing policy pricing. The number of death claims experienced by a company can be expressed as a percentage—actual number of death claims divided by the number of priced-for death claims. If the percentage is 100 percent, the number of actual claims equals the number priced and projected by the insurance company. A higher than 100 percent mortality ratio assumes that the rates of death will not remain as high in the future. It, therefore, indicates an expectation that the company experienced more death claims than it had projected. Clients and their advisors may then wonder what the underlying basis is for this anticipated change. A 90 percent mortality ratio means that actual claims experience was 10 percent less than what was priced and projected. Such a result would provide a 10 percent cushion for future adverse mortality experience. If more than 10 percent tolerance is experienced, the pricing level will invariably be changed in the future.

If the insurance company over time does not exhibit a fundamental ability to produce favorable mortality experience, the policyholders will ultimately be asked to assume this risk. Since policyholders have no control over the underwriting rules used by the insurance company, the assumption of that risk may be unacceptable to many policyholders.

4. Expense Ratios

The fourth factor influencing policy pricing is the company's expense ratio. A lapse is a discontinuance of insurance coverage by a policyholder. The lapse ratio compares actual lapse rates to anticipated or priced-for lapse rates. Early lapses can produce gains for the insurance company under some type of insurance products. These gains can often be used to subsidize loss of profits in the product, which typically occurs for the first few years that the policy is being maintained. If lapse-support is a pricing factor and lapses do *not* occur as projected and priced-for, the original illustrated results may not be achieved and price adjustments (changes in future premium costs) will have to be made.

Policy Illustration Questions

In the end there may be as much art as science involved in evaluating insurance policies and their illustrations. Both analyses begin with knowing what questions to ask. Here is a sample list of questions that the retirement distribution specialist can ask to help their clients more fully understand the insurance illustration being shown. If the insurance specialist is unable to answer these questions, the chances that the policyholder or their other advisors will know the answers to these questions is nil.

- How is the designated risk class defined? Are there progressive risk categories?
- Are ages determined on an *age nearest* or *age last birthday* basis?

- Are any optional benefits included?
- Are death benefits illustrated on an *end-of-year* or *beginning-of-year* basis?
- What methods are available to access policy cash values without having to surrender the policy?
- What is the effect on the death benefit of borrowing against the cash value?
- Are the illustrated gross premiums guaranteed?
- Do the illustrated cash values represent actual surrender values net of all other expenses?
- What is the effect on future premiums in a vanishing premium illustration if the interest rate should drop by 1 percent or 2 percent?
- Is the total death benefit provided through a base policy, or is a term rider used for a portion of the insurance coverage? (With term riders, the annual outlay is initially lower, but the level of guarantee is also reduced, thereby increasing the policy's sensitivity to changes in dividends or other non-guaranteed elements.)
- What interest rate is charged on policy loans?
- What is the difference between the rate charged and the rate credited on borrowed portions of the cash value?
- Is the mortality assumption underlying the illustration based on current experience, or does it include projected improvements in experience?
- What services are provided after issue (either by the carrier and/or by the producer) of updated projections of in-force policies or to administer a changing patter of premiums, withdrawals, and loan illustrations?

For whole life policies and survivorship whole life policies, the following questions should also be asked:

- If the interest rate drops after premium payments have been made from earnings, what options are available to the policyholder—resume premium payments, decrease death benefits, shorten the period of insurance coverage, or a combination of these three?

- Who will monitor the policy values to provide an early warning that additional premiums are needed? Will the warning be given in enough time before the resulting amounts become unmanageable?
- For the past five years, what has been the gross interest rate underlying the dividend scale (for traditional participating whole life policies)?
- What have the interest rates been for the past five years (for interest-sensitive whole life policies)?
- Is the whole life product banded? If so, list the banding levels.
- Is a Portfolio Rate or a New Money Rate used in the dividend scale? Describe.
- Is a gross rate or a net rate used in the dividend scale? Describe.
- What interest rate is used in calculating the guaranteed values?
- Does the insurance company allow the policy to be split into two single life policies in the case of a divorce or a change in the tax law?
- If the insurance company allows the policy to be split into two single life policies, is evidence of insurability required at the time of the split?
- Does the insurance company charge for the policy split option? If so, what is the charge?
- What is the guaranteed annual premium on a 100 percent whole life policy?
- On what basis is the insured's age determined—attained age or nearest age?
- Do the policy values change after the first death? If so, what assumption was made in the illustration about the timing of the first death?

If universal life insurance and survivorship universal life insurance policies are being considered, the following questions should also be asked:

- What is the minimum premium which must be paid in each of the first few policy years?
- For how many years is the minimum premium necessary?
- After the minimum premium period, what events trigger a policy lapse?

- When can the policy face amount be decreased or increased?
- How long is the surrender charge period?
- Does the illustration reflect bonuses with respect to the crediting of interest? Are the bonuses guaranteed?
- What are the current cost-of-insurance charges per $1,000?
- What is the current interest rate?
- Is the current interest rate a gross rate or net rate?
- Is the current interest rate tied to a Portfolio Rate or a New Money Rate? Describe.
- What interest rate is used in calculating the guaranteed values?
- Are old policyholders credited with the same interest rate as new policyholders?
- What is the interest rate persistency bonus used in the illustration? In what year is it effective? What criteria must be met to earn the persistency bonus?
- What are the current annual mortality charges used in the projection and the guaranteed annual mortality charges at ages 55, 60, 70, and 80?
- On what basis is the insured's age determined—attained age or nearest age?
- Does the insurance company allow the policy to be split into two single policies? Is there a cost associated with the split? Is evidence of insurability required at the time of the split?
- Does the insurance company have a maturity extension rider? Describe the conditions and costs associated with the use of the rider.

For individual, survivorship variable, and variable universal life insurance decisions, the following questions should also be asked:

- What investment funds are available?
- What are the premium loads, mutual fund expenses, and policy fees?
- Does the policy have mortality and expense risk charges? Describe current and guaranteed amounts.
- Does the policy have a guaranteed interest account? Describe current and minimum rates.

- Does the policy have any policy enhancement bonuses that are credited to cash values?
- Do the available funds use outside fund managers?
- What has been the past performance of the investment fund?
- What has been the spread between gross yields and net yields, and what portion is guaranteed?
- What total return is assumed in the illustration?
- Is there a guaranteed minimum death benefit that applies regardless of fund performance?
- How large should the variable separate account fund be?
- Is the product banded? Describe.
- What are the current annual mortality charges used in the projection and the guaranteed annual mortality charges at ages 55, 60, 70, and 80?
- On what basis is the insured's age determined—attained age or nearest age?
- Does the insurance company allow the policy to be split into two single policies? Is there a cost associated with the split? Is evidence of insurability required at the time of the split?
- Does the insurance company have a maturity extension rider? Describe the conditions and costs associated with the use of the rider.

Choosing the Right Insurance Company

At the completion of the above analysis, the advisor should be able to identify the type of insurance policy that best meets the client's objectives, in terms of projected price and performance and overall suitability for its intended purposes. The next step in locating the right policy for the right price is to look at the insurance companies themselves.

From the end of World War II until the late 1980s, most major insurance companies seemed equally financially secure. The 1980s brought enormous changes in the financial service industry, intense competition for investment and premium dollars, and nearly unrestrained creativity in insurance company product development. However, insurance company *projected* product performance eventually had to be backed up by actual increased product performance. This inevitably led the insurance companies down certain investment paths that were riskier than they traditionally had been. When California regulators seized Executive Life Insurance Company, one of the most creative insurance companies around from an investment perspective, the public learned for the first time that it was possible for a major life insurance company to fail.

The seizure of several other insurance companies followed over the next several years, as regulators decided that the insurance companies could not realistically meet the guarantees they had made to policyholders. The causes for these failures included high-risk investment strategies, large mortgage loans in a declining real estate market, critical imbalances between higher credited policy returns and reduced premiums, and, finally, unrestrained consumer panic.

Unlike the consumers of certain other financial service institutions which had failed in the 1980s, life insurance policyholders generally were made whole throughout the seizure process, with all insurance death benefits being paid in full. Guaranty funds established by the various state regulatory agencies, subject to state-legislated caps and supported by the life insurance companies themselves, provided a source of additional funds to further back up the policyholders. In most cases, the insurance policies of the seized companies were sold to healthy life insurance companies. In the process, some benefit payments were delayed, while some policyholders were unable to access their funds for extended periods of time, creating havoc in the personal financial planning of some individuals.

However, as startling as these developments were, customers and the life insurance industry were somehow able to successfully weather the crisis. In hindsight, perhaps the real surprise may have been that, shortly before the crisis had emerged, few of these companies were perceived as being at risk. Because the industry historically had enjoyed such a long period of stability and growth, most watchdogs entirely missed the early warning danger signs.

Since the 1980s, the possibility of an insurance company's failure has been the focus of industry analysts and consumers alike. Today a comparative analysis of the relative financial strength of life insurance companies has become a critical element in the life insurance decision-making process for any competent life insurance professional. Company evaluations center on the following issues:

- Ratings
- Surplus
- Assets
- Liquidity
- Earnings
- Quality and continuity of management

The objective in analyzing a particular insurance company is to determine the right balance between performance and safety. Acceptable ratings to a client will depend upon their particular risk tolerance and objectives as identified by their insurance advisor. Ratings are expressed as codes of letters or numbers intended to convey different evaluation objectives. For example, here are some of the valuation companies and the criteria that they measure:

- A.M. Best—overall rating classification
- Duff & Phelps—ability to pay claims
- Moody's—financial strength
- Standard & Poor's—ability to pay claims

It is suggested that an insurance company's particular rating be used to establish a minimum threshold level of acceptability. For example, if the insurance company receives an acceptable rating from two or more ratings services, as well as no rating below investment grade from the other rating services, it should make the cut-off list. An analysis of the insurance company, however, should not be dependent *solely* upon ratings, even when they far exceed an acceptable minimum level. The following questions should always be asked:

1. Is the company's surplus adequate?

Actual surplus must be compared to benchmark requirements and to the risk characteristics inherent in the company's particular assets and liabilities.

2. Are the company's assets of a high quality and properly diversified?

Assets should be diversified by type, size, industry, and region. There should not be too many high-risk assets in relation to the company's surplus. The ratio of all high risk assets to adjusted surplus should total below 150 percent. High-risk assets include below-investment-grade bonds, delinquent mortgages, and real estate acquired by foreclosure.

3. Does the company have sufficient liquidity?

Insurance company liquidity refers to the degree to which the current value of marketable investments is sufficient to cover a potentially high and sudden withdrawal request. Such liquidity can go a long way toward preventing a run-on-the-bank scenario.

4. How consistent are the company's earnings?

The advisor should look for stable to increasing total earnings over the past five years, as well as a stable to increasing ratio of earnings to premiums, total assets, and insurance. The analysis should also be made among a significant major product lines. A major problem product in one line can have a negative impact on the non-guaranteed elements in the individual life insurance area, and can also af-fect overall company solvency.

Finally, an assessment of the quality of the insurance company's management team should also be undertaken. This analysis should include the management's understanding of its business, its ability to identify and solve problems, and its strategic perspective. The success of the management team affects the overall financial strength of the company, and also indicates its commitment to certain product lines and business development strategies.

The Right Source of Funds

Once the client has been made to understand each of the important considerations to be weighed in selecting the proper insurance product type and issuing company, there is still the problem of where the money should come from to pay the yearly insurance premiums. In deciding where the premium dollars should come from, two questions should be answered. The first question is: Should a policy be used whose internal structure provides for the build-up of tax-advantaged funds which can then be used to pay the premiums? The second question is: Are there any existing tax-advantaged structures in the client's personal situation—primarily a business—which can be used to pay the premiums?

The flexibility inherent in many policies allows the policy to be designed to fit specific client needs. A skilled insurance advisor can walk the client through a series of decision factors that in the end can lead to the construction of an ideal prototype policy for the client's particular situation. From that prototype, the insurance advisor can then negotiate with various life insurance companies to find a range of policies that match the given criteria. Each broad category of policies can be made to favor one or more of these criteria.

With a traditional whole life policy, the premiums will be level each year. Premium payments go to cover the cost of insurance—the pure term foundation of the policy—and to build the investment of the policy component. Eventually, the cash value in the policy will equal its death benefit, due to the accumulation of premium amounts paid over and above the pure cost of insurance, together with dividends and interest credited to those funds. This phenomenon will occur at age 95 or 100. At that time, the policy will be fully paid up.

The traditional whole life policy is a vehicle with the least amount of risk. Policy values are based on the highest guarantees. Premium payment amounts are also guaranteed. With this product, the buyer takes on almost no risk. The tradeoff for this lower level of risk is a higher level of required yearly cash outlay. Premiums are generally higher with whole life policies than with other types of life insurance, all other factors being equal.

The client must decide whether or not this is the position he or she wants to be in with respect to the retirement distribution plan. Based on the multigenerational approach, the retirement distribution plan can be structured to last for decades. It can take into account the remaining life expectancy of the IRA owner, the remaining life expectancy of the spouse beyond the IRA owner's life expectancy, and the remaining life expectancy of their children and then grandchildren. However, the life insurance policy need only last as long as the end of the life expectancy of the IRA owner and spouse, assuming a survivorship structure, because that is when the estate tax liability on the IRA asset arises, and, accordingly, that is when the death benefit is needed. Although it is critical that the policy last until that time, it is not critical that the policy contain guarantees of each one of its elements.

If a traditional whole life policy payment structure is not the most appropriate type of policy to be used, then perhaps a more flexible, less guaranteed policy structure (such as universal or variable life policy) may be more appropriate, especially where the client may be willing to take on some of the policy performance risk.

With universal life insurance, the client pays the full pure cost of insurance, but then is allowed to decide how much of the remaining amount of premium he or she wishes to pay each year. The minimum amount of premium to be paid each year is the amount calculated to continue the policy in force each year, using whatever amounts had been paid into the cash value component of the policy, together with the dividends and interest which had accumulated thereon. With this form of insurance, the client assumes the risk for keeping the policy in force. The risk that the policy will be canceled should not be underestimated. If the policy lapses, all the premiums paid to date will have been wasted. Allowing a universal life policy to lapse can spell disaster to an individual's estate plan or retirement distribution plan. Nevertheless, the value of the flexible premium payment arrangement, such as is allowed with universal life insurance, may ideally suit a particular client's circumstances.

The client may be willing to take on another form of risk—investment risk—as an additional trade-off for more favorable contract provisions in a policy. Variable life and variable universal life give the client some discretion in choosing among a variety of investment choices, instead of having to rely on the insurance company's overall investment policies. This perhaps represents the ultimate application of the "buy term and invest the difference" admonition that was leveled against the stodgy whole life insurance policies that had existed in the 1970s. In the past decade, variable policies have achieved exceptional results for many individuals, due in large part to the unprecedented run-up in the bull market in the 1990's. Since investment returns inside a life insurance policy are not subject to income tax, the earnings on the policy when applied to the internal cost of insurance, in effect pay the premiums on a pre-tax basis. This makes the cost of insurance for this type of policy considerably less than paying premiums with all after-tax dollars.

A knowledgeable and ethical life insurance advisor should be able to effectively communicate all of these options to the client. Although the commission level associated with a traditional whole life insurance policy may be the highest, a quality insurance advisor will frame recommendations to the client in terms of what type of policy is best suited to the client, and not what type of policy will pay the highest commission. The professional insurance advisor sees his or her role as sitting on the client's side of the table. If the advisor perceives a desire on the client's part for high guarantees, the advisor will find the appropriate insurance product which stresses those guarantees. If flexibility is the dominant factor in the client's mind, the insurance advisor will find an insurance product which satisfies that goal.

Paying for Life Insurance

Once the right insurance policy has been designed and located, the next question to ask is: What is the best way to pay for it? Actually, the best policy for this purpose may already be owned by the client. The better insurance advisors will look at the broader planning issues associated with the client to determine whether existing coverage that previously was put in place to solve other problems can be utilized in the retirement distribution plan. The result of that analysis might be the avoidance of having the purchase additional insurance coverage by using existing insurancc policies or by redeploying existing policies. However, in order to effectively use existing policies for retirement distribution planning purposes, it is necessary that the policies be structured in such a way as to not be subject to estate tax in the estate of the IRA owner, or in the estate of the IRA owner's spouse. The income- and estate-tax-free benefits of life insurance can be used to dramatically reduce the effect of the double tax syndrome associated with retirement assets.

In most instances, the insurance should be owned by an irrevocable life insurance trust, which should also be designated as the beneficiary of the policy. Each year the individual makes gifts to the trust on behalf of the beneficiaries—in this case, the beneficiaries of the multigeneration IRA, which gifts should be structured in such a way as to qualify for the annual gift tax exclusion. The amount contributed into the trust each year is then used by the Trustees of the Trust to pay the yearly premiums due on the insurance policy owned by the trust. Upon the individual's death the trust receives the insurance benefit free from any estate tax or income tax. Although the estate taxes which are due will be paid by the estate, the trust can provide liquidity to the estate to pay the estate taxes, by either lending cash to the estate or by purchasing estate assets. In order to preserve estate tax excludibility, the trust must be irrevocable, with the insured having no ownership or control of the policy, including no right to borrow from the policy and no right to surrender it for cash. If an existing policy owned by the insured is transferred to the trust, the policy proceeds will *not* be excluded from the individual's estate until three years have passed from the date of the transfer. The trust document should *not* require that the policy proceeds be used to pay estate taxes. For the yearly gifts to qualify for the $10,000 annual gift tax exclusion, the beneficiaries of the trust must be given a present interest in the gifts—i.e., a limited right to withdraw from the trust the amounts contributed to the trust. Typically, this right exists for 30 days from the date on which the funds were contributed to the trust. This withdrawal right is known as the "Crumney Powers," a name taken from the family that had first litigated this issue with the IRS.

If a charitable remainder trust has been named as beneficiary of one of the multigeneration IRAs, the income stream paid by the charitable trust can be used to fund the life insurance policy which is to be used to help meet the estate tax liabilities of the children and/or grandchildren or used to replace the value of the IRA asset given to charity, so that the heirs can still inherit the full value of the individual's estate.

Another source of funding for the life insurance premiums could be the IRAs themselves. If the IRAs are earning more than was initially projected in the retirement distribution plan, the additional earnings could be withdrawn from the IRAs, with a portion of the after-tax funds being used to pay the life insurance premiums.

Finally, for business owners, one of the best sources for funding life insurance premiums is the privately held corporation. A business owner has the option of structuring an insurance plan using split dollar arrangements to pay a portion or all of the premiums due. A split dollar arrangement is a payment method structured to take advantage of what may be significant differences between the corporate income tax bracket and the personal income tax bracket of the business owner. If the corporation's tax bracket is lower than that of the business owner, life insurance premiums can be paid at the corporation level with dollars that are taxed at lower marginal tax rates. The split dollar arrangement can be structured to provide tax-deferred growth of cash values and generally income-tax-free death proceeds.

If the company is a Subchapter S corporation, there will be no income tax benefit associated with the use of a split dollar arrangement, in that a Subchapter S corporation is merely a conduit entity, with all of its profits automatically taxed each year to the business owner. However, a split dollar arrangement may still be an effective way of paying premiums, even under those circumstances. The benefit of using a split dollar arrangement to pay premiums with an S corporation is that it allows the individual to avoid having to use his or her annual gift tax exclusions and/or Unified Credit Amount, had the individual's personal dollars been used to pay the premiums. Under the split dollar arrangement, premiums are paid by the corporation, allowing the individual to make their annual tax-free gifts in addition to providing a fund to make the annual premium payments.

A tax-exempt split dollar arrangement apportions the various components of an insurance policy into separate parts allocable to each party in accordance with their needs and circumstances. The components include ownership, premiums payments, death proceeds, cash values, and dividends. In the typical split dollar arrangement, the corporation advances all of the money each year to pay the premiums on the policy insuring the life of the business owner/employee. In exchange, the corporation receives a share of the policy cash values and death benefit. The business owner, employee, and heirs are entitled to the *balance* of the cash values and death benefit. The rights and obligations of each party to the arrangement are defined in a split dollar agreement, drafted by the legal advisors and signed by both parties.

The split dollar agreement defines how the premiums are to be split. Several options are available, including the following:

- The corporation pays a premium each year equal to the annual increase in the policy's cash value, while the business owner/employee pays the balance of the premium due.
- The corporation pays all premiums.
- The business owner/employee pays a premium each year equal to the economic benefit the individual derives that year by virtue of the insurance coverage, with the corporation paying the balance.
- The corporation and the business owner/employee each pay a set portion of the premium amount each year.

One of the factors to consider in determining specifically how the split dollar arrangement should be structured to apply to a particular client's circumstances is the potential tax advantage to be gained by splitting the various components of a policy between the two parties to the agreement—the corporation and the individual. Where there is a difference between the corporate and personal income tax rates—for instance, where the corporation is *not* a Subchapter S corporation, the split dollar approach can allow for the purchase of life insurance coverage with dollars that are taxed at the lower marginal rates.

Under the typical split dollar arrangement, premiums are not deductible by the corporation. However, certain other tax issues relating to the use of split dollar life insurance arrangements have *not* been the subject of clear guidance from the IRS. It is, therefore, essential before adopting a split dollar arrangement that the advisor and client engage the services of an individual who specializes in this area, and who is thoroughly familiar with the most recent tax rulings applicable to this type of arrangement.

The Right Underwriting

There is one final factor to be considered in this life insurance discussion. The ability to use life insurance as a tool to fund the estate tax liability associated with retirement assets is often dependent upon the insurability of the IRA owner, and also possibly of the IRA owner's spouse. If retirement distribution planning is ignored until the last minute, individuals who need this life insurance coverage may already be in their late 60s, or even age 70, $70^1/_2$, or beyond. This is a time when health concerns can arise for many, and when ill health may have already overtaken others. Insurance underwriting at that time can become a significant problem in the planning process.

Underwriting problems can arise when non-insurance advisors try to do their clients a favor by putting out bids for life insurance coverage. From the advisors' perspective, this is a reasonable way to obtain the necessary coverage. It protects the clients' interests by seeking the lowest cost for the insurance coverage. One problem associated with this approach is that very few advisors—and virtually no clients—will be able to break down life insurance policy and illustration assumptions to get each of the proposed insurers to provide meaningful bid specifications.

Still more subtle problems can arise to undermine the ideal of bidding in the life insurance area. The insurance industry, through an independent information bureau, shares data on work in progress. When several agents are working on the same case, the same insurer may see the identical case several times. The insurance company will reason that the case is probably being submitted to other companies as well. That rightfully leads the company to doubt the client's commitment to their company alone, thereby causing the company's underwriters not to give the case their fullest consideration or best efforts.

At the same time, agents, who otherwise may have outstanding track records with a particular insurance company for submitting quality business, are put in a weaker bargaining position, causing them to lose their ability to receive favorable contract quotes and specifications for their clients. The ability to independently negotiate favorable underwriting terms with the insurance company is generally restricted to insurance advisors with excellent relationships with the company's management and underwriters. In contrast, a weaker agent who attempts to slip a high-risk client past underwriting simply for the sake of achieving an insurance sale will, in short order, get a bad reputation. The insurance company's hands will then be tied by the fact that multiple agents have submitted the same case, effectively preventing it from considering subjective criteria provided to them by the respected agent.

Another problem which arises frequently in the context of large insurance policies is the issue of the dollar amount of risk that the insurance company is willing to assume. This is an issue which virtually no one outside the insurance industry and few agents within it ever see. Life insurance company underwriters evaluate insurance applications (including the medical histories of the applicants), not only to determine *whether* to accept the risk of coverage, but also to determine *how much* of the risk to accept. This issue is not health-related. It has nothing to do with the life expectancy of the particular applicant. Instead, it focuses on the fact that the coverage needed may simply be too great for one insurance company to handle on its own. The insurance company may accept an insurance application for an amount of coverage considerably in excess of what it is willing to underwrite on its own because it has the ability to cede the excess risk to a reinsurance company.

Reinsurance

Reinsurance is a way for insurance companies to capitalize their accounts receivable. It relieves the company of the need to maintain a surplus to cover large underwriting risks, and spreads the risk over many carriers. Reinsurance is issued by major international reinsurance syndicates through treaty arrangements. The treaties contain very specific underwriting guidelines, with certain reinsurance companies favoring certain kinds of underwriting criteria over others.

In a large case—such as the typical case involving retirement distribution planning—the insurance company underwriter may seek to secure reinsurance from a reinsurance company because the company underwriting criteria for that client may make it a perfect match for that reinsurance company. By treaty, once the reinsurance company receives the application, it is prohibited from negotiating the case to any other source. The reinsurance is locked in. The agent cannot then shop the case to other insurance company in the hope of getting a better rating for the client, since the next carrier will be unable to obtain the same reinsurance commitment. Only experienced life insurance advisors will know how to successfully navigate this maze for their clients.

On the positive side, well-respected insurance agents can assist their clients immeasurably in the underwriting process, in a way that the broader population of agents cannot, due to their ability to negotiate the various underwriting factors with the insurance company on terms more favorable to their clients. While underwriting standards are generally accorded sacred status at most insurance companies, they are not immutable. Accepting or not accepting a particular insurance risk is a business decision which takes into account many factors. Even though insurance companies keep an ideal client profile in mind as the basis of its profitable business, in many instances they will accept less profitable business in order to preserve their relationships with their insurance agents and for the sake of revenues. Every business makes those types of risk/reward analyses, including insurance companies—especially when they are trying to meet certain established premium goals at year's end. Under those circumstances, the seasoned insurance advisor that the company trusts and listens to can prove to be a substantial asset on the client's side. In such situations, the agent's reputation and clout with the insurance company may be almost as important as the state of the client's health.

CHAPTER 11
INTEGRATING ESTATE PLANNING AND RETIREMENT DISTRIBUTION PLANNING

CONTENTS

11 INTEGRATING ESTATE PLANNING AND RETIREMENT DISTRIBUTION PLANNING

The first step in integrating the estate plan with the retirement distribution plan is to provide for a long-term commitment to tracking each plan. Since the two transfer strategies in all likelihood had been developed at different times through different planning processes and led by different advisors, some effort must be made to ensure that the right effects take place at the right time for the heirs. This is especially important when clients have expressed concerns about the effects of inheriting unearned income on their younger family members.

As part of this planning process, it is usually helpful to view the client's assets as a whole, and to elicit from the client the dollar amount or the percentage amount of the total pie which is to be allocated to each family member. Once the client has decided on the dollar amount or percentage amount of each beneficiary's share, the advisor should help the client identify which type of asset should be used to satisfy each intended bequest.

It is a good idea for the advisory team to develop a schedule of exactly how and when the heirs will receive each of the various estate assets and streams of income. The schedule can also serve as a benchmark to determine whether the estate plan still meets the overall planning objectives of the clients after the process has been completed.

The first problem associated with integrating clients' retirement distribution plan with their other estate planning efforts is that *estate planning* tends to be a very loosely defined term. No matter what

Note: Readers should refer to the Introduction for a discussion of issues and concepts covered in Chapter 11 that may be affected by the IRS's issuance of the Revised Proposed Regulations governing Required Minimum Distributions and by the passage of EGTRRA 2001. These include: changes in Federal estate tax amounts and rates; the Uniform Distribution Period Table; the elimination of irrevocable elections at the individual's Required Beginning Date; and the determination of the beneficiary by December 31 of the year following the year of the individual's death.

the true state of their estate planning might be, most clients will think they have fully completed the process. The second problem associated with this process is that most clients will not realize, however sophisticated their estate plans may be, that without frequent and periodic reviews of their personal and financial circumstances, as well as of the current status of relevant tax laws, their estate plan may no longer be viable. This is precisely why a long-term commitment to tracking each plan is so essential.

> **Example:** Grant and Susan had just recently completed a substantial update of their estate plan through a major law firm in New York City. A short time thereafter their accountant referred them to a retirement distribution specialist to add some specialized planning to their overall estate plan. Their total taxable estate was than valued at $8 million. Each had $250,000 in retirement assets. There was a $800,000 policy on Grant's life and a $200,000 policy on Susan's life. Included in the comprehensive estate plan which they had just completed was an update to their Wills, revocable trusts, and irrevocable life insurance trusts, and the creation of a family limited partnership, a QPRT, a private foundation trust, and a Charitable Remainder Trust. Grant and Susan had spent a significant amount of their time, effort, and money with their estate planning attorneys to protect their accumulated wealth from estate taxes, and to ensure that, upon their death, their assets would be distributed according to their wishes. After all that time and money spent with their legal experts, however, the retirement distribution specialist discovered two areas of extreme vulnerability in the estate plan—the $500,000 retirement assets and $1 million in life insurance coverage.
>
> Unbeknownst to Grant and Susan, the ownership of the $800,000 insurance policy on Grant's life and the ownership of the $200,000 insurance policy on Susan's life had never been transferred into the name of their respective irrevocable life insurance trusts. This planning lapse constituted a disaster waiting to happen. On their premature deaths, both policies would be fully taxable in their estates.

Clients often feel a tremendous sense of security in owning significant insurance policies on their lives. But that security is misplaced when this potentially estate-tax-free asset is required to be included in their estates for estate tax purposes, because they had not parted with the requisite ownership interests in the policies.

The retirement assets represented another disaster waiting to happen. The named beneficiary of each of their retirement assets was none other than their respective estates. Rather than using creative beneficiary designations and dual life expectancy options, Grant and Susan had simply designated their estates as beneficiary of their retirement assets, under the belief that in so doing, the various trusts established in their Wills would be funded. They did not realize that under this approach, their retirement assets after their death could no longer remain sheltered in the retirement vehicles, but would have to be almost immediately paid out of the shelter of the retirement vehicles, and then would be subject to immediate income taxation. Under their simplistic retirement distribution plan, the government would receive a full 80 percent in combined federal and state estate and income taxes of their retirement assets—$400,000 of the $500,000 value of those assets.

The tax erosion based on these two planning lapses alone was enormous, despite the fact that the estate planning attorney had designed and implemented for them some of the most sophisticated estate planning techniques available. The real problem was that the attorney—although a specialist in trusts and estates—was not familiar with the retirement distribution rules applicable to qualified plans and IRAs, and was not familiar with the various retirement distribution strategies that could have been implemented.

On an individual's death their assets can pass to their heirs from many different sources and directions. Some assets will pass through the Will, other assets may pass by contract or beneficiary designation (such as retirement assets or life insurance proceeds), while still other assets may pass throughout joint ownership. The above example demonstrates why, in all this confusion, the integration of retirement distribution planning with estate planning is so critical.

The Two Goals of Estate Planning

Estate planning can be defined for clients as a set of integrated strategies that will achieve for them the following two objectives:

1. The transfer of their assets at their death to the people or entities that they have selected, and in the manner in which they want them to be received.
2. The transfer of their assets at their death with the least possible loss in the value to estate or income taxation or to other expenses.

A comprehensive estate plan will attempt to achieve both objectives. What clients may not realize at first is that the government has stacked the deck against achieving *both* of these goals. In order to realize both goals, affluent clients typically have to make hard choices between preserving control over their assets during their lifetime, or preserving the value of those assets for their heirs by disposing of their assets prior to their date of death. Achieving both of these goals usually involves coordinated planning through a team of knowledgeable advisors who are each expert in the different but complementary tax and financial disciplines. Estate planning from the advisor's perspective is the assiduous search for solutions that maximize the realization of the client's two goals, with the least amount of compromise or tradeoffs.

For many clients, the estate planning process can tend to be irritating, incomprehensible, and emotionally draining. For this reason, many estate planning efforts remain incomplete during the client's lifetime. Certainly no one would want to go through this exercise more than once. Clients can also become complacent about the estate planning process, because they mistakenly believe that estate planning is simply a matter of completing and updating their Wills. They believe that, with a Will alone, their assets are assured of going to the people or entities that they have designated, and in the manner that they have chosen. In addition, clients may also resist revising their estate and retirement distribution plan under the mistaken belief that their asset, family, and tax circumstances will remain the same indefinitely, making any re-examination of those issues unnecessary.

Ordinarily, clients can get by for quite some time with a head-in-the-sand approach. After all, they are probably not going to die tomorrow. However, once they reach age 70½, some amount of planning *must* be done. At that point, the retirement distribution planning efforts can and should go forward to completion, independent of the status of the estate planning process as a whole. The retirement distribution specialist should make sure that retirement distribution issues are adequately and completely addressed at that time. Any separation of those two planning components, however, must eventually give way to the full integration of the two plans into one coordinated plan.

It is more than likely that certain problems will arise during the process of integrating retirement distribution planning with the existing estate plan. At that stage in the process, it is often discovered that certain changes have taken place to make the estate plan out of date. Often the estate plan must then undergo substantial revisions before it can be fully integrated with retirement distribution planning. However, this coordination of the two planning processes can also create the potential for new opportunities to achieve the clients' goals.

Ownership of Assets

One method in which property is transferred upon death is referred to as transfer by operation of law. Some examples of transfers by operation of law are discussed below.

Transfers made pursuant to state intestate distribution statutes: This type of transfer applies in those cases in which an individual had died without a Will. The intestacy laws of the state of the individual's domicile as of the date of death determine the heirs of the individual's property.

Transfers pursuant to state right of election statutes: Under the laws of all states, a spouse cannot be entirely disinherited by an individual. The laws of all states provide certain minimum amounts that must be paid to a surviving spouse, unless the surviving spouse has previously agreed to waive those rights or had agreed not to assert those rights. These statutes must be taken into account in designating beneficiaries of retirement assets. If the surviving spouse is *not* to be the beneficiary of those benefits, great care should be taken to see to it that the surviving spouse is given sufficient other assets from the estate, so that the spouse's exercise of his or her right of election after the retirement assets owner's death does not work to defeat the retirement distribution plan.

Other problems in the estate plan may arise over the issue of how certain estate assets are owned or titled. The Will might not be able to achieve its anticipated results unless the couple's assets are properly titled. In each case the question should be asked: Can the existing title to certain assets interfere with the testamentary plan to fund the Unified Credit Amount with certain assets at the first death, thereby causing the imposition of unnecessary estate taxes on the death of the second spouse to die? This question illustrates the difference between assets which pass by operation of law and assets which pass by the Will through the probate process. The titling of assets must be consistent with both state law and the estate plan.

The following example illustrates how the current ownership of assets may work to defeat a testamentary estate plan:

Assume that a couple owns the following assets:

Assets	*Value*
House—jointly held	$300,000
Cash, stocks—all jointly held	$500,000
Husband's IRA	$750,000
Wife's IRA	$450,000
Total	$2,000,000

In a basic estate planning situation, on the death of the first spouse to die, their Will would establish a Credit Shelter Trust for the benefit of the survivor, in an amount equal to the Unified Credit Amount available for that year ($675,000 for 2000 and 2001). Accordingly, if the Wills of the husband and wife were each drafted to include language to establish those Credit Shelter Trusts, many estate planning attorneys would think that they had completed the estate planning process. However, then an additional step must be taken. That step is to determine which assets are to be used to fund the Credit Shelter Trust in each Will following the death of the first spouse to die. Each of the above-listed assets is a designated asset, in that it is to be paid either pursuant to the title held on the asset, or pursuant to a beneficiary designation. Accordingly, because of the way in which each asset is now owned, on the death of either the husband or wife, *none* of those assets would be payable into their Wills or used to fund the Credit Shelter Trusts which each had established in their Wills for the survivor.

A better practice would have been for the advisor to have counseled the clients to divide their jointly held property (their house, cash, and stock) into two equal shares, with each owning outright assets worth $400,000. Each Will could then affect each of those $400,000 shares, but would still be missing $275,000 in assets to maximize the use of the $675,000 Unified Credit Amount for 2000 and 2001.

Next, each of the couple's IRA assets should then be configured so that the beneficiary of the *first* $275,000 of each IRA asset is the Credit Shelter Trust designated in their Wills. A thorough review of each of the rules applicable to the use of trusts as designated beneficiaries should be completed before implementing this particular planning strategy to ensure that the life expectancies of the various trust beneficiaries could then be used to maximize deferrals and increase accumulations in the retirement assets.

Several warning signs that advisors should look at which can raise doubts about the efficacy of a particular estate plan may involve a client's move from one state to another, or the sale or acquisition of certain property since the last time the estate plan had been reviewed. Real estate, which a client may own in more than one state, could present other estate planning issues. Community property states treat the ownership of certain assets differently from states which are common law states. Accordingly, property which is subject to a state's community property rules could pose still further estate planning problems, and could also create retirement distribution planning issues.

The Beneficiary Method of Transferring Property

Another method of transferring property upon death is the beneficiary method, often referred to as *transfer by contract* method. As part of their retirement distribution plan, clients may have executed properly drafted beneficiary designations for both their IRAs and other retirement assets. However, what about the beneficiary designations on their life insurance and annuities? Were these designations all completed correctly? Have changing circumstances made those designations out-of-date? Have the clients themselves been named as the owners of the insurance policies on their own lives, with their spouses named as beneficiaries? In each case, the proceeds from those assets would be included in their estates with an unnecessary estate tax liability thereby being incurred.

Many assets do not pass through the Will because they are jointly held. A typical example type of ownership would be a house owned jointly by husband and wife with rights of survivorship. Additional examples would be joint bank accounts, joint stock brokerage accounts, or stocks and bonds held in joint name. Other forms of designated assets are accounts held Payable On Death (POD) or "In Trust For" certain individuals. In each instance, it is not necessary to look to the Will or to the intestacy laws of the state of the individual, in order to ascertain to whom the asset is to be paid on the individual's death. In each case, those assets will be paid to the surviving joint tenant, POD individual, or the "In Trust For" beneficiary, regardless of how the Will is worded.

Family Circumstances and Transfer of Assets

Blended Families

In addition to specific ownership problems and beneficiary designation issues, special family circumstances can further complicate the planning process and, unless handled correctly, may influence whether the client's assets will go where he or she wants, and in the manner that he or she wishes. The most common problem in this area involves blended family situations. This may entail a second, third, or even fourth marriage, as well as intended heirs from the first marriages. In the context of a blended family situation, a Will which may seem perfectly clear and unambiguously drawn on its face may cause legal issues to arise or may have the inadvertent effect of disinheriting a party. The result may be post-death challenges to the Will and estate plan—and perhaps an expensive, protracted, and public legal battle.

Spouses Who Are Not United States Citizens

Less common, but equally problematic in the area of estate planning, is the situation in which a spouse is not a United States citizen. Several common estate planning devices (most notably the unlimited marital deduction) do not apply to non-citizen spouses, making alternative planning approaches necessary in order to achieve the same estate conservation results.

Minor Children

Children who are minors can pose significant estate planning issues. Often, control of the money allocable for the benefit of a minor child vests in one individual (as Trustee), while the guardianship of the physical person of the minor child resides in another. Special needs may arise in families in which the children are intellectually or artistically gifted. Parents may need to make special bequests or gifts to provide educational and suitable training to maximize these talents. On the other hand, families with emotionally or physically handicapped children who are not capable of caring for themselves must plan for the future medical, financial, and custodial care of those individuals, or face the possibility that those individuals will not be properly cared for or will be cared for at the lowest subsistence level provided by government or charitable organizations.

Under those circumstances, trusts tailor-made to the particular needs of each child should be crafted. Assets that the child is to inherit through the estate should be paid into that trust, as should the retirement assets allocable to that child which had been accumulated in the qualified plans and IRAs of the parents. In most families, the children will, at some point, have achieved sufficient emotional and financial maturity as to be fully capable of making intelligent tax and financial decisions on their own. At that time, the trust can end, with all subsequent tax and investment decisions, including Required Minimum Distribution decisions, made by the then–adult child.

In cases in which a child has a severe psychological or physical disability, the trusts should probably be continued for longer periods of time, perhaps for the remaining life expectancy of the child. In such cases, the structuring of their trust to qualify as a Supplemental Needs Trust, which is expected to continue for the life of the child, should perhaps also be considered. If grandchildren are to inherit the assets, the same factors that were considered with respect to the payment of inherited wealth to young children should be considered—how, when, and to what extent grandchildren should be paid any inherited wealth. This analysis should include whether the grandchildren's inheritance should be paid to them directly, or paid indirectly for their benefit through some form of trust vehicle. In the case of grandchildren, the preferences and financial security of the grandchild's parent—especially the parent who is the client's child—should be considered.

Comprehensive Estate Planning

Once clients are ready to integrate their retirement distribution planning with their estate plan, they should appreciate how by applying successive layering of estate planning strategies—systematically ceding a little bit of control over their assets in order to achieve ever-increasing estate tax savings—they can significantly reduce their overall potential estate tax liability. They should be made to realize they can take the process as far as they would like to go, even reaching a point where no estate taxes will be due, or where all estate taxes due will be paid from pre-arranged non-estate sources (most notably, insurance proceeds) payable either directly to their children or indirectly through payments to trusts established for the benefit of their children. If clients have strong philanthropic goals, a zero-estate-tax plan can also be achieved through certain charitable gift-giving strategies. These strategies were discussed in Chapter 8.

Clients need to see that the estate planning process is not simply a goal-line stand against an unrelenting government. In truth, the exact amount of estate taxes which will be due on their death is entirely a matter of their choice. Because there are virtually no limits on the amount of insurance coverage individuals can obtain on their lives, the amount of their ultimate estate tax liability can be entirely pre-funded through adequate insurance coverage, assuming that insurability issues are not a factor and assuming further that the clients have the requisite assets to pay the yearly insurance premiums. Similarly, charitable gifting, either before death or at death can also be used to reduce the value of the taxable estate to a level at which there will be no estate taxes due.

In many instances, it can truly be said that the family picks the level of estate taxes that will be due, either through the level of planning they have implemented prior to death or, more commonly, through their lack of planning. After the client has grasped this concept, the advisor should then begin to discuss the specific estate tax-saving devices and techniques which are available.

Unlimited Marital Deduction

The Internal Revenue Code provides an unlimited estate tax marital deduction to married couples who leave assets to each other on their death. The use of the unlimited marital deduction is probably the single most important estate planning strategy. If each spouse is an American citizen, regardless of who dies first, and regardless of the level of their wealth, all of the assets of the first spouse to die can be left to the survivor with no estate taxes due at the first death.

Unified Credit Amount

The next most important estate planning strategy involves the use of the Unified Credit Amount. (As noted earlier, the Unified Credit Amount is also known as the "Applicable Exclusion Amount," the "Credit Shelter Amount," the "Exemption Equivalent Amount," and the "Applicable Credit Amount.") As a result of the passage of the Taxpayer Relief Act of 1997, the Unified Credit Amount has

Table 11-1. Unified Credit Against Estate Tax

In the case of decendents dying, and gifts made, during	Amount of estate or gift exempt from tax
1998	$625,000
1999	$650,000
2000 and 2001	$675,000
2002 and 2003	$700,000
2004	$850,000
2005	$950,000
2006 or thereafter	$1,000,000

risen from $600,000 in 1997 to $675,000 in 2000 and 2001, and is scheduled to continue to rise until it reaches $1 million by the year 2006. There are currently several proposals before Congress to increase the Federal Unified Credit Amount to $1 million prior to the scheduled 2006 date. In addition, it is expected that, in the near future, legislation will be passed which raises the Federal Unified Credit Amount to a level considerably higher than the $1 million threshold amount established in the Taxpayer Relief Act of 1997. The progress of each of the various pending bills will be tracked with great interest by all advisors in this area.

Most wealthy clients have by now read numerous articles and attended several seminars dealing with the effective use of the Unified Credit Amount, and are familiar with the concept. This strategy allows individuals to leave a certain amount of their assets to non-spouse beneficiaries with no federal estate tax liability. A standard strategy recommended by virtually all legal and estate advisors is for the couple to retitle their assets, so that $675,000 (the amount corresponding to the Unified Credit Amount for 2000 and 2001) shown in Table 11–1 will be owned individually by each spouse. The $675,000 amount is then placed in a trust upon the death of the first spouse to die. The trust is typically a testamentary trust found in the Will of the first spouse to die, although a Credit Shelter Trust can be contained in an *inter vivos* trust. In a properly structured Credit Shelter Trust, the surviving spouse can receive income for life from the trust assets. Upon the surviving spouse's death, the principal amount of the trust is not included in his or her gross estate, but instead passes directly to the beneficiaries free from all estate taxes. An example will explain how this works:

> **Example:** Paul and Anne, a married couple, own assets aggregating $1,350,000. Were Paul to die (in 2001) leaving his entire estate to Anne, no estate tax would be due, owing to the operation of the unlimited marital deduction. However, on Anne's death (in 2001) an estate tax would be due to the extent that her estate exceeded $675,000 (the Federal Unified Credit Amount for 2001). The estate tax on her $1,350,000 estate would be $270,750.
>
> However, if Paul had established a Credit Shelter Trust in his Will for the benefit of Anne in the amount of $675,000, on his death, the trust would be funded with $675,000. There would be no estate tax due on Paul's estate, because the $675,000 amount used to fund the Credit Shelter Trust did not exceed the Unified Credit Amount applicable in the year of Paul's death. Anne would then own the remaining $675,000 of assets outright in her own name. On Anne's death, the $675,000 which she owned outright would pass directly to their children free from estate tax, due to the operation of the Unified Credit Amount in her estate. The $675,000 Credit Shelter Trust would also pass to the children free from estate tax, because that trust was entitled to a $675,000 Unified Credit Amount in Paul's estate and the value of that trust was not included in Anne's estate. In this way,

> both Paul and Anne would be able to utilize their Unified Credit Amount, thereby reducing estate taxes to the children to zero, and saving the children $270,750 in potential estate taxes.

It is a basic tenet of estate planning that, wherever possible, clients should make full use of their Unified Credit Amounts, including full use by both husband and wife. In integrating the estate plan with the retirement distribution plan, advisors should ensure that all federal and state estate tax credits and exemptions have been carefully considered and effectively utilized. This certainly includes the full use of the Unified Credit Amount by both spouses.

In some cases, particularly with professionals and executives, the advisor may find that the retirement assets make up the single largest asset in the client's estate. Moreover, clients may not have sufficient other assets in their estate to be able to fully utilize the Unified Credit Amount without having to use some or all of the qualified plan or IRA assets. In that case, the client may seek to fund the Unified Credit Amount, either partially or entirely with retirement assets. However, the use of retirement assets to fund a Credit Shelter Trust immediately brings up two important tax issues that must first be considered and weighed.

The first issue has to do with the use of pre-tax assets in a Credit Shelter Trust. Pre-tax retirement assets may be used to fund the Unified Credit Amount shelters assets from estate taxes that will, at some point, be subject to income taxes. The ultimate beneficiaries of the Credit Shelter Trust will, therefore, not be in a position to enjoy 100 percent of the value of the assets in the trust, because they will lose a certain percentage of those assets to income taxation. As a result, the value of the estate tax shelter is reduced by the amount lost in income taxes. For instance, if the beneficiaries were to withdraw the full $675,000 amount from an IRA that was being used to fund a Credit Shelter Trust, they would net only $405,000 of the asset, *after* a 40 percent loss to income taxes. Accordingly, $270,000 ($675,000 minus $405,000) of the $675,000 Credit Shelter Amount was lost to income taxes, and, on the death of the second spouse to die, only $405,000 would be exempted from estate taxation. In contrast, using all after-tax assets to fund a Credit Shelter Trust shelters the full value of the Unified Credit Amount from subsequent estate taxes.

The second issue has to do with the effective use of the income in respect of a decedent (IRD) deduction. Using retirement assets to fund a Credit Shelter Trust will result in a loss of the IRD tax deduction. This concept may be difficult for both advisors and clients to fully understand. When federal estate taxes are paid on IRD items, a corresponding federal income tax deduction becomes available. The deduction is computed based on the portion of the federal estate taxes which were attributable to the IRD item. The IRD deduction is then used to reduce the income tax bite on the IRD item. Qualified plan and IRA assets qualify as IRD assets. When they are sheltered from estate tax, the IRD deduction is lost. The deduction is lost because no federal estate tax had been due in the first estate. Because no federal estate tax had been due, no deduction becomes available for the payment of federal estate tax. The client cannot take a deduction for an amount that was not paid.

> **Example:** Dr. Dexter has a stronger bias against estate taxes than he does against income taxes. The bulk of his net worth consists of retirement assets. He has carefully quantified the amount of retirement assets he wants to pass along to his children and grandchildren to equal his Unified Credit Amount. The rest of his retirement assets are to go to his wife. This strategy accomplishes his first goal in estate planning—passing the right assets to the right people in the right manner, without the imposition of any estate taxes being due in his estate. If the amount of retirement assets that he wanted to pass along to his children and grandchildren had been considerably larger, it would have exceeded the Unified Credit Amount in his estate, causing an estate tax to be due on his death. This was the very possibility that he was trying to avoid.
>
> In implementing this strategy, Dr. Dexter sacrificed a portion of his second goal—income tax reduction—by using pre-tax rather than after-tax assets to fund his Unified Credit Amount. However, he reasoned that the grandchildren would be in a low income tax bracket for many years to come and would not be likely to itemize deductions on their personal income tax returns. Given these facts, the value of the IRD deduction to the

grandchildren did not seem worth the trade-off of the loss of an immediate reduction in estate tax liability by funding his Unified Credit Amount with retirement assets. The estate tax savings would have been lost because there were no other assets available to fund the Unified Credit Amount. Many clients whose retirement assets make up a large percentage of their total net worth may reach the same conclusion as did Dr. Dexter.

Although the IRD deduction is a valuable tool in reducing income tax liability to recipients of certain qualified plan and IRA benefits, the IRD rules themselves remain complicated and, in some respects, unclear. Moreover, IRS pronouncements in this area have not been especially helpful in resolving certain recurring IRD issues. However, an example should help clarify some of the details.

Example: David has estate assets sufficient to put his estate into the 55 percent marginal federal estate tax bracket. The estate contains an IRA worth $1 million. This means that the IRA asset will generate $550,000 in federal estate taxes upon his death. David reasons that the IRD deduction which will be available to his beneficiaries should, therefore, reduce the amount of the IRA asset which is subject to federal income tax to $450,000 ($1 million minus $550,000). At a 40 percent marginal federal income tax rate, $180,000 of the $450,000 net IRA asset remaining should go to the IRS by way of income taxes due on that asset when the IRA is paid to his heirs, leaving $270,000 of the original $1 million IRA asset payable to his beneficiaries. This analysis has produced a total tax shrinkage of 73 percent of the value of the IRA asset, a truly upsetting result. However, the above example has *understated* the level of tax erosion.

David's tax advisor then informs him that the federal government allows state governments to receive as much as 16 percent of a decedent's taxable estate, which would otherwise be due to the IRS, depending on the size of the estate. This allowance is known as the

"Credit for State Death Taxes." Since the payment of this amount represents a windfall to each state, with no extra estate taxes due from their citizens, each state eagerly claims this credit amount whenever it is applicable. David computes that, upon his death, the state in which he lives will be entitled to claim 16 percent of his IRA as their State Death Tax Credit. David's tax advisor then explains to him that the IRD deduction which will be available to his heirs is *only* available on amounts payable in estate taxes to the federal government, and is not available with respect to any estate taxes which are paid to any state government.

Based on this latest information, David redoes his computations, this time using the correct formulas. Of the $1 million in retirement assets, federal estate taxes methodology will account for only $390,000 ($550,000 minus the $160,000 payable to the state). Therefore, on his death, the IRD deduction amount will be only $390,000, with income taxes due on the remaining $610,000. At a 40 percent marginal income tax rate, the income tax bite comes to $244,000. That leaves only $206,000 of the original $1 million IRA asset, after all federal and state estate taxes and income taxes have been paid. The shrinkage has suddenly got bigger—it is now more than 79 percent.

One may ask why the shrinkage became larger or, stated another way, why the IRD deduction become smaller. The answer is that the IRD deduction applied only to the federal estate taxes. Even though the overall estate tax attributable to the retirement asset was at a 55 percent rate, only 39 percent (out of 55 percent) represented federal estate taxes, which were paid. The remaining 16 percent represented state estate taxes.

IRD Calculation

Income taxes are due on IRA distributions only as distributions are received. However, without proper planning, many IRAs are required to be entirely distributed at the IRA owner's death, thereby triggering the full income tax liability and the full use of the IRD tax deductions. However, if a multigeneration IRA strategy had been implemented, the IRA would be paid out over many years, perhaps over 50, 60, or even 70-plus years. In that case, income taxes due on the IRA payment would be deferred, with a portion of the IRD deduction recovered in each year. If the multigeneration IRA strategy is followed, each year the heirs will receive their portion of the Required Minimum Distribution payments and will pay their share of income taxes due thereon. Under the Proportionate Method for recovering the IRD deduction each year, a proportionate amount of the 39 percent IRD tax deduction will be applied to each year's distribution. Once the full IRD deduction has been recovered, the remaining IRA distributions will be fully taxable to each beneficiary without the ability to off-set further income tax liability by any further IRD deduction.

The above analysis has highlighted one crucial estate and retirement distribution planning issue: the monitoring and tracking of the IRD deduction each year to ensure that it is used by each beneficiary to reduce his or her income tax liability in each year in which it is available to the beneficiary. Surprisingly, many accountants are unaware of the IRD deduction, do not routinely ask their clients questions that will elicit sufficient information to determine whether the deduction is available to them in any given year, and do not have either administrative or computer systems in place to track and monitor this important deduction. Nor does the IRS especially alert practitioners to the possible availability of this deduction. The IRS does not have a separate line on the 1040 form, or on any of its schedules, for the deduction. Instead, the deduction is to be aggregated with other deductions on Schedule A, "Itemized Deductions," under "Other Miscellaneous Deductions" and labeled as "Federal estate tax on income in respect of a decedent."

Even more troubling, though, is that the IRS rules developed for calculating the IRD deduction apply in only two circumstances—when the full IRD is covered in a single year and when all IRD is received in even installments over a period of years. The authors are aware of no rules or formulas that the IRS has as yet developed for calculating the IRD deduction when IRD is received in uneven amounts over many years or for multiple beneficiaries, yet these are each scenarios that will doubtless occur in the context of most multigeneration IRAs. In such a case, IRD will likely be only a portion of the overall distribution. One portion of the distribution would, therefore, generate an income tax deduction as income in respect of a decedent, while the other portion would not. The total amount available to be recovered as the IRD income tax deduction is known, based on the prior estate tax calculations. However, a complete list of the acceptable methodologies for recovering the IRD deduction each year has never been issued by the IRS, nor has the IRS ever listed proposed recovery methods for the IRD deduction which it considers not to be acceptable. Until this problem is cleared up by IRS legislation, regulation, ruling, or case precedents, most accountants will probably continue to use either a Proportionate Recovery Method or a FIFO (first in-first out) in computing the recovery of the IRD amounts. At least each of these two recovery methods has a basis somewhere in the tax law.

Qualified Domestic Trusts

For non-citizen spouses, a different trust mechanism is available to defer estate taxation until the death of the second spouse to die. This trust mechanism is known as a Qualified Domestic Trust (Q-DOT). As noted earlier, the federal government is usually content to wait until *both* husband and wife have died before exacting the federal estate tax. When the surviving spouse is not a United States citizen, however, the fear is that the surviving spouse will return to his or her home country and die, with the family wealth being taxed in the surviving spouse's native country, thereby escaping U.S. estate tax.

The tax code addresses this issue in two ways. The first way is to deny an unlimited marital deduction to the non-citizen surviving spouse. In this way the issue of estate taxes will often have to be addressed by the family unit on the death of the *first* spouse to die, and cannot be deferred until the death of the second.

The second way in which this issue is handled is by allowing the non-citizen surviving spouse a marital deduction but only in those limited instances in which the inherited assets which otherwise were to be payable to the surviving spouse are instead held in a Q-DOT. One of the requirements of a Q-DOT is that at least one trustee of the trust must be a United States citizen or domestic corporation. An additional Q-DOT rule is that not more than 35 percent of the assets in the Q-DOT can be invested in real estate located outside of the United States. A third Q-DOT rule requires that when a principal distribution is made from the Q-DOT, the United States trustee is required to withhold and pay a portion of the amount of the distribution to the federal government as representing the deferred federal estate taxes which were due from the first estate. This rule prevents wholesale distributions of assets from the Q-DOT *without* the federal estate tax being paid that otherwise would have been due in the first estate. The last general rule applicable to Q-DOTs is that the executor of the decedent's estate must elect to treat the inherited property as a Q-DOT.

Certain additional and stricter rules apply if the value of the assets in the Q-DOT exceeds $2 million. There are also provisions that apply in the event that the surviving spouse subsequently becomes a United States citizen. Under those circumstances, once citizenship has been obtained, the Q-DOT can be ended, with outright distribution to the surviving spouse of all of the assets in the trust *without* the imposition of any federal estate tax. The idea behind this rule is that if the individual has become a United States citizen by that time, he or she will in all likelihood remain in the United States until their death, with their assets subject to federal estate tax at the time of their death.

The Q-DOT rules are quite involved and can be found in Internal Revenue Code §2056A and the regulations thereunder. The Q-DOT rules also contain special sub-rules in the event that retirement assets are to be inherited by the surviving spouse. It is interesting to note that those rules, under certain circumstances, will allow the marital deduction in those cases in which the assets are left in the shelter of the retirement vehicle and have not been paid into the Q-DOT. A fuller discussion of the various Q-DOT rules and their applicability to retirement assets is beyond the scope of this text.

Annual Gift Tax Exclusion

Just as most clients will recognize the existence of the Unified Credit Amount and its use as an estate tax deduction strategy, most clients will also be familiar with the use of the $10,000 annual gift tax exclusion amount. The government grants each individual the right to make $10,000 in gifts annually, and as indexed for inflation, to as many individuals as they want, without reducing their lifetime Unified Credit Amount. By using this annual gifting strategy, clients may be able to pass a significant portion of their estate to their heirs during their lifetimes, significantly reducing the estate tax liability which otherwise would have been imposed on their estates.

The value of this right to make any number of tax-free $10,000 gifts per year should not be underestimated. A couple with three children, six grandchildren, and three sons-in-law, or three daughters-in-law, each year could make $240,000 in totally non-taxable gifts ($10,000 times 12 times 2). Over a ten-year period of time, the couple could pass $2,400,000 of their assets to their heirs on a totally tax-free basis ($240,000 times 10).

Perhaps less well known, however, are the gift tax exclusions available for the payment of the tuition and medical expenses of an individual. As in the case of the $10,000 annual gift tax exclusion amount, this gift tax exemption applies regardless of the familial relationship between the donor and donee. Accordingly, this exemption would apply to the payment of tuition and/or all medical expenses by parents for their children, by grandparents for their grandchildren, by uncles and aunts for their nieces and nephews, by godfathers or godmothers for the benefit of their godchildren, or in fact by any individual for the benefit of any other individual. A limitation of this rule with respect to the payment of tuition expenses is the fact that the exemption does not apply to payments made to cover room and board. Accordingly, if a grandchild is enrolled in an Ivy League school with a yearly tuition, room, and board cost of $30,000, grandparents who had paid the full $30,000 amount would be able to exclude only the portion of the $30,000 payment that was attributable to tuition, but not that portion attributable to room and board.

Many college students live off campus and pay for their own food. Colleges are well aware of these developments, and of these gift tax exemption rules, and structure their payments each year in such a way that tuition constitutes the bulk of the yearly required bill, with a much smaller portion of the yearly bill attributable to room and board. In addition, a family member wishing to take advantage of this additional gift tax exemption would still be able to make a $10,000 non-taxable gift to the student in the year in which the tuition payment had been made without using up any portion of their Unified Credit Amount.

> **Example:** Zachary, grandson of Arthur and Lenore, has been accepted to an Ivy League school. The yearly cost to attend is $30,000, of which $24,000 is allocated to tuition, with $6,000 allocated to room and board. Arthur and Lenore can pay the $24,000 tuition amount directly to the school and are entitled to a gift tax exemption for the entire amount. If they choose, they can *also* each make $10,000 non-taxable gifts each year for the benefit of Zachary. In this way, they can provide funds to pay the $6,000 room and board charge, saving Zachary's parents that expense and leaving $14,000 to go to Zachary over and above the yearly $30,000 education cost. Each of those payments could be made by Arthur and Lenore without using up one dollar of their federal Unified Credit Amounts.

The tax laws, therefore, force each client to make a choice between continued control over their assets on the one hand and gifting strategies and estate tax reduction on the other. For many clients there will be two significant emotional hurdles to overcome before gifting strategies can be implemented. First, what if they will need the money later? If they attempt to retain any control over the gifts, the goal of estate tax reduction may be compromised. Second, will a gift of unearned income prove detrimental to the character formation and professional development of the heirs?

A client may want to maximize his or her annual gifting program, but may lack the cash or other assets to do so. Each year that goes by and annual non-taxable gifts have not been made is a year in which the client has lost an opportunity to reduce his or her overall estate and, therefore, to save on estate taxes. As pretax money, retirement assets cannot be gifted. However, suppose the retirement asset's growth has been unexpectedly large in a recent years. Why not take additional distributions each year from the retirement asset, pay the income tax, and gift the net amount remaining, so that maximum annual gift giving can be achieved? With this strategy, the client will have given up further income tax deferral on the retirement asset and will have incurred a current income tax liability on the extra IRA distributions. However, by making non-taxable gifts, the client has reduced the value of his or her overall estate, provided the heirs with a valuable economic benefit, and reduced overall estate taxes.

The Crummey Powers

As noted above, individuals are allowed to make gifts of $10,000 annually to any number of individuals of their choosing, without incurring any federal gift tax and without using up any of their Federal Unified Credit Amount. The $10,000 exemption, however, is available only for gifts of present interests. If gifts have been made into a trust and the enjoyment of the gift by the beneficiaries is, therefore, to be postponed until the future, the annual $10,000 gift tax exclusion is denied and the value of the gift then reduces the Federal Unified Credit Amount that is then available to the donor. The ultimate effect of the reduction of the individual's Federal Unified Credit Amount is higher estate taxes on their death.

However, many years ago, clever tax practitioners devised a strategy in which a gift into a trust could qualify for the annual $10,000 gift tax exclusion amount, despite the deferred date on which the beneficiaries of the trust would actually benefit from the gift. The scenario they devised was to transfer $10,000 into a trust, giving the trust beneficiary the immediate right for 30 days to elect to withdraw the $10,000 amount. The educated beneficiary knew not to exercise that right. The right to withdraw the $10,000 amount then expired, and the $10,000 stayed in the trust. Next year another $10,000 contribution was made to the trust and another election afforded to the beneficiary, who similarly opted not to withdraw that year's contribution. This went on year after year, with significant assets accumulating in the trust. Because in each instance the beneficiary had been given the immediate right to receive in cash the full yearly contributions made to the trust, the argument was that each gift, although not made outright to the beneficiary, nevertheless constituted a gift of a *present* interest and was thus eligible for the annual

$10,000 gift tax exclusion. This opinion eventually prevailed after subsequent litigation with the IRS in a case involving the Crummey family. Accordingly, this technique is now known as the "Crummey Powers."

Many trusts, especially life insurance trusts, have been funded using these Crummey Powers. In each instance, amounts up to the annual gift tax exclusion amount are contributed to the trust. Beneficiaries are then provided with written election forms, advising them of the dates and amounts of the contributions to the trust, their withdrawal rights associated with the contributions, and the dates on which their withdrawal rights must either be elected or will lapse. The beneficiaries are also given election forms on which they can elect to receive or not to receive the contributions. As in the case involving the Crummey family, educated beneficiaries know not to elect to withdraw any of the yearly contributions.

Life Insurance

Many clients have purchased life insurance coverage to provide financial protection to their heirs in the event of their death, to equalize estate assets, and to provide liquidity for the payment of estate taxes upon their death. These uses of life insurance are well known to most clients. However, less well known is the fact that the insurance proceeds will be included in the individual's estate if the policies are owned by the individual. This fact may come as a great surprise to many clients, who, for the most part, do not view insurance on their life as one of their assets. After all, the policy's death benefit is not generally available to them while they are alive, as are their other assets. Moreover, estate taxes can eat up approximately one-half of the value of the insurance death benefit. Many clients have been advised to place their life insurance in an irrevocable trust to avoid this problem. However, if the trust has been poorly drafted, or if the insured has retained certain incidents of ownership in the policy, the problem may still remain. One such test of policy ownership is whether the insured has retained the ability to change the beneficiary on the policy. If the beneficiary can be changed by the insured, the policy will be considered as if it were still owned by the insured and will be included in his or her estate, notwithstanding the fact that the trust is now its legal owner.

Generation-Skipping Exemption

Generation-skipping transfer trusts (GST) can be used to save substantial transfer tax costs, while passing an individual's assets to his or her grandchildren. For decades, a GST trust was one of the most widely used estate conservation techniques for the wealthy. These trusts existed even before estate taxes and before estate planning was a professional discipline. In those early days, the goal of the GST Trust was to preserve family wealth from generation to generation, protecting it against any ill-conceived financial plans or excessive spending habits of any of the descendants. However, once estate taxes became law—even at the low level of taxation that had existed initially—these trusts began to play a crucial role in protecting family wealth for succeeding generations from the ravages of the estate tax.

Earlier tax law allowed individuals to establish GST trusts by Will or by gift. Estate or gift tax was first paid on the amount going into the trust. The yearly earnings from the trust were used to provide the children with a lifetime income interest, while the principal was left intact, accumulating in value for the grandchildren, great-grandchildren, or even more distant levels of descendants. When the trust eventually dissolved, all the principal, as well as the growth, was distributed to the descendants free of any further estate or gift tax. The assets in the trust had, therefore, been subject to tax only once, at the time of the creation of the trust, even though several generations of descendants may have enjoyed the benefits derived from the trust. Often the assets which had been transferred in the trust and preserved from one generation to the next consisted of stock in a family business. In many cases, those family businesses had gone on to become multinational corporate giants.

Current tax law looks askance at GST Trusts. Since 1986, outright transfers which skip generations and GST Trusts have been subject to a special generation-skipping tax of 55 percent. The tax imposed is *in addition* to the regular estate tax, which is assessed on the asset transferred. Fortunately, each individual is afforded a \$1 million generation-skipping exemption (indexed by inflation, and up to \$1,030,000 in 2001). Accordingly, if both husband and wife wish to avail themselves of the full \$1 million GST exemption amount, together they can transfer up to $2 million ($2,120,000 in 2001) in assets to their grandchildren, great-grandchildren, or more remote descendants, free of the GST tax. In GST Trusts, clients can place reasonable controls on their grandchildren's (or more remote descendants') access to the funds during the individual's minority and beyond, while providing enough discretionary control in the hands of the trustees of the Trust, as to not create a stranglehold on the trust assets or unduly limit the family's financial freedom during the period in which the GST Trust is in existence.

Are retirement assets the right assets to use to take advantage of the GST exemption? For many clients without sufficient other assets to utilize the full GST exemption, the answer is likely to be yes. If these clients had already decided that the multigeneration IRA approach using their grandchildren as their IRA beneficiaries made sense to them from both a personal and financial perspective in implementing such a strategy for their retirement assets, they were already creating a vehicle similar in form and effect to that of the typical trust. The $1 million GST exemption allows them to effectuate such a strategy with a significant portion of their retirement assets, while sheltering these assets from the imposition of any estate taxes in the estates of their children.

Using retirement assets to fill up the generation-skipping transfer exemption amount presents the same type of problem as discussed in the case of using retirement assets to fill up the Unified Credit Amount. The main problem once again has to do with using before-tax dollars to fill up an exemption amount. If $1 million in retirement assets is transferred into a GST Trust for the benefit of a grandchild, once the assets have been paid out of the GST Trust to the grandchild, there will be a significant income tax loss attributable to the payout, with the grandchild not having netted the benefit of the full $1 million inheritance.

If, on the other hand, the GST Trust had been funded with all after-tax non-retirement assets, the distribution to the grandchild of 100 percent of the assets in the trust would result in the grandchild's netting the full $1 million. It is for this reason that the use of retirement assets to fill up a GST Trust should be very carefully weighed.

However, the advisor may find that in many instances there are no other assets available which the clients can use to fund the GST Trust. Accordingly, under those circumstances, the retirement assets should be used for this purpose. However, any time retirement assets are to be used to fund a GST Trust, great care should be taken that the beneficiary designation forms and Retirement Asset Will each have been properly constructed. These documents should specify that only the Required Minimum Distribution amounts are to be paid out each year from the shelter of the retirement asset (absent a year in which there is some financial emergency affecting the beneficiaries). This will allow the retirement asset to continue to grow in value each year, and will not cause the decimation of that asset by being so inarticulately drawn as to require that all amounts to be immediately paid out of the retirement asset on the individual's death.

Moreover, if retirement assets are to be used in conjunction with a GST Trust, the trust has to be structured for this specific purpose. First, all of the assets in the trust should qualify for the GST exemption. This means that the value of the assets in the GST Trust should not exceed the available GST exemption amount. The trust should be established during the lifetime of the client, specifically by the individual's Required Beginning Date, so that the right beneficiary designations and life expectancy elections will have been timely made.

If the client has one IRA and wants to designate a trust for the benefit of the grandchildren as beneficiary of the IRA, the children should not also be named as beneficiaries of that trust. The life expectancy to be used for Required Minimum Distribution purposes whenever a trust has been named as a beneficiary of a retirement asset is the life expectancy of the oldest beneficiary of the trust. Naming a child as one of the beneficiaries of the GST Trust will force the child's life expectancy, and not that of the grandchildren, to be used for Required Minimum Distribution purposes. If it is the client's intention to benefit a child or children with a portion of the retirement assets, then in that case the IRA should be split into two IRAs, with one established for the benefit of the children and one established for the exclusive benefit of the grandchildren. The grandchildren's IRA collectively should be funded with $1 million in retirement assets. In this way, the $1 million GST exemption amount can be fully realized. The remaining retirement assets will go into the IRA in which the children have been designated as beneficiary.

If it is the intention of the IRA owner to leave all IRA assets to the spouse, with the spouse doing a spousal rollover at the time of the IRA owner's death, the separation of the IRA assets into two IRAs can take place after the death of the IRA owner. Naturally, this strategy will work only if the spouse has survived the IRA owner. A properly drawn simultaneous death clause in the Retirement Asset Wills may be necessary in order to increase the probability of that outcome.

When a husband and wife have died virtually at the same time, if the wife had been named as beneficiary of the IRA and had predeceased the husband owner by even a few minutes, a spousal IRA will not be permitted. Similarly if the couple has truly died at the same time, or if it cannot be established which one had died first, the simultaneous death provisions contained in the state law applicable to those individuals may apply. State law under those circumstances may indicate that the spouse has either not survived, or had survived but with respect to only one-half of the value of the IRA asset.

Generally, it is the client's intention under such circumstances to have it assumed that the spouse of the IRA owner has survived. To ensure that the client's wishes in this regard are carried out, a simultaneous death provision should be included in the Retirement Asset Will applicable to the IRAs. The Retirement Asset Will shows that, in the case of a simultaneous death, the spouse of the IRA owner is deemed to have survived. With that documentation in place, the wife will be deemed to have survived, and the spousal rollover will be capable of being effectuated. Once the spousal rollover IRA has been established, the GST Trust should be designated as beneficiary for the first $1 million of IRA assets. The balance of the IRA amounts should then be established in a second IRA in which the children outright, or trusts established for their benefit, have been named as beneficiaries.

Alternatively, the client, by the Required Beginning Date, could have established separate multigeneration IRAs under the Participant Direct Approach previously described, naming each grandchild as the sole beneficiary of each separate IRA. The IRAs for each grandchild beneficiary would total $1 million, in the aggregate, with the GST tax exemption claimed for these IRAs collectively. While requiring multiple IRAs, this strategy creates maximum income tax deferral, since the actual age of each individual grandchild could then be used for life expectancy purposes rather than being required to use the life expectancy of the oldest grandchild.

One administrative problem associated with this approach is that the IRAs will probably continue to grow during the owner's lifetime. Once the IRAs collectively have grown to an amount in excess of the GST tax exemption amount, all excess amounts will be subject to the GST tax. Since GST tax rates are set at 55 percent, in addition to the regular estate taxes due on those assets, the cumulative tax bite will be considerable.

The solution to this potential problem involves careful monitoring of the growth of the IRAs each year and making corrective distributions from the IRAs or corrective trustee-to-trustee transfers from the IRAs at regular intervals during the IRA owner's lifetime, in amounts sufficient to ensure that at no time will the total value of the IRAs collectively exceed the available GST tax exemption amount.

Family Limited Partnerships

Another device which families may use to transfer wealth effectively is the family limited partnership. As noted earlier, one of the major objections clients raise against transferring their assets while they are still alive is the perceived risk inherent in surrendering control over those assets. However, what if there were a device in which the client could transfer assets while retaining control over those assets? Surely, such a device would be welcomed by individuals who, with the security of continued control over their assets, would then be able to easily commit to substantial transfers of their wealth, thereby significantly reducing their projected estate tax liability.

One such device is the use of a family limited partnership. Under this approach, the couple creates a company (the partnership) and transfers the ownership of their investment assets, stocks, bonds, real estate, etc. into the company. They then create two classes of ownership interests in the partnership. The first class is a general partnership ownership interest which carries with it voting rights. The second class of ownership interest is a limited partnership interest which carries with it no voting rights. Typically, 6 percent general partnership interests and 94 percent limited partnership interests are then created (totaling 100 percent), with the husband and wife sharing half of the interest in each class. The parents then make gifts of substantial portions of the limited partnership interests to their children and/or grandchildren.

Because the transfer of those interests confers no voting rights on the children or grandchildren, the value of the limited partnership interests that the children and grandchildren receive will be subject to a substantial minority interest discount to reflect the lack of voting rights. Similarly, it would be extremely difficult for the children or grandchildren to sell their limited partnership interests on the open market for a price approaching the net asset value of their underlying percentage interests. Accordingly, in valuing the limited partnership assets transferred to the children and grandchildren, the value of the gift will also be afforded a substantial lack of marketability discount.

In this way, parents can transfer significant portions of their wealth to subsequent generations through discounted giving without using up all of their Unified Credit Amount (and, therefore, subjecting the gift to current gift taxes) and without even using up their $10,000 annual gift tax exclusion amounts.

> **Example:** Mitchell and Rita establish a family limited partnership with $2 million of their investment-grade assets. They create a 6 percent general partnership interest in the partnership and a 94 percent limited partnership interest. Mitchell then owns a 3 percent general partnership interest and a 47 percent limited partnership interest, with Rita owning the same percentage amounts of general and limited partnership interests. Each of them then transfers 46 percent of their 47 percent limited partnership interest to their children. Based on a net asset value of partnership assets of $2 million, the 46 percent interest looks like a transfer, which will be valued at $920,000 ($2,000,000 times 46 percent). However, when a cumulative 30 percent discount for minority interest and lack of marketability is applied to the $920,000 figure, the resulting net value of the gift is reduced to only $644,000 ($920,000 times 70 percent), less than the federal Uni-

fied Credit Amount available in 2001. Accordingly, no current federal gift tax will be due on the transfers, and Mitchell and Rita will have retained their right to use their $10,000 annual gift tax exclusion amounts for that year.

As general partners of the partnership, Mitchell and Rita will control all partnership investment decisions each year and will control also whether and to what extent any partnership distributions are to be made in any given year. All of these decisions will be made without any vote of any of the children, even though the children collectively own 92 percent of the partnership.

In this way, Mitchell and Rita will have transferred $1,840,000 ($920,000 times 2) of the value of their assets to their children, while still maintaining virtually 100 percent control over those same assets.

Other Strategies

Other efficient strategies that advisors may use to transfer wealth usually involve the use of some form of discounting device for purposes of valuing the amount of the gift made. Those devices typically are keyed into the life expectancy of the donor, the life expectancy of some other individual, or a term of years.

If a donor makes a current gift of $100,000, the value of the gift received by the donee would be $100,000. However, if the donor had wanted to make a gift of $100,000 to the donee, with the *enjoyment* of the gift by the donee deferred until some later date, for instance, five, ten, or 15 years in the future, or until the end of the life expectancy of the donor, in determining the value of the gift to the donee, the future value of the assets transferred would have to be reduced to their present value. Present value, in turn, would be dependent on both the length of the period that the beneficiary would be required to wait before enjoyment of the gift would begin and the interest rate that would be applied to the gift during the waiting period.

When such strategies are applied with respect to the transfer of the ownership of a personal residence, the strategy takes the form of the adoption of a Qualified Personal Residence Trust, or QPRT. When this strategy involves the use of assets *other* than personal residences, Grantor Retained Annuity Trusts (GRATS), or Grantor Retained Unitrusts (GRUTS) are used.

A detailed discussion of the application of each of these types of trusts is beyond the scope of this book. However, each depends on the use of a life expectancy or fixed-period factor to discount the present value of the gift to its current value in order to reflect the deferred enjoyment date by the donee. An important point for the advisor to remember, however, is that where a donor wishes to avail him- or herself of one of these strategies, unless the QPRT, GRAT, and GRUT rules have been strictly followed, no discount is afforded to the value of the gift. From a tax point of view, the gift will be considered as if an outright transfer had been made of the entire value of the asset, rather than a transfer in trust of the value of the remainder interest in the asset. Therefore, the advisor would do well to ensure that each of the requirements set forth in the Internal Revenue Code and regulations thereunder with respect to the use of QPRTs, GRATs, and GRUTs have been strictly complied with. Any deviation from those rules will result in the value of the gift being taxed at its 100 percent current value without any discount. This in turn may cause a transaction, which was thought to be entirely exempt from any current gift tax, to be subject to significant current federal gift taxes.

Charitable Giving

Linking charitable planning and estate planning can yield substantial estate tax reductions—sometimes resulting in a zero estate tax liability. Some significant income tax benefits may also be associated with this approach. The key to understanding this estate planning opportunity is to view the charitable disposition not solely for its philanthropic or educational purposes, but also as another tool available to substantially reduce overall estate taxes. See Chapter 8 for a detailed discussion of charitable giving and retirement distribution strategies.

The Use of Trusts in Integrating Estate Plans and Retirement Distribution Plans

The estate plans of many clients may already incorporate the use of trusts to realize certain planning objectives. Trusts allow clients to retain indirect control over their assets at a time when they have been forced to give up direct control due to death or disability or to further some estate tax, income tax, or retirement distribution strategy. Because the client may have previously created *inter vivos* trusts, he or she may want to use those trusts in the retirement distribution planning process, believing it logical to name those trusts as the beneficiaries of the IRA assets.

As discussed earlier, this desire for efficiency can cause serious problems when planning a multigeneration IRA distribution strategy. Using a trust as a beneficiary of retirement assets carries with it certain inherent risks. A trust which fails to follow certain trust rules is deemed to have no life expectancy, meaning that the life expectancies of the individual beneficiaries of a non-qualifying trust cannot be used for the purposes of determining Required Minimum Distributions payable each year. The inability to use the life expectancies of the trust beneficiaries can seriously disrupt a retirement distribution strategy by requiring the immediate payment of all retirement assets.

The rules applicable to trusts named as designated beneficiaries of retirement assets were first enunciated in proposed IRS regulations issued in 1987. At that time, one of the rules required the trust to be irrevocable by the Required Beginning Date in order for the life expectancies of the trust beneficiaries to be used for Required Minimum Distribution. This rule was intended to promote certainty in the individual's choice of beneficiary by the Required Beginning Date. A revocable trust that could be amended at any time to change the beneficiaries makes designated beneficiary elections uncertain, and certainty is needed if the designated beneficiary and life expectancy elections are to be set at the individual's Required Beginning Date. Therefore, under the prior trusts, if a trust were still revocable at the individual's Required Beginning Date, the individual was considered as having no designated beneficiary, thus eliminating the individual's opportunity to use joint life expectancy in determining Required Minimum Distribution.

In 1997, amendments were made to the proposed regulations that modified the irrevocability rule. Under these new rules, trusts can remain revocable until an individual's death, even where death occurs after the individual's Required Beginning Date. Therefore, the fact that a trust remains revocable during an individual's entire lifetime will not now prevent the life expectancies of the beneficiaries of that trust from being used for Required Minimum Distribution purposes.

In promulgating the proposed regulations in 1987, the IRS faced the issue of how to handle trusts which had been named as beneficiaries of retirement assets. The IRS could have adopted a strict conduit theory with respect to the use of such trusts. Under a strict conduit theory, all Required Minimum Distribution amounts payable each year into a trust from a qualified plan or IRA are required to be distributed out of the trust that same year to the trust beneficiaries. In this way, the trust would act as a mere conduit for the yearly retirement assets payments and could never be used to accumulate any Required Minimum Distribution amounts paid in any year. Such a view was flatly rejected by the Internal Revenue Service. In Question H-7 of the 1987 proposed regulations, the IRS indicated as follows:

> A payment by a plan after the death of the employee will not fail to be treated as a distribution for purposes of section 401(a)(9) solely because it is made to an estate or a trust. As a result, the estate or trust which receives a payment from a plan after the death of an employee need not distribute the amount of such payment to the beneficiaries of the estate or trust in accordance with section 401(a)(9)(B).

Based on a plain reading of this rule, practitioners for many years felt comfortable structuring trusts which were to serve as designated beneficiaries of retirement assets in virtually any way they wanted. Accordingly, some trusts were prepared which did, in fact, serve as mere conduits for the Required Minimum Distribution amounts that were payable into the trust each year, in that the amounts received by the trust each year from the retirement asset were paid out that same year to the trust beneficiaries. Other trusts were prepared in which all of the Required Minimum Distribution amounts payable into the trust each year were accumulated each year in the trust, and eventually paid out at some later date to the trust beneficiaries. Still other trusts were designed in which a combination of these two approaches was taken.

Until relatively recently, each of these approaches was thought to be acceptable. However, an IRS Private Letter Ruling in 1998 cast significant doubt on the use of trusts as designated beneficiaries in those cases in which the trust does not serve as a mere conduit. In those cases in which the current trust income beneficiary is either not paid the full amount of the Required Minimum Distributions out of the trust each year or does not have the ability to direct that said payments be made, there is a chance that the life expectancies of the contingent beneficiaries of the trust will be required to be taken into account for purposes of computing the Required Minimum Distribution amounts which are due each year. In those cases in which the contingent beneficiaries are individuals who are all younger than the primary beneficiaries, the requirement to consider those additional life expectancies will present no problem. However, in those cases in which any of the contingent beneficiaries is *older* than the primary beneficiaries, the result of including those extra life expectancies will be a *shortening* of the payout period and *higher yearly* Required Minimum Distributions payments.

More significant, however, are those instances in which any of the contingent beneficiaries is a non-individual—for instance, an estate or a charity. The aggregation of the life expectancy of a human being with the zero life expectancy associated with an entity (for instance, a charity or an estate) results in no life expectancy capable of being used. This forces all distributions while the individual is alive to be payable based solely on the individual's own life expectancy. In addition, were the individual to die prior to his or her Required Beginning Date, all benefits would be required to be paid out of the retirement asset by December 31 of the calendar year containing the fifth anniversary of the individual's death. Therefore, whenever a trust is to be designated as a beneficiary of retirement assets, advisors should take great care to either draft the trust so that the trust serves as a mere conduit for the yearly Required Minimum Distribution payments or, if it does not, that the life expectancies of the contingent beneficiaries which must be taken into account are considered in each case, and are used in place of the life expectancies of the primary beneficiaries if the contingent beneficiaries' life expectancies are shorter than those of the primary beneficiaries. Advisors should also be sure that no non-individual entity is named as a primary beneficiary of the trust, or named as a contingent beneficiary of the trust in those cases in which the life expectancies of contingent beneficiaries are required to be taken into account.

Estate As Beneficiary

This approach will trigger the application of the Five-Year Rule where the IRA owner has died before the Required Beginning Date. Often the advisor will find that the client has named his or her estate as the beneficiary of the retirement assets. Naming an estate as beneficiary is the most common error in retirement distribution planning today. By naming the estate as beneficiary, an individual, at his or her Required Beginning Date, loses the ability to base yearly Required Minimum Distribution on a two life expectancy payout. In addition, in those cases in which the individual has died before reaching his or her Required Beginning Date, the Five Year Rule applies. Under the Five-Year Rule, all benefits must be paid out of the shelter of the plan or IRA by December 31 of the calendar year containing the fifth anniversary of the individual's death. Under this approach, the real value of the retirement assets—extended tax deferral—has been largely wasted. See Chapter 12 for a fuller explanation of the Five-Year Rule.

However, suppose a client intends to use a testamentary trust as the beneficiary for the retirement assets. How is this to be accomplished? If the individual names the state as beneficiary, the testamentary trust in the Will will be funded, just as the individual had wanted. However, in structuring the beneficiary designation in that way, the individual has lost the ability to use the life expectancies of the trust beneficiaries for Required Minimum Distribution purposes. The better way to designate a testamentary trust as the beneficiary of retirement assets is to list the beneficiary as "Robert Smith as Trustee of the John Smith Trust contained in Article Five of the Last Will and Testament of Paul Smith dated July 1, 1999." In this way, the testamentary trust will be the beneficiary of those retirement assets, but, most importantly, the life expectancies of the trust beneficiaries will be capable of being used for Required Minimum Distribution purposes. Under this approach, the individual has preserved the right to base yearly distributions on a two life expectancy payout beginning at his or her Required Beginning Date, and has avoided the application of the Five-Year Rule, if death should occur *before* their Required Beginning Date.

Credit Shelter Trusts

Credit Shelter Trusts can be funded with retirement assets in one of three ways. One way is to establish a separate IRA in which the Credit Shelter Trust has been designated as beneficiary, with care being taken to ensure that on a year-to-year (or more frequent) basis the amount in that separate IRA does not exceed the Federal Unified Credit Amount applicable for that year.

A second way to fund a Credit Shelter Trust with retirement assets is to have one IRA, with a formula clause in the beneficiary designation form or Retirement Asset Will which specifies that a portion of the assets in the IRA, up to the available Federal Unified Credit Amount for that year, is to be paid into the Credit Shelter Trust, with the balance payable to another beneficiary, usually the surviving spouse.

Either method is acceptable. The first method will require yearly (or more frequent) adjustment of the amounts in the IRA accounts. This may necessitate trustee-to-trustee transfers throughout the year to maintain the IRA at the right level. The second method will tie in the life expectancies of two sets of beneficiaries—the beneficiaries of the Credit Shelter Trust portion of the IRA and the beneficiaries of the non–Credit Shelter Trust portion. Because of the complexity of the second approach, many IRA Custodians may reject this approach.

By the time of the retirement asset owner's death, considerable growth may have swelled the retirement assets beyond the amount of the Unified Credit Amount applicable in that year. If the assets in the IRA upon the individual's death are larger than the Unified Credit Amount, the Credit Shelter Trust may be structured to allow the excess amount to flow outright to the surviving spouse. In this way, a marital deduction can be secured for the balance of the IRA over the Unified Credit Amount. This approach avoids estate taxes on the death of the first spouse to die.

In order to accomplish this, a formula which ties into the remaining available Unified Credit Amount should be contained in the beneficiary designation form or Retirement Asset Will. The formula used should always be a fractional share formula and not a pecuniary amount formula. A fractional share formula would read, "X percent of my estate payable to . . .," while a pecuniary formula would read, "$Y amount payable to . . . " The reason to avoid the use of a pecuniary formula is that an extremely technical income tax rule may require the acceleration of income on IRD items used to fund a pecuniary bequest in a Will. This situation could arise if a Will provision were to state, "The first $675,000 of assets shall be used to fund the Credit Shelter Trust in my Will." If non-IRD assets are used to fund that trust, there is apparently no problem, while if IRD items are used to fund that trust there may be a problem. As noted earlier, retirement assets are IRD items. Accordingly, if $675,000 in retirement assets were used to fund that pecuniary bequest, the full $675,000 amount might be subject to income tax immediately, even though the assets may still reside in the shelter of the qualified plan or IRA and are not even scheduled to be paid out of the shelter of that tax-favored vehicle until some later point.

Apparently, the problem does *not* arise when the assets are not first paid into the Will, or are not first paid through a Will into a trust, but instead are paid *directly* into the trust by operation of the designation of beneficiary form. Procedures for avoiding this potential problem have never been fully developed by the Internal Revenue Service. There are several views among top practitioners in the area about which devices will avoid the potential problem. Some practitioners doubt that this potential problem exists at all under any circumstances. Nevertheless, advisors should keep in mind that a potential problem may arise when retirement assets are used to fund a pecuniary bequest in a Will. Wherever that possibility exists, great care should be taken to be sure that the issue of the acceleration of retirement income has been properly addressed.

A third way in which retirement assets can be used to fund a Credit Shelter Trust is through the use of a disclaimer (or renunciation, as the device is known under certain State laws). With the disclaimer approach, an individual typically designates his or her spouse as the beneficiary of 100 percent of the retirement asset. An *inter vivos* Credit Shelter Trust or testamentary Credit Shelter

Trust is then listed as the contingent beneficiary, in the event that the spouse survives, but then disclaims (or renounces) a portion or all of the retirement assets. Typically the children are designated as the next contingent beneficiaries, who will be paid the retirement assets if the spouse predeceases the retirement asset owner.

On the death of the retirement asset owner, the surviving spouse determines the maximum amount needed to fully utilize the Unified Credit Amount in the estate of the first spouse to die. If, for example, non-spouse beneficiaries are to receive $100,000 in Will bequests or in testamentary substitutes (for instance, as surviving joint tenants on bank or brokerage accounts), the surviving spouse after the first spouse's death would determine that $575,000 would be the optimum amount to be used to fund the Credit Shelter Trust ($675,000 Unified Credit Amount for 2001 minus $100,000). If the retirement assets consisted of an IRA worth $2,000,000, the spouse, within nine months of the IRA owner's death, would disclaim $575,000 of his or her interest in the IRA, electing to receive the balance of the $1,425,000 in IRA assets ($2,000,000 minus $575,000) as the primary beneficiary of those assets. The $1,425,000 amount would then be paid outright to the spouse, who would then roll over that amount into a spousal roll-over IRA, naming new beneficiaries and making new method of payment elections at that time. The $575,000 portion of the IRA which had been disclaimed would then be used to fund the Credit Shelter Trust.

This approach is extremely popular because it preserves flexibility in the hands of the surviving spouse and obviates the need to keep one or more IRAs exactly at the remaining available federal Unified Credit Amount at all times. Under this approach, the maximum federal Unified Credit Amount is used up in the first estate, with a marital deduction taken for any amounts in excess of the federal Unified Credit Amount, thus ensuring that no estate taxes will be due in the first estate. The one drawback to this approach could arise in the case where a surviving spouse has refused to disclaim any portion of the retirement asset. If this situation were to occur, a portion or all of the federal Unified Credit Amount in the estate of the first spouse to die will have been wasted, thereby eventually increasing overall estate taxes to the family unit upon the death of the surviving spouse. Accordingly, advisors should probe the underlying psyche of both the client and spouse in order to assess whether there are any hidden emotional issues which might arise in the future that would prevent the surviving spouse from disclaiming the proper portion of the retirement asset, or whether the spouse currently harbors any secret reservations about carrying through with this approach upon the death of the first spouse. Assuming, however, that these potential obstacles can be overcome, clients may find this to be a particularly desirable approach.

Q-TIP Trusts

So far, this chapter has covered the topic of the use of trusts as designated beneficiaries of retirement assets, many of the rules applicable to their use, and the conduit theory as it applies to trusts. However, when dealing with Q-TIP Trusts, a new and secondary level of issues rise. (See Chapter 8 for a discussion of Q-TIP Trusts in the context of charitable dispositions.)

A Q-TIP Trust is a device used to provide a surviving spouse with an income interest in an asset, while preserving to the original owner of the asset the right to dispose of the asset in the way in which the original owner sees fit, without any control over that asset by the surviving spouse. It is typically used in the context of a second (or third or fourth) marriage. In the typical Q-TIP Trust situation, the asset owner wants the spouse to have an income interest in the asset, but wants his or her own children (typically those from their first marriage) to receive that asset upon the death of the spouse. Upon the asset owner's death, the assets are placed in a Q-TIP Trust, which usually is contained in the individual's Will, but can also be contained in an *inter vivos* trust. The Q-TIP Trust, because it follows certain IRS rules, is eligible for a marital deduction in the individual's estate. The Q-TIP Trust pays the surviving spouse a lifetime annual income from the trust. On the death of the surviving spouse, the assets in the Q-TIP Trust are paid to the children of the asset owner. Because the surviving spouse had no right to the principal amount in the Q-TIP Trust, the surviving spouse cannot direct how and to whom the assets in the Q-TIP Trust will be paid upon his or her death. Through the use of the Q-TIP Trust, the asset owner has, therefore, retained control over the asset after his or her death, has secured a marital deduction for the value of the Q-TIP Trust in his or her estate, and has provided a lifetime annual income interest for the benefit of the surviving spouse, while *still* being able to direct who is to receive the assets in the Q-TIP Trust upon the death of the surviving spouse.

In order for the assets in the Q-TIP Trust to be eligible for the federal estate tax marital deduction, the Q-TIP Trust must follow certain rules set forth in Internal Revenue Code §2518. The failure to follow *any* of those rules will result in the loss of the marital deduction. This, in turn, will subject those assets to estate tax in the estate of original asset owner, to the extent that the value of the estate then *exceeds* the Unified Credit Amount applicable for that year, after all other estate tax deductions and credits have been taken into account.

One of the rules that Q-TIP Trusts must follow in order to be eligible for the federal estate tax marital deduction is that all of the income earned on the Q-TIP Trust must be paid each year to the surviving spouse and not to anyone else, with no person having the power to appoint any part of the property in the Q-TIP Trust to anyone other than the surviving spouse during the surviving spouse's lifetime.

Another Q-TIP Trust rule is that the surviving spouse must be given the right to have nonproductive assets in the Q-TIP Trust made productive. This issue could arise were the assets in the Q-TIP Trust to invest exclusively in vacant land. Vacant land typically generates no income each year and, in fact, represents a cash drain, in that real estate taxes and other upkeep expenses must be paid each year to maintain the property. A surviving spouse who is the beneficiary of a Q-TIP Trust which had invested exclusively in vacant land can compel the Trustees of the Trust to sell the land, investing the sales proceeds instead in cash, stocks, bonds, or other assets which will generate *realized* earnings, dividends or profits each year.

Whenever a Q-TIP Trust has been designated as the beneficiary of retirement assets, *two* separate and distinct sets of rules must be followed. In the first instance, the Q-TIP Trust rules contained in Internal Revenue Code §2056(b)(7) and the regulations thereunder must be followed in order for the marital deduction to be available. In addition, the Required Minimum Distribution rules set forth in Internal Revenue Code §401(a)(9), §403(b)(10), §408(a)(6) and §408(b)(3) and the regulations thereunder must *also* be followed in order for the retirement assets to retain their qualified tax-exempt status and for the taxpayer to be able to avoid the 50 percent excise tax under Internal Revenue Code §4974 for the failure to have received the Required Minimum Distribution payments in any year.

Practitioners faced with the issue of how to coordinate the various Q-TIP Trust rules with the Required Minimum Distribution rules were provided with guidance from the Internal Revenue Service in 1989 with the issuance of Revenue Ruling 89-89. Specifically, the question had been asked: What amounts are required to be distributed to the surviving spouse each year in order to conform with *both* sets of rules? Under the Q-TIP Trust rules, the spouse is required to be paid all of the income *realized* from the Q-TIP Trust each year, while under the Required Minimum Distribution rules the surviving spouse each year is required to receive that year's Required Minimum Distribution amount. The Ruling answered this question by requiring the surviving spouse to receive, each year, the *greater* of the *realized* trust income for the year *or* the Required Minimum Distribution amount due for that year. The ruling also stated that, in order for the federal estate tax marital deduction to be available, the retirement asset *and* the Q-TIP Trust must *both* conform to the Q-TIP Trust rules. An example will explain how this rule works.

> **Example:** Michael had designated a Q-TIP Trust which he had established for the benefit of his wife, Sandy, as the beneficiary of his $1 million IRA. By his Required Beginning Date, he had elected a dual life expectancy payout using a term certain method of payment for both his life expectancy and the life expectancy of Sandy, who was 67 at the time. That designation called for a 22-year payout of his IRA benefit.
>
> Michael died two years later. In the year of Michael's death, the Q-TIP Trust was required to receive 1/20th of the amount in the IRA, in order to satisfy the Required Minimum Distribution rules for that year. Therefore, if the amount in the IRA account as of December 31 of

the prior year was $1 million, the Required Minimum Distribution rules would be satisfied if the IRA paid $50,000 ($1,000,000 divided by 20). However, if the IRA had earned 8 percent in realized income tax the year of Michael's death, the Q-TIP Trust rules would require that $80,000 be paid from the IRA that year into the Q-TIP Trust, with the $80,000 amount then distributed that year out of the Q-TIP Trust and paid to Sandy.

Each year both the Q-TIP Trust rules and the Required Minimum Distribution rules must be satisfied in order for the payment arrangement to work. Therefore, each year the IRA must pay out all of the realized income earned from the IRA that year or the yearly Required Minimum Distribution amount, whichever is greater. In the above example, the amount necessary to satisfy the Required Minimum Distribution rules for that year was $50,000. However because the IRA had realized income of $80,000 for that year, the greater of $50,000 or $80,000 was required to be paid from the IRA that year. Since the greater of $50,000 or $80,000 is $80,000, $80,000 is required to be paid out of the IRA to the Q-TIP Trust for that year, with the $80,000 amount then required to be paid out of the Q-TIP Trust to Sandy that year. If instead the IRA had realized earnings of only $40,000 for that year, under the applicable rules, the greater of the $50,000 amount necessary to satisfy the Required Minimum Distribution rules or the $40,000 amount in realized earnings would require that $50,000 be paid out of the IRA that year into the Q-TIP Trust.

However, in this example the full $50,000 amount would *not* be required to be paid out of the Q-TIP Trust to Sandy that year. Instead, only $40,000 would be required to be paid to her that year. The reason for this is that the IRS, in *rejecting* the conduit theory of Required Minimum Distributions, does *not* require that any Required Minimum Distribution amounts paid out of an IRA each year into a trust be paid out of the trust that year to the trust beneficiaries. Because $40,000 was the amount of the IRA's *realized* earnings for that year, the payment of that amount *first* into the Q-TIP Trust and *then* out to Sandy satisfied the Q-TIP Trust rules for that year, with *both* the IRA and Q-TIP Trust complying with those rules. Therefore, the payment of $50,000 from the IRA to the Q-TIP Trust, and then the payment of only $40,000 from the Q-TIP Trust to Sandy, satisfied *both* the Q-TIP Trust rules and the Required Minimum Distribution rules for that year.

It should be noted that the above example represents a somewhat simplified version of the facts that an advisor may see on a typical case. It assumed that there were no other assets in the Q-TIP Trust, other than amounts which had been paid into the Q-TIP Trust that year from the IRA. Had there been other assets in the Q-TIP Trust that year, the Q-TIP Trust rules would have required that all of the realized earnings on those *other* assets be paid out of the Q-TIP Trust to the surviving spouse that year, *in addition to* the surviving spouse being paid all of the realized earnings on the IRA asset for that year. Alternatively, the Q-TIP Trust rules would have been satisfied had the surviving spouse been given the right each year to *elect* that such payments be made.

In 2000, the Internal Revenue Service substantially modified its prior position regarding the interaction between the various Q-TIP Trust rules and the Required Minimum Distribution rules. The change was contained in Revenue Ruling 2000-2. In that Ruling, the Internal Revenue Service indicated that although the amount paid from the retirement asset to the Q-TIP Trust each year must still include, at a minimum, the Required Minimum Distribution amount which was due for that year, it no longer requires the surviving spouse to *receive* all of the realized income earned from the retirement asset each year. Instead, as long as the surviving spouse is given the right each year to compel the Trustees of the Q-TIP Trust to pay to the surviving spouse, each year, all of the realized income earned by both the retirement asset and by the Q-TIP Trust, the Q-TIP Trust rules will have been satisfied. Under this new ruling, the surviving spouse is free to decide each year to keep in the Q-TIP Trust all of the realized income from the retirement asset. Under this new ruling, the Required Minimum Distribution amounts must still be paid each year from the retirement asset into the Q-TIP Trust. However, now with the spouse's approval, no additional amounts are required to be paid each year from the retirement asset into the Q-TIP Trust, and any assets paid into the Q-TIP Trust can remain there, continuing to accumulate in value each year. In Revenue Ruling 2000-2, the IRS indicated that taxpayers wishing to continue the scenario outlined in Revenue Ruling 89-89 would be allowed to do so, without any problem. In that ruling, the *greater* of the Required Minimum Distribution amounts or the realized earnings on the retirement asset were required to be paid out of the retirement asset each year into the Q-TIP Trust, with the realized earnings on *both* the retirement asset and on the other assets in the Q-TIP Trust required to be paid out to the surviving spouse each year.

Obviously, this new ruling will allow much greater flexibility in estate and retirement distribution planning. It will allow for greater potential growth in the retirement assets, by no longer requiring that all realized earnings on the retirement assets be paid out each year. This is especially important in the first several years of Required Minimum Distributions, when the realized earnings on the retirement assets may far exceed the Required Minimum Distribution amounts due for that year. However before practitioners begin celebrating the liberalization of this rule, they should bear in mind the fact that a Q-TIP Trust has generally been created in the context of a blended family situation, involving a second (or third or fourth) spouse and children from prior marriages. The fact that, under the revised ruling, a spouse can decide in any given year *not* to receive the realized income on the retirement assets or on the other Q-TIP Trust assets is *not* a guarantee that the surviving spouse will make that choice. One can easily imagine a second marriage situation in which the IRA owner has died and the second spouse is at odds with the individual's children. Will the second spouse in that case decide to leave in the Q-TIP Trust each year all of the realized earnings on the retirement assets and on the other assets in the Q-TIP Trust, allowing all of those assets to pass to the deceased spouse's children on the surviving spouse's death? Probably not. Therefore, advisors should realize that the liberalization of this rule will be helpful only in certain situations, usually involving elderly spouses of first marriages, where the Q-TIP Trust had been established as an asset protection device, designed to shield those assets against an elderly spouse's mental or physical infirmity. However, in those cases involving second, third, or fourth marriages, any benefits associated with the liberalization of this rule may prove to be more illusory than real.

Obviously, many IRA Custodians will not be equipped to deal with these kinds of detailed issues, complications, and computations, and accordingly may not even permit Q-TIP Trusts to be named as IRA beneficiaries. However, where the IRA Custodian permits this type of designation, the IRA beneficiary designation forms, Retirement Asset Will and Q-TIP Trust must each be carefully crafted, to ensure that both the Q-TIP Trust rules and Required Minimum Distribution rules have been followed. If the requisite Q-TIP Trust rules are not followed, the federal estate tax marital deduction will be lost. Similarly, if the Required Minimum Distribution rules are not followed, the client will be subjected to the 50 percent excise tax, to the extent that Required Minimum Distributions amounts have not been taken.

In addition to its inherent complexity, there are certain other drawbacks associated with naming a Q-TIP Trust as beneficiary of a retirement asset. We noted earlier that, whenever a spouse has been named as beneficiary, the spouse, regardless of his or her age, can roll over the distribution into a new IRA, making *new* beneficiary elections and *new* method of payment elections at that time. This Spousal Rollover Approach permits a multigenerational payout of retirement benefits *after* the original retirement asset owner and spouse have each died. The surviving spouse as beneficiary can also avail himself or herself of the Spousal Deferral Rule, in which the commencement of benefit payments from a retirement asset can be deferred until the year in which the retirement asset owner would have reached age 70½, had he or she not died. With the Q-TIP Trust approach, the surviving spouse will lose the ability to roll over the retirement asset into his or her own IRA, and distributions will be required to start by December 31 of the calendar year following the calendar year of the first spouse's death. The surviving spouse's life expectancy will then have to be used to compute the Required Minimum Distribution amount payable each year. The ability to use the combined life expectancies of the surviving spouse *and* the children and grandchildren will be lost forever.

A final problem associated with naming a Q-TIP Trust as the beneficiary of a retirement asset has to do with the likely payout over time of Required Minimum Distribution amounts and realized retirement asset earning amounts. During the early years, the Required Minimum Distribution amounts will probably represent a fairly low percentage of the retirement assets, based on the age of the spouse at the time of the IRA owner's death. However, in later years, as the retirement distribution denominator reduces, the distribution percentage becomes larger, increasing yearly Required Minimum Distribution each year. Eventually, advisors may find that, if the surviving spouse lives long enough, the application of both the Q-TIP rules and the Required Minimum Distribution rules have caused all benefits to have been paid out of the IRA into the Q-TIP Trust and, if the Q-TIP Trust has not been properly worded, for all assets in the Q-TIP Trust to have been paid out of the Q-TIP Trust to the surviving spouse. When this situation involves a second marriage and the goal of the original retirement asset owner was to preserve the principal of the retirement asset for the benefit of his or her children, this planning objective will have been entirely defeated by the prior payout to the surviving spouse. Advisors should, therefore, take great care when using retirement assets to fund a Q-TIP Trust and should thoroughly explain to their clients the possible consequences of certain payout scenarios, including ones in which the surviving spouse dies prematurely, but also including ones in which the surviving spouse survives to and perhaps beyond the end of his or her projected life expectancy.

As noted earlier, specific provisions must be included in the Q-TIP Trust for both the retirement asset and Q-TIP Trust to qualify for the federal estate tax marital deduction. Q-TIP Trust rules are often strictly monitored and enforced by IRS estate tax examiners. In those instances in which a marital deduction has been disallowed, the extra bite of estate taxes can be substantial. The disallowance of such potentially large amounts provides sufficient motivation to the IRS estate tax examiners to scrutinize the terms of beneficiary designation forms, Retirement Asset Wills, and Q-TIP Trusts to determine whether they have been prepared to assure compliance with each of the applicable Q-TIP Trust rules, thus entitling both the retirement assets and the Q-TIP Trust to be eligible for the federal estate tax marital deduction. If there is any set of circumstances under which those rules could be violated—for instance, any set of circumstances under which the surviving spouse would not be entitled to all of the income earned each year by the retirement asset and by the Q-TIP Trust—even if it was subsequently determined that the surviving spouse had been paid all of the income each year—the marital deduction can be disallowed. Practitioners are, therefore, advised to pay close attention to the various Q-TIP Trust rules and should proceed with extreme care when using retirement assets to fund a Q-TIP Trust.

Irrevocable Life Insurance Trusts

Clients may be tempted to name their previously established irrevocable life insurance trusts as the beneficiary of their retirement assets. However, the use of those trusts for that purpose may pose certain problems. Those trusts had typically been established by the clients years ago, primarily to provide cash to their heirs to pay the estate taxes due on the death of the second spouse to die. The life insurance death benefit allows other assets—such as the client's businesses, real estate, or collectibles—to be preserved so that they will not have to be sold at sacrifice prices to pay the estate taxes. The irrevocable nature of these trusts, and the specifications that went into the drafting of those trusts at the time, might not be compatible with the client's current goals with respect to multigenerational retirement distribution planning. The many safeguards which the clients may now want to build into the trust to protect the income stream from the retirement assets, which may be payable for decades to come, cannot now be added to a preexisting irrevocable trust, because, by its definition, the trust is irrevocable and cannot be amended or changed.

Death of the IRA Owner

So far we have discussed the different types of trusts that can be named as beneficiaries of retirement assets and the relative advantages and disadvantages of using each different approach. It is important to bear in mind, however, that in each case the retirement asset owner is entirely free to change any of those designations in any year, even if the individual is then beyond his or her Required Beginning Date. The only negative effect associated with a change in beneficiary designation occurring *after* the individual's Required Beginning Date is a possible increase in subsequent Required Minimum Distribution amounts. However, once the individual has died, the beneficiary designations in effect at the time of the individual's death become irrevocable.

If the retirement asset is an IRA, at the individual's death the IRA is no longer owned by that individual. Instead, the designated beneficiary, in effect, becomes the owner of the IRA. Where the beneficiary is the individual's spouse, the spouse can roll over the IRA into a new IRA, making *new* beneficiary choices and *new* method of payment elections at that time. However, where the beneficiary is someone *other* than the surviving spouse, or where the beneficiary is an entity (such as a trust), the IRA must remain in the decedent's name. The removal of the decedent's name from the IRA and the substitution of the name of the beneficiary in its place will be interpreted by the IRS as a complete distribution of the IRA, with all amounts in the IRA being currently taxable to the beneficiary. There will be no further tax-deferred growth of the asset, and the beneficiary will find that there is no way to get the assets back into the shelter of an IRA.

The questions then arise: If the beneficiary, following the IRA owner's death, *cannot* be listed as the owner of the IRA, how is the IRA Custodian to know that the IRA owner had died, and that the beneficiary is, therefore, now in charge of the IRA? How is this change of equitable ownership to be documented? The answer is that the IRA at that time should be retitled as an Inherited IRA. A preferable way to retitle the IRA as an Inherited IRA would be to change the name on the IRA to read as follows: "Martin Green, deceased, Inherited IRA for the benefit of Rose Green, as beneficiary." The descendant's's name has thus been left on the IRA, and no distribution has occurred.

Although the beneficiary is not permitted to roll the IRA over into another IRA or into a new IRA, the beneficiary is free at any time to *transfer* the IRA from one IRA Custodian to another, unless prohibited from doing so by the terms of the IRA Custodial Agreement. This can be accomplished by a direct "Trustee to

Trustee" transfer in which one IRA Custodian sends the funds or assets *directly* from the IRA in which they are now being maintained to a *new* IRA established with the *new* IRA Custodian. In a Trustee to Trustee transfer, at no time are any of the assets paid out of the IRA or paid to the beneficiary. The name on the IRA *after* the Trustee to Trustee transfer has been completed should still read the same, "Martin Green, deceased, Inherited IRA for the benefit of Rose Green, as beneficiary."

It is preferable to leave the decedent's Social Security number on the IRA. However, the IRA Custodian is required by law to report to the IRS each year distributions made during the year to the beneficiary. Accordingly, the IRA Custodian will need the beneficiary's Social Security number in order to comply with that reporting requirement. If the Inherited IRA has been properly retitled, the mere use of the beneficiary's Social Security number in connection with the IRA should *not* be interpreted by the IRS as a distribution of all of the assets in the IRA.

What happens then when an IRA owner has died and a trust had been named as the designated beneficiary? The answer once again is that the IRA should be retitled as an Inherited IRA, this time along the following lines: "Martin Green, deceased, Inherited IRA for the benefit of the Rose Green Trust dated June 1, 1995, as beneficiary." The omission of the decedent's name and the substitution of the name of the trust on the IRA will once again be considered by the IRS as a complete distribution of all of the assets in the IRA. In that case, the trust will be fully funded. However, all further opportunity for tax-deferred growth will have been lost, and the IRA will have become fully taxable.

How then does one fund a trust which has been named as the designated beneficiary of an IRA *without* causing a complete distribution of all of the assets in the trust? The answer is twofold. First, the IRA itself should be retitled as an Inherited IRA for the benefit of the trust, and as outlined above. Secondly, the IRA beneficiary designation form, Retirement Asset Will, and trust agreement should each be worded to allow all of the assets to remain in the shelter of the IRA, with only the Required Minimum Distribution amounts required to be paid out of the IRA each year. If each of those documents has been set up correctly, the trust will be "funded," even though all of the assets will still remain in the IRA.

An example will illustrate how this works.

> **Example:** Arthur has an IRA worth $500,000. He divides the IRA into two IRAs of $250,000 each. He designates two *inter vivos* trusts, one for each of his two grandchildren, Traci and Zack, as beneficiary of each separate IRA. Each trust has been designed and is administered in such a way that it qualifies as a "designated beneficiary" of each respective IRA. This means that Arthur is allowed to use the life expectancies of the primary beneficiaries of each trust for purposes of computing Required Minimum Distribution amounts which are due each year.
>
> Prior to his death, Required Minimum Distribution amounts are paid to Arthur each year based on the joint life expectancy of himself and the beneficiary of each separate trust. Due to the operation of the MDIB Rule, this requires payments to be made over a period initially determined to be 26.2 years. However, following Arthur's death, the MDIB Rule is no longer applicable. For each year thereafter, Required Minimum Distributions can be paid out based on the *actual* remaining life expectancies of each of his two grandchildren.
>
> Assume that Traci was ten and Zack six at the time that Grandfather Arthur had attained age $70^1/_2$. Grandfather Arthur dies five years later, when the grandchildren are 15 and 11, respectively. At that time each IRA is properly retitled as an Inherited IRA for the benefit of each respective trust.
>
> In computing Required Minimum Distributions due after Arthur's death, one must look to the life expectancy of the grandchildren determined when Arthur had attained age $70^1/_2$. At that time, the grandchildren's life expectancies were 71.2 and 75.6 years respectively. In the years following Arthur's death, the applicable divisors are now 65.7 years and 69.6 years respectively, because six years have now elapsed since the year Arthur atttained age $70^1/_2$. Accordingly, in that sixth

year, 1/65.7th of the amount in the IRA for Traci must be payable into the trust for the benefit of Traci, with 1/69.6th of the IRA for Zach.

Because the Internal Revenue Service has never adopted a strict conduit theory for the payment of Required Minimum Distribution amounts into trusts, the Required Minimum Distribution amounts can be accumulated each year in each trust for the benefit of each of the grandchildren until each has reached majority. At that point, each trust indicates that each yearly Required Minimum Distribution amount paid into each trust each year is to be paid out of each trust directly to each grandchild. Each trust ends when the grandchild/beneficiary reaches age 30. At that time, all amounts which had been paid into the trusts in each prior year and which are still in the trust are then paid out of the trust to each respective grandchild/beneficiary. Starting with the next year, the Required Minimum Distribution amounts due for that year are paid out *directly* to the grandchild/beneficiary, thereby bypassing the trust, which by that time had ended. Each *subsequent* year's Required Minimum Distribution is then paid directly from the IRA to each grandchild each year, until there are no assets left in the IRA to be paid. Presumably that date would be 71.7 years and 75.6 years respectively after Arthur's Required Beginning Date, assuming that in each year after Arthur's Required Beginning Date, first the Trustee of each grandchild's trust, and then each grandchild had withdrawn only the Required Minimum Distribution amounts due from his or her IRA.

The key to the multigenerational payout of the IRA benefits in the above example was that each document—the beneficiary designation form, the Retirement Asset Will and each trust itself—permitted the assets to remain in the shelter of the IRA, paying out only the Required Minimum Distribution amounts which were due each year. This was allowed because the two trusts which had been named as the beneficiaries of the IRAs were qualified as "designated beneficiaries." This allowed the life expectancies of each of the two grandchildren to be used for Required Minimum Distribution purposes, both *before* the IRA owner's death and afterwards. Had the trusts *not* qualified as "designated beneficiaries," benefits payable during the IRA owner's life would have been based on a single life expectancy payout, which, if paid on a recalculation basis, would have required all of the amounts in the IRA to be paid out by the December 31 of the calendar year immediately following the calendar year of the IRA owner's death—in effect, the death knell of each IRA. Had those benefits instead been payable based on a single life term certain method of payment, the maximum payout period would have been only 16 years, the original life expectancy of the IRA owner at age 70½. Contrast this with the 71.7 year and 75.6 year payouts which were used in the above example.

Accordingly, it is imperative, whenever a trust has been named as the beneficiary of retirement assets, for the trust to qualify as a "designated beneficiary." Once again, the five requirements which trusts must comply with in order to qualify as "designated beneficiaries" are as follows:

1. The trust beneficiaries must each be individuals, and not corporations, estates, charities, or nonqualifying trusts.
2. The trust must be irrevocable initially or, by its terms, must become irrevocable upon the death of the trust creator.
3. The beneficiaries must each be identifiable from the terms of the trust instrument.
4. The trust must be valid under state law.
5. A copy of the trust instrument must be provided to the plan administrator or IRA Custodian.

Failure to meet these requirements will mean that the benefits must be payable while the individual is alive and after his or her death, as if there were no designated beneficiary. However, if each of the above five rules *have* been followed, the trusts *will* qualify as designated beneficiaries, allowing for the multigenerational payout of the IRA benefits, which, in the above example, produced a stream of IRA distributions which lasted in excess of 70 years.

In the above example, until each grandchild reaches age 30, each year the Required Minimum Distribution amounts due from their IRAs will be paid into the Trust established for his or her benefit. The Trustee each year will have control over the IRA assets. If there are years in which a grandchild needs extra funds, the Trustee, under the terms of the designation of beneficiary forms, Retirement Asset Wills, and Trust agreements, will be able to withdraw additional funds from the IRA of that particular grandchild in the amounts needed. Those amounts may be considerably in excess of the Required Minimum Distribution amounts due for that year. Such a scenario could easily present itself in years in which a grandchild were to incur substantial college tuition expenses. The Trustee, in those years, would withdraw from the IRA of that grandchild an amount sufficient to pay the tuition expenses. From a mechanical point of view, what would happen in each of those years is that the Trustee would withdraw an amount from that grandchild's IRA, depositing that amount into the Trust established for that grandchild. The Trustee would then establish a reserve to pay the income taxes which would be due on that IRA distribution. The Trustee would then make the tuition payment with the *net* amount remaining after the anticipated tax payment had been subtracted from the gross amount of the IRA distribution.

A trust is entitled to a distribution deduction in the year in which a distribution has been made to a trust beneficiary or for the benefit of a trust beneficiary. The tuition payment would constitute an expenditure for which a distribution deduction would be available. This shifts the income tax liability on that amount from the trust to the grandchild. Accordingly, it may be a good idea for the Trustee to distribute to the grandchild the entire amount of the reserve which had been established for taxes. This will eliminate (due to the operation of the distribution deduction) any tax on the IRA distribution for that year at the trust level, where the income tax rates are presumably higher, and will shift the entire income tax liability to the grandchild level, where the income tax rates are presumably much lower.

By designating the grandchildren trusts as the IRA beneficiaries, the IRA owner will have created a scenario in which the retirement assets can be paid out over a period of more than 70 years to his grandchildren, allowing those assets to continue to grow in value each year on a tax-deferred basis for decades into the future. Until each grandchild reaches age 30, those assets will be protected by being paid into a Trust established for each grandchild, with the Trustee of each Trust having control over the IRA assets during that time. This means the Trustee has control over the investment of the IRA assets each year, and Trustee control over the amount of the distributions made from the IRA each year, but the Trustee is careful each year to withdraw from the IRA at least the Required Minimum Distribution amount due for that year. Once the grandchild has reached age 30, the Trust will end. At that time, Required Minimum Distribution payments will continue each year, but will then be made *directly* to each grandchild, and *not* into their respective Trusts. Each grandchild at that time will then gain complete control over their respective IRA assets. This means that each grandchild could then elect to close out his or her IRA, receiving a lump-sum payment for the entire amount in that IRA. This would end all further tax-deferred growth on that asset. However, by the time the grandchild has reached age 30, he or she should be mature enough to realize that it is in his or her best long-term interest to keep the IRA intact, withdrawing only the Required Minimum Distribution amounts each year or only those small amounts *in excess* of the Required Minimum Distribution amounts which the grandchild truly needs to live on.

CHAPTER 12
DEATH BENEFITS AND DISTRIBUTIONS BEFORE THE REQUIRED DATE

CONTENTS

12 DEATH BENEFITS AND DISTRIBUTIONS BEFORE THE REQUIRED BEGINNING DATE

The focus of this book so far has been on retirement distribution planning at the Required Beginning Date and afterwards. This chapter will focus on other options and rules governing the period before the Required Beginning Date.

Importance of Planning Before the Required Beginning Date

Many individuals are aware that they must make elections by the time they reach their Required Beginning Date (generally April 1 of the calendar year following the year in which they reach age $70^1/_2$) and that those elections will govern all subsequent distributions to them from their qualified plans and Individual Retirement Accounts (IRAs) for the remainder of their lifetime and after their death to their named beneficiaries. The individuals may also realize that those elections, once made, are irrevocable, in the sense that at the Required Beginning Date, no subsequent change in elections can lengthen the payout period or reduce Required Minimum Distribution amounts otherwise payable each year. Accordingly, many individuals take great care to ensure that they have made all of the proper elections by their Required Beginning Date, and that all elections have been properly documented.

Note: Readers should refer to the Introduction for a discussion of issues and concepts covered in Chapter 12 that may be affected by the IRS's issuance of the Revised Proposed Regulations governing Required Minimum Distributions and by the passage of EGTRRA 2001. These include: increased rollover opportunities; the determination of the beneficiary by December 31 of the year following the year of the individual's death; the elimination of irrevocable elections at the individual's Required Beginning Date.

On the other hand, there is no time limit for completing a retirement distribution plan before the individual's Required Beginning Date. Most individuals assume that they will survive until age $70^1/_2$ and thus reason that they can complete their retirement distribution planning on or shortly before that date. They do not realize that their untimely death could wreak havoc on an otherwise well-thought-out retirement distribution plan that has not yet been fully implemented.

These same individuals may have met with their attorneys and other estate planning advisors years earlier to have their Wills drafted and other estate planning documents adopted and estate planning devices implemented—with the retirement assets often having been overlooked by the attorneys or other estate planning advisors. This oversight may be due to the advisors' lack of information about the retirement assets or to the mistaken belief that the retirement assets will be entirely consumed before the individual's death. This lack of proper planning with respect to the retirement assets could spell the difference between a multi-generational payout of those assets for 40, 50, 60, or 70 years *after* the individual has died (with the retirement assets compounding ten to 15 times in the process) and a requirement to pay out all retirement assets shortly after the individual's death, thereby eliminating the possibility of future tax deferrals on those assets.

When dealing with a client who is in his or her 40s, 50s, or 60s, the retirement distribution planning specialist will often have to overcome the client's natural tendency to feel that there is plenty of time left to complete planning for retirement distributions. One effective way to overcome this hurdle is to ask the client, "Do you have a Will?" The client will typically answer, "Yes, I do." The retirement distribution planning specialist can then ask, "Why did you feel it was important to have a Will in place now, if you believe you will live at least until age $70^1/_2$?" The client will then usually say, "I thought it was important to have a Will in place now just in case I should die prematurely." The retirement distribution planning specialist can then point out that the client's answer is precisely why it is important for the requisite retirement distribution plan to already be fully implemented.

Often, retirement distribution planning is precipitated by a client's medical crisis. If the medical crisis is severe enough, the client may be physically or mentally unable to execute the necessary retirement distribution planning documents. Therefore, perhaps the most important retirement distribution planning document that should be in effect *before* an individual's Required Beginning Date is his or her Durable Power of Attorney. This document, if properly drafted, will allow the individual's representatives to make the appropriate choices of beneficiaries and method of payment options with respect to the individual's retirement assets, notwithstanding the individual's physical disability and/or mental incompetence. The topic of Durable Power of Attorney is discussed in Chapter 13.

Distributions Before the Required Beginning Date

A change in an individual's employment status often triggers a distribution from the qualified plan in which the individual had participated. Although the Employee Retirement Income Security Act of 1974 (ERISA), the Federal pension law, allows Plan Sponsors to keep a former employee's plan benefits until the former employee would otherwise have reached the Plan's Normal Retirement Age (typically age 65), most defined contribution plans (401(k) plans, profit sharing plans, and money purchase plans) pay out benefits to the participant soon after the participant's employment with the plan sponsor has ended. More and more defined benefit plans (especially those sponsored by closely held companies) are also paying out plan benefits soon after the participant's termination of employment, although they are not required to do so by law.

Individual Retirement Account Rollovers

Where the participant is not in immediate need of the plan benefits, the entire amount of the plan distribution should usually be rolled over into an IRA as a means of continuing tax deferrals. The law allows an individual who has received a plan distribution 60 days to roll over the distribution into an IRA, an Individual Retirement Annuity, or another qualified employee benefit plan. An individual who rolls over the distribution into an IRA or Individual

Retirement Annuity *after* the 60-day period has expired will have forever lost the chance to create a valid rollover. If the individual leaves the rollover distribution in the IRA or Individual Retirement Annuity *beyond* the due date (plus extensions) for filing his or her Federal income tax return for the year of the rollover, the distribution will be subject to a 6 percent penalty tax on excess contributions to an IRA. In addition, the 6 percent penalty tax will be asserted *each year* on the excess IRA contribution *until* the year in which it is withdrawn. Moreover, earnings on the excess IRA contribution will also be subject to the 6 percent excise tax each year until they too have been withdrawn (IRC § 4973).

Advisors should be aware that not all amounts received as plan distributions are eligible to be rolled over into an IRA, Individual Retirement Annuity, or another qualified plan. First, distributions from tax-sheltered annuities (403(b) plans) can be rolled over *only* into another tax-sheltered annuity (403(b) plan), IRA, or Individual Retirement Annuity and *cannot* be rolled over into a qualified plan. Similarly, distributions from qualified plans can be rolled over *only* into a qualified plan, IRA, or Individual Retirement Annuity and *cannot* be rolled over into a tax-sheltered annuity (403(b) plan). In addition, for the rollover to be valid, the distribution must have come from a *qualified* plan. If the plan had previously lost its qualified tax status (i.e., it no longer conforms to the requirements of IRC § 401(a) either in form and/or in administration), the rollover will not be permitted.

If the distribution from the qualified plan was made in cash, then the rollover should be made in cash as well. If the distribution has been made in kind (e.g., in stocks, bonds, mutual funds, or other assets), the individual may roll over the exact assets received as part of the distribution or sell those assets and roll over the net sales proceeds. The individual is not allowed to use a cash distribution to buy new assets and then to roll over those newly purchased assets. In addition, the individual is not allowed to sell and/or exchange the non-cash assets received as part of a distribution for new non-cash assets which are then rolled over into the IRA.

After-tax amounts which are returned to the participant cannot be rolled over into an IRA, Individual Retirement Annuity, or qualified plan. The after-tax items may include the P.S.-58 costs on life insurance purchased by the qualified plan (see Chapter 15 for a discussion of P.S.-58 costs and the recapture of those amounts). They may also include voluntary or non-deductible contributions which the participant had previously made to the qualified plan. After-tax amounts may also include amounts returned to the participant from a qualified plan due to problems associated with the language of the qualified plan itself or the way in which it is administered in practice. For instance, if the participant had made an excess contribution to a 401(k) plan (more than $10,500 for 2000), no portion of the excess contribution which had been returned to the participant would be permitted to be rolled over. Amounts received by the participant from his or her 401(k) plan as a hardship distribution are also ineligible for rollover treatment (IRC § 402(c)(4)(C)). If the participant in the past had defaulted on a plan loan, and the amount of the loan had previously been taxed to him or her, the participant is not permitted to roll over the amount of the plan distribution attributable to the previously taxed amounts. Similarly, if the entire plan had been disqualified, no part of the plan distribution received by the participant may be rolled over.

There are also at least two instances in which distributions from qualified plans *cannot* be rolled over, even where they represent all *before*-tax items. The first such case involves distributions which are Required Minimum Distributions—in other words, distributions which are required to be made under the Required Minimum Distribution rules set forth in the Internal Revenue Code (IRC § 401(a)(9), § 408(a)(6), or § 408(b)(3)) and for which a 50 percent excise tax (IRC § 4974) will be imposed, to the extent that the distribution has not been made. In addition, distributions which are payable over a specified period of ten years or more, or which represent a series of substantially equal periodic payments payable over a period measured by the life (or life expectancy) of the participant or the joint lives (or joint life expectancies) of the participant and designated beneficiary (IRC § 402(c)(4)(A)) *cannot* be rolled over, even where those amounts do *not* represent Required Minimum Distribution amounts. Virtually all other amounts received from qualified plans are eligible to be rolled over.

When Rollovers Should Be Made

Individuals who are interested in effecting the longest possible payout of their qualified plan benefits after their death may find themselves frustrated in achieving that objective if their retirement assets are held in a qualified plan at the time of their death. Many can large companies do not permit the multigenerational payout of plan benefits. Smaller companies that do permit the multigenerational payment of plan benefits may fail to be in existence for the requisite number of years (40, 50, 60, or 70-plus years) needed to complete all scheduled distributions. A closely held business controlled by the individual may come to an end at or shortly after the individual's death. In each instance, all benefits will be required to be distributed from the qualified plan. This requirement could spell disaster for the beneficiaries of those benefits, who may be forced to pay income taxes on the full value of the plan benefits soon after the individual's death.

An example will illustrate the devastating effect on a retirement distribution plan when the company that sponsors the qualified plan either terminates the plan or goes out of business.

> **Example**. Mark, a widower, owns a small company, the Ellicott City Patio Company, which manufactures patio furniture. The business has been in the family for years. It is Mark's expectation that, on his death, his two children, Benjamin and Emily, will continue the business for at least one or two more generations. Mark's company sponsors a 401(k) plan which allows Mark to pay out plan benefits following his death for the entire remaining life expectancy of Benjamin, the eldest of his two beneficiaries. It is Mark's expectation that, following his death, his two children will pay themselves only the Required Minimum Distribution amounts each year, thereby allowing his $500,000 account balance to grow ten to 15 times over Benjamin's remaining 40-year life expectancy payout. Mark had been told by his retirement distribution specialist that it is safer to roll over the 401(k) benefits into an IRA, because the IRA Custodian has perpetual life and the retirement distribution plan will not be at risk of premature termination due to the possible failure of the company to continue to sponsor the qualified plan in the future. Mark ignores this advice and keeps his entire $500,000 account balance in the qualified plan.

> Mark dies in 2000. Within two years of his death, Benjamin and Emily, while building up the value of the business tremendously, have opted to sell the company to a regional furniture company, which immediately terminates the 401(k) plan, causing all of Mark's benefits in the plan to be immediately payable in full to his two children. This act terminates all further tax deferrals on the retirement assets.

The above scenario would also have occurred had Benjamin and Emily *not* been successful in operating the family business, causing the business to cease operations within two years of Mark's death. In the first case, without a willing successor plan sponsor, the plan *must* come to an end and fully pay out its benefits. In this second case, it was the initial plan sponsor (the Ellicott City Patio Company) that went out of business, causing the plan to end prematurely.

All of this could have been avoided had Mark, prior to his death, rolled over the entire amount of his plan benefits into an IRA. Because of the perpetual life of IRA Custodians and the greater flexibility in payment options typically afforded to benefits in IRAs, it is usually the retirement vehicle of choice for individuals interested in implementing multigenerational retirement distribution planning. (See Chapter 4 for a more detailed discussion of the flexibility of an IRA.)

Individuals who would like to name several beneficiaries for their plan benefits, with each beneficiary's life expectancy used for purposes of determining yearly Required Minimum Distribution amounts, will find it nearly impossible to accomplish this objective while the assets are still held in a qualified plan. The IRS allows an individual's plan benefits to be paid out after his or her death, based on the beneficiaries' different life expectancies, but only if the participant had divided his or her account into separate accounts or separate subaccounts. Virtually no qualified plan or IRA permits or is administratively capable of creating separate subaccounts for each individual beneficiary of the participant. However, the separate account option can easily be implemented if thc participant rolls over his or her plan benefits into multiple IRAs, each of which names a different individual beneficiary as the primary beneficiary. In this way, on the individual's death, Required Minimum Distribution amounts can be based on the actual remaining life expectancy of each primary beneficiary of *each* separate IRA.

Generally, where the participant's employment with the plan sponsor is continuing, no distribution from the qualified plan would be made. However, it often is possible to amend the plan document to permit in-service distributions. This provision allows a participant to receive his or her entire interest in the plan and then to roll over the entire amount of that distribution into an IRA, even though the participant has not terminated his or her employment. In fact, the plan document could even permit the participant to continue to earn additional contributions and/or benefits in the plan, even though these additional accruals, too, could be rolled over into the IRA each year as they are earned by the participant. (See Chapter 4 for a more detailed discussion of in-service distributions.)

When Rollovers Should Not Be Made

Although in most instances it is advisable to make IRA rollovers of qualified plan distributions in order to implement a multigenerational IRA distribution planning strategy, there are certain instances in which the alternatives to an IRA rollover strategy should be seriously considered.

Creditor Protection Issues

By far the most significant reason for *not* effectuating an IRA rollover involves creditor protection. For the most part, while the participant's retirement assets remain in the shelter of an ERISA-qualified plan, they are protected from the claims of the participant's judgment and bankruptcy creditors. Although this exemption from creditor claims does *not* apply to certain alimony and child support claims, certain voluntary assignments of a portion (up to 10 percent) of any plan benefit payment (IRC § 401(a)(13)), and claims by the IRS for back taxes owed by the participant, the exemption does bar most other creditors from being able to attach the participant's plan benefits. However, ERISA (the Federal pension law which created these exemption rules) did *not* extend similar protection to assets in IRAs or Individual Retirement Annuities. Instead, the rules governing the protection of IRAs and Individual Retirement Annuities from bankruptcy and from creditor claims instead are based on the provisions of State law applicable to the individual's IRA or Individual Retirement Annuity.

Fortunately, many states extend to IRAs the same type of blanket ERISA-qualified plan creditor protection. This protection often applies not just to traditional IRAs and Individual Retirement Annuities, but to the far newer Roth IRAs. However, many states do *not* offer IRAs the same type of blanket protection from creditors that Federal law extends to benefits in qualified plans. Many states place a dollar limitation on the exemption of IRAs and Individual Retirement Annuities from bankruptcy and from creditor claims ranging from $100,000 in North Dakota to $500,000 in Nevada, while other states tie in the exemption to an amount considered reasonably necessary to provide for the support of the individual and/or his or her other family members. Still other states limit their exemption to amounts *other* than those amounts contributed into the IRA or Individual Retirement Annuity within a certain number of days preceding a certain triggering date or event. The triggering date or event is typically measured from the date of the institution of a lawsuit, the date of the entry of a judgment, or the date of the filing of the bankruptcy petition (ranging from 90 days in Connecticut, to five years in Massachusetts).

Employer Securities and Net Unrealized Appreciation

Another situation in which it might not be advisable for the participant to roll over the entire amount of the distribution from a qualified plan into an IRA occurs if a participant receives a plan distribution which consists of Employer securities. Employer securities are defined as stock in the company which is sponsoring the qualified plan. Where a participant's distribution from a qualified plan consists of Employer securities, the participant is not required to pay income tax on the full fair market value of the Employer securities received as part of that plan distribution. Instead, the participant is required to pay income tax only on the plan's "cost basis" in the stock, which may be far less than the current fair market value of the stock. The difference in value between the plan's cost basis in the Employer securities and the fair market value of those securities as of the date of the plan distribution is known as the "net unrealized appreciation", or NUA. The NUA is *not* taxed to the participant until the Employer securities are sold, at which time the NUA is taxed at long-term capital gains rates.

On the other hand, if the Employer securities received as part of the plan distribution were rolled over into an IRA, the ability to pay tax on the cost basis only of the stock would be lost forever. All distributions from the IRA, either of the Employer securities themselves or of the cash proceeds from the prior sale of those securities, would then be subject to tax at ordinary income tax rates, and *not* at favorable capital gains tax rates. It may, therefore, be to the participant's advantage to hold the Employer securities and pay the small amount of current income tax associated with the plan's cost basis in those assets, rather than to avoid paying any current income tax on the distribution of Employer securities by rolling over into an IRA the entire amount of the Employer securities received as part of the plan distribution. This may especially be the case where the participant has no present intention of selling the stock and, in fact, may intend to hold the Employer securities for many years, or even decades, into the future. The topic of Employer securities and NUA is discussed in greater detail in Chapter 15.

Ten-Year Averaging and Capital Gains Treatment for Those Born Before January 1, 1936

Still another situation in which it might not be advisable for the participant to roll over the entire amount of the distribution received from a qualified plan into an IRA involves the case of a participant who was born before January 1, 1936. In some cases, those individuals may be entitled to ten-year averaging and/or capital gains treatment for a portion or all of their plan distribution.

The idea behind ten-year averaging is that the distribution from the qualified plan typically represents the accumulation of Employer contributions and earnings credited to the participant's account over many years. It was, therefore, thought to be unfair to tax this amount, which may have taken many years to accumulate, all in one year, and at the Internal Revenue Code's (IRC's) progressive income tax rates, which move up in income tax brackets the higher the amount of income received. Instead, under the ten-year averaging rules, a participant is allowed to divide by ten the amount of the plan distribution received. The participant then computes the amount of the tax attributable to this one-tenth portion as if that amount had been the *only* item of income received for that year. Once the amount of the tax attributable to the one-tenth portion has been computed, the participant then multiplies that tax figure by ten and adds the amount of that tax to his or her other income for the year. The enormous benefit of this approach is that, by dividing the distribution amount by ten and then computing the tax on each of the one-tenth pieces *separately* from the individual's other income received for that year, the entire amount of the plan distribution is in effect taxed at the *lowest* marginal Federal income tax rates, rather than at the *highest* marginal Federal income tax rates. It should be noted that, while certain distributions from qualified plans can be eligible for ten-year averaging tax treatment, distributions from IRAs are *never* eligible for this favorable tax treatment, even if all of the assets in the IRA had originated from a rollover distribution from a qualified plan.

One obvious disadvantage to this approach is that it is not available for individuals born *after* December 31, 1935. Another major disadvantage is that it is available only where the distribution received by the participant from a qualified plan consisted of a lump sum distribution (IRC § 402(e)(4)(D)). A "lump sum distribution" is a distribution of a participant's entire interest in a qualified plan that is received within one taxable year of the recipient and where the distribution has been made on account of the participant's:

- Death
- Attainment of age 59½
- Separation from service (except for self-employed individuals) or
- Disability (self-employed individuals only)

Where the plan distribution occurred because of some *other* reason—for instance, the termination of the plan or through a "garden variety" termination of an individual's employment *before* he or she had at-tained age 59½—ten-year averaging will *not* be available. In addition, in order for the plan distribution to constitute a lump sum distri-bution, the individual seeking lump sum distribution tax treatment must have been a participant in the plan for at least five years *prior* to the year of the plan distribution (IRC proposed regulation § 1.402(e)-2(e)(3)). This five-year participation rule on lump sum distributions is waived for beneficiaries of deceased participants. Becauseof the many requirements which must be met before a plan distribution can be considered to be a lump sum distribution, practitioners will often find that *most* plan distributions do not qualify as lump sum distributions.

Another major disadvantage of this approach is that the Tax Reform Act of 1986 (which allowed for the grandfathering of the ten-year averaging rules to continue to apply under certain circumstances to those individuals who had attained age 50 as of January 1, 1986) requires the continued use of the Federal income tax rates that were in effect for 1986 when computing the amount of the Federal income taxes attributable to the lump sum distribution under the ten-year averaging method, even where the lump sum distribution is being made in a subsequent year. The income tax rates which were in effect for 1986 are considerably *higher* than the rates that are in effect today, or that were in effect even a short time thereafter, due to significant changes to the income tax rate structure bought about by tax law changes enacted in the second half of the Reagan Administration. The Tax Reform Act of 1986, which eliminated the ability of individuals (other than those individuals who had attained age 50 by January 1, 1986) to elect ten-year averaging tax treatment for their qualified plan distributions, originally replaced those rules with five-year income averaging on lump sum distributions. The five-year averaging rules were to be applied thereafter to all participants who had received lump sum distributions from their qualified plans. However the five-year averaging rules were entirely eliminated by the Small Business Job Protection Act of 1996, effective for all taxable years beginning after December 31, 1999, regardless of the participant's date of birth. The elimination of the five-year averaging rules left only the ten-year averaging rules applicable to participants who were born before January 1, 1936 and who had received a lump sum distribution from their qualified plan.

Even in those few cases in which ten-year averaging tax treatment *can* be elected by the participant, the participant may find that it is still advantageous to roll over the entire amount of their plan distribution into an IRA, thereby avoiding the payment of *any* current income taxes on the plan distribution and allowing the *full* amount of their plan distribution to continue to grow on a tax-deferred basis in the shelter of the IRA. This is especially the case where the participant has no immediate need for the money and intends to accumulate the amount of the plan distribution indefinitely for future use. In addition, ten-year averaging tax treatment is not especially helpful should the lump sum distribution exceed $300,000 or $400,000. This is true because at that level and under the tax rate structure which was in effect for 1986, and which is still required to be used today for ten-year averaging purposes, the Federal income tax rates attributable to the plan distribution are already at sufficiently high marginal income tax rates (34 to 38 percent), as to make the ten-year averaging election not especially advantageous.

Individuals who were born before January 1, 1936 also have the ability to elect capital gains tax treatment, at a flat 20 percent long-term capital gains tax rate (the rate in effect in 1986), for a portion of their distributions from their qualified plans. Where this option is available, it may be to the participant's advantage to elect capital gains tax treatment and to *not* roll over the entire plan distribution into an IRA, because capital gains tax treatment will *not* be available for distributions from the IRAs. However, as with the case of ten-year averaging, capital gains tax treatment is *not* available unless the plan distribution qualifies as a lump sum distribution. See the above discussion on ten-year averaging for the requirements as to what types of qualified plan distributions constitute lump sum distributions. Moreover, the portion of the plan distribution that is eligible for capital gains tax treatment is *only* the portion of the distribution attributable to the individual's participation in the plan *prior* to 1974. The pre-1974 period of participation in the plan is determined by multiplying the total benefit in the plan by a fraction, whose numerator is the number of months of plan participation *prior* to 1974 and whose denominator represents the total number of months of total plan participation (including *both* pre-1974 and post-1973 participation). Accordingly, as time goes on, the option to take capital gains tax treatment for a portion of a qualified plan distribution will become less and less desirable as fewer and fewer participants find that they have significant periods of plan participation *prior* to 1974.

Participants born before January 1, 1936 who receive lump sum distributions from their qualified plans can also mix and match the ten-year averaging and capital gains tax treatment approaches. Therefore, those individuals will find that they can elect any one of the following options:

1. All ordinary income tax treatment for their entire plan distribution;
2. All ten-year averaging for their entire plan distribution;
3. Capital gains treatment for the portion of their distribution attributable to their pre-1974 participation in the plan, while electing ten-year averaging for the post-1973 portion of their plan distribution; or
4. Rolling over a portion or all of their plan distribution into an IRA.

Accordingly, when dealing with a client who was born before January 1, 1936 (especially where the client had participated in a qualified plan for a considerable period of time prior to January 1, 1974), tax computations and asset value projections under each of the four tax option scenarios above should be performed, so that the client and his or her advisors will have all of the relevant tax figures needed to determine if a portion or all of the plan distribution should be rolled over into an IRA. If the plan distribution is *not* to be rolled over into an IRA, the client and his or her advisors should determine whether capital gains or ten-year averaging tax treatment is to be afforded to a portion or all of the plan distribution. It should be noted that if *any* portion of the plan distribution was rolled over into an IRA, no portion of the plan distribution that was *not* rolled over into an IRA will be eligible for ten-year averaging.

Distributions Before Age 59½ and the 10 Percent Penalty Tax

One of the announced goals of ERISA (the Federal pension law of 1974) is to promote the accumulation and growth of amounts in qualified plans and IRAs, so that those amounts can be available to provide individuals with retirement income, once their periods of employment with their employers have ended. With this objective in mind, the Internal Revenue Code provides numerous current tax benefits to companies that sponsor qualified plans, and also provides numerous current tax benefits to the participants in those plans, all with the goal of facilitating contributions to and accumulations of amounts in qualified plans and IRAs. For instance, employers are entitled to current income tax deductions for the amounts of their contributions to qualified plans, while those amounts, as well as the earnings on those amounts, are not currently taxable to the participants as long as those amounts are retained in the shelter the qualified plan or IRA. In addition, individuals who make contributions to 401(k) plans or IRAs are entitled to receive current income tax deductions for the amounts of their contributions in certain circumstances. Finally, distributions from these qualified plans or IRAs can also enjoy certain favorable income tax treatment—such as rollover tax treatment, ten-year averaging or capital gains tax treatment. However, where an individual has withdrawn money from an IRA or qualified plan *prior* to age 59½, the Internal Revenue Code penalizes this behavior as running contrary to the stated objective of continuing the accumulation process until the individual has reached what Congress has determined to be the desired retirement years. The Internal Revenue Code defines those favored retirement years as the years *after* the individual has attained age 59½.

One way in which the Internal Revenue Service actively discourages individuals from receiving distributions from their qualified plans or IRAs before age 59½ is to impose a 10 percent excise tax on the amount of their qualified plan or IRA distribution. The amount of this penalty tax is in addition to the ordinary income tax which the individual is also required to pay on his or her qualified plan or IRA distribution. The authority for the 10 percent excise tax on pre-mature distributions from qualified plans and IRAs is contained in Internal Revenue Code Section 72(t). Fortunately, the Internal Revenue Code also contains numerous exceptions to the 10 percent penalty tax. Those exceptions, which can also be found in Internal Revenue Code Section 72(t), have come to be known as the "72(t) rules." It should be noted that the 10 percent penalty tax and each of the exceptions to the 10 percent penalty tax also apply to distributions from tax-sheltered annuities (403(b) plans).

There are at least 14 known exceptions to the 10 percent penalty tax on premature distributions. Those exceptions are as follows:

1. Distributions which are made after the individual has attained age 59½;
2. Distributions which are not subject to tax because they have been timely rolled over into another qualified plan, IRA, or tax-sheltered annuity;
3. Distributions which are made to a beneficiary following the death of the participant;
4. Distributions which are made on account of the permanent disability of the participant;
5. Distributions which are part of a series of substantially equal periodic payments;
6. Distributions which are made to an employee after separation from service after attaining age 55;
7. Distributions which are used to pay for certain higher education expenses:
8. Distributions which are used to pay for certain first time home purchases;
9. Distributions which are made to an alternate payee pursuant to a Qualified Domestic Relations Order (QDRO);
10. Distributions which are made to pay for certain medical expenses;
11. Distributions which are made to an unemployed individual to pay health insurance premiums;
12. Distributions which represent corrective distributions from qualified plans or IRAs of prior excess contributions;

13. Distributions which represent a dividend payment with respect to certain stock held by an Employee Stock Ownership Plan (ESOP); and
14. Distributions made directly to the Internal Revenue Service to satisfy a prior IRS levy.

The typical retirement distribution client is one who has deferred taking any distributions at all from his or her qualified plan or IRA until well into his or her retirement years, with distributions not usually beginning until the attainment of age 65 or beyond. However, the situation does arise frequently enough that a retirement distribution specialist is asked to assist an individual who wishes to receive a plan or IRA distribution considerably *earlier* than those dates. It is, therefore, important for the advisor to be aware of each of the 14 exceptions to the imposition of the 10 percent penalty tax, so that the client is not put into a position in which the 10 percent excise tax is imposed when it possibly could have been entirely avoided.

Under these circumstances, the retirement distribution specialist should advise the client to spend some of his or her *other* assets to pay for any needed expense item rather than to use retirement assets for that purpose. The reasons are twofold. First, all distributions from the retirement assets used to pay an expense item will be subject to ordinary income tax (unless eligible for ten-year averaging or capital gains tax treatment), while the use of the client's *other* assets to pay an expense item may not be subject to any current income tax at all (e.g., where the client has withdrawn money from his or her bank account to pay the expense item). Even where a client may have to sell some stocks or bonds to pay for an expense item, the sale of those assets may generate no current income tax liability or, at worst, a small tax on the profit derived from the sale of those assets (the net price realized from the sale of those assets minus the individual's cost basis in those assets). That profit would then taxed at favorable capital gains tax rates, not at ordinary income tax rates. Secondly, any distribution of retirement assets used to pay for an expense item will no longer be an asset which can continue to accumulate in the retirement vehicle on a tax-deferred basis, producing subsequent substantial tax-deferred earnings for the individual which can be used to support the individual and his or her spouse during their retirement years and, after the death of the individual and spouse, can then be used to create a legacy for the individual's children and grandchildren.

However, in those cases in which the client cannot be dissuaded from using retirement assets for this purpose, the retirement distribution specialist would do well to advise the client how to structure the qualified plan or IRA distribution so that, to the greatest extent possible, the distribution will be exempt from the imposition of the 10 percent penalty tax on premature distributions.

Distributions Made After Age 59½

Distributions made to an individual from a qualified plan, IRA, or tax-sheltered annuity *after* the date on which the individual has attained age 59½ will be exempt from the application of the 10 percent penalty tax. An individual turns 59½ six months after the day on which he or she turned age 59. Accordingly, an individual who turned age 59 on January 1, 2001 would turn 59½ on July 1, 2001. An individual who turned age 59 on August 8, 2001 would turn 59½ on February 8, 2002. Clients who need money from their retirement assets and who are very close to their age 59½ date should make every effort to postpone taking the retirement assets *after* that date, even if it means securing short-term bridge loan financing to cover the cost of the expense item on a temporary basis.

Distributions Which Are Rolled Over

Most individuals will find that they can entirely avoid the imposition of any current income tax liability (and any current excise tax liability) on any qualified plan or IRA distribution by rolling over the full amount of the distribution within 60 days of its receipt into an IRA. Qualified plan distributions can also be rolled over within the 60-day period into another qualified plan. Distributions from IRAs *cannot* be rolled over into a qualified plan, unless the entire amount in the IRA had been attributable originally to a rollover from a qualified plan, with no regular IRA contributions ever made to that IRA. Distributions from tax-sheltered annuities (403(b) plans) *cannot* be rolled over into a qualified plan, but can be rolled over within the 60-day time period into either another tax-sheltered annuity or into an IRA. Distributions from 457 plans (certain deferred compensation plans of a state or local government or tax-exempt employer) can be rolled over into another 457 plan, but cannot be rolled over into either a qualified plan, IRA, or a tax-sheltered annuity. In addition, no after-tax amount in a qualified plan, or amount which is required to be paid out in any year from any retirement plan, IRA, or tax-sheltered annuity pursuant to the Required Minimum Distribution rules can ever be rolled over into any form of retirement vehicle. Pending legislation before Congress would great-ly liberalize these rollover rules by permitting greater rollover ability between qualified plans, IRAs, tax-sheltered annuities, and 457 plans, and would also permit after-tax amounts in qualified plans to be similarly rolled over to IRAs under certain circumstances. See the beginning of this chapter for a discussion of certain other rules applicable to IRA rollovers.

Surviving spouses who receive distributions from the qualified plans, IRAs, or tax-sheltered annuities of their deceased spouses are permitted to roll those assets over into one or more spousal rollover IRAs. However, surviving spouses are *not* permitted to roll over these types of distributions into any qualified plan in which they currently participate. Non-spouse recipients of distributions from qualified plans, IRAs, or tax-sheltered annuities of a deceased individual are *not* permitted to roll over those distributions into a qualified plan, IRA, or tax-sheltered annuity.

Distributions Made on Account of the Death of an Individual

Distributions made to a beneficiary following the death of an individual are exempt from the application of the 10 percent penalty tax, even in those cases in which the decedent had been younger than age 59½ at his or her date of death, and even in those cases in which the beneficiaries themselves are younger than age 59½.

As noted above, surviving spouse beneficiaries are permitted to roll over the qualified plan, IRA, and tax-sheltered annuity benefits from their deceased spouses into one or more spousal rollover IRAs. However where the surviving spouse is younger than age 59½ at the time of the spousal rollover, the spouse may be waiving a valuable right if the entire amount of the retirement benefit is rolled over into the spousal rollover IRA. Where a surviving spouse needs to use a portion of the inherited retirement assets *before* attaining age 59½, he or she should consider leaving a portion of the retirement asset in the name of the deceased spouse and receiving certain distributions *directly* from that retirement vehicle, rather than rolling over the full amount of the retirement asset into his or her own spousal rollover IRA, and then receiving *all* distributions from that spousal rollover IRA. In this way, distributions to the surviving spouse from the inherited retirement vehicle will *not* be subject to the 10 percent penalty tax on premature distributions, because the distributions to the spouse will be made on account of the death of an individual. An example will help to explain how this can work.

> **Example.** John dies at age 60, with $500,000 in his IRA and with his wife, Jean, named as his designated beneficiary. Jean, who is age 56 at the time of John's death, expects that she will probably need approximately $25,000 each year from John's IRA. Instead of rolling over the full $500,000 into a spousal rollover IRA, Jean should consider rolling over only $425,000. The remaining $75,000 amount should continue to be kept in John's IRA. Should Jean need the $25,000 per year from the IRA, she can withdraw that amount from the $75,000 in the IRA that is still in John's name. Because these distributions are being made to a beneficiary on account of an individual's (John's) death, they will *not* be subject to the 10 percent penalty tax, even though Jean will not have attained age 59½ at the time she receives any of those distributions. Once Jean has attained age 59½, she can withdraw amounts from her *own* rollover IRA free from the imposition of the 10 percent penalty tax. Had Jean rolled over the full $500,000 amount into her own spousal rollover IRA, any distributions which she may have taken from that IRA *before* she attained age 59½ would have been subject to the 10 percent penalty tax.

Distributions Made on Account of the Disability of an Individual

Distributions made to an individual who has not yet attained age 59½ will not be subject to the 10 percent penalty tax, if they are made on account of the individual's disability. However, not every form of disability is considered severe enough to trigger the application of this exception. Internal Revenue Code Section 72(m)(7) defines disability, for this purpose, as the inability of an individual to "engage in any substantial gainful activity by reason of any medically determinable physical or mental impairment which can be expected to result in death or to be of long-continued and indefinite duration."

Accordingly, not all physical or mental impairments will be deemed to be serious enough or permanent enough to fall within this rather strict definition of disability. Illnesses or injuries from which the individual is reasonably expected to eventually recover will *not* qualify, nor will illnesses or injuries which will permanently prevent the individual from engaging in their *prior* occupation, but which will *not* prevent them from engaging in some other occupation to which they are suited due to their education, training, and prior work experience. In addition, the Internal Revenue Code places the burden of proof on the individual to show that his or her illness or injury is substantial enough and permanent enough to fall within this exception to the imposition of the 10 percent penalty tax. Advisors may frequently find that their clients, though physically or psychologically unable to continue working at their prior job, are not so severely ill or disabled as to exempt their qualified plan, IRA, or tax-sheltered annuity (403(b) plan) distributions from the imposition of the 10 percent penalty tax.

Distributions Which Are Part of a Series of Substantially Equal Periodic Payments

Distributions made to an individual who has not yet attained age 59½ will not be subject to the 10 percent penalty tax if the distributions are part of a series of substantially equal periodic payments. This exception to the 10 percent penalty tax is an extremely important one, in that it is one of the few exceptions which can be created by the client and his or her advisor, regardless of the client's prior circumstances, and which can be tailored to suit the client's particular situation and circumstances at the time. IRS Notice 89-25 provides three alternative methodologies for complying with the substantially equal periodic payment rules. Although the Internal Revenue Service has indicated that these three methodologies are *not* the only methodologies which may be used, it has never illustrated any other methodology which it considers acceptable.

The way this device typically works is that the client tells his or her advisor that he or she will need a certain amount of money from retirement assets in each of a number of years before the attainment of age 59½. The advisor then selects one of the three substantially equal periodic payment methodologies, as well as the amount of the retirement assets to be committed to this device. The client then isolates the amount of the retirement assets to be used for this purpose into a separate retirement vehicle, usually an IRA. Substantially equal periodic payments are then taken by the client from that IRA each year in the amounts determined each year, based on the selected methodology. This arrangement typically continues for five years or until the individual has attained age 59½, whichever is *later.*

The statute (Internal Revenue Code § 72(t)(4)) provides that, if the arrangement is terminated or modified prior to that date, all prior distributions which had previously been exempt from the imposition of the 10 percent penalty tax will be retroactively subject to that tax. This means that a 55-year-old who has set up a substantially equal periodic payment arrangement must continue that arrangement for at least five years, or else be subject to the imposition of the special recapture rules. On the other hand, a 40-year-old who has set up a substantially equal periodic payment arrangement must continue that arrangement for 20 years in order to avoid the recapture rules. Interest on the 10 percent penalty tax will also be imposed by the Internal Revenue Service on any recaptured amounts. The special recapture provisions, however, are not applicable if the substantially equal periodic payment arrangement has prematurely ended due to the death or disability of the individual. Disability for purposes of this rule is the strict definition of disability (discussed earlier in this chapter) as an exception to the 10 percent penalty tax.

The three acceptable methodologies for making substantially equal periodic payments are as follows:

1. Minimum Distribution Method;
2. Amortization Method;
3. Annuity Factor Method.

Each of these three methods requires at least yearly payments. In addition, substantially equal periodic payments under each of the three methods *cannot* be made from a qualified plan unless the participant has first terminated his or her employment with the plan sponsor. However, each of the three methods do permit substantially equal periodic payments to be made from an IRA, regardless of the individual's current employment status.

Minimum Distribution Method

Under the Minimum Distribution Method, substantially equal periodic payments are calculated from the retirement vehicle each year in exactly the same way as Required Minimum Distribution amounts are determined each year for the individual's retirement assets and beginning at the individual's Required Beginning Date. The one exception is that, in the case of substantially equal periodic payments, the individual has not yet attained age 70½—or even age 59½. Under this methodology, substantially equal periodic payments typically gets larger and larger each year as the value of the individual's retirement asset typically grows each year and as the life expectancy divisor which is to be applied each year gets higher and higher. However, of the three acceptable methods for computing substantially equal periodic payments each year, this method produces the *lowest* amount which can be withdrawn each year from the retirement vehicle free of the 10 percent penalty tax. Accordingly of the three methodologies, this methodology is the least favored.

Amortization Method

Under the Amortization Method, substantially equal periodic payments are computed each year in much the same way in which one would amortize a mortgage. Under this method, the balance in the individual's retirement asset is, in effect, amortized over the remaining life expectancy of the individual or of the individual and his or her designated beneficiary, at an assumed reasonable interest rate selected by the individual. Under this methodology, life expectancy is to be determined based on the use of the Internal Revenue Service life expectancy tables. Because this methodology assumes an interest rate for the payout of the retirement assets, and then amortizes *both* principal and interest each year, substantially equal periodic payments under this methodology are *higher* than they would be under the Minimum Distribution Method. Substantially equal periodic payments under the Amortization Method are generally in a set amount each year, regardless of any fluctuations in the value of the underlying retirement assets, much as a mortgage payment is typically a set amount each month or each year. However, yearly payments under the Amortization Method can apparently be increased pursuant to a predetermined cost-of-living factor or standard.

Annuity Factor Method

Under the Annuity Factor Method, substantially equal periodic payments are computed each year based on an annuity factor selected by the individual. The annuity factor assumes both a reasonable rate of interest as selected by the individual and a life expectancy table. However, unlike the case of the Amortization Method, the life expectancy table can be one which has been developed privately (e.g., by an insurance company or actuarial organization) and need not be one developed by the Internal Revenue Service. Typically, the life expectancy tables used in connection with the Annuity Factor Method are those used by actuaries each year to compute contributions due to qualified defined benefit pension plans. As in the case of the Amortization Method, yearly payments under the Annuity Factor Method are generally in set amounts each year, but apparently can also be adjusted each year pursuant to a predetermined cost-of-living factor or standard.

How to Apply the Substantially Equal Periodic Payment Rules

An example will help to illustrate how to apply the substantially equal periodic payment rules.

Example. Paul is age 50 and has $500,000 in his rollover IRA. Paul's elderly mother has just entered an adult retirement community home, requiring higher monthly housing costs than she can reasonably afford. Paul figures that he will need another $20,000 in before-tax income each year in order to be able to help his mother defray these anticipated increased yearly housing costs. Due to his mother's current age of 75, Paul now estimates that he may have to continue these increased payments at least for the next ten years. Paul has no other liquid assets with which to make these payments and asks his retirement distribution specialist, Kevin, to assist him in this regard. Kevin suggests a 72(t) solution for Paul (substantially equal periodic payments under Internal Revenue Code § 72(t)).

Kevin instructs Paul to divide his one IRA into two IRAs, with the first IRA containing $222,180 and the second IRA containing the balance of the $500,000 amount, or $277,820. Paul then commits to using the *first* IRA only for the 72(t) arrangement. Kevin instructs Paul that he will be using the Annuity Factor Method to compute yearly substantially equal periodic payments, with an assumed interest rate of 8 percent, and with the use of the UP-1984 Mortality Table. That interest rate and mortality table produce a factor of 11.109. Kevin then divides the initial balance of $222,180 in the first IRA by the factor of 11.109 to produce a yearly required distribution amount of $20,000 under the 72(t) arrangement ($222,180 divided by 11.109). Kevin then instructs Paul to withdraw $20,000 from the *first* IRA each year until Paul is age 59½, at which time the 72(t) arrangement can end. Kevin tells Paul that under the 72(t) arrangement, although Paul will have to pay regular income tax on the amount of each yearly distribution of $20,000, no 10 percent penalty tax should be applicable to any of the yearly payments. However, Kevin reminds Paul that, should Paul modify or end the 72(t) arrangement at any time *before* he reaches age 59½, the 10 percent penalty tax, together with interest thereon, will be retroactively applied to *all* prior distributions, including all prior distributions made while the 72(t) arrangement was still in effect and *before* the arrangement had been modified or ended.

Had Paul used the Minimum Distribution Method for computing substantially equal periodic payments, he would have had to commit $662,000 to the arrangement, an amount in excess of Paul's $500,000 IRA balance. The $662,000 amount was arrived at by multiplying the $20,000 yearly amount needed by Paul by his life expectancy factor of 33.1 years, as determined for a 50-year-old under the Internal Revenue Service single life expectancy table. Had Paul used the Amortization Method for computing substantially equal periodic payments, he would have had to commit $230,441 to the arrangement. The $230,441 amount was arrived at by multiplying the $20,000 amount which Paul needs each year by a factor of .08679. The .08679 factor, in turn, was derived from an assumed interest rate of 8 percent, when amortized over Paul's remaining life expectancy of 33.1 years and based on the IRS life expectancy table for a 50-year-old.

One of the nice features of a 72(t) arrangement is that if Paul were to find, five years into the arrangement, that he needed another $10,000 per year to assist his mother, he could structure a *second* 72(t) arrangement with the assets in his second IRA (which was initially worth $277,820). If that IRA had grown in value by 8 percent per year, five years into the first 72(t) arrangement the second IRA would be worth $408,209. Paul could then have his advisor structure a *second* 72(t) arrangement for him, with as much of the assets in the second IRA as would be necessary to generate the additional $10,000 in desired yearly income. The remaining amount in the second IRA that would *not* be needed for this second 72(t) arrangement would be transferred into a *third* IRA. Paul would then have three IRAs. The first IRA would be making yearly substantially equal periodic payments of $20,000 to Paul, while the second IRA

> would be making yearly substantially equal periodic payments to him of $10,000. Paul would, therefore, be receiving $30,000 in yearly payments from his first two IRAs. Although Paul would have to pay income taxes each year on the $30,000 total amount received, there should be no 10 percent excise tax attributable to any of those payments. No yearly payments would be made to Paul from his third IRA (which IRA was not subject to any of the 72(t) arrangements) until after he had reached age $59^1/_2$.

Among the reasons for the popularity of 72(t) arrangements are the ability they grant an individual to isolate only those retirement assets needed to establish the substantially equal periodic payment device in the yearly desired amount and the enormous flexibility this entails. In addition, the individual's ability to establish multiple 72(t) arrangements (and to have the several arrangements running simultaneously) significantly adds to their utility. In fact, there appears to be no limit to the number of 72(t) arrangements an individual can run simultaneously. There also appears to be no minimum age at which an individual can establish a 72(t) arrangement. However, the younger the individual is at the time that the 72(t) arrangement is established, the greater the number of years the arrangement has to continue (for five years or until age $59^1/_2$, whichever is longer) before the arrangement can be terminated or modified without the retroactive imposition of the 10 percent penalty tax.

When advising clients in this area, practitioners should be aware that several software companies sell off-the-shelf programs which can develop the substantially equal periodic payment numbers under each of the three acceptable methodologies. These companies are generally the same companies that have developed software programs to generate the Required Minimum Distribution amounts which are due each year.

Section 72(t) arrangements have become especially popular in those cases in which individuals with large IRA balances find that they are cash poor and need to tap into their retirement assets in order to pay for certain yearly expense items. Where those individuals are younger than age $59^1/_2$, the 72(t) arrangement allows them the ability to receive yearly distributions from their retirement assets, *without* having the 10 percent penalty tax apply to their yearly distributions.

Distributions Made to an Employee Following Separation from Service After Attaining Age 55

An additional exception to the imposition of the 10 percent penalty tax applies in the case of an individual who had received a distribution from a qualified plan before attaining age 59½ and had separated from service from the employer *after* attaining age 55. In order for this exception to apply, the employee's separation from service must have occurred after he or she had attained age 55, with the plan distribution having occurred *after* their employment status had ended. Under these rules, an individual could not (1) terminate his or her employment at age 52 and then wait three years to receive his or her plan distribution after age 55 or (2) receive a distribution at age 55 or older while still employed. A distribution under either of those two circumstances would be subject to the 10 percent penalty tax. However the employee need not have exactly attained age 55 before termination of employment has occurred. It is sufficient for this purpose if the individual's separation from service occurred during or after the calendar year in which he or she attained age 55. Moreover, once this exception applies, if in some later year the individual were to return to employment with their original employer, the 10 percent penalty tax would *not* be reinstated retroactively to the original plan distribution. It should also be noted that this exception to the imposition of the 10 percent penalty tax is applicable only to distributions from qualified plans and from tax-sheltered annuities (403(b) plans) and is *not* applicable to distributions from IRAs, regardless of the date on which the IRA owner had terminated his or her employment.

Distributions Used to Pay for Certain Higher Education Expenses

This exception to the imposition of the 10 percent penalty tax applies to the payment of tuition, books, fees, supplies, and equipment required as part of any post-secondary college, university, vocational school, graduate or professional degree course, and for any other post-secondary educational institution, whether public, private, or non-profit. The exception also covers room and board expenses, provided that the student is enrolled on at least a half-time basis. The exemption is available for the payment of these qualified higher education expenses for the individual or his or her spouse, or for the children or grandchildren of the individual or spouse. This exception, however, is available only for distributions from IRAs, and is not available for distributions from either qualified plans or tax-sheltered annuities (403(b) plans).

The amount of the IRA distribution that is eligible for this exception to the imposition of the 10 percent penalty tax is required to be reduced by the amount of any tax-free scholarship, Pell Grant, or tax-free distribution from either an Education IRA or an Employer-provided educational assistance plan that are used to pay for any of these expenses. However, any payment made by the student himself or herself, from his or her own personal assets or savings, are *not* required to be used to reduce the amount of the IRA distributions that are eligible for this exception.

Advisors should not confuse distributions from traditional and rollover IRAs that are used to pay these "qualified higher education expenses" with distributions from Education IRAs that are used to pay these same expenses. Distributions from Education IRAs that are used to pay for qualified higher education expenses are exempt from any current Federal income taxation and are also exempt from the imposition of any 10 percent penalty tax. Distributions from traditional IRAs and rollover IRAs, on the other hand, that are used to pay these qualified higher education expenses, while exempt from the imposition of the 10 percent penalty tax, *are* subject to ordinary Federal income tax on the amount of each distribution.

Distributions Used to Pay for Certain First-Time Home Purchases

This exception to the imposition of the 10 percent penalty tax applies to distributions from an IRA that are used to acquire, construct, or reconstruct the individual's primary residence and also includes IRA distributions that are used to pay the usual or reasonable settlement, financing, and closing costs associated therewith. The exception applies only to those housing expenses that are used, within a 120-day period after the IRA distribution has been received, for the benefit of the individual or spouse, or for the benefit of any child, grandchild, or ancestor of the individual or spouse. A qualified first-time home buyer is defined as someone who had no present interest in a principal residence at any time during the two-year period ending on the date of the acquisition of the current principal residence to which the IRA distribution is being applied. The exception contains a lifetime limitation of $10,000 on the amount of an individual's IRA distributions that are eligible for this exception. In addition, the exception is available *only* for distributions from IRAs, not for distributions from either qualified plans or tax-sheltered annuities (403 (b) plans) that are used to pay these expenses.

Distributions Made to an Alternate Payee Pursuant to a QDRO

Ordinarily, distributions from qualified plans or from tax-sheltered annuities can be made only to the participant while the participant is alive, or to the participant's beneficiaries, following the participant's death. However, Internal Revenue Code Section 414(p) permits an individual's qualified plan or tax-sheltered annuity benefits to be paid to the individual's spouse, former spouse, child, or other dependent, even where the participant is still alive, where the payment is required to be made pursuant to a QDRO.

The QDRO rules are not applicable to distributions from IRAs. However Internal Revenue Code Section 408(d)(6) permits an individual's IRA to be divided up and transferred to the IRA of the individual's spouse or former spouse as part of the individual's divorce or separation agreement or decree, without the transfer being subject to any current Federal income tax by either the participant, spouse, or former spouse. In addition, these IRA divisions are not subject to the 10 percent penalty tax on premature distributions, even in those cases in which the IRA owner, spouse, or former spouse of the IRA owner were each younger than age 59½ at the time of the division of the IRA. (IRC § 72(t)(2)(C))

A QDRO is a court order affecting the participant's qualified plan or tax-sheltered annuity benefits. It generally is issued as part of an alimony award or property settlement agreement relating to a current divorce or separation action affecting the participant. QDROs typically provide for certain alimony, child support, or marital property rights of a spouse, former spouse, child, or other dependent of the participant, in a portion or all of the participant's qualified plan or tax-sheltered annuity benefits. The non-participant recipients of the retirement benefits pursuant to the QDRO are known as alternate payees. QDROs typically assign a portion of the participant's retirement benefits to the alternate payees, with payments to the alternate payees beginning either currently or at some later date, when those benefits would ordinarily first come into pay status for the participant.

Where a distribution from a qualified plan or tax-sheltered annuity is made pursuant to a QDRO, the distribution will not be subject to the 10 percent penalty tax on premature distributions, even where the participant or other payee (alternate payee) of the plan distribution was younger than age 59½ at the time of the distribution. However, a spouse or former spouse recipient of the QDRO payment will be subject to ordinary Federal income tax on the amount of the plan distribution received. Where the recipient of the QDRO payment is someone other than the spouse or former spouse of the participant (e.g., where the alternate payees are the children of the participant), the participant will be required to pay the Federal income taxes that are due on the plan distribution.

In order for a QDRO to be valid, the terms of the domestic relations order must be approved by both the plan administrator of the plan and by the court having jurisdiction over the matrimonial matter. Any distribution from a qualified plan or tax-sheltered annuity to an alternate payee which is *not* made pursuant to the terms of a valid QDRO will subject the participant to ordinary Federal income tax on the amount of the distribution, even where the distribution was made to the individual's spouse, former spouse or children. In addition, because the payment was not made pursuant to a valid QDRO, the distribution will be subject to the 10 percent penalty tax in those cases in which the participant had been younger than age 59½ at the time of the payment. Moreover, any distribution to an alternate payee that is *not* made pursuant to a valid QDRO runs the risk of disqualifying the entire qualified plan or tax-sheltered annuity for all plan participants.

A spouse (or former spouse) who receives a plan distribution pursuant to a QDRO may have the right to roll over the amount of that distribution into a spousal rollover IRA, provided that the distribution is otherwise eligible for rollover tax treatment. However, any distribution which the spouse (or former spouse) were then to receive from the spousal rollover IRA before age $59^1/_2$ would be subject to the 10 percent penalty tax on premature distributions, unless one or more of the 14 exceptions to the imposition of that tax were to be applicable. Non-spouse (or non-former spouse) recipients of QDRO payments are not permitted to roll over those QDRO payments into an IRA.

Distributions Made to Pay for Certain Medical Expenses

Distributions which are used to pay for certain medical expenses are exempt from the imposition of the 10 percent penalty tax. Distributions for purposes of this exception include distributions from qualified plans, IRAs, and tax-sheltered annuities (403(b) plans). Medical expenses that qualify for this exemption are those which are deductible on the individual's Federal income tax return for the year or which would have been deductible on the individual's Federal income tax return for the year had the individual itemized deductions for the year. Those deductible medical expenses apply to the individual's own medical expenses, as well as to the medical expenses of the individual's spouse and dependents. However, there is a limit on the amount of the individual's medical expenses that fall within this exception. The limit is the amount of the individual's medical expenses that are *deductible* for the year. Because medical expenses are deductible each year only to the extent that they exceed 7½ percent of the individual's adjusted gross income (AGI) for the year, this exception to the imposition of the 10 percent penalty tax is limited to only that portion of the medical expenses that are deductible for the year.

An example will help to explain how this limitation works.

> **Example.** Frank received a $10,000 distribution from his IRA for the year. Frank is only age 50 and fears that he will have to pay not only the regular Federal income tax on the amount of the distribution, but the 10 percent penalty tax as well on the full $10,000 amount. His AGI for the year is $60,000, inclusive of the $10,000 IRA

distribution. If Frank had incurred $8,000 in medical expenses for the year, $3,500 of his $10,000 IRA distribution would be exempt from the imposition of the 10% penalty tax. The $3,500 amount was computed by multiplying Frank's $60,000 AGI for the year by 7.5 percent, the percentage limit on deductible medical expenses for the year. The product of those two numbers is $4,500. Of the $8,000 in medical expenses incurred for the year, $4,500 would *not* be deductible, leaving $3,500 ($8,000 minus $4,500) as the deductible amount. Accordingly, even though Frank will have to pay Federal income tax on the full $10,000 IRA distribution received for the year, only $6,500 of the $10,000 amount will be subject to the 10 percent penalty tax ($10,000 minus $3,500). The remaining $3,500 amount will be exempt from that tax.

Distributions Made to an Unemployed Individual to Pay Health Insurance Premiums

Distributions from IRAs which are used to pay the health insurance premiums for the individual, or for the individual's spouse or dependents, will be exempt from the imposition of the 10 percent penalty tax, where the individual is unemployed and had been receiving Federal or State unemployment benefits for at least 12 consecutive weeks, and where the IRA distribution had either been received in the same year in which those unemployment benefits had been received or had been received in the following year. This exception can apply to self-employed individuals, if under applicable Federal or State law, the individual *would* have been entitled to the unemployment benefits, but for his or her status as a self-employed individual. There is also a dollar limitation on the amount of the IRA distributions that are eligible for this exception. The dollar limitation is the amount of the health insurance premiums which are deductible on the individual's Federal income tax return for the year.

The exception to the imposition of the 10 percent penalty tax does not apply to distributions from either qualified plans or from tax-sheltered annuities (403(b) plans). In addition, this exception does not apply if, at the time the individual received the IRA distribution, the individual had already worked for at least 60 days following the date of his or her original termination of employment, even if the individual should subsequently become unemployed again and is not currently working at the time he or she receives the IRA distribution.

Distributions Which Are Corrective Distributions of Prior Excess Contributions from Qualified Plans or IRAs

As discussed earlier in this chapter, there are certain circumstances under which either after-tax amounts in qualified plans or in IRAs, or excess contributions made by a participant to a 401(k) plan, could be distributed or returned to the participant, and any amounts so distributed or returned would not be eligible for rollover tax treatment. The distribution of any after-tax amount in either a qualified plan or IRA is not subject to the 10 percent penalty tax, even if the plan participant or IRA owner was younger than age 59½ at the time of the distribution. Similarly, the return to the plan participant or IRA owner of any prior excess contribution amount would not be subject to the 10 percent penalty tax.

The excess contributions in a 401(k) plan could have been attributable to excess aggregate contributions, excess deferral contributions, or excess aggregate contributions. The return of employee contributions previously made to a qualified plan in order to correct a possible excess annual addition problem would also come under this exception. The excess contributions in an IRA could have been attributable to amounts previously contributed to the IRA in excess of the amounts allowed as deductible, non-deductible, or rollover contributions.

Distributions Which Are a Dividend Payment with Respect to Certain Stock Held by an ESOP

If the qualified plan in which an individual participates is an Employee Stock Ownership Plan (ESOP), the plan has the ability to distribute to plan participants their pro rata share of any dividends earned during the year by any qualifying Employer securities held by the ESOP. Under certain circumstances, those dividend payments to plan participants may be exempt from the imposition of the 10 percent penalty tax, even where the plan participants are younger than age 59½ at the time the distribution of the dividend payments were made. See Chapter 15, which discusses ESOPs and the tax benefits associated with receiving qualifying Employer securities as part of a plan distribution.

Distributions Made Directly to the IRS to Satisfy a Prior IRS Levy

The last exception to the imposition of the 10 percent penalty tax on premature distributions occurs where an individual is unfortunate enough to have an IRS levy placed against his or her retirement assets. Any payments made directly to the IRS in satisfaction or partial satisfaction of that levy will not be subject to the 10 percent penalty tax on premature distributions, even where the plan participant or IRA owner had been younger than age 59½ at the time of the payment to the IRS. Even though the 10 percent penalty tax will not apply to that distribution, the individual will still be required to pay the regular Federal income taxes due on the full amount distributed from the qualified plan or IRA and paid to the IRS.

This exception applies to distributions from both qualified plans and IRAs. However, the exception does *not* apply where the individual owes money to the IRS and then *voluntarily* withdraws money from his or her qualified plan or IRA to pay the IRS. Instead, the exception is applicable only in the case of *involuntary* payments made to the IRS. Involuntary payments are those made to the IRS *after* the IRS has placed a levy on the individual's retirement assets.

Death Benefit Rules

Required Minimum Distributions Before the Required Beginning Date

Chapter 4 discussed the various Required Minimum Distribution rules that applied once the individual had reached his or her Required Beginning Date. Those rules then operate to govern all subsequent distributions due from the retirement vehicle for the remainder of the lifetime of the individual and for the remainder of the lifetime of the individual's beneficiary (where the beneficiary's life expectancy is to be taken into account). However, where the retirement asset owner has died *before* his or her Required Beginning Date, a second set of rules is to apply. Those rules are known as the "Death Benefit Rules." The Death Benefit Rules, although similar in some respects to the rules that apply once the individual has reached his or her Required Beginning Date, represent a separate set of rules and should not be confused with the "Living Payout Rules," which are applicable once the individual has reached his or her Required Beginning Date.

Determining the Required Beginning Date

Many people assume that, because an individual has died, the Death Benefit Rules must be operative. Such is the case *if* the individual has died *before* reaching his or her Required Beginning Date. For instance, where an individual dies at age 60 or at age 65, clearly the Death Benefit Rules are applicable, in that the individual had clearly not reached his or her Required Beginning Date. However, many people become confused as to how to apply this rule where the individual dies at age 70 or at age 70½. Under each of those cases, the Death Benefit Rules would *still* be applicable, because the individual had *still* not reached his or her Required Beginning Date. The Required Beginning Date is April 1 of the calendar year immediately following the calendar year in which the individual reached age 70½. Therefore, in order for an individual to have reached his or her Required Beginning Date, it is not enough for the individual to have attained age 70 or even age 70½. Instead, the individual must have survived until April 1 of the calendar year immediately following the calendar year in which he or she attained age 70½. An example will help to explain the application of this rule.

> **Example.** Larry was born on July 10, 1930. He reaches age 70 on July 10, 2000, and age 70½ on January 10, 2001. Accordingly, his Required Beginning Date is April 1, 2002, the April 1 immediately following the calendar year (2001) in which he had attained age 70½. Were Larry to die at any time in 2000 or in 2001, the Death Benefit Rules would be applicable to his retirement assets, in that he had *not* survived until his Re-

> quired Beginning Date of April 1, 2002. Even if Larry had died at age $70^1/_2$ on March 1, 2002, his benefits would still be payable under the Death Benefit Rules because he *still* had not survived until his Required Beginning Date. In fact, Larry could die as late as March 31, 2002, and still have his benefits payable after his death subject to the Death Benefit Rules and not the Living Payout Rules. It is only if Larry were to die on April 1, 2002 or after, that the Death Benefit Rules would *not* be applicable to the payment of his retirement benefits.

See Chapter 4, which discusses in greater detail the topic of determining an individual's Required Beginning Date, including the discussion of certain exceptions to the age $70^1/_2$ rule (e.g., the exceptions under the Small Business Job Protection Act of 1996, the exception for benefits in tax-sheltered annuities (403(b) plans) that had been earned by December 31, 1986, and the exceptions applicable to the TEFRA § 242(b)(2) elections).

Five-Year Rule and the Life Expectancy Rule

Where an individual has died *before* his or her Required Beginning Date, his or her retirement benefits will be payable to their beneficiaries under either the Five-Year Rule or the Life Expectancy Rule, except in those cases in which the spouse is the beneficiary. Certain additional special rules which are applicable when the spouse is the beneficiary are discussed later in this chapter.

Five-Year Rule

Under the Five-Year Rule, the individual's benefits are required to be paid out in full from the retirement vehicle by December 31 of the calendar year containing the fifth anniversary of the individual's death. There is no requirement under the Five-year Rule that any benefits be paid before that date, or in any one or more of the five years, as long as the entire amount in the retirement vehicle has been paid out by that outside date.

The Five-Year Rule is required to be used in each case in which an individual has died before his or her Required Beginning Date, *and* where the beneficiary of the retirement asset is either an estate, a charity, or a trust which does not qualify as a "Designated Beneficiary." (See Chapter 11, which discusses the four rules which a trust must comply with, in order to qualify as a Designated Beneficiary.) An example will help to explain how the Five-Year Rule works.

> **Example.** Richard dies at age 60 on March 20, 2002, and his estate is named as his IRA beneficiary. Following his death, all of the benefits in his IRA are required to be paid pursuant to the Five-Year Rule. Under that Rule, all amounts in Richard's IRA must be paid out in full by December 31, 2007. It is not a requirement of the Five-Year Rule that any particular amount be paid out of the IRA in either the year of Richard's death, or in any of the following five years, as long as the *full* amount in the IRA has been paid out by the December 31, 2007 date. Richard's beneficiaries have decided that they would like to withdraw one-fifth of the amount in Richard's IRA each year beginning with 2003. Such a withdrawal methodology fully complies with the Five-Year Rule in that, under this methodology, the entire amount in the IRA will have been withdrawn by December 31, 2007. Alternatively, Richard's beneficiaries could have decided to withdraw the full amount in the IRA in one lump-sum payment on January 1, 2003. That withdrawal methodology would also have fully complied with the requirements of the Five-Year Rule. Finally, if Richard's beneficiaries had decided to leave all of the amounts in the IRA *until* December 31, 2007, and to withdraw the entire balance on that date, that withdrawal methodology would also have fully complied with the requirements of the Five-Year Rule because, again, all amounts would have been withdrawn from the IRA by the December 31, 2007 date.

Life Expectancy Rule

Where an individual has died before his or her Required Beginning Date, his or her benefits, instead of being paid pursuant to the Five-Year Rule, could be paid pursuant to the Life Expectancy Rule. Under the Life Expectancy Rule, distributions following the individual's death are based on the life expectancy of the beneficiary, determined as of December 31 of the calendar year immediately *following* the calendar year of the individual's death. Under this Rule, the first distribution from the retirement vehicle is required to be made by December 31 of the calendar year immediately *following* the calendar year of the individual's death. All subsequent distributions are required to made by December 31 of each succeeding year, with the beneficiary's life expectancy reduced by one for each year that has since elapsed. An example will help to explain how the Life Expectancy Rule works.

> **Example.** Richard dies at age 60 on March 20, 2002, and has named his daughter, Wendy, as his IRA beneficiary. Under the terms of Richard's IRA, his benefits can be paid pursuant to the Life Expectancy Rule. Wendy was born on May 25, 1976, and will reach age 27 on December 31, 2003, which is December 31 of the calendar year immediately *following* the calendar year of Richard's death. If the balance in Richard's IRA on December 31, 2002 were $300,000, Wendy would be required to withdraw $5,444.65 from the IRA by December 31, 2003, in order to comply with the requirements of the Life Expectancy Rule. The $5,444.65 amount was determined by dividing the IRA balance of $300,000 as of December 31, 2002 by Wendy's life expectancy of 55.1 years, determined from the IRS single life expectancy table for an individual who will be age 27 on December 31, 2003. If the IRA were to grow in value by 8 percent for the 2002 year with a value of $318,555 as of December 31, 2003, Wendy's Required Minimum Distribution from the IRA for 2004 would be $5,888.26 ($318,555 divided by 54.1). In each subsequent year, Wendy would calculate her Required Minimum Distribution amount based on the *prior* year's December 31st remaining balance in the IRA, and by dividing that amount by her yearly reducing life expectancy divisor of 53.1 for 2005, 52.1 for 2006, 51.1 for 2007, 50.1 for 2008, and so on.

> The Required Minimum Distribution rules do not prevent Wendy from taking distributions from the IRA in any given year or years *in excess* of these Required Minimum Distribution amounts, or in taking her yearly distributions well in advance of the year-end December 31 date of each year. Instead, those rules are only concerned with whether or not the *minimum* amounts have been taken from the IRA each year, not with whether or not amounts in *excess* of the minimum amounts have been withdrawn. If Richard had been concerned about Wendy's taking *more* than the Required Minimum Distribution amounts from his IRA each year after his death, he could have prevented her from doing so by designating a trust for her benefit as the IRA beneficiary, instead of having named Wendy as the outright beneficiary of those benefits. The terms of the trust could then have limited the yearly withdrawals from the IRA to only the Required Minimum Distribution amounts which are due each year. (See Chapter 11, which discusses the use of trusts as IRA beneficiaries.)

Where an individual has designated more than one beneficiary for his or her retirement benefits, the Life Expectancy Rule requires that the life expectancy of the beneficiary with the *shortest* life expectancy must be used. An example will help to illustrate this point.

> **Example.** Andrew has designated his three children—Thomas, Jill, and Steven—as the three equal beneficiaries of his one IRA. Andrew dies at age 68, survived by his three children, who, as of December 31 of the year *following* the year of his death, are the following ages: Thomas is age 40, Jill is age 37, and Steven is age 35. In applying the Life Expectancy Rule following Andrew's death, the three children would each be required to use Thomas's life expectancy, because Thomas was the oldest of the three beneficiaries and, accordingly, has the shortest life expectancy. Therefore, Thomas's life

> expectancy of 42.5 years (the life expectancy of a 40-year-old) would be required to be used each year for the payment of *all* benefits from the IRA, whether those benefits were payable to Thomas, Jill, or Steven.

If instead of maintaining only one IRA, however, Andrew could have divided his IRA up into multiple IRAs prior to his death, with each separate IRA now containing one-third of the value of the original IRA and with each of his three children named as the 100 percent beneficiary of each separate IRA. Under this scenario, each of his three children, following his death, would be able to apply the Life Expectancy Rule to the payment of their benefits from their own Inherited IRAs, based on their *own* individual life expectancies, and without having to base all payments on the life expectancy of Thomas, the oldest of the three.

This planning technique may not have appeared to be especially advantageous in the prior example, because, in that example, the age differential between the three beneficiaries was only five years. Suppose, however, that the three beneficiaries had been Thomas, age 40, and Thomas's two children—Beth, age 8, and Howard, age 5. Although the benefits payable to Thomas would still be required to be paid out over a 42.5-year period, it is possible to structure a retirement distribution strategy in which the remaining benefits, payable to Beth and to Howard, could be paid out over a 73.7-year period with respect to Beth, and over a 76.6 year period with respect to Howard. To accomplish this, the IRA would have to be divided into separate IRAs for each beneficiary.

If Andrew had continued to maintain only one IRA, with his son Thomas and his two grandchildren, Beth and Howard, as his three IRA beneficiaries, and if the value of that one IRA was worth $1,000,000 on December 31 of the calendar year of Andrew's death, the first yearly Required Minimum Distribution amount that would be due to each of his three beneficiaries for the following year would be $7,843 ($1,000,000 divided by 42.5 equals $23,529, divided by the 3 beneficiaries equals $7,843 per beneficiary). However, if Andrew prior to his death, had divided the one IRA up into three equal IRAs, with each of his three beneficiaries named as the 100 percent beneficiary of each separate IRA, the yearly Required Minimum Distribution amounts that would be due to Beth and Howard would be significantly reduced each year. For the first year following the year of Andrew's death, the Required Minimum Distribution amount due to Thomas would still be $7,843 ($333,333 divided by 42.5 equals $7,843). However, the first year's Required Minimum Distribution amount due to Beth would be $4,523 ($333,333 divided by 73.7 equals $4,523), while the first year's Required Minimum Distribution amount due to Howard would be $4,352 ($333,333 divided by 76.6 equals $4,352).

This technique of dividing the IRA into separate IRAs for each IRA beneficiary prior to the individual's death (and before their Required Beginning Date), reduced the yearly Required Minimum Distributions to Beth and Howard by over 42 percent (from $7,843 to $4,523 for Beth and to $4,352 for Howard). Over time, this technique can double, triple, or even quadruple the ultimate payouts which Beth and Howard can receive over their lifetimes from their Inherited IRAs.

Therefore, whenever it appears that the Life Expectancy Rule is likely to be used, it is usually a good idea to divide the IRA up into separate IRAs for each IRA beneficiary. This will allow each IRA beneficiary the right, following the IRA owner's death, to base all of his or her Required Minimum Distribution payments on each one's life expectancies alone, without being required to use the life expectancy of any older IRA beneficiary.

Suppose that instead of selecting his three children as his IRA beneficiaries, Andrew had decided to give 25 percent shares of his IRA to each of his three children, and to his favorite charity. Under the Life Expectancy Rule, where there are multiple beneficiaries, the life expectancy that is required to be used is the life expectancy of the beneficiary with the *shortest* life expectancy. Of the four IRA beneficiaries in this example, the beneficiary with the shortest life expectancy was the charity, which has no life expectancy for Required Minimum Distribution purposes. Accordingly, because no life expectancies can be used, it would appear as if, under the Life Expectancy Rule, all benefits would be required to be paid out in full from the IRA by December 31 of the year immediately following the year of Andrew's death. However, such is not the case. Where *any* of the beneficiaries of the retirement asset have no life expectancy (e.g., where an estate, charity, or trust that does not qualify as a "Designated Beneficiary" has been named as one of the beneficiaries), the

Life Expectancy Rule *cannot* be used. Instead, all benefits from the retirement vehicle would be required to be paid out pursuant to the Five-Year Rule.

The harsh effect of the application of this rule can be ameliorated if the IRA owner divides the IRA into multiple IRAs prior to his or her death. Had Andrew taken this step prior to his death—although all benefits in the IRA in which the charity had been named as beneficiary would be required to be paid out in full by December 31 of the calendar year containing the fifth anniversary of Andrew's death pursuant to the Five-Year Rule—the benefits in the three *other* IRAs in which his son, Thomas, and his two grandchildren, Beth and Howard, had been named as beneficiaries could continue to be paid out based on their own life expectancies under the Life Expectancy Rule.

Accordingly, another good rule of thumb is that whenever a beneficiary with no life expectancy is to receive a portion of the retirement assets, it is usually a good idea to isolate the value of the retirement assets that are to go to that beneficiary in a separate retirement vehicle, usually an IRA, for the benefit of that particular beneficiary. In this way, the failure of that beneficiary to have any life expectancy will not *taint* the balance of the retirement assets and will not prevent the *other* beneficiaries who have life expectancies from using their own life expectancies for Required Minimum Distribution purposes.

Five-Year Rule or Life Expectancy Rule: Which One Will Apply

One can readily see that an individual who wished to create the largest possible legacy effect with his or her retirement assets would generally prefer to have those benefits paid out over the life expectancy of his or her beneficiary under the Life Expectancy Rule, rather than under the Five-Year Rule. Under the Life Expectancy Rule, the smallest yearly distributions are required, allowing the bulk of the retirement assets to remain in the shelter of the retirement vehicle, compounding ten, 15, or perhaps even 20 times over the remaining 50-, 60-, or 70-plus-year life expectancy of the beneficiaries. Such a dramatic impact *cannot* be achieved under the Five-Year Rule, where the entire amount in the retirement vehicle is required to be paid out in full by December 31 of the calendar year containing the fifth anniversary of the death of the retirement asset owner.

The question then arises: Under what circumstances would an individual's retirement benefits be *required* to be paid out under the Five-Year Rule or under the Life Expectancy Rule? The answer can often cause great consternation to clients and their advisors.

The simplest and most obvious answer to this question arises in the case in which an individual had designated an estate, a charity, or a trust that does not qualify as a Designated Beneficiary as the beneficiary or as one of a number of beneficiaries for the retirement asset. In those cases, there is no choice but that the Five-Year Rule will apply to the payment of all retirement benefits, even if such was not the intent of the client or his or her advisors.

However, where the client has selected only individuals as beneficiaries, it is frequently assumed that in *all* cases the beneficiaries will be able to use the Life Expectancy Rule in paying out the retirement assets over their remaining life expectancies. Such is not always the case. The plan document or IRA Custodial Agreement determines whether the Five-Year Rule or the Life Expectancy Rule is to apply under those circumstances. Some plan documents and IRA Custodial Agreements allow the plan participant or IRA owner the choice of electing whether the Five-Year Rule or the Life Expectancy Rule is to apply following their death. Other plan documents and IRA Custodial Agreements allow the beneficiaries, following the death of the plan participant or IRA owner, to select which of the two rules are to apply, with the beneficiary's decision required to be made by December 31 of the calendar year immediately following the calendar year of the plan participant or IRA owner's death. Still other plan documents and IRA Custodial Agreements allow the beneficiaries the right to make that choice, but *only* in the event that the plan participant or IRA owner had *failed* to make such election before his or her death. Finally, some plan documents and IRA Custodial Agreements do not permit *any* elections to be made by the plan participant, IRA owner, or beneficiaries in this regard, but instead compel the use of either the Five-Year Rule or the Life Expectancy Rule in all cases.

In those cases in which the plan participants, IRA owners, or their beneficiaries are given the choice of electing either the Five-

Year Rule or the Life Expectancy Rule, which of these two rules will apply where the plan participant, IRA owner, or beneficiary had *failed* to make any such election? The answer is that the plan document or IRA Custodial Agreement typically contains a "default provision" which would apply in that event. The default provision could then *require* the use of *either* the Five-Year Rule or the use of the Life Expectancy Rule. However, what happens when the plan participants, IRA owners, or their beneficiaries either have failed to make any election in this regard, or where the plan document or IRA Custodial Agreement does not provide them with this choice, *and* where the operative document itself fails to indicate which one of the two methods is to apply? Under those circumstances, the default provisions in the Internal Revenue Service proposed regulations themselves provide the answer. The proposed regulations provide that, where the plan document or IRA Custodial Agreement is silent on this issue, the default rule is the Five-Year Rule, where the beneficiary is someone *other* than the individual's spouse. Where the individual's spouse is the beneficiary, the default rule in the Internal Revenue Service proposed regulations is the Life Expectancy Rule.

It may be especially dangerous for a plan participant or IRA owner to rely on these default provisions, because the operation of the default provisions may work to frustrate the client's entire retirement distribution plan. An example will explain why this may be so.

> **Example.** Margaret, a widow, has designated her daughter Paula, who is 45 years old, as the beneficiary for her $1,000,000 IRA. Margaret dies at age 70 in 1999 *without* taking advantage of her right, under the IRA Custodial Agreement, to elect to have either the Five-Year Rule or the Life Expectancy Rule apply to her IRA benefits following her death. The IRA Custodial Agreement does *not* give the beneficiaries the right to make this choice following the IRA owner's death and, instead, defaults to the Five-Year Rule. Accordingly, the entire $1,000,000 interest in the IRA must be paid out in full to Paula by December 31, 2004 (December 31 of the calendar year containing the fifth anniversary of Margaret's death), even though both Margaret and Paula would

> have much preferred for Paula to have taken out the IRA benefits over her remaining life expectancy of 37.7 years, and as determined under the Internal Revenue Service single life expectancy table for a 45-year-old.

Wherever possible, advisors should review the terms of their clients' qualified plans and IRA Custodial Agreements to ascertain whether the client, or the client's beneficiaries following the client's death, have the ability to make this important election of the Life Expectancy Rule. Where the client *has* the ability to make this election during his or her lifetime, the advisor should ensure that the election is immediately made and properly documented. Where the IRA Custodial Agreement does *not* give either the IRA owner or his or her beneficiary, following the IRA owner's death, the option of electing the use of either the Five-Year Rule or the Life Expectancy Rule, but instead automatically defaults to the use of the Life Expectancy Rule, a client who would like to have the Life Expectancy Rule apply to his or her benefits following his or her death should have no problem, *unless* the plan sponsor or IRA Custodian should subsequently amend the document, changing the default provision to that of the Five-Year Rule. However, if the IRA Custodial Agreement had defaulted to the use of the Five-Year Rule, the client's entire retirement distribution plan would be defeated by the requirement that all benefits in the IRA be paid out in full by December 31 of the calendar year containing the fifth anniversary of the IRA owner's death.

Where the advisor has been able to ascertain this fact in advance, the advisor can inform the client of the disastrous consequences associated with the application of the Five-Year Rule to their retirement benefits and can then have their client immediately move his or her IRA account to another IRA Custodian whose forms and documents permit the use of the Life Expectancy Rule following the IRA owner's death. Where the plan document does not allow either the plan participant or beneficiary, following their death, the choice of using the Life Expectancy Rule, and where the plan document then defaults to the use of the Five-Year Rule, it may be possible for the advisor to arrange for the client's benefits in the qualified plan to be rolled over into an IRA, where the IRA Custodial Agreement or the IRA forms will permit the application of the Life Expectancy Rule following the IRA owner's death.

Another good rule of thumb when dealing with retirement assets before the individual's Required Beginning Date, is to ensure that the Five-Year Rule will *not* apply to retirement benefits should death occur before the Required Beginning Date. If the Five-Year Rule is the default rule in the plan document or IRA Custodial Agreement, the advisor should make sure that the individual has opted out of the application of that rule, wherever possible, and has affirmatively elected that the Life Expectancy Rule will apply to his or her retirement assets following his or her death. This election should be filed with the Plan Administrator of the individual's qualified plan or with the IRA Custodian, and with the filing of the election duly acknowledged and recognized by the Plan Administrator and IRA Custodian as constituting an election that they will honor.

However, even in those cases in which the client, working with his or her advisor, has taken all of these precautions, there is at least one circumstance in which the Five-Year Rule could still apply to the payment of retirement benefits following the client's death. That circumstance could occur accidentally under the following scenario: Assume that the client had designated an individual as beneficiary, and had even elected to have the Life Expectancy Rule apply to the payment of benefits following the client's death, but had named no contingent beneficiary. If the primary beneficiary should predecease the client, with no contingent beneficiary named, the plan document or IRA Custodial Agreement may then default to the client's estate as contingent beneficiary. The retirement assets, in that case, may eventually go through the estate and then out to the same intended contingent beneficiaries that the client would have named, had he or she known about this issue, and had he or she taken the time to name contingent beneficiaries. However, because their estate has no life expectancy, all benefits from the retirement vehicle would be required to be paid out pursuant to the Five-Year Rule. In order to avoid this harsh result, the client should have named *both* a primary beneficiary *and* multiple levels of contingent beneficiaries so that there would always be living human beings who would be named under *all* circumstances, and so that there would never be a case in which the client had run out of beneficiaries, causing the client's estate to become his or her default beneficiary.

Spouse As Beneficiary: Spousal Rollover Rule and Spousal Deferral Rule

As discussed earlier in this chapter, the spouse is the only beneficiary who is permitted to roll over inherited retirement assets into his or her own IRA. This rollover right extends to distributions from qualified plans, IRAs, and tax-sheltered annuities (403(b) plans). No other beneficiary is afforded this right. This rollover right is especially advantageous where the surviving spouse is considerably younger than age $70^1/_2$ at the time of the death of the retirement asset owner, and where the surviving spouse wishes to allow the inherited retirement asset to continue to grow each year on a tax-deferred basis, with no distributions to be made from the retirement asset until the surviving spouse's own Required Beginning Date. Where the retirement asset owner had already reached his or her Required Beginning Date at the time of death, without this spousal rollover right, the surviving spouse would be required to begin distributions from the retirement asset by December 31 of the calendar year immediately following the calendar year of the spouse's death. An example will help to illustrate how this can work.

> **Example.** Matthew dies at age 71, survived by his wife Karen, age 61. Karen is the primary beneficiary of Matthew's IRA. Were Karen to leave the IRA in Matthew's name, each year following the year of his death, she would be required to take Required Minimum Distributions from his IRA. If on the other hand, she immediately rolled his IRA over into a spousal rollover IRA, she could defer taking any distributions from her rollover IRA until she reached her Required Beginning Date, which is not for another nine years. During that time, the IRA could be growing in value on a tax-deferred basis, unreduced by any yearly distributions. At an 8 percent annual interest rate over the nine-year period, the IRA could double in value, providing Karen with much higher yearly distributions once she reached her Required Beginning Date, and distributions from the IRA were required to begin. In addition, under this approach, the IRA would also

produce a much higher legacy for her beneficiaries, following her death.

An additional right afforded to the surviving spouse as beneficiary, which is *not* afforded to any other beneficiary, is the Spousal Deferral Rule. As noted earlier in this chapter, under the Life Expectancy Rule the first Required Minimum Distribution payment is due by December 31 of the calendar year immediately following the calendar year of the death of the retirement asset owner, with yearly distributions required to be made each year thereafter. However, where the spouse is the beneficiary and where the retirement asset owner had *not* reached his or her Required Beginning Date as of the date of his or her death, the spouse is allowed to defer the first Required Minimum Distribution payment until December 31 of the calendar year in which the retirement asset owner would have reached age 70$^{1}/_{2}$, had they survived. This is an especially valuable right, where the deceased spouse had died *before* his or her Required Beginning Date, and where the surviving spouse is already older than age 70$^{1}/_{2}$. An example will help to illustrate this point.

> **Example.** In the prior example, Matthew had died at age 71, survived by his wife, Karen, who was then age 61. Suppose, however, that Karen had died at age 61, survived by her husband, Matthew, who was then age 71. If Matthew were to have immediately rolled over Karen's IRA benefits into a spousal rollover IRA, he would be required to begin yearly Required Minimum Distributions from the spousal rollover IRA by December 31 of the calendar year immediately following the calendar year of Karen's death. If Matthew instead had allowed the IRA to remain in Karen's name, he would *not* be required to take any distributions from that IRA until December 31 of the calendar year in which Karen would have turned age 70$^{1}/_{2}$, had she survived. In this example, Matthew's use of the Spousal Deferral Rule will allow him to defer having to take *any* Required Minimum Distributions from Karen's IRA for nine years.

CHAPTER 13
INVESTING FOR THE FUTURE

CONTENTS

13 INVESTING FOR THE FUTURE

In the past, most Americans did not invest; they saved. In other words, they let *other* people invest for them, by depositing their excess funds with financial institutions that then invested the funds in assets which optimized the financial institution's growth. Even those who invested their assets in financial markets generally delegated the investment decisions to their brokers. It would be hard to claim that in those days the average investor had a personal investment philosophy.

Today, however, everyone has a personal investment philosophy—if only an innate or instinctive one. For those who are interested in researching their various investment options, there are a multitude of books, magazines, newsletters, talk shows, and Web sites from which to derive current investment information. Moreover, the depth and breadth of investment choices today are much larger than had been available to previous generations.

Some people take their investment philosophy and all available financial information to the next level by memorializing a specific investment plan which defines both the sources and uses of their income and their specific short-term and long-term investment goals. For most people, however, their own investment philosophy remains largely unfocused. They continue to allow their investment decisions to be made by their financial advisors.

Personal investment philosophy becomes of critical importance to those with significant retirement assets who are committed to a multigenerational retirement distribution plan. The very nature of multigenerational retirement distribution planning causes an evolution in one's personal investment philosophy. The generation which now owns the retirement assets today winds up investing those assets for

---

Note: Readers should refer to the Introduction for a discussion of issues and concepts covered in Chapter 13 that may be affected by the IRS's issuance of the Revised Proposed Regulations governing Required Minimum Distributions—particularly a discussion of those rules and strategies that have *not* been changed by the Revised Proposed Regulations.

the benefit of their children and/or grandchildren, who will own and invest those assets in the future.

What is the financial impact of this intergenerational use of the retirement assets from an investment perspective? The investment philosophy of the older generation is often entrenched in certain strong emotional issues and certain long-held beliefs. The era in which one grew up plays a vital role in how those feelings and principles were formed. Most older-generation clients were children during the Great Depression and spent their teenage years in the shadow of World War II. Even if their family did not experience a catastrophic loss as a result of those two historic events, people of that era often still harbor a fear of losing everything, a fear reinforced throughout their early childhood and teenage years, as they saw what happened to other families. Not surprisingly, these clients tend to invest with an eye toward security as their overriding financial objective. They are also at a stage in their lives when preservation of principal seems of paramount importance.

Meanwhile, the next two generations—the ones who will inherit the tax-deferred retirement assets in the multigenerational retirement distribution plan—have experienced from birth a very different world. In their lifetimes, America has been transformed from an isolationist manufacturing-based society to a preeminent global service-based superpower. The two world wars which took place in the first half of the last century have been replaced with localized regional conflicts, most with limited impact on American lives, cultural ideals, or political interests. These family members in the next two generations do not fear for their own lives, or for the lives of their family members, as did their parents and grandparents when confronted with such real and imminent enemies as Hitler and Stalin. The investment philosophy of these last two generations is tied less to preserving principal than to mitigating the debilitating effect which inflation can exert over time, and to achieving prolonged rates of return that are high enough to constitute real inflation-adjusted growth. As medical advances have continued to increase longevity, and preserve health and well-being for many individuals in their 80s, 90s, or beyond, long-term asset growth becomes even more important.

Personal investment philosophies are neither right nor wrong. They simply create a framework within which all investment decisions are made. The key to making sound investment decisions from a multigenerational perspective is, first, understanding the differences in generational outlook and, then, developing strategies that effectively address what may often be complex and diverse goals. It is not necessary to abandon one family member's investment philosophy in order to pursue another, nor is it necessary to attempt to merge inherently contradictory investment philosophies. This advice, although easy to articulate, may be quite difficult to put into practice. Even if the advisor's professional practice does not include a financial planning component, the advisor should alert the clients to the type of investment decisions that are inherent in any multigenerational distribution strategy, and should then direct the clients to the plan, appropriate professionals, and resources to help them further develop and implement the multigenerational investment strategy.

Under such a scenario, it may be best for the advisor to go back to the basics, reviewing with the clients the fundamentals of financial planning and alternative investment philosophies. The considerations and concerns of the clients and those of their children and grandchildren should also be taken into account. Neglecting this step may cause difficulty later on in administering the multigenerational retirement distribution plan.

The Variables of Investment Philosophy

The differences in personal investment philosophies among individuals of different generations may stem from two sources. The first possible source is the differences between the cultural experiences of the two generations, as briefly discussed above, that gave rise to different attitudes and expectations that affect investment philosophy. The second possible source is the differences in life experiences that project into differing short-term and long-term investment goals.

For members of the older generation, three distinct but significant financial objectives will need to be realized over the course of their retirement years. The first financial objective is to realize their income goals so that both husband and wife can comfortably support themselves during their retirement years. This financial objective is often paramount during the early part of their retirement years. The latter portion of their retirement years may involve a period in which living expenses have increased dramatically due to the declining health of one or both of the couple, and as home healthcare aides, nurses, physicians, hospitals, prescription medication, and perhaps even nursing home expenses, can begin to consume significant portions of their monthly income. The third financial objective of the couple during their retirement years is their attempt to create a legacy for their family, by passing on a significant inheritance to them after they have died.

Individuals in the younger generation, on the other hand, have a lifetime of events ahead, both planned and unplanned, that may have a significant impact on their financial well-being, and on the financial well-being of their spouse and children. One such unplanned event is the untimely death of the individual or spouse. This event could prove to be financially devastating for the immediate family of the deceased, especially in those cases in which the family's breadwinner had died. Obviously, there is a compelling need for income and asset protection devices to be put in place to insure against the risk of the family's breadwinner becoming disabled or dying. Certain planned events which will require significant funding by the young couple include the purchase of a home, the education of their children, and providing a retirement nest egg for themselves.

Traditionally, these three significant funding events were undertaken in sequence. However, today that may no longer be the case. At one time, a married couple's first financial planning goal was saving enough money for a down payment on the purchase of their first home. Once this first financial goal was realized, the couple often had another ten to 15 years before they needed to make the first pay-ments for college tuition for their first child. However, those tuition payments eventually might double or triple as their younger children graduated from high school and went off to college. Once the couple's mortgage had been paid off, and their children had each completed college and then moved out on their own, their monthly lifestyle expenses would, presumably, be significantly reduced and retirement funding could commence in earnest, becoming at that time their one remaining investment goal.

However, more and more frequently, American couples are moving away from the norm in which they graduated from high school or college, got their first job, changed jobs infrequently during their early working years, until they inevitably found long-term employment with a large company that would employ them for the rest of their lives. In this norm, the individual, early in the work cycle, married, purchased a first home almost immediately, and then almost immediately after that began the process of raising children, staying in the same community until their retirement years, and often until death.

Today the typical scenario can be quite different. Individuals now experience many more changes of jobs and changes of careers during their working lifetime than ever before, with many changes occurring late into their working years, and with some individuals changing careers during midlife and beyond. Many of these job changes or career changes involve relocating to different cities. Additionally, many people are now deferring marriage until their late twenties, thirties, or even forties, or are deciding not to marry at all. Married couples are also deferring the time at which they begin child rearing, often preferring to develop their careers before children are born, and allowing them to accumulate more of a financial nest egg before undertaking the financial responsibility of raising children. Moreover, it is no longer as certain that a child will marry and raise his or her own children. Many couples today are deciding not to have any children, while many single individuals are deciding to have children, either by birth or through adoption. More and more, gay individuals are deciding to openly establish their own households, in many instances raising their own children, who may be their biological children or their adopted children.

For those now in their 60s and 70s, these alternative lifestyle choices made by their children may be bewildering. Some parents in that generation may be entirely willing to support these alternative lifestyle choices, continuing their emotional, and perhaps financial, support of their children. However, some of that generation will choose *not* to support those lifestyle choices, especially if those choices go against ingrained religious or societal beliefs, such as in the case of marriages out of one's religion, interracial marriages, or unions involving individuals of the same sex.

The second, third, or even fourth marriages of the retirement asset owner or of their children may increase the complexity of the financial arrangements exponentially, by factoring in one or more ex-spouses who, in some cases, must continue to be supported, along with the plethora of varying degrees of stepsons and stepdaughters, some of whom may eventually be adopted by the individual.

In short, each of the lifestyle choices made by the clients, their children, and grandchildren will affect on the personal investment philosophy of each individual in the family unit, and on each family member's relationship to each other, financial or otherwise. It will be up to the financial advisor to assist the client in sorting through this maze in order to arrive at a point where the client's financial goals can be clarified sufficiently to be translated into specific investment decisions to fit the clients' investment objectives.

The Element of Risk

Advisors need to accurately assess risk, whenever assisting a client in developing and implementing their financial plan. However, risk is a more complex subject than most people realize. Advisors typically talk about a client's risk tolerance as if there were only one type of risk. In fact, there are several components of investment risk, each of which must be thoroughly analyzed before the client decides on a particular investment plan. A client's limited understanding of risk usually focuses on those risks that cause the most immediate pain and anxiety.

Inflation Risk

One risk that most people are aware of, but often severely underestimate, is inflation risk. Inflation can put purchasing power at extreme risk, especially over an extended period of time. However, the debilitating effects of inflation may take so long to take effect that it is often not perceived as a risk factor at all. A multigenerational retirement distribution plan may span seven decades or more. The retirement assets, over that period of time, will have to be insulated from the effects of inflation, or else risk severe erosion of the purchasing power of those assets for the second and third generations. Combating inflation usually involves balancing the retirement asset portfolio mix heavily in the direction of long-term investments that historically have outpaced inflation, for instance by investing in common stocks.

Volatility Risk

One risk that can produce real worry for investors, especially those of the older generation, is volatility risk. Conventional wisdom states that if one invests in the stock market for the long term, volatility risk becomes less and less significant over time, eventually reaching a point where there is virtually no volatility risk at all. However, not many people can watch with equanimity as the value of their stock portfolio plummets in value. Statistical studies have shown that for common stocks to mitigate volatility risk entirely, an individual should hold their stock an average of 20 years or more.

For many members of the older generation, volatility risk is not so much a function of the periodic up-and-down swing in asset values over time, but of the risk that their assets will be not at full value at the moment when liquidity is necessary, when the asset *must* be sold as part of their overall strategy to liquidate their assets over time. Rather than facing this potential risk, they prefer to invest in federally insured deposits and government bonds over investments in the stock market. After all, they reason, why give up the stability of government backing and insurance security? Their children and grandchildren, on the other hand, are not tied in to this ultra-conservative outlook. The children's investment horizon can be three or four times longer than that of the older generation. They can be justifiably worried when they see the funds which represent their potential inheritance being eaten away each year by inflation. Given the choice, they would prefer having those funds invested in domestic and global stock markets, where real growth can be achieved, and where there is a more realistic chance that the effects of inflation can be entirely overcome, thereby enabling their asset portfolio to fund their future lifetime expense needs.

Business Risk

Investing in corporate stocks and bonds can carry with it still another risk—that the business itself will experience a downturn, producing irreversible losses. Investors who act on information about a particular business and who invest a substantial portion of their investment portfolio in one company's future are especially susceptible to this type of business risk. Many members of the older generation may vividly recall the worst nightmare years of the Great Depression, when otherwise promising businesses and ventures failed and investors who had staked their entire portfolio in one company's stock saw their assets wiped out.

Those who grew up in later generations may not be able to imagine business failures on such a massive scale. They have grown up confident in the belief that the financial world has all but eliminated the conditions that had caused such financial catastrophes in the United States stock markets in the past. Regulatory oversight committees, Blue Sky laws, and certain built-in fail-safe market mechanisms, they reason, now operate together to ensure that an overall stock market crash can no longer occur. One business may fail, but surely they cannot all now go at once. Those in the later generation believe that the obvious way to mitigate business risk is through a proper diversification of their investment assets.

Market Risk

Those in the older generation are not always as sanguine about the long-term prospects of the stock market increasing in value decade after decade. Their early childhood memories of the Great Depression cause them to contemplate a darker possibility, based on their actual experience. Diversification makes sense to them, but not as an absolute safe harbor. For them, of far greater concern is market risk—the perception that sooner or later the *entire* stock market will fall.

Those in the younger generations should be sensitive to market risk and should not dismiss this concern as the paranoid delusion of their elders, especially since several precipitous market declines have occurred within the past two decades. However, also within recent memory are two developments of perhaps even greater significance. The first is that in each recent case of precipitous market decline, the financial markets have come back more quickly, and in short order achieved higher levels than had existed immediately before the decline. The second development is that, in each instance, not all markets declined at the same time—in fact, there are certain homeostatic relationships that exist between markets. Therefore, one strategy that can be used to substantially mitigate market risk is to diversify among asset categories. Most financial planners use as an illustration, a pyramid of investment categories to assist them in explaining to their clients this investment strategy. In this methodology, a decreasing portion of the investment resources are allocated as one move up the investment risk pyramid, with the most conservative investments at the base of the pyramid and constituting the *largest* asset category, and with the most aggressive and risky investments occupying the very top of the pyramid, and constituting the smallest asset category.

Marketability Risk

Among various asset categories are certain types of assets, such as real estate, that are less subject to volatility risk, business risk, or market risk, and may even be helped by inflation risk. A danger associated with these types of investments is the risk of marketability—when the asset needs to be sold, no one will be around who wants to buy it.

The most effective way to deal with marketability risk is to choose investments according to a projected investment time horizon. In the projected investment time horizon, it is pre-determined when certain assets are to be sold. The projected sales dates are based on estimations of the optimum time to sell a particular investment and are entirely independent of the timing of any specific life event or other financial milestone. The projected investment time horizon creates a *flexible* time frame in which it is anticipated that an asset will be sold. However, because there is no absolute requirement or compelling financial crisis which forces the sale of the asset at any particular point in time, the client is entirely free to take advantage of favorable market conditions to determine the actual best date on which the asset is to be sold.

Interest Rate Risk

Bonds, the investments perhaps most favored by those of the older generation, carry with them still another type of risk—interest rate risk. As a bond matures, rising market interest rates will cause its value to decline, even if the bond is a fully guaranteed government bond. In fact, if interest rates have risen high enough, the bond issuer (frequently a municipality) may choose to call the bond and redeem it.

The most universally accepted method of reducing interest rate risk is to purchase a block of the same type of investments, but with each particular asset in the block possessing a different maturity date, or stated differently, with the assets having "staggered" maturity dates. With this approach, each bond can then be sold at its maturity date when it will realize its full face value, regardless of any prior fluctuations in its value which may have occurred in the past, due to changing market interest rates. The individual in this way will, therefore, have achieved the equivalent of asset diversification, but with the diversification factor in this case being time.

Currency Risk

The historic progression toward a truly global economy has made currency risk an increasingly important factor in a client's investment strategy. As more and more foreign securities are owned by American investors, greater reliance may in the future be placed on the various monetary hedge strategies of professional money managers or mutual fund managers.

Death of Owner Risk and Variable Annuity with Guaranteed Death Benefit

While it is not within the scope of this book to make any specific investment recommendations, one type of investment in particular deserves mention—the variable annuity with guaranteed death benefit. There are two reasons why this investment deserves special consideration for those interested in multigenerational retirement distribution planning. First, its risk factors closely match the risk factors involved in multigenerational investing. Second, it has gone largely unnoticed by much of the investment community.

One risk that has not been touched on so far, and that is perhaps unique to multigenerational investing in the context of retirement distribution planning, is the risk of the death of the IRA owner. In a multigenerational plan in which multiple life expectancies are involved, the time period over which many investments will be held will in many instances be far longer than is typically contemplated in most standard investment strategies. In the typical multigenerational retirement distribution plan, the holding period for many of the assets may actually exceed the life expectancy of the IRA owner.

One way in which the certain eventual death of the IRA owner can be exploited to maximize the rate of return on the IRA assets is to invest the IRA assets in a vehicle which offers a more aggressive portfolio mix than many older generation investors may initially feel comfortable with, but which at the same time provides a guarantee that at the death of the IRA owner the full value of the original investment plus earnings will be returned, less any prior distributions which had been made. In other words, by contract guarantee with the insurance company, the IRA owner at his or her death can do no worse than provide their heirs with the full value of the original contract purchase price, less the Required Minimum Distributions, and any other prior distributions which may have been made. This guaranteed death benefit is provided regardless of the annuity's value as of the date of death of the IRA owner, and accordingly is provided *regardless* of how successfully the IRA owners had selected the various annuity investment options within the contract during their lifetime.

Life insurance companies for many years have been providing guaranteed death benefits through annuity products. These annuity products historically have been used for the investment of retirement assets. Today, many mutual funds are now offering these same type of guaranteed death benefit features, targeting the sale of this new investment product to the large-IRA market.

The annuity contract guarantee typically takes one of three forms. The basic annuity contract guarantee provides that, at the IRA owner's death, the beneficiaries will receive the original annuity contract principal amount less any distributions which may have been made. A second and more attractive version of this type of annuity contract guarantees the *highest* account value realized by the IRA owner on a predetermined prior anniversary date, typically, annually, creating a new valuation benchmark which is to be used. The third and most attractive version of this annuity contract provides at the IRA owner's death, the accumulated interest rate, typically 5 or 6 percent compounded annually.

Naturally, there is a steep mortality expense built into this product. However, even giving up 50 to 60 basis points initially to obtain this product will be viewed by many clients as a small price to pay to guarantee the principal amount (plus earnings) of their retirement assets, especially when in the back of their mind they are still expecting a stock market crash and their retirement assets to be wiped out.

Asset Allocations with Multiple IRAs

As the IRA allocation example below illustrates, the typical multigenerational IRA distribution plan will involve the creation of several *different* IRAs, each established for a *different* IRA beneficiary, in different amounts, payable over *different* periods of time and therefore with each having a *different* financial objective. The challenge of the investment advisor is to develop an individualized investment strategy unique to each particular IRA, taking into consideration the investment philosophies of both the IRA owner and each *different* IRA beneficiary. In the ideal family situation, the IRA owner will welcome the input which the particular IRA beneficiary will want to make over the way in which the IRA allocable to that beneficiary is to be invested. In that case, the IRA owner and beneficiary will work together with the investment advisor and retirement distribution specialist, to formulate an overall investment plan for that particular IRA, which *both* IRA owner and beneficiary agree on. However, the IRA still belongs solely to the IRA owner, who is entirely free each year to invest the IRA in any way in which he or she chooses, without accepting *any* investment advice from any intended IRA beneficiary. In fact, the IRA owner is entirely free to close out any IRA in any year, or to change the beneficiary on any IRA in any year.

Figure 13-1

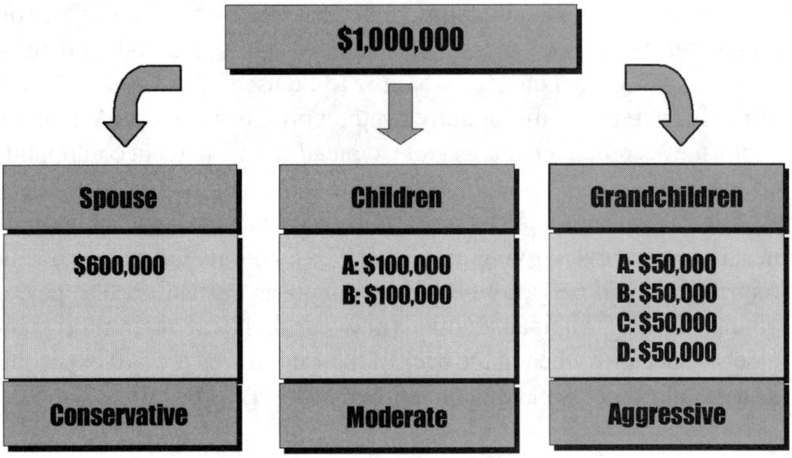

Drawing Up the Investment Plan

The Issue of Control Over Investments

At this stage in the process, the clients should decide how much control they would like to retain over investment decisions regarding the retirement assets—and for how long. Part of their stewardship over the retirement assets involves exercising control over the investment decisions and distribution decisions, with a view toward optimizing the value of the retirement assets for the benefit of the family unit as a whole. However, part of their stewardship over the retirement asset means that they must relinquish some measure of control, so as to provide transition to the time *after* their death, when their heirs will be administering the retirement assets on their own.

Control can be exercised directly by the clients during their own lifetimes by making the specific investment decisions themselves. Control to a certain extent can be extended beyond their lifetimes by designating trusts as beneficiaries for those retirement assets, and by putting appropriate trust mechanisms in place to safeguard those assets for the benefit of their children and grandchildren after they have died.

These after-death control issues arise after careful consideration has been made of the beneficiaries' ages and maturity levels. Are the children and the grandchildren capable of making informed investment decisions on their own? Are they especially vulnerable to the undue influences of others? Will their prior lifestyle choices work to impair their judgment? Will the yearly income stream generated by the IRA assets, or the possible access to the full value of the IRA itself create a disincentive for the beneficiaries, dissuading them from pursuing and accomplishing certain educational, vocational, and professional objectives? Will the yearly income stream generated by the IRA be sufficient to ensure the funding of those life events that the beneficiaries might otherwise not have been able to achieve, or achieved only through extraordinary effort?

The client's stewardship over that retirement asset need not be confined to those decisions which the clients make alone during their lifetime, or those decisions which the trustees of any trust designed as beneficiary of the retirement assets may make alone. Early on, the clients may have structured the investment decision process as a collaborative family effort, with each beneficiary providing input, where and when appropriate. With the proper beneficiary designations, Retirement Asset Wills, and trust documents in place, the clients can determine to a great extent the degree of control that the beneficiaries will be able to exercise over the retirement assets initially, as well as the time frame for increasing and ultimately ceding total investment control over those assets.

If, in the client's mind, the children or grandchildren are each fully capable of handling the retirement asset income stream and investment authority over the assets, the clients should then take the responsibility for assuring that their beneficiaries will enjoy maximum flexibility and control over the retirement assets. Remember, however, that on the IRA owner's death title to the IRA does not pass to the beneficiaries. Instead, at that time the IRA is merely retitled as the IRA of the deceased, for the benefit of the beneficiaries. The owner of the IRA, while he or she is alive, is entirely free to limit the beneficiaries' subsequent access and control over the retirement assets. For example, the beneficiaries may need to change the Custodian of the IRA after the IRA owner has died. If this right is not specified in the beneficiary designation forms, Retirement Asset Will, or underlying IRA Custodial Agreement, the right may not exist. Accordingly, the IRA owner *prior* to his or her death should specify in the appropriate documents which rights he or she would like the beneficiaries to have *after* his or her death and, as important, which rights he or she would *not* like the beneficiaries to have.

The Best Multigenerational Investment Plan

Once the advisor has completed the work of gathering and interpreting all of the relevant financial and family data, the advisor should then create a summary of the various investment philosophies which are to be reflected in the investment plan. The summary can then serve as a starting point for discussion with the IRA owner and with the other family members who are to be included in the decision-making process. In designing the multigenerational investment plan, the advisor should keep in mind that the best multigenerational investment plans will have certain characteristics. They will be comprehensive, well managed, flexible, and responsive to change.

Before deciding on any specific investment choices, it is a good idea to discuss the three alternative investment strategies: conservative, moderate, and aggressive. Discuss which of the three models would be the best choice to achieve the specific goals of the various family members involved in the retirement distribution plan. Next, an asset allocation model should be decided upon for the specific investment alternatives which are to apply within each IRA.

The client—acting alone or in conjunction with other family members—will then allocate the overall IRA assets among the various IRAs established for each individual beneficiary, choosing the appropriate asset allocation model—conservative, moderate, aggressive—for each individual IRA, based on the specific investment profile established for the particular family member who is the beneficiary of that IRA.

Over time, clients may decide to maintain the various predetermined asset allocation mixes through periodic ratio transfers, also known as portfolio rebalancing. Many mutual fund, brokerage, and insurance companies will automatically rebalance a diversified portfolio at pre-determined intervals established by the clients. Alterna-

Figure 13-2

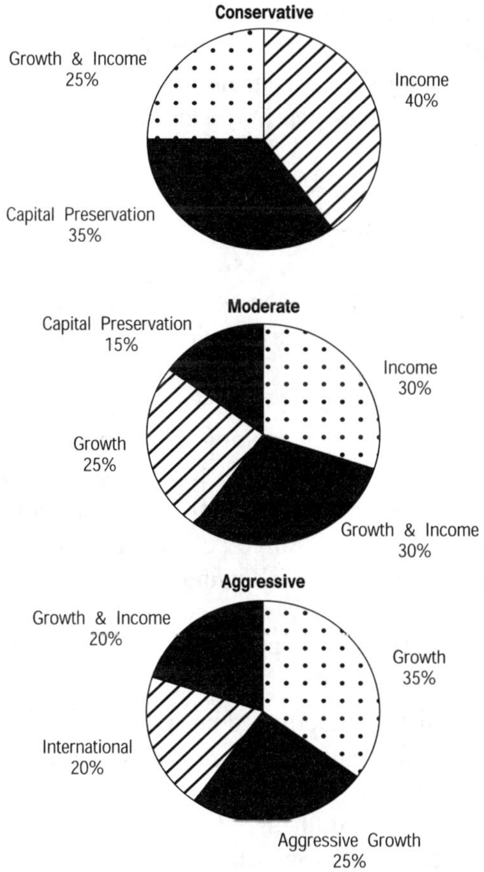

tively, the rebalancing of an asset allocation mix can be done manually with an investment advisor. The client may also decide periodically to adjust the asset allocation mix applicable to one or more of the IRAs. Either way, the following issues should be reevaluated at least annually:

- Is the investment allocation mix still appropriate to each particular beneficiary?
- Will anticipated independent performance accomplish the stated objectives?
- Did the investment strategy perform as modeled? Better or worse?
- What adjustments must be made?

The advisor should also periodically review the family situation to determine whether any changes in financial or personal circumstances have occurred among the beneficiaries or in the financial environment at large that would necessitate any changes in the multigenerational investment plan.

Distribution Allocation

The retirement distribution specialist should meet at least annually with his or her clients. The yearly review should take place *before* the client is scheduled to take his or her yearly IRA Required Minimum Distributions payment. One of the purposes of the yearly review will be to assist the client in determining which portion of the Required Minimum Distribution amount due for that year is to be paid from each IRA involved in the multigeneration plan at retirement distribution. The distribution allocation to be made from each IRA each year can be based on either of the following:

- Pre-set proportions from each of the IRAs which are subject to review and adjustment each year
- Proportions that are determined anew each year, based on the particular family and financial circumstances existing at that time

There will also be certain IRA Custodial issues which will have to be dealt with each year. (See Chapter 14, which discusses many of these custodian issues.) It is extremely convenient from an administrative point of view to have the client maintain all of the IRAs with one IRA Custodian—preferably one that has demonstrated the rare combination of a proactive service standard with the requisite knowledge and expertise. Of course, the Custodian of the IRA must have previously agreed to accept the beneficiary designation form, Retirement Asset Will, and Trust Agreement (where applicable) that had all previously been executed. If those documents are not being followed, the annual review process can become an exercise in frustration and futility, with the efficacy of the entire retirement distribution plan potentially at risk. Advisors may therefore have to monitor the IRA Custodians to ensure that the retirement distribution plan is being administered correctly, and that the interests of their clients are being protected.

Monitoring the Investment Plan

Once the multigenerational investment plan has been put in place, it will have to be monitored closely for any needed changes or adjustments. This takes the stewardship of the retirement asset to another level. Because of the longevity of the plan and the number of people involved, clients may be tempted to either micromanage the plan or to leave the plan entirely alone without reviewing it periodically. Both ends of the spectrum could be potentially devastating. An annual review of the multigenerational investment plans seems to strike a reasonable balance between these two extremes.

A Radical Alternative

Throughout this book, the objective of preserving tax deferral has been assumed as the highest goal—provided that tax-deferral strategies do not interfere with or conflict with certain psychological and family factors involved in wealth transfers. The desirability of tax deferral is based on the premise that the compounded growth of *pre-tax* assets will always far outperform the compounded growth of *after-tax* assets, even when the income tax bill finally comes due.

Under certain circumstances, however, it may make sense to actually *accelerate* certain retirement distributions in order to take advantage of certain income tax benefits that perhaps would not otherwise be available to the individual. One example of this involves the use of the income in respect of a decedent (IRD) deduction, and the ability which the beneficiary of the retirement asset may have to reduce the effective tax rate applicable to their retirement distributions by the amount of the IRD deduction. (See Chapter 9, which discusses the IRD deduction and its creation when the owner of a retirement asset has died, and the value of the retirement asset increased the Federal estate taxes which were due in the individual's estate.)

Many individuals who are the recipients of retirement distributions will not be able to take advantage of the IRD deduction. Consider, for example, the case of a young grandchild who does not itemize deductions. Such an individual will not be able to use the IRD deduction. For such individuals, minimizing retirement distributions in order to preserve the tax-deferred growth of the asset will usually make the most sense. Similarly, for those beneficiaries with no other opportunity to defer current income taxes on their current earned income, it makes more sense to spend *after-tax* dollars while preserving the growth potential of all *pre-tax* dollars. Moreover, if the estate of the retirement asset owner did not owe any Federal estate taxes on the retirement assets, for instance because the total estate was less than $675,000, no IRD deduction is even available. Accordingly, the beneficiary under those circumstances would not be able to minimize income taxes due on any retirement distributions by employing any IRD deduction. Under those circumstances, it may make more sense for the beneficiary to take retirement distributions over as long a period of time as possible in order to avoid the income tax bite on those payments for as long as possible.

However, what about older children or grandchildren, with successful careers, who, because of their current cash flow needs, have thus far been unable to maximize their contributions to a retirement plan in which they would participate? If they do not have sufficient excess income from other sources after the payment of their lifestyle expenses to make the maximum use of these tax-deferral opportunities for their own income, it may be to their advantage to accelerate their distributions from the multigeneration IRA in order to free up their own retirement plan opportunities. In many instances the income tax otherwise due on the distributions from the multigeneration IRA may be largely offset by the IRD deduction, effectively reducing the tax rate applicable to the receipt of that asset to a very low level. The income tax rate applicable to their earned income that year, on the other hand, is not reduced by any IRD deduction. Accordingly, individuals under those circumstances may want to consider receiving IRD distributions each year *in excess of* the Required Minimum Distribution amounts. The individuals should then contribute the amount of the IRA distribution which they had received that year into a 401(k) plan, in which they now participate. They will then receive a current income tax deduction for the full amount of the contribution to the IRA distribution, due to the availability of the IRD deduction.

An example will illustrate the application of this rule. In an example given in Chapter 9, the Participant Direct Approach had been used, with the children receiving IRA assets worth approximately $1.87 million. If the Federal estate tax due on that asset was $410,040, then the potential overall income in respect of a decedent deduction would be the $410,040 amount. Under the Proportionate Recovery Method for recovering the IRD deduction, 41 percent ($410,040 divided by $1 million) of every dollar of IRA benefit received by the beneficiary would be deductible. Accordingly, if the beneficiary were in a 40 percent marginal income tax bracket, a $10,000 distribution from the IRA would incur only $2,760 in taxes ($10,000 times (40% x (1-41)%), while a $10,000 contribution to the 401(k) plan would generate a current income tax deduction of $4,000. The individual is, therefore, $1,240 ahead, with the $10,000 IRA distribution in effect moved over into the 401(k) plan. Accordingly, where IRA distributions can be taxed at a *lower* rate than an equivalent dollar derived from current compensation or taxable investments, the receipt of larger IRA distributions than would otherwise be due represents a tax savings—as long as the IRA distributions are then contributed into a qualified pension or profit sharing plan. In such a case, the tax-favored dollars received from the Inherited IRA effectively funded tax-deferred savings for the beneficiary's own retirement plan. Alternatively, if the extra amount of the IRA distribution is not contributed by the beneficiary into a qualified plan, or does not stay there until at least age 59½, this tax advantage is lost. Moreover, the above strategy must dovetail with the beneficiary's particular financial objectives—both short-term and long-term—in order to warrant serious consideration.

The Benefits of Multigenerational Investing

The retirement distribution plan, if constructed and administered correctly, will have enormous beneficial effects on the families' overall financial well being. Moreover, the process of retirement distribution planning itself often facilitates family unity and cohesiveness by encouraging the involvement of the children and grandchildren in the planning and decision-making process. Often, the children and grandchildren will be informed about the extent of the retirement assets and the portion of the retirement assets allocable for their benefit. Frequently, as the retirement asset owner ages, the children and grandchildren are given a more active role each year in monitoring and continuing to refine the retirement distribution plan and in investing the retirement assets. Through the retirement distribution plan, the retirement asset owner has an opportunity not only to provide financial security and asset growth potential to his or her children and grandchildren, but also to pass along to those succeeding generations the knowledge and wisdom to help them successfully manage the family wealth.

CHAPTER 14
THE CHALLENGE OF THE IRA CUSTODIAN

CONTENTS

14 THE CHALLENGE OF THE IRA CUSTODIAN

A recurring theme throughout this book is that one of the major obstacles to comprehensive retirement distribution planning is the client's mindset. This chapter, however, discusses an even more significant obstacle—the difficulties advisors and clients often encounter in dealing with IRA Custodians. This obstacle may be even harder to deal with because it may surface only after a significant portion of the tax, financial, and personal issues have already been resolved.

Many clients who have accumulated large assets in their qualified plans have been accustomed to administering those assets each year themselves as either the Plan Administrator or trustee of the plan, or as both. If those assets have been invested through financial institutions, which they invariably are, the financial institutions, especially in the context of qualified plans for closely held businesses, typically serve as mere depositories for the assets and do not hold any fiduciary position with respect to the plan assets. However, in the area of IRAs, this is not the case.

Internal Revenue Code §§408(a)(2) and 408(n) define who can qualify to be an IRA Trustee (Custodian). The regulations expressly indicate that the Trustee (Custodian) "cannot be an individual." Accordingly, individuals cannot serve as custodians for their own IRAs. Only banks or other financial institutions that meet the requirements set forth in the above-cited Code and regulation sections can qualify as IRA Custodians. A client who wishes to establish any form of IRA—whether it be a regular contribution (traditional) IRA, a rollover IRA,

Note: Readers should refer to the Introduction for a discussion of issues and concepts covered in Chapter 14 that may be affected by the IRS's issuance of the Revised Proposed Regulations governing Required Minimum Distributions and by the passage of EGTRRA 2001. These include: the Uniform Distribution Period Table; the elimination of irrevocable elections at the individual's Required Beginning Date; the determination of the beneficiary by December 31 of the year following the year of the individual's death; and IRA Reporting.

an Inherited IRA, a SEP IRA, a Simple IRA, a Roth IRA, an Education IRA, or a Multigeneration IRA—will need to select a custodian institution in which the IRA funds will be deposited.

Virtually every major brokerage firm, bank, trust company, and insurance company seems to advertise itself as having substantial expertise in the area of retirement distribution planning. If fact, nothing could be further from the truth. The most common source of misinformation clients typically receive in this area is from the sales and service representatives of these same financial institutions. While these institutions may actually possess significant expertise in the product sales area of retirement distribution planning, they typically demonstrate only a vague awareness of the many technical tax rules relating to retirement distribution planning. In fairness, many financial institutions have taken the necessary steps to adequately train their employees in this area. Some have established departments, usually at the main office, where individuals can be found who are highly qualified to advise the local account executives correctly. Unfortunately for clients and advisors alike, there is no easy way to tell the difference between an institution whose personnel are up on all of these rules, and one in which they are not. Typically, it is at the account executive level where most misinformation is disseminated. This can be particularly troublesome when clients embark on the complex and comprehensive decision-making process of retirement distribution planning, only to find at the point of implementation that they must deal with an account executive at the IRA Custodian institution who is misinformed. Clients may feel confident about the planning decisions they have made, but may not feel competent to effectively communicate these decisions to the account executives, who often have no prior experience in this area. Nor do clients always know the questions to ask that will reveal whether or not the account executive really understands the client's decisions and knows how to implement those decisions.

In addition, the institution itself may have certain policies and procedures that are incompatible with the implementation of any multigenerational retirement distribution strategy, let alone the one designed by the clients and their advisory team. When account executives at these institutions respond by saying that their custodial institution does not allow such an arrangement, the entire retirement distribution plan can come crashing down. Now the clients' confidence level has taken several steps backward, erasing whatever prior gains may have been made.

Adoption Agreement/Beneficiary Designation

In establishing an IRA, an individual will be asked to complete what is often referred to as an "Adoption Agreement" or "Beneficiary Designation" form. Many individuals, especially many account executives, believe that this *one* document constitutes the entire IRA agreement. They fail to recognize that the Adoption Agreement/Beneficiary Designation form is roughly the equivalent of an insurance application. In the insurance application, the owner of the policy is listed, the primary and contingent beneficiaries are named, the level of insurance sought is specified, and the individual's medical history is elicited.

Once the insurance policy is issued, however, the application becomes an Addendum to the policy itself. The policy constitutes a contract between the policy owner and the insurance company. The form of the contract is the policy itself, which frequently runs ten to 15 pages in length, and which sets forth all of the rights, liabilities, and obligations of both the insured and the insurance company.

A similar arrangement exists in the case of IRAs. Each IRA consists not only of the Adoption Agreement/Designation of Beneficiary form, but also of a Custodial Agreement, which typically runs anywhere from six to 15 pages. The Custodial Agreement defines all of the rights, liabilities, and obligations between the IRA owner and the financial institution as IRA Custodian. The advisor may have to do some sleuthing to find this document. It is often difficult to get a copy of the IRA Custodial Agreement because the account executives themselves may not be aware that such a document exists.

Where the IRA is held in a trust account, the underlying agreement will be a Trust Agreement instead of a Custodial Agreement. Similarly, where the IRA is held as an Individual Retirement Annuity, the underlying agreement will be an Individual Retirement Annuity Contract. However, in each case the result is the same. There is an underlying legal document that sets forth all of the rights, liabilities, and obligations of both parties.

Three Choices

Individuals with IRAs need to address the following three issues with respect to the payout of those benefits:

1. Who are the primary and contingent beneficiaries of the IRA?
2. If the individual lives to his or her Required Beginning Date, will one life expectancy or two be used to compute Required Minimum Distributions each year? Will the individual's life expectancy and/or a spouse beneficiary's life expectancy be recalculated each year, or will their life expectancies be based on a term certain method of payment or on a hybrid method?
3. If the individual dies before his or her Required Beginning Date, will the death benefit payout be based on either the Five-Year Rule or the Life Expectancy Rule? (See Chapter 12 for a complete discussion of these rules.)

The elections and decisions that a client makes with respect to each of the above three issues will have a dramatic impact not only on who the IRA will eventually be paid to, but also on the period of time over which benefits will be paid, both before and after the individual's date of death. Despite the significance of these three elections, the majority of Adoption Agreement/Designation of Beneficiary forms from various financial institutions fail to ask the clients each of these three important questions.

The typical Adoption Agreement/Designation of Beneficiary form will inquire as to the individual's choice of primary and contingent beneficiary. However, it frequently will *not* ask whether one life expectancy or two will be used for purposes of computing Required Minimum Distributions payable each year after the individual has reached his or her Required Beginning Date. In addition, it frequently will *not* ask whether one, two, or no life expectancies, are to be recalculated each year. Most Adoption Agreement/Designation of Beneficiary forms also ignore the issue of whether, if the individual dies prior to his or her Required Beginning Date, the payout of his or her benefits will be made pursuant to the Five-Year Rule or the Life Expectancy Rule.

One way to address each of these three issues is for the clients or their advisor to locate an IRA Custodian whose Adoption Agreement/

Designation of Beneficiary elicits the requisite information. In most cases, however, clients already have a long-term relationship with their account executive. The natural choice is to keep the IRA with the IRA Custodian which currently employs that account executive, or which currently engages their services. In fact, when account executives change their employment or their relationship to that of another financial institution, clients typically will move their IRA funds to the new custodian institution.

Locating an IRA Custodian whose forms ask all the right questions may seem to many clients like putting the cart before the horse. Even suggesting this approach to certain clients may severely disrupt the otherwise effective existing relationship which the retirement distribution planner may have already established with the client. The next best thing is to have the existing IRA Custodian accept a form, prepared for the client, that does in fact address each of the three issues that the Adoption Agreement/Designation of Beneficiary form of the IRA Custodian had failed to address. This document is, therefore, merely an expanded version of the IRA Custodian's own Adoption Agreement/Designation of Beneficiary form. This supplemental document has been referred to consistently throughout this text as the "Retirement Asset Will."

The real value of the Retirement Asset Will lies in its ability to deal in a comprehensive way with each of these issues (e.g., choice of beneficiary and certain payment options) both before and after the individual's death and to deal with certain other related issues as well. Armed with a Retirement Asset Will, the retirement distribution specialist can approach a particular custodial institution and can determine in advance what limitations and obstacles their client will face in implementing their retirement distribution plans with that particular IRA Custodian. Many of the obstacles can be found in the various default provisions of the IRA Custodial Agreement and in the administrative policies promulgated by the custodial institution, many of which are likely to be thoroughly out of sync with the current planning environment. The Retirement Asset Will, if accepted by the custodial institution, can then operate to "fix" each of the problems contained in the Custodial Agreement and in the custodial institution's administrative policies.

Default Provisions of the Proposed Regulations

Once an individual reaches his or her Required Beginning Date, benefits will be paid out under the methodology selected by the individual with respect to whether one life expectancy or two will be used, and whether or not one, two, or no life expectancies are to be recalculated. Similarly, if the individual dies before the Required Beginning Date, payouts will be made under either the Five-Year Rule or the Life Expectancy Rule, depending again on which choice the individual had previously made. If an individual has failed to address any of these vital issues, his or her benefits will be paid out based on the default provisions contained in the IRA Custodial Agreement.

Most IRA Custodial Agreements contain the requisite default provisions which are to operate in those cases in which the individual has failed to make any elections with respect to those issues. However, sometimes the IRA Custodial Agreement does not contain any default provisions, or does not contain all of the necessary default provisions. The proposed regulations under Internal Revenue Code Sections 401(a)(9) and 408(a)(6) indicate that where the individual has failed to make the appropriate elections in a timely manner (i.e., by their Required Beginning Date or by their date of death), and where the IRA Custodial Agreement is also silent on the answer to those issues, then the default provisions contained in the proposed regulations themselves are to apply. The default provisions in the proposed regulations are as follows:

- With respect to the issue of the use of one or two life expectancies at the Required Beginning Date, the proposed regulations indicate that the individual, in timely naming a beneficiary who will receive their benefits upon their death (other than an estate, charity, or non-qualifying trust), will automatically be allowed to use the life expectancy of that beneficiary for purposes of computing Required Minimum Distribution amounts payable at the Required Beginning Date and beyond.
- With respect to the issue of a term certain or recalculation payout, the proposed regulations require that both the life expect-

ancy of the individual and the life expectancy of a spouse beneficiary are to be recalculated each year.

- With respect to the payment of death benefits before the individual's Required Beginning Date, the default provisions in the proposed regulations indicate that if the individual and IRA Custodial Agreement are each silent on the issue of whether the Five-Year Rule or the Life Expectancy Rule is to apply after the individual's death, benefits are to be paid under the Five-Year Rule, if an individual other than the spouse has been designated as beneficiary. However, if the individual's spouse is the beneficiary, the default provisions in the proposed regulations provide that the death benefits are to be paid under the Life Expectancy Rule.

Default Provisions in IRA Custodial Agreements

From a practical point of view, one hardly ever needs to go to the IRS proposed regulations to learn of their default provisions, because virtually every IRA Custodial Agreement contains the requisite default provisions with respect to each of these issues. However, the drafters of those Custodial Agreements, when faced with alternative choices on how to word the default provisions in their particular Custodial Agreements, initially opted in most instances to conform those default provisions to the default provisions contained in the IRS proposed regulations.

Although this policy might sound like a sensible one from the custodial institution's point of view, in fact the default provisions in the proposed regulations in most instances hurt the IRA owner by dramatically precluding the possibility of both multigenerational IRA distributions and continued tax deferrals. After all, the IRS wants its deferred taxes. The custodial institutions probably did not intend to put the IRS's interests ahead of the interests of its own clients. Instead, the drafters of those Custodial Agreement default provisions were probably unaware of the harmful effects of incorporating the IRS default provisions into the Custodial Agreements. However, the unfortunate result of that policy is that, unless individuals affirmatively answer each one of the above issues in completing an IRA Adoption Agreement or Designation of Beneficiary form, there is no assurance that their retirement distribution choices will be entirely implemented, due to the operation of the default provisions in their IRA Custodial Agreement, which may work to thwart their retirement distribution plan.

That outcome, though bad enough, can get worse.

Again, the default provisions in the IRS proposed regulations indicate that the mere designation of an individual as an IRA beneficiary entitles the IRA owner to use the life expectancy of that individual for purposes of computing Required Minimum Distribution amounts payable at the individual's Required Beginning Date. Fortunately for most IRA owners, the default provisions in most IRA Custodial Agreements mirror this liberal rule. Therefore, an individual with this somewhat standard IRA Custodial Agreement, in merely selecting a person—in other words, spouse or children—as beneficiary, without doing anything further, will automatically be allowed to use the life expectancy of that person for purposes of computing the Required Minimum Distribution amounts due each year.

However, some IRA Custodial Agreements, including one by a nationwide brokerage firm, are written so poorly that the provisions require an individual to affirmatively elect to use a second life expectancy before that option can be honored. Individuals adopting the Custodial Agreement of that financial institution would, therefore, be relegated to the use of only one life expectancy, unless they had selected an individual beneficiary (or beneficiaries) for their benefits and had also affirmatively elected to use the life expectancy or life expectancies of those individuals for purposes of measuring Required Minimum Distribution amounts payable each year. Without this second affirmative election at the Required Beginning Date, the individual's payout would be limited to one based on his or her life expectancy alone—a potential disaster for the individual's retirement distribution payout strategy.

With respect to life expectancy calculation alternatives, the proposed regulations contain a default provision that the life expectancy of both the individual and individual's spouse beneficiary are to be recalculated, unless an affirmative election to the contrary has been made. This requirement is anathema to individuals who are interested in multigenerational IRA payouts and continued tax deferrals. When both the individual's and spouse's life expectancies are being recalculated, all benefits must be paid out of the IRA by December 31 of the calendar year following the calendar year of the second death, where death has occurred *after* the Required Beginning Date.

The tragedy here is that, in the case of individuals with IRAs sponsored by those IRA Custodians, unless those individuals have affirmatively elected to use either a term certain or hybrid method of payout for their benefits, both the individual's life expectancy and the life expectancy of the individual's spouse beneficiary will be required to be recalculated each year. Although this disaster situation can be saved in a case where the spouse survives the IRA owner and creates a spousal rollover IRA, should the spouse predecease the IRA owner, on the IRA owner's death, all amounts in the IRA will be required to be paid out by December 31 of the year following that death.

Next come the five-year and one-year payout provisions for death benefits. As noted earlier, the proposed regulations provide a different default provision, depending on whether the beneficiary is a spouse or non-spouse. In those instances in which a spouse is the beneficiary, the default provision is the Life Expectancy Rule. This means that benefits can be paid over the remaining life expectancy of the spouse after the individual's death, with the first payment required to be made by December 31 following the calendar year of the individual's death (unless the spouse can elect the Spousal Deferral Rule, in which case the first payment can be deferred until December 31 of the year in which the IRA owner would have turned $70^1/_2$). However, in the case of a non-spouse beneficiary, the default provisions in the proposed regulations require the operation of the Five Year Rule. Under the Five-Year Rule, the entire amount of the retirement assets must be paid out by December 31 of the calendar year containing the fifth anniversary of the individual's death.

Here again, the default provisions in many IRA Custodial Agreements mirror those contained in the proposed regulations. For non-spouse beneficiaries, the default provisions in most IRA Custodial Agreements call for the application of the Five-Year Rule. This default provision flies in the face of multigenerational planning, which, through the use of the Life Expectancy Rule, would allow those benefits to be payable over the entire remaining life expectancy of the beneficiaries—often the individual's children or grandchildren, and would not require that the amounts be paid out over such a short period.

Some IRA Custodial Agreements contain a default provision stating that, on the individual's death, benefits payable to a non-spouse beneficiary will be paid under the Five-Year Rule unless the beneficiary has elected the Life Expectancy Rule. Under that default provision, at least the beneficiary will be afforded the opportunity to elect the Life Expectancy Rule, after the individual's death, rather than being stuck with the far more restrictive Five-Year Rule.

Default Beneficiaries

Finally, there is the issue of the default beneficiary. Most IRA Adoption Agreements/Designation of Beneficiary forms provide space to designate both a primary and a contingent beneficiary. The question then arises: Who will be the beneficiary of the IRA if an individual had failed to designate a beneficiary, or had designated a beneficiary (and/or contingent beneficiary) only to have that individual predecease the IRA owner?

Most IRA Custodial Agreements indicate that the spouse is to be the default beneficiary, with the individual's estate as the contingent default beneficiary. However, many IRA Custodial Agreements require the individual's estate to be the first default beneficiary. Because an estate has no life expectancy, were the individual to die prior to the Required Beginning Date, all benefits would have to be paid out of the retirement asset by December 31of the fifth calendar year following the calendar year of the individual's death.

If the individual had elected a term certain method of payment, with the estate as beneficiary, upon the individual's death after the Required Beginning Date, payments could still continue over the remaining portion of the term certain. However, if the individual had elected to have life expectancy recalculated, or had not elected out of the default provisions in the IRA Custodial Agreement that may have required the recalculation of life expectancy, all benefits would be required to be paid out of the IRA by no later than by December 31 of the calendar year following the calendar year of the individual's death.

Lessons Learned

For the most part, the default provisions contained in the various Custodial Agreements were written in a way that is unfavorable to multigenerational planning and continued tax deferral and should be superseded wherever possible. The only real assurance for a retirement distribution specialist that their clients' retirement distribution plans will be implemented is to select an IRA Custodian whose Custodial Agreement contains the proper default provisions or whose Adoption Agreement/Designation of Beneficiary form allows their clients the opportunity to select the specific beneficiary choices and method of payment elections called for in the retirement distribution plan.

The most practical solution to this problem, therefore, probably lies not in finding the proper IRA Custodian with the proper documents and administrative policies, but in finding the account executive who has the authority to work within the framework of the clients' plans. Simply stated, this means accepting a Retirement Asset Will ("Designation of Beneficiary and Method of Payment Election Form") which contains the proper elections for that particular client. The reluctance of an account executive or IRA Custodian to accept this document can often be attributed to lack of knowledge or understanding of multigenerational planning concepts, and the mistaken belief that acceptance of a tailor-made Retirement Asset Will somehow will increase the IRA Custodian's liability and exposure with respect to the assets in the IRA account.

Objections from IRA Custodians to proposed retirement distribution strategies commonly center on the following issues:

1. Multiple IRAs. The most powerful multigenerational retirement distribution planning tool for achieving maximum tax-deferred growth is the Participant Direct IRA Approach described earlier, which splits the individual's retirement asset into separate IRAs, with different children and grandchildren named as the primary beneficiary of each separate IRA. This technique allows the distributions from each separate IRA to be based on the life expectancy of the sole beneficiary of each separate IRA. This strategy will naturally depend on the ability of the IRA Custodian to break up the client's IRA into multiple IRAs. Some IRA Custodians are unwilling to do this because they believe that it is illegal for an individual to have more than one IRA with the same IRA Custodian. This belief is false.

Other IRA Custodians believe that the only effective way of tracking and recordkeeping with respect to the IRAs which are maintained at their financial institution is based on a system keyed in to either the individual's name or Social Security number. Since individuals have only one name and one Social Security number, the antiquated computer and recordkeeping systems of some IRA Custodians apparently have no way of keeping track of multiple IRAs of the same individual that are maintained with them. These administrative shortcomings will no doubt soon be resolved, as the computer and recordkeeping systems of these financial institutions become more sophisticated, and they begin to realize the cost of passing up the management of assets of this magnitude.

2. Splitting Up an IRA After Death. One multigenerational strategy is to divide an IRA into separate IRAs for different children or grandchildren after the death of the IRA owner. Some IRA Custodians have refused to permit the splitting up of the IRA after the individual's death, absent a specific prior direction to that effect made by the IRA owner.

3. Formula or Percentage Allocations. Some IRA Custodians have refused to allow percentage or formula allocations for the payment of IRA benefits to multiple beneficiaries. A typical formula bequest might be 40 percent to child A, with 20 percent each to grandchildren B, C, and D. The perceived danger here seems to be that the distribution plan is too complex and that disputes or litigation might ensue. There is no rational basis for this argument, insofar as most people who have IRAs have designated their spouse as primary beneficiary, with their children collectively as contingent beneficiaries. An individual with two children would be dividing the IRA in half on his or her death, should the individual's spouse predecease the individual; with three children, the IRA account would be divided in thirds, etc. In those cases, there is no reason why the IRA Custodian cannot perform the basic mathematical computations involved in a division of the IRA along specific percentage lines, or on the basis of a formula clause contained in the individual's Will or testamentary trust.

4. Charitable Beneficiaries. Some IRA Custodians will not allow charities to be named as primary or contingent beneficiaries. No doubt this prohibition has to do with a confused sense of measuring life expectancies. As noted earlier, when a charity has been named as the beneficiary—or as one of several beneficiaries—a second life expectancy cannot be used. However, that rule does not preclude a charity from being a beneficiary. All the rule does is to preclude the use of a second life expectancy for Required Minimum Distribution purposes.

5. Successor Beneficiaries. Several IRA Custodians have limited the choices an individual can make with respect to the designation of their IRA beneficiaries. Some IRA Custodians do not allow the IRA owner to designate the individuals who will receive the IRA assets, should the primary beneficiaries and initially designated contingent beneficiaries each predecease the IRA owner, or should those individuals survive the IRA owner but subsequently die before all amounts have been paid out of the IRA.

6. Inherited IRA Issues. An Inherited IRA, as noted earlier, is the remaining amount payable to the beneficiary which is left in an IRA after an IRA owner has died. A spouse beneficiary who elects to treat the IRA as his or her own can roll over the IRA into a new IRA in his or her own name. The surviving spouse will then have the opportunity to make new beneficiary elections and new method of payment elections.

With the spousal rollover, the IRA ceases to be an Inherited IRA and becomes the IRA of the surviving spouse, almost as if the IRA had always been the IRA of the surviving spouse. Were a non-spouse beneficiary to attempt to establish a rollover IRA, the IRS would consider the retitling of the IRA as a distribution to the beneficiary, thereby causing the full value of the IRA to be immediately taxable to the beneficiary.

Because beneficiaries other than spouses are not allowed to establish rollover IRAs, an incorrectly retitled IRA would be subject to full and immediate income taxation on the beneficiary's income tax return. This catastrophe makes it imperative that the IRA Custodian, following the death of the IRA owner, continue the IRA in the name of the decedent, with the continued use of the decedent's Social Security number wherever possible.

There have already been cases on record in which an IRA Custodian, when asked to establish an Inherited IRA for the benefit of a beneficiary, had erroneously retitled the IRA as the IRA of the beneficiary. This problem can easily arise in two ways. In the more simple case, an IRA owner dies, having previously named an individual as beneficiary. The beneficiary leaves the IRA with the same IRA Custodian, but in providing information to the IRA Custodian for its internal records (i.e., address, Social Security number, and date of birth of the beneficiary), the IRA Custodian, acting on its own or perhaps at the mistaken direction of the beneficiary, puts the beneficiary's name on the IRA account, removing that of the original IRA owner.

The problem could also arise in the context of an IRA owner who has died, with the beneficiary then wanting to transfer the IRA from one IRA Custodian to another. A direct Trustee-to-Trustee transfer from one IRA Custodian to another is permitted by law, even in the context of an Inherited IRA. However, in the transfer process, the transferred IRA in the hands of the new IRA Custodian sometimes becomes mislabeled as the IRA of the beneficiary, and not of the deceased IRA owner.

Clients may meet significant resistance from IRA Custodians when attempting to establish an Inherited IRA. Most account executives have never heard of the term Inherited IRA, and are often surprised to learn that there have been IRS pronouncements on this subject. Even if the account executive has heard of and understands the concept of the Inherited IRA, errors can still occur. The IRA Custodian may insist on being provided with the Social Security number of the IRA beneficiary. This is a legitimate request, since the IRA Custodian will be required to report to the IRS, at each year-end, the amount of any distributions made to the beneficiary from the IRA that year. The form that is used to report this information is Form 1099-R, "Distributions from Pensions, Annuities, Retirement, or Profit-Sharing Plans, IRAs, Insurance Contracts, Etc."

However, unless great care is taken, sometimes the beneficiary's Social Security number finds its way onto the title of the IRA. Such a posting should be avoided to the same extent as the avoidance of placing the individual beneficiary's name on the IRA. The title on the Inherited IRA should read "John Smith, deceased, Inherited IRA for the benefit of Paul Smith as beneficiary," with the decedent's Social Security number, wherever possible, still listed on the account.

If the IRA Custodian has made an error in this retitling process, the error should be immediately called to the attention of the IRA Custodian and corrected retroactively in the IRA Custodian's internal administrative records, so that, upon any subsequent audit of the case by the IRS, the IRA Custodian's records will be consistent with the position that at all times the IRA had remained in the name of the decedent and un-der the decedent's Social Security number.

Approval of the Retirement Asset Will

The most carefully thought-out retirement distribution plan will be of no benefit to the client or the client's family unless it is properly im-plemented. This book should have demonstrated to every advisor and reader that the one document critical to that implementation effort is the Retirement Asset Will. Because of the comprehensive nature of the Retirement Asset Will, and the fact that in certain areas it supersedes the terms of the underlying IRA Custodial Agreement, it is crucial to obtain the approval of the Retirement Asset Will by the IRA Custodian. The approval should be obtained no later than the time when the retirement distribution plan is to be implemented.

Most IRA Custodial Agreements require that any designation of beneficiary or method of payment election be made on a form prepared by the IRA Custodian and that no other form will be accepted. Unless the client has some evidence that the Retirement Asset Will has been approved for use by the IRA Custodian, the IRA Custodian may be on solid legal ground in denying the provisions of the Retirement Asset Will executed by the client but not previously approved for use by the IRA Custodian in favor of the more restrictive default provisions of the IRA Custodial Agreement. Those provisions will be made to apply to the IRA, despite the client's written direction (through the Retirement Asset Will) to the contrary.

The approval process typically is handled in one of two ways. Where the IRA Custodian is sympathetic to the wishes of the client and has some familiarity with the terms to be contained in the Retirement Asset Will, the client can simply execute the Retirement Asset Will and forward it to the IRA Custodian, who will approve it.

However, in those instances in which the IRA Custodian is not especially sympathetic to the concerns of the client or is not familiar with the terms to be contained in the Retirement Asset Will, the approval process may need to go through two stages. In the first stage, the law firm that is drafting the Retirement Asset Will typically sends the IRA Custodian a generic version of the Retirement Asset Will. In the generic Retirement Asset Will, none of the personal information regarding the client or his or her family members is included. Instead, the generic Retirement Asset Will is for the fictitious clients, John Smith, Jane Smith, and their children. However, the generic Retirement Asset Will, which is submitted to the IRA Custodian, is similar to the final Retirement Asset Will that will be used for that client in that it specifies the same types of beneficiaries. For instance, if a Q-TIP Trust established for the benefit of the spouse is to be the beneficiary in the final Retirement Asset Will, the generic Retirement Asset Will forwarded to the IRA Custodian should name a fictitious Q-TIP Trust as beneficiary. Similarly, for a client who wishes to name a trust for the benefit of a grandchild as the IRA beneficiary, the generic Retirement Asset Will should name a fictitious trust for the benefit of a grandchild as beneficiary.

IRA Custodians often want to add additional exculpatory language to the Retirement Asset Will. The suggested additions may run anywhere from three or four sentences to a page and a half. The exculpatory provisions which the IRA Custodians typically ask to add to the Retirement Asset Will make it clear that, in approving the Retirement Asset Will, the IRA Custodian is assuming no additional responsibility with respect to the calculation of the Required Minimum Distribution amounts which are payable each year and is not responsible to see that any Minimum Required Distribution payment is, in fact, made in any year. These additional exculpatory provisions, in the opinion of the authors, are entirely unnecessary, insofar as the IRA Custodial Agreements already contain similar exculpatory provisions which are usually more than adequate to put the IRA owner and beneficiary alike on notice of these requirements.

However, in order to facilitate the approval of the Retirement Asset Will, these additional exculpatory provisions should almost always be agreed to and included in the final version of the Retirement Asset Will, unless there is some technical problem with the particular wording sought by the IRA Custodian.

Once the IRA Custodian has approved the Retirement Asset Will, the client should execute the Retirement Asset Will and simultaneously should establish the multiple IRA accounts with the IRA Custodian. The Retirement Asset Will should then be filed with the IRA Custodian, who should sign the last page of the Retirement Asset Will as evidencing its approval and acceptance. In those instances in which the IRA beneficiary is a testamentary or *inter vivos* trust, a copy of the

Will or *inter vivos* trust should also be provided to the IRA Custodian at that time. Alternatively, a list of the beneficiaries of the trust can be filed with the IRA Custodian, in lieu of filing the actual trust agreement with the IRA Custodian. However, in order for this alternative filing to be acceptable, the list of beneficiaries should include contingent and remainder beneficiaries and a description of their entitlement. Whatever filing requirement is to be used (i.e., the filing of the *actual* trust document or the filing of the list of the trust beneficiaries), in each case, the IRA Custodian should acknowledge the receipt of those documents.

Chapters 5 and 11 discussed the use of trusts as beneficiaries of retirement assets. Included in those discussions was a reference to the fact that if the trust qualifies as a "Designated Beneficiary," the life expectancies of the trust beneficiaries can be used for Required Minimum Distribution purposes, both at the individual's Required Beginning Date and with respect to death benefits, which are payable if the individual does not survive until the Required Beginning Date. One of the rules that a trust must follow in order to qualify as a Designated Beneficiary is that a copy of the trust agreement be provided to the plan administrator or, alternatively, that a list of all of the beneficiaries of the trust (including contingent and remainder beneficiaries) be provided to the plan administrator, along with a description of their entitlements. In at least two early Private Letter Rulings, the IRS had unofficially ruled that the plan administrator of an IRA is the IRA owner, and that the filing requirements associated with the use of trusts as beneficiaries of retirement assets, which must ordinarily be made to the plan administrator, are automatically satisfied when the IRA owner has kept a copy of the trust document in his or her records. However, despite those two early Private Letter Rulings, the IRS has now moved away from that position. Accordingly, the better practice now would be to file all Wills and trust documents serving as beneficiaries of IRA accounts with the IRA Custodian.

The client should also send a letter to the custodian agreeing to provide the IRA Custodian within a reasonable time with copies of any future amendment changes to the Will or trust. The IRA owner should also agree that, by the end of the nine-month period following the individual's death, the beneficiaries of the IRA account will provide the IRA Custodian with a final certification as to who the ultimate beneficiaries of the Will or trust will be.

Typically, multiple copies of the IRA Custodian-approved Retirement Asset Will are secured, with the IRA Custodian keeping one fully executed copy, the client keeping one fully executed copy, and the retirement distribution specialist and the client's estate attorney each keeping an additional fully executed copy.

One additional IRA custodial issue that should be touched on involves the loss of the retirement distribution documents. Clients and advisors may assume that, with the computerization of the IRA Custodian office, each of the relevant retirement distribution documents would be preserved in the IRA Custodian's records on microfiche or on a computer disc in a permanent memory file, with appropriate computer backups and duplications of all essential files.

Unfortunately, experience has shown that this is often not the case. A smart practice, therefore, would be for the client and the client's estate and retirement advisors each to retain a duplicate of both the Designation of Beneficiary form and Retirement Asset Will. This will prevent a situation from arising in which the IRA Custodian has lost the designation of beneficiary form and the Retirement Asset Will and it cannot be proved what elections the individual had made at his or her Required Beginning Date (or prior to his or her death, in the event that the individual had died prior to his or her Required Beginning Date).

Power of Attorney

Retirement distribution specialists frequently become involved in situations in which a recent medical crisis of a family member has motivated a client or family to begin or complete a retirement distribution plan or estate plan. If the crisis is severe enough, the individual on whose behalf the planning is desired may lack the requisite mental acuity to understand the nature and extent of his or her assets, and may be incapable of executing the necessary legal documents.

An important document which all individuals should have in place is a binding and comprehensive Durable Power of Attorney. This document allows people, while they still have their mental and physical capacity, to designate another individual or individuals to manage their financial affairs, typically after they have suffered a disability or incapacitating injury. The Power of Attorney is said to be "Durable" in that it survives the subsequent disability of the individual who has made the Power of Attorney. Clients should execute this document before any others, so that, in the event of a subsequent disability, the retirement distribution plan, and often the estate plan as a whole, can be implemented.

Armed with a legally binding and enforceable Durable Power of Attorney, family members who are interested in implementing a comprehensive retirement distribution plan for their disabled family member will find that the Power of Attorney allows them not only to designate beneficiaries for the retirement assets of the individual, but also to select the method of payment and period over which the benefits will be paid. Family members who have been given the Power of Attorney will then be able to make these beneficiary and method of payment choices exactly as the individual would have.

Perhaps the biggest issue associated with the use of Powers of Attorney is that too few individuals execute them prior to the onset of a disability. If the disability is severe enough, it may not be possible for the individual to execute a Durable Power of Attorney at that time, thereby relegating the individual and the family members to the various retirement distribution elections, or lack of elections, which were in place prior to the onset of the disability.

An additional problem that can arise in connection with the use of a Power of Attorney is the acceptance of the Power of Attorney by the IRA Custodian. Most attorneys, especially most elder law and estate planning attorneys, are quite familiar with Durable Powers of Attorney and have been preparing them for years to cover, in an omnibus way, all of their client's assets. However, financial institutions during the same period have developed their own Power of Attorney forms, which are specific to a particular financial institution and which an institution's account executives would like the individual to sign.

Elder law and estate planning attorneys, on the other hand, do not want to limit the client to signing the Power of Attorney of the one financial institution at which some of the client's assets are held at that time. Rather, they would prefer that a general Durable Power of Attorney be signed which addresses all of the client's assets, wherever they are now or may be moved to in the future.

Financial institutions, when faced with an omnibus general Durable Power of Attorney, have in the past been slow to recognize its legal effect. A financial institution may have insisted that the client instead sign the institution's own Power of Attorney form. Rather than fight with the financial institution, the client will often accede to those demands. However, if the client had already lost his or her mental or physical capacity, the execution of the financial institution's Power of Attorney form may not be possible. A battle may then ensue between the holders of the omnibus general Durable Power of Attorney and the financial institution, whose legal department may be advising the institution not to recognize any Power of Attorney unless it is the institution's pre-approved form.

Many states have statutes on their books requiring financial institutions to honor omnibus general Powers of Attorney forms. The problem is that, typically, no penalties are associated with the failure of the financial institutions to comply with the rules. Accordingly, many financial institutions honor only Powers of Attorney which have been created on their pre-approved form.

One way around this potential problem is to have the financial institution approve the omnibus general Power of Attorney form before the client's disability—for instance, at the time the client executes the omnibus general Power of Attorney when their Will and estate plan are being updated. If the financial institution refuses to accept the form at that time, the client will have an opportunity to remove all assets from that financial institution and move them to a more accommodating financial institution. Therefore, a smart practice would be to have the client take the general Power of Attorney, once executed, to each of the financial institutions in which the client then maintains assets, to have the omnibus general Power of Attorney pre-approved by each financial institution. In this way, the family can preserve the flexibility needed to implement and periodically adjust a comprehensive retirement planning strategy, notwithstanding the subsequent disability of the retirement asset owner.

CHAPTER 15

OTHER PLANNING STRATEGIES—ROTH IRAs, EMPLOYER SECURITIES AND NET UNREALIZED APPRECIATION, AND TAX-FREE RECOVERY OF PS-58 COSTS

CONTENTS

15 OTHER PLANNING STRATEGIES—ROTH IRAs, EMPLOYER SECURITIES AND NET UNREALIZED APPRECIATION, AND TAX-FREE RECOVERY OF PS-58 COSTS

The focus of this book has been retirement distribution planning at the Required Beginning Date and afterwards as well as planning before the Required Beginning Date. This chapter will focus on certain alternative planning strategies which may present themselves at either time under certain circumstances.

Roth IRAs

In 1974, Congress created the IRA as a device in which eligible individuals could make deductible contributions to their own private retirement vehicles. All subsequent growth in the IRA would be tax-deferred, with all subsequent distributions from the IRA generally 100 percent includible in income.

In 1986, Congress created nondeductible IRAs, for those individuals not eligible to make deductible contributions to their IRAs in any given year. Contributions to nondeductible IRAs accumulate on a tax-deferred basis. Distributions from nondeductible IRAs are generally taxed based on a recovery percentage determined by comparing the

---

Note: Readers should refer to the Introduction for a discussion of issues and concepts covered in Chapter 15 that may be affected by the IRS's issuance of the Revised Proposed Regulations governing Required Minimum Distributions and by the passage of EGTRRA 2001. These include: the Uniform Distribution Period Table; the elimination of irrevocable elections at the individual's Required Beginning Date; the determination of the beneficiary by December 31 of the year following the year of the individual's death; changes in Federal estate tax amounts and rates; and issues that were *not* resolved by the Revised Proposed Regulations.

total non-deductible contributions made to the IRA to the expected number of monthly payments over which benefits are expected to be paid.

In 1997, enter William V. Roth, Jr., the Republican Senator from Delaware. His idea was to create a new class of IRAs in which *no* deductions would be allowed going in and *no* growth would be currently taxable. However, unlike the case with all other existing forms of IRAs, all distributions from these new IRAs would forever be 100 percent exempt from all Federal income taxes. This dream IRA, now known as the Roth IRA, was enacted as part of the Taxpayer Relief Act of 1997, effective as of January 1, 1998.

Why has the creation of the Roth IRA been heralded in so many quarters? Its appeal stems from two factors. The first is the fact that the Roth IRA rules do not require a taxpayer to receive any distributions from the Roth IRA while the taxpayer is alive. The second is the staggering effect of the compounding value of investments over time.

The combination of these two factors produce startling results for those individuals who do not wish to receive distributions from their IRAs while they are alive.

> **Example:** Suppose Ian, age 30, contributes $2,000 per year to a deductible IRA. Assuming an 8 percent yearly growth of those contributions, at age 70, the $80,000 amount contributed to the IRA over the 40 years would grow to $518,113. That amount will provide Ian with $58,535 in yearly income for the remaining 16 years of his IRS assumed life expectancy. If we assume a 33⅓ percent combined Federal and State income tax rate, Ian would net $39,023 in each year of the 16-year payout.
>
> Were Ian to have made 40 years of contributions to a Roth IRA, instead of to a traditional IRA, at age 70 his Roth IRA would again aggregate the $518,113 amount, but all distributions from the Roth IRA would be entirely exempt from all Federal income taxes, thereby allowing Ian to net the full $58,535 yearly distribution amount each year.
>
> If Ian instead wanted to receive payments each year of only $39,023—the net amount he would have received each year had he made 40 years of contributions to a traditional IRA and not to a Roth IRA—at the end

of the 16-year payout, instead of his IRA balance being zero, it would equal $1,429,617.

Moreover, if Ian were disposed to leaving his entire Roth IRA to his children or grandchildren and did not wish to and did not need to withdraw any amounts from the IRA while he was alive, the balance in his Roth IRA at his death at age 86 would equal $1,775,026.

If his children and grandchildren were to pay that amount out over their remaining life expectancies of 25 years, over the 25-year period of time, the $1,775,026 amount would produce $5,015,867 in totally tax-free distributions to the children and grandchildren. This represents a growth of over 2.8 times the original $1,775,026 amount.

In other words, by foregoing the yearly tax deductions on the 40 $2,000 yearly IRA deductions—deductions worth $88,298 cumulatively at 8 percent at age 70½, and worth $755,425 by the end of the children's and grandchildren's 25 year payout—Ian would be affording his heirs over $5 million in entirely tax-fee distributions.

Because individuals are allowed to convert existing traditional IRAs into Roth IRAs, older taxpayers may be able to reap these substantial benefits for their family members without having to make yearly Roth IRA contributions for many years.

Example: Edith, age 70, converts her $1,000,000 traditional IRA to a Roth IRA in 1998. She pays the Federal and State income tax on the conversion of the IRA from other assets. She now has $1,000,000 in her Roth IRA. If she is disposed to leaving her entire Roth IRA to her children and grandchildren without drawing down any distributions while she is alive—assuming again an 8 percent yearly growth rate—at her death the Roth IRA would be worth $3,425,943. If the children and grandchildren then pay this amount out to themselves over a remaining 25-year period of time, their total tax-free payout would equal $9,681,029. Once again, this is a growth of over 2.8 times the original $3,425,943 amount.

What about the tax bite on the $1,000,000 conversion? If the taxpayer's tax rate was 33⅓ percent, that amounts to $333,333 in

Federal and State income taxes to be paid. Doesn't that amount mitigate to a great extent the benefits of converting the taxpayer's traditional IRA into a Roth IRA, and besides, whose clients would want to pay $333,333 in taxes now while they are alive, if they don't have to? Isn't it better to defer as much of the income tax bite until sometime after the taxpayer has died if that were possible?

The answer is yes, if the taxpayer either needs to spend the bulk or the entire IRA balance for his support while he is alive, or if he is not disposed to leaving as much of the IRA balance to his children and grandchildren as he can. However, if neither of those two cases applies, and the taxpayer wants to leave as much of his IRA assets to his children and grandchildren as possible, then converting to the Roth IRA is a good choice.

A special Roth IRA rule allowed for the Federal income tax due on the conversion of a traditional IRA to a Roth IRA to be paid over four years, if the conversion had occurred in 1998. The deferral was accomplished by assuming that one-quarter of the amount converted in 1998 had been received by the taxpayer in each of the years 1998, 1999, 2000, and 2001. Therefore, a taxpayer who converted $1,000,000 of his traditional IRA to a Roth IRA in 1998 only added $250,000 to his 1998 taxable income (or one-quarter of the total amount converted), with $250,000 added to his income in each of the years 1999, 2000, and 2001. If we assume that the tax payments, if not made, would have grown at 5.33 percent per year—8 percent minus a $33\frac{1}{2}$ percent yearly income tax rate applicable each year—at the taxpayer's death in year 16, the future value of those four tax payments would equal $606,680, compared to a gross value of $3,425,943 in the Roth IRA at that time.

Despite this enormous potential benefit to the families of individuals who convert traditional IRAs into Roth IRAs, will clients really want to pay the income tax up front now, rather than years later, when distributions would ordinarily *first* be payable from their traditional IRAs? The answer is often yes. Many older clients with significant IRA assets, vividly recall the Great Depression and World War II. This client profile usually carries with it a predisposition to biting the bullet now, paying the income tax on the conversion of a traditional IRA into a Roth IRA, and then sitting back and watching this money tree grow for their children and grandchildren, entirely free in the future from all Federal income taxes.

Adjusted Gross Income

So far, the Roth IRA story sounds almost too-good-to-be-true. Regrettably, it turns out to be just that for most affluent clients, because the rules governing Roth IRAs contain an income cap. Individuals whose adjusted gross income (AGI) for the year exceeds $100,000 are precluded from converting their traditional IRAs into Roth IRAs for that year. Moreover, all individuals whose AGI exceeds $160,000 are precluded from making the $2,000 contribution to a Roth IRA in that year.

The experience of most financial advisors has shown that the number one reason why clients are *not* currently making yearly $2,000 Roth IRA contributions and are *not* converting their traditional IRAs into Roth IRAs is that their projected AGI is simply too high. However, if clients are able to successfully reduce their AGI, using the strategies their advisors can offer them, a higher percentage of those clients apparently would be willing to go the Roth IRA route. Moreover, recent proposed legislation would seek to eliminate the AGI limitation entirely on making regular contributions to a Roth IRA and would seek to increase the limitation to $1 million on Roth IRA conversions. Therefore, if that proposed bill were to be passed, the enormous potential benefits associated with a client establishing a Roth IRA or converting a traditional IRA into a Roth IRA would then be available to a much larger class of individuals.

Currently, regular full Roth IRA contributions up to $2,000 per year can be made by married couples filing a joint return, whose combined AGI does not exceed $150,000 for that year. The $2,000 maximum contribution is phased down for married couples filing a joint return, whose combined AGI is between $150,000 and $160,000, with no regular Roth IRA contribution permitted if their AGI exceeds $160,000 for that year.

For single individuals, $95,000 is the maximum AGI amount up to which full regular Roth IRA contributions can be made, with a phasedown of the maximum contribution for single individuals with AGIs for the year between $95,000 and $110,000. Single individuals whose AGI exceeds $110,000 for the year are not currently permitted to make any regular Roth IRA contributions for that year.

Married individuals who file separately are not currently permitted a full $2,000 Roth IRA contribution and can make no Roth IRA contribution if their AGI exceeds $10,000. In addition, married individuals who file separately are not currently permitted to convert a traditional IRA into a Roth IRA, regardless of their AGI for the year. Single and married individuals whose combined AGI exceeds $100,000 for the year are not permitted to make the Roth IRA conversion in that year. For purposes of computing the individual's AGI for the year, amounts withdrawn during the year from traditional IRAs and converted into Roth IRAs are not counted for taxable years beginning after 2004. Required Minimum Distribution amounts received during the year are *not* required to be included in AGI for purposes of determining entitlement to contribute to or to convert to a Roth IRA.

Operating Rules for Roth IRAs

1. Limits on Contributions. Individuals may not contribute more than $2,000 to a regular contribution Roth IRA in any year. Contributions are limited further to earned income for those individuals whose earned income is less than $2,000 for the year. Therefore, individuals with no earned income for the year cannot make any regular Roth IRA contributions for the year.

However, as is the case with traditional deductible IRAs, a special exception applies for spouses. As long as one spouse has earned income of at least $4,000, both spouses can contribute up to $2,000 to a regular contribution Roth IRA for the year, regardless of the level of "earned income" of any particular spouse for the year. However, no individual is permitted to contribute more than $2,000 in any year to all IRAs that they maintain (other than rollover IRAs). Therefore an individual who has already contributed $2,000 to a regular deductible IRA for the year will not be permitted to make any contributions to a regular contribution Roth IRA for that year.

2. Age Limitations. There are no age limits on when an individual can make either a regular Roth IRA contribution or a conversion of a traditional IRA into a Roth IRA. Therefore individuals who have passed age 70½ can still make regular Roth IRA contributions, in any year, if they are otherwise eligible to do so—in other words, if their AGI is not too high for that year, and if the Roth IRA contributions do not exceed the amount of their earned income for the year. Similarly, minors of any age with earned income can make Roth IRA contributions up to $2,000 or the amount of their earned income for that year, whichever is less.

3. Active Participation Rules. Unlike traditional IRAs, Roth IRA contributions can be made each year regardless of an individual's status as an active participant in any one or more qualified employee benefit plans for the year. This same rule also applies in the case of the conversion of a traditional IRA into a Roth IRA, with the individual's participation status being entirely irrelevant to his or her ability to make the conversion in any year.

4. Deadline. Contributions to a regular Roth IRA must be made each year by the original due date, *exclusive* of any extensions, for filing the individ-ual's Federal personal income tax return for that year.

How to Establish a Roth IRA

A taxpayer wishing to establish a regular contribution Roth IRA or wishing to convert an existing traditional IRA into a Roth IRA can do so by completing either Form 5305-R, "Roth Individual Requirement Trust Account," Form 5305-RA, "Roth Individual Retirement Custodial Account," or Form 5305-RB, "Roth Individual Retirement Annuity Endorsement (see IRS Notice 98-49).

Distributions from Roth IRAs

Distributions from Roth IRAs are generally 100 percent free from all Federal income taxation. However, in order to qualify for this benefit, a distribution must be a "Qualified Distribution." This is a distribution which is made after the individual had attained age 59½, became disabled, or died. It could also be a Qualified First-Time Homebuyer Distribution—a distribution not in excess of $10,000 for certain first-time homebuyers.

In addition, in order for a distribution to be a Qualified Distribution, it must satisfy a five-year holding rule. The five-year rule is satisfied if withdrawals are made *after* the end of the five-year period beginning with the first taxable year for which the first regular Roth IRA contribution had been made or for which an amount had first been converted from a traditional IRA into a Roth IRA, whichever is sooner. For instance, if an individual first made a regular Roth IRA contribution on April 15, 1999 *for 1998*, the five-year rule would be satisfied if the first distribution from the Roth IRA occurred after December 31, 2002. All distributions from the Roth IRA occurring after that date would be deemed to be in compliance with the five-year holding period rule.

All Roth IRAs are aggregated for purposes of the five-year holding rule, regardless of whether or not the Roth IRA was a regular contribution Roth IRA or a converted Roth IRA. Accordingly, individuals thinking of establishing a Roth IRA should do so at the earliest possible date, and perhaps with relatively modest amounts, in order to immediately begin the running of the five-year holding period.

A special basis recovery rule dramatically reduces the instances in which distributions from Roth IRAs will be included in income. The rule states that distributions from Roth IRAs are deemed to be made from contributions *before* they are considered as being made from the earnings on those contributions. Because all Roth IRA contributions are made on an after-tax basis, until an individual recovers his or her cost basis, no amount is generally includible in income. For instance, assume that an individual age 60 converts $100,000 of traditional IRA assets into a Roth IRA in 1999. In 2000, the individual withdraws $30,000 from the Roth IRA. Because the 2000 withdrawal is deemed to be made entirely from after-tax contributions, no portion of the $30,000 amount withdrawn in 2000 would be subject to Federal income taxation, despite the fact that the five-year rule had not been satisfied. The application of this ordering rule makes it a low risk proposition for an individual who is over age 59½ to convert his or her traditional IRA into a Roth IRA, even if the individual is concerned about the immediate access to his Roth IRA assets.

It should be noted, however, that the above result would *not* have been the same if the same if the individual in 2000 had been younger than age 59½, and had not been disabled or deceased at the time he had withdrawn the $30,000 from his Roth IRA.

Recharacterization of Roth IRA Contributions and Conversions

So far, we have discussed many reasons why an individual would want to establish a Roth IRA and make $2,000 yearly contributions to that account, or would want to convert his or her traditional IRA to a Roth IRA. Suppose, however, that the individual, after establishing a Roth IRA, decided that he or she did not want to categorize the contributed amount or converted amount as being established in a Roth IRA, but instead preferred to have that amount considered as having been contributed *initially* into a traditional IRA. Perhaps the individual did not want to pay a current income tax liability on amounts converted from a traditional IRA to a Roth IRA for that year, or perhaps the individual had decided that it was more advantageous for the contribution to the Roth IRA to be entitled to a current income tax deduction, as would be the case had the contribution been initially made to a traditional IRA and *not* to a Roth IRA. Fortunately, the IRS has provided a mechanism, whereby the establishment of a Roth IRA can, in effect, be retroactively "undone" and recharacterized as assets still maintained in a traditional IRA. In order for the recharacterization to be valid, however, the recharacterization must be done by the due date, plus extensions, for filing the individual's Federal income tax return for the year in which the Roth IRA contribution or Roth IRA conversion was made. A special rule applies to Roth IRA contributions and conversions made for the year 1998. For that year (which was the first year that Roth IRAs were available), the IRS allowed taxpayers until December 31, 1999 to recharacterize their 1998 Roth IRA contributions and conversions.

Assuming that a Roth IRA recharacterization has been properly made (see IRC § 1.408A-5, Q&A-6), no Federal income tax will be due on any amounts that the individual had previously converted to a Roth IRA for that year. In addition, if the recharacterization applied to a contribution which was made to a Roth IRA for the year, by recharacterizing the contribution as a contribution to a traditional IRA for the year instead of as a contribution to a Roth IRA for the year, the individual may be able to secure a Federal income tax deduction for the amount of the contribution, provided that the rules governing the deductibility of contributions to traditional IRAs were followed.

The ability to recharacterize a Roth IRA contribution amount or conversion amount is an especially important feature of Roth IRAs, because an individual may want to contribute an amount or convert an amount to a Roth IRA for any given year, but may not know until after the year has ended whether his or her AGI for that year allowed the individual the right to make the Roth IRA contribution or Roth

IRA conversion. Because the recharacterization of those amounts contributed or converted into a Roth IRA is allowed— and because the recharacterization may be made until as late as the due date, plus extensions, for filing the individual's Federal income tax return for the year—the individual in most instances can be fully protected from the potential adverse tax consequences of contributing amounts to a Roth IRA or converting amounts to a Roth IRA in years in which the applicable AGI limitations were inadvertently exceeded. However, there are certain instances in which an individual will have contributed or converted amounts to a Roth IRA when they were *not* entitled to do so, and where the recharacterization rules are not available to help them. Such a situation could easily occur if the individual, by the due date for filing of his or her Federal income tax return for the year, plus extensions, concluded that his or her AGI for the year was well within the limits for having made the contribution or conversion into the Roth IRA for the prior year, only to find—perhaps two years later and perhaps upon the IRS audit of the individual's income tax return for that tax year—that his or her AGI for that year was increased by the IRS, making the individual ineligible for the Roth IRA contribution conversion for the year. Because this discovery was not made until sometime *after* the due date for filing the individual's Federal income tax return for the year, it is too late for the recharacterization rules to be applied retroactively to help the individual. Although this type of scenario is probably uncommon, it does point out the extreme caution that advisors should use when rendering advice in this area, especially when they are dealing with clients whose AGI for the year is close to the applicable threshold amounts.

Having allowed taxpayers the right to recharacterize their Roth IRA contributions and conversions, the IRS very quickly encountered an unanticipated development. Apparently, some individuals were converting a significant portion or all of the assets in their traditional IRA into a Roth IRA early into the year, and then watching the investment performance of those Roth IRA assets. If the assets appreciated substantially in value, then those individuals were required to pay Federal income tax only on the value of the Roth IRA at the time that it had been initially converted from the traditional IRA, which was at its initial lower value. However if the assets in the Roth IRA *de-creased* significantly in value from the time of the Roth IRA conversion, those assets would be worth far less than they were when the Roth IRA was established. In that case, the individual would elect to recharacterize the Roth IRA as a traditional IRA, and would then immediately re-establish the traditional IRA as a Roth IRA. The re-characterization of the Roth IRA as a traditional IRA and then the immediate re-establishment of the Roth IRA allowed the individual to pay income taxes on the conversion of the traditional IRA into the Roth IRA at a time when the value of the Roth IRA was at its most depressed level, rather than at the initial date, when the Roth IRA had been established. In fact, some individuals were known to go through the conversion, recharacterization, and reconversion process a number of times throughout the year and until the due date for filing the individual's Federal income tax return for the year, all the while watching the value of their portfolio as it increased or decreased in value, hoping to peg the final conversion from the traditional IRA into Roth IRA at the IRA asset's lowest value established during the year, and until the due date for filing the individual's Federal income tax return for that year.

As one might guess, the IRS considered this practice to be abusive. Accordingly, the IRS issued regulations in this area (IRC § 1.401A-5, Q&A-9) which limited the number of times during the year in which an individual could contribute or convert amounts from a traditional IRA into a Roth IRA, and then recharacterize that amount back to a traditional IRA. A contribution or conversion to a Roth IRA, followed by a recharacterization back to a traditional IRA, can only be made once in any calendar year. Once the Roth IRA has been recharacterized as a traditional IRA, the assets cannot be recontributed or reconverted back into a Roth IRA until the later of the beginning of the calendar year following the calendar year in which the amount had initially been contributed or converted into a Roth IRA, or the date that is 30 days after the date on which the Roth IRA had been recharacterized as a traditional IRA.

Required Minimum Distributions

As explained previously, individuals who are participants in traditional IRAs must begin to receive their IRA benefits beginning by April 1 following the year in which they attain age 70½—their Required Beginning Date—with benefits payable over a period of time measured initially by their life expectancy alone or by their life expectancy and the life expectancy of their beneficiary.

Upon their death after that date, benefits must be payable at least as rapidly per year as prior to death. If one life expectancy was being used, the application of this rule requires distributions to be initially calculated over a maximum 16-year life expectancy payout period. When a second non-spouse life expectancy was being used, distributions were generally initially required to be made based on a 26.2-year maximum life expectancy payout period.

Roth IRAs, on the other hand, are not subject to the Required Minimum Distribution rules applicable while an individual is still alive. Therefore, individuals who are age 90 with assets in Roth IRAs need not receive any distributions from their Roth IRA in that year or in any prior year, unless they wanted to. This allows the individual to defer or eliminate entirely all distributions while he or she is alive. As noted earlier, the application of this rule can result in huge payouts to the children and grandchildren of the Roth IRA owner after he or she has died.

Upon the death of a Roth IRA owner, benefits must be payable over the life expectancy of the beneficiary of the Roth IRA. This rule is the same as with distributions from traditional IRAs, in those instances in which the IRA owner had not yet reached his or her Required Beginning Date. However, if the IRA owner had reached his or her Required Beginning Date, on his or her death, with a traditional IRA, benefits could not be paid over a period of time longer than the remaining period elected by the individual while he or she was alive. For instance, with a traditional IRA, if an individual had elected to use his or her life expectancy alone without recalculation each year, to compute the maximum period over which benefits were to be paid, benefits would have to be paid over a period of time not exceeding 16.0 years. Therefore, if the individual had died after 12 years of payments had been made, his or her beneficiary would be required to be paid the remaining benefits in the IRA over the remaining four years of the initial 16-year payout.

With a Roth IRA, on the individual's death, if the beneficiary's life expectancy was then 30 years, the amounts in the Roth IRA could be payable to the beneficiary over that 30-year period of time. This rule accordingly allows for the payment of benefits over a much longer period of time than with traditional IRAs, and permits the compounding aspect of investments over time to produce a dramatic effect.

Who Should Contribute to a Roth IRA?

Several types of clients make excellent candidates to make yearly $2,000 Roth IRA contributions:

- Individuals past age 70½ who want to accumulate more money in their IRAs, and who have earned income of at least $2,000 for the year, but who because of their age are precluded from making either traditional deductible or nondeductible IRA contributions
- Generation Xers who, by making regular Roth IRA contributions, will have all future growth and appreciation in their IRA accounts forever 100 percent exempt from Federal income taxes, regardless of how large their IRA accounts should eventually become
- Stock market speculators who feel that they can make a killing with one IRA purchase. If the investment pans out, all growth, appreciation, earnings and dividends on that Roth IRA investment will be forever 100 percent exempt from Federal income taxes. An extreme application of this would be to have bought a winning lottery ticket with Roth IRA assets.
- Individuals whose taxable income for the year is low enough, or whose deductible expenses for the year are high enough, that the deduction associated with making traditional deductible IRA contributions is of no economic benefit to them. For those individuals, future tax-free distributions from the Roth IRA will be worth far more than current useless income tax deductions.

Who Should Convert a Traditional IRA into a Roth IRA?

Those individuals who do not need to live off their IRA benefits and who wish to accumulate the largest possible inheritance for their children and grandchildren make excellent candidates for Roth IRA conversions. For those individuals, Roth IRAs are ideal, because no benefits need be paid to the individual from the Roth IRA while the individual is alive, thereby allowing for the tremendous tax-exempt growth of the Roth IRA investments over time, for the benefit of the children and grandchildren.

Another category of clients who should convert their traditional IRAs into Roth IRAs consists of individuals who are past age 70½ and who had erroneously elected to have their life expectancy recalculated each year in computing benefits payable to them from their traditional IRAs. One rule applicable to the Required Minimum Distribution payouts from traditional IRAs states that if the IRA owner, by his or her Required Beginning Date, had elected to have benefits payable over his or her life expectancy alone, with that life expectancy to be recalculated each year, in the year following the year of that individual's death, his or her life expectancy would be deemed to be zero. That rule requires the payment of *all* benefits in the IRA to the individual's beneficiaries by December 31 of the year following the year of the individual's death. The individual, once having made the recalculation election by his or her Required Beginning Date, is therefore later powerless to rescind this election and is stuck with its consequences to the beneficiaries.

The Roth IRA can be used to prevent the application of this rule. By converting the traditional IRA to a Roth IRA, even after age 70½, no distributions will be required to be made while the individual is still alive. Once the individual dies, benefits can be paid out over as long a period of time as the beneficiary's then remaining life expectancy, regardless of what election the individual had previously made at his or her Required Beginning Date, when perhaps the Roth IRA assets were still in the form of a traditional IRA.

Additionally, virtually all individuals who are good candidates for making regular $2,000 yearly contributions to Roth IRAs are probably also good candidates for converting a portion or all of their traditional IRA assets into Roth IRAs, subject of course, to the AGI limitations applicable to those conversions, and as discussed previously.

Roth IRAs and Estate Planning

It was previously pointed out that in those cases in which a significant portion of a couple's assets consist of qualified Plan or IRA assets, the entire estate planning process becomes far more complicated. If the overall estate plan requires the establishment and funding of a Credit Shelter Trust and/or a marital deduction Q-TIP Trust, and if there are insufficient non-Plan and non-IRA assets to fully fund those trusts, then Plan and IRA assets must instead be used.

The temptation is to have the Plan and IRA assets, upon the death of the first spouse, immediately payable into those trusts. However, the payment of amounts out of the shelter of the qualified Plan or IRA immediately subjects those distributions to income taxation. Moreover, the qualified Plan and IRA assets would then be subject to the Required Minimum Distribution rules.

Great skill is therefore required in assisting clients in their estate planning to comply with these Required Minimum Distribution rules each year, all the while keeping the bulk of the qualified Plan and IRA assets maintained in the shelter of the qualified Plan and IRA, but while still adequately funding the Credit Shelter Trust and/or the Q-TIP Trust.

There is also a tax on tax problem to consider. This problem arises when a significant amount of estate taxes must be paid, and there are insufficient non-Plan and non-IRA assets with which to make the payment. The payment of estate taxes with qualified Plan or IRA assets can cause an income tax on estate tax problems, which in turn can cause an income tax on income tax problem, which together can immediately reduce the value of the qualified Plan or IRA assets by more than 75 percent.

> **Example:** Assume Dean dies with a total taxable estate of $3,000,000, which consists of $2,000,000 in IRA assets and $1,000,000 in an illiquid family business, which business cannot be sold, converted to cash or used as a security to raise cash. If the estate tax is $1,000,000 and that amount is paid from the IRA assets, the $1,000,000 IRA distribution—at combined Federal and State income tax rates of 33.8425 percent—will generate an income tax liability of $338,425.
>
> If the estate cannot pay this liability with other assets, then an additional $338,425 must be withdrawn from the IRA, which distribution in turn will cause the imposition of further income taxes due of $114,531. This income tax on income tax problem does not end until the

estate has distributed $511, 544 from the IRA to pay income taxes on the estate and income taxes, in addition to the original $1,000,000 amount the estate withdrew from the IRA to pay the estate taxes. The original $2,000,000 IRA is then left with only $488,455 in assets, a shrinkage of over 75.5 percent.

Note that, for the sake of simplicity, this example had ignored the effect of the income in respect of a decedent deduction (IRD) discussed previously.

Because distributions from Roth IRAs are not generally subject to any income tax, this entire income tax on estate tax, and income tax on income tax problem is avoided, even in the undesirable case in which IRA assets have to be used to pay estate taxes. Moreover, because Roth IRAs are not subject to the Required Minimum Distribution rules while the taxpayer is alive, it is far easier to use Roth IRAs to fund either a Credit Shelter Trust or Q-TIP Trust than it is to use qualified Plan or traditional IRA assets for these purposes.

It may also be possible to exclude the Roth IRA asset from estate taxation altogether. As was explained above, it is possible for a taxpayer with a Roth IRA to decide never to take any distributions from the Roth IRA while he is alive. What happens if that taxpayer were to sign an irrevocable election agreeing never to take any distributions from the Roth IRA while he is alive, and giving up forever his right to change the current Roth IRA beneficiary? At lease one commentator has suggested that if a taxpayer were to do this, he would have made an immediate gift of the entire amount in the Roth IRA, with the possible imposition of gift tax at that time, but with the prospect that all subsequent growth of the Roth IRA should then be entirely exempt from estate taxes in the taxpayer's estate.

Example: Curtis, who has $500,000 in his traditional IRA, converts the IRA to a Roth IRA when he is age 50, and pays the income tax on the conversion from other sources. Because the $500,000 amount is less than the current Federal credit shelter amount of $675,000, no current Federal gift tax is owed on the gift.

Curtis then signs an irrevocable election agreeing never to take any distributions from the Roth IRA while he is alive and agreeing never to change the individuals then designated as the beneficiaries of those benefits. If by the time of his death at age 85 the Roth IRA has grown to $7,392,672—assuming a yearly 8 percent growth rate—-the entire growth of $6,892,672 may be 100 percent exempt from estate taxes in his estate.

Although the IRS has indicated that this technique would constitute a taxable gift of the entire amount in the Roth IRA and would then immediately disqualify the asset as a Roth IRA (see IRC § 1.408A-6(A-19)), Congress has not yet officially closed down what may still prove to be a rather large loophole in the Roth IRA rules.

Unlikely Roth Candidates

The following types of clients will probably *not* benefit from the conversion of a traditional IRA into a Roth IRA:

- *Spendthrift clients*. Clients who consume all IRA income and substantial IRA principal each year should probably *not* convert their traditional IRAs to Roth IRAs, because they are likely to consume the entire Roth IRA balance before their death. The conversion in that case will therefore *not* serve the purpose of preserving assets for their children and grandchildren and will only cause the acceleration of the income tax liability on the amount in the traditional IRA at the time of its conversion.
- *Clients who do not wish to benefit close family members or who wish to benefit charities*. For those clients, the idea of accumulating significant assets for their heirs after they have died may be of little or no importance. Moreover, distributions to charities of IRA benefits can be structured in such a way that the benefits will be entirely free from all income tax liability anyway, without the need for first converting the traditional IRA into a Roth IRA. Therefore, for those clients, the conversion of the traditional IRA to a Roth IRA will once again only cause the acceleration of income tax liability, with no attendant benefit to the charity, and with an economic benefit only to those individual beneficiaries that the IRA owner is *not* especially interested in enriching.

- *Clients whose Adjusted Gross Income exceeds the applicable limits.* A client who converts a traditional IRA to a Roth IRA in a year in which his or her AGI exceeds $100,000 will in all likelihood be subjecting the entire amount converted to ordinary Federal income tax in that year and with no deferral of the tax over four years in the case of a conversion occurring in 1998. Moreover, if the distribution had been made before the individual had attained age 59½, the entire distribution would be subject to a 10 percent excise tax on early distributions. In addition, a 6 percent excises tax will apply in the case of an "excess" contribution to a Roth IRA. Therefore it is important to be certain that any particular client's AGI will not exceed the $100,000 threshold amount *before* recommending the conversion of their traditional IRAs to Roth IRAs in any given year.

It may be prudent to counsel the client to wait until December of the year of the planned conversion, and after a detailed and thorough analysis of the client's estimated AGI for the year has been completed, *before* advising the client as to whether or not the conversion should take place.

Roth Potential Problems

There are still some potential problem areas associated with the use of Roth IRAs. Accordingly, an advisor must thoroughly explore with the client, all of the possible pros and cons of contributing to or converting to a Roth IRA, including discussing each of the remaining unresolved issues associated with the use of Roth IRAs, *before* the advisor can categorically recommend this option to a client. Two such potentially problematic areas are the following:

- *State Income Tax Concerns.* Advisors should carefully check their State income tax rules to determine to what extent their States have conformed all of their income tax rules to the Federal income tax rules relating to Roth IRAs, including the rules on recharacterization of a Roth IRA back into a traditional IRA. Will all earnings in Roth IRAs and all payouts from Roth IRAs be forever exempt from State income taxes? Will the States allow for the deferral of any State income taxes over four years, in the case of a conversion of a traditional IRA to a Roth IRA in 1998? If the States do conform their laws to the Federal laws, when will those changes be implemented, and what will the effective dates of each of those changes be? What if the advisor's client subsequently moves to a State in which each of these rules are *not* followed? The answers to many of these questions must be thoroughly explored by the advisor before the client decides on using a Roth IRA.

- *State Creditor Laws.* Many States at this time exempt all IRA assets, regardless of their initial source, from the claims of all non-governmental creditors. However, the Federal statutory authority that created the Roth IRA did so by adopting a new Internal Revenue Code section (§ 408A), rather than by amending the already existing Internal Revenue Code § 408 relating to traditional and regular rollover IRAs. Consequently, most State laws dealing with IRA benefits and the exemption issue did *not* initially apply to Roth IRAs and this new Internal Revenue Code section. Will all States modify their current exemption laws to similarly exempt assets in Roth IRAs from the claims or creditors? If such changes are to be made, when will those statutory changes be made, and what will the effective date of those changes be? In addition, what if the advisor's client moves from a State in which Roth IRAs are entirely exempted from creditors' claims to a State in which there is no exemption for Roth IRAs? Once again, the answers to many of these questions must also be thoroughly explored by the advisor before recommending a Roth IRA for any of the advisor's clients.

Final Thoughts on Roth IRAs

Given the right set of circumstances, using a Roth IRA as a tool for multigenerational planning can produce tremendous results. Often the children and grandchildren of the taxpayer will receive a larger inheritance—even net after all estate taxes have been paid—when the taxpayer has converted his or her traditional IRAs into Roth IRAs and especially into multigenerational Roth IRAs. Therefore, for clients whose primary objective is to maximize the inheritance to their heirs, the Roth IRA is an excellent idea. This is especially so if the growth on the Roth IRA assets, subsequent to the date of conversion, can be exempted from all Federal and State estate taxes.

For clients whose primary objective is to maximize payouts for themselves while they are alive, the decision to convert their traditional IRAs to Roth IRAs is a closer call. The various factors to consider are the client's age, the growth rate applicable to the assets in the traditional and Roth IRA, the client's current and future income and estate tax brackets, and the client's desired yearly distribution amounts from the IRA.

One major concern that all clients have is whether or not the Roth IRA rules will continue indefinitely into the future or whether those rules will be severely curtailed or eliminated by a subsequent Congress and President dealing with a Federal budget once again out of balance.

Much of the benefit of converting a traditional IRA to a Roth IRA, as has been shown, is only realized over an extended period of time, as the assets in the Roth IRA continue to grow on a tax-exempt basis. If Congress and the President were to eliminate Roth IRAs in ten years, for example, will it have been to anyone's benefit to have made the conversion? Will the assets in Roth IRAs at that time be grandfathered, with respect to their perpetual exemption from Federal income taxation?

It may be hard to imagine subsequent legislation being passed which either taxes Roth IRA assets or the earnings on Roth IRA contributions, each of which would severely penalize the owners of Roth IRAs. Remember that taxpayers with Roth IRA accounts had either voluntarily agreed to forego current income tax deductions in order to establish their Roth IRA accounts or had voluntarily pre-paid the full Federal income taxes due on their traditional IRA assets at the time that they had converted their traditional IRAs into Roth IRAs. To tax those individuals at some point in the future on their Roth IRA assets or on the growth of their Roth IRA assets seems manifestly unfair and in some instances, tantamount to a double taxation of those assets. However, those who argue that Congress and the President would never impose such an unfair result would do well to remember the days when Social Security and unemployment benefits were each entirely exempt from all Federal income taxes.

In summary, the complexity of the Roth IRA rules, the AGI limitations on its use, the unknown variables with respect to the client's future personal and economic needs and expenses, and the possibility of significant changes in future tax legislation, are all formidable obstacles in the road leading to the establishment of a Roth IRA by any particular client. However, a well-informed objective advisor, armed with the relevant Roth IRA rules and with all of the details of the client's current and anticipated financial circumstances, can be of enormous assistance to the client in helping the client make this most important tax decision.

Employer Securities and Net Unrealized Appreciation

When a participant is entitled to benefits from a qualified plan, the distribution to the participant can be made entirely in cash, entirely "in kind" with non-cash assets, or in any combination of cash or in-kind assets (see Chapter 12). As explained previously, there is no problem in rolling over an all-cash distribution into an IRA, as long as the rollover was completed within 60 days of the date of the plan distribution, and provided further that the distribution is not one of those few distributions that are not eligible to be rolled over into an IRA. Where the distribution consists of all in-kind assets (or part cash, part in-kind assets), the participant has the option of selling the non-cash assets and contributing the cash proceeds into the IRA, or directly contributing the in-kind assets themselves into the IRA. Current IRS rules, however, prevent the individual from taking a cash distribution from a qualified plan, purchasing assets with that cash distribution, and then contributing those newly purchased assets into the IRA. Similarly, current IRS rules do not allow a participant who has received an in-kind distribution to sell the assets constituting that distribution, take the net cash proceeds from the sale and buy new assets, and then contribute those new assets into the IRA. Simply stated, cash distributions from qualified plans can be rolled over into IRAs, in-kind distributions from qualified plans can also be rolled into IRAs, but no new assets purchased with either the cash received from a qualified plan distribution or from the sale of in-kind assets received as part of a qualified plan distribution can be rolled over into an IRA.

It would, therefore, seem that in most cases, participants will usually favor an all-cash distribution from their qualified plans. This type of distribution can easily be rolled over into an IRA, and as soon as the cash has been credited to the IRA account, the individual will decide how best to reinvest that cash amount in the IRA. Even in those instances in which the participant wishes to maintain the same investment in the IRA as had been maintained in the qualified plan, it is usually a simple matter for the participant to direct the IRA Custodian to purchase those same investments with the cash amount in the IRA. The sale charges and commissions associated with the purchase of those assets will be lost in the process. However, those sales charges and commissions typically represent a very small percentage of the value of the assets purchased and, in most instances, will not represent a significant expense to the participant. However, in those few cases in which the sales charges and commissions associated with the purchase of the same asset are significant, it would be to the participant's advantage to receive a distribution from the qualified plan of the asset itself, which can then be rolled over within the 60-day period into the shelter of the IRA, where it can be maintained indefinitely. Such a situation could easily occur with a mutual fund which charges a 5 percent or 6 percent sales charge for new purchases up to $25,000, but which charges only 1 percent or no fee at all, once cumulative purchases have exceeded $100,000. This situation frequently occurs with 401(k) plans, which, relatively early on in their administration, easily reach the breakpoint at which sales commissions and charges have been reduced to 1 percent or to nothing. However, a participant receiving an all-cash distribution from that same 401(k) plan who wishes to purchase that same mutual fund with their rollover IRA assets may find that the sales charges and commissions associated with that purchase are still at the 5 percent or 6 percent level (insofar as the purchase by the IRA is considered to be a purchase by a *new* client of the mutual fund), with no credit given for the prior volume purchases made by the 401(k) plan.

Participants will also favor an in-kind distribution from a qualified plan in those instances in which the qualified plan had owned an insurance policy on the life of the participant and the participant now wishes to continue the insurance coverage outside of the plan, or wishes to recover the cumulative PS-58 costs associated with the policy on a tax-free basis from the plan. This topic will be discussed in greater detail later in this chapter.

Where the qualified plan distribution consists of employer securities, an additional substantial potential tax benefit is available to the participant. Ordinarily, when a participant receives a distribution from a qualified plan and does not roll over that distribution into an IRA within the 60-day period, the participant is taxed on the full fair market value of the plan distribution, whether the distribution had consisted of all cash, all in-kind assets, or a combination of cash and in-kind assets. However, where the distribution consists of employer securities, a special rule becomes operative. Instead of being taxed on the then-current fair market value of the employer securities received as part of the plan distribution, the participant is only taxed based on the plan's cost basis in the company stock. The difference between the current fair market value of the employer securities received as part of the plan distribution and the plan's cost basis in the company stock is not currently taxed to the participant. That amount is not taxed to the participant until the stock is actually sold by the participant. The portion of the value of the stock which is not taxed to the participant until the stock is later sold by the participant is known as the "net unrealized appreciation" or NUA. When the employer stock is sold, the gain on the sale of the stock is determined by computing the difference between the plan's cost basis in the asset and the final sales price of the asset. This gain is then taxed at capital gains rates to the participant. This rule represents a significant departure from the ordinary income tax rules, which generally taxes all distributions from qualified plans at ordinary income tax rates and not at capital gains rates. This difference in tax rate, and the ability of the participant to defer the income taxes due on the company stock until the company stock has been sold, can prove to be an enormous tax benefit to the participant.

An example illustrates how this complex tax rule works:

> **Example:** Mark, age 60, has been a participant in the Employee Stock Ownership Plan (ESOP) of Amalgamated, Inc. for 30 years. He is retiring and is entitled to a distribution from the plan. The plan pays him a cash distribution of $100,000, and he receives a distribution of stock in Amalgamated, Inc., which is worth $400,000. If Mark chooses to, he can roll over the $100,000 cash distribution into an IRA, thereby avoiding any current income tax liability on that portion of his plan distribution. In addition, Mark may also roll over the stock in Amalgamated, Inc. into the IRA. In that way, Mark will

> have avoided any current income taxation on the two portions of his plan distribution. However, were Mark to pursue this route, all subsequent distributions from the IRA would be subject to ordinary income taxation, and the ability to receive capital gains treatment on the sale of the Amalgamated, Inc. stock would have been lost forever. Moreover, once Mark has reached his Required Beginning Date (RBD), distributions from the IRA must begin based on the full value of the IRA, as of December 31of the year immediately preceding the year in which Mark turned age 70½.

Instead of the above route, Mark could have immediately sold all of the shares of stock in Amalgamated, Inc. which he had received as part of his plan distribution, rolling over the $400,000 net sales proceeds into his IRA. However, had Mark pursued this route, he would have been subject to ordinary income tax on the full $400,000 value of the company stock.

Alternatively, Mark could have decided to roll over into his IRA only the cash portion of the plan distribution he had received, while at the same time accepting a distribution of the company stock directly to him, and not rolling over any of the company stock into an IRA. If the plan's cost basis in the stock was $50,000, Mark would have to pay income tax only on the $50,000 cost basis in the stock. That tax would be imposed at ordinary income tax rates, but Mark would not have to pay any income tax on the $350,000 NUA in the value of the stock. In addition, by rolling over the $100,000 cash distribution into the IRA, Mark would have avoided any current income taxation on that portion of his plan distribution.

Once Mark reached his RBD, distributions from the IRA would be required to begin. However yearly Required Minimum Distribution (RMD) amounts from the IRA would be relatively small, since only $100,000 of the total plan distribution had been rolled over into the IRA initially, instead of the full $500,000 value of the plan distribution which Mark had received. Mark could decide to hold on to the com-pany stock indefinitely, even if he was then well past age 70½. In fact, if he wanted to, Mark could hold on to the company stock until his death, without any requirement that he sell any portion or all of the stock at any time while he was alive. In this way, during his lifetime,

Mark would have entirely avoided any income taxation on the NUA of the value of the stock. At some point in the future, were Mark to have decided to sell some or all of the stock, he would then be taxed on the NUA of the stock which was sold, plus any subsequent appreciation in the value of the stock which had occurred after the date on which Mark had received the distribution of the stock from the plan. However, all such tax would be imposed at capital gains rates, and not at ordinary income tax rates.

It would seem from the above example that any participant in Mark's situation should decide not to roll over into an IRA any portion of a plan distribution that consisted of employer securities. By paying only the relatively small current ordinary income tax on the plan's cost basis in the stock, Mark was able to entirely avoid any of the RMD rules on the value of the company stock and was never taxed at ordinary income tax rates on any portion of the value of the company stock (other than on the plan's cost basis in the stock). Moreover, by deciding when to sell any portion or all of the company stock, Mark retained complete control over the point at which any income taxation would be imposed on any sale of the company stock. It may, therefore, seem that this scenario represents the best of all possible worlds. However, there are potential problems and obstacles associated with this approach.

In the first instance, many individuals in Mark's position who potentially could receive a distribution of company stock, and who potentially could elect not to roll over the stock into an IRA, do not do so because they have not been informed by either their company or their tax advisor of their ability to avail themselves of this favorable tax treatment. Strange as it may seem, many plan trustees or plan administrators of qualified plans which hold employer securities are unaware of the tax benefits available to the participants in receiving employer securities as part of their plan distribution. In fact, many plans which are permitted to distribute employer securities as part of a plan distribution often do not do so, but instead may make an all-cash distribution to the participant, unaware that a valuable tax benefit to the participant will have then been lost forever.

In the second instance, the vast majority of qualified plans in the United States do not hold *any* employer securities as part of their plan assets. In fact, most qualified plans are prohibited from investing any portion of their assets in employer securities. The only types of plans which are permitted to invest any portion of their plan assets in employer securities are certain profit sharing plans, with ESOPs being the only type of qualified plans which are permitted to invest *primarily* in employer securities. Employer securities are defined as stock in the company that is sponsoring the plan. Typically, companies that sponsor ESOPs are publicly traded companies. However, closely held companies that maintain ESOPs are also permitted to invest primarily in employer securities. Many advisors may find located in their community one or more companies that employ a substantial percentage of the local workforce. These companies often maintain ESOPs. Advisors in that type of community may find that a relatively high percentage of their client base is or was employed by that one company and thus are eligible to receive distributions of employer securities from their company's ESOP upon retirement.

In addition, employees may not want to hold onto employer securities outside of an IRA because they may find that the qualified plan's cost basis in the stock is relatively high and that, accordingly, they would have to pay a significant ordinary income tax amount were they to decide not to roll over the company stock into an IRA. On the other hand, employees who saw the value of their company stock plummet over the past few years will often welcome an all-cash distribution from their plan, so that they will not have to bear any further losses in value should the company stock continue to decline further in value, even if they intend to sell the stock shortly after receiving it.

Probably the single largest reason why many employees do not want to hold employer securities outside of an IRA is that the value of the employer securities received as part of a plan distribution may represent the major portion, if not all, of the plan distribution. Ideally, during the participant's retirement years, his or her retirement assets should be conservatively invested for the long term, with the participant's retirement portfolio properly diversified between cash, stocks, mutual funds, bonds, Treasury bills, annuities, and other holdings, as well as being diversified geographically and across multiple industry groups. By continuing to hold onto a significant portion of employer securities, the participant is relegating himself or herself to an investment posture in which his or her retirement portfolio—or at least a significant portion of it—is not only *not* invested in different types of assets, geographically diversified over multiple industry groups, but is largely or exclusively invested in only one company. If the stock in that one company continues to grow each year at a significant rate, all will go well. However, the investment risk associated with this approach, especially in the long run, is extremely high in many instances. It is simply too risky and too dangerous a strategy for the participant and spouse to maintain—even if the participant has residual goodwill toward his or her former employer and even if, over a lengthy period in the past, the employer's stock had appreciated at a consistent and significant rate. Especially during the last decade, many highly successful Fortune 500 companies that in the past had enjoyed perhaps decades of continued and measured growth, suddenly fell on hard times, and may now be in a state of substantial decline. Were a participant's retirement income largely dependent on that company's continued financial success, the participant could well find that his or her retirement nest egg, instead of continuing to grow incrementally during the participant's retirement years, has already begun to drop precipitously in value as the prognosis for the company's financial turnaround proves more and more bleak.

When dealing with a client who is eligible to receive a distribution of employer securities, the advisor should perform a careful analysis to determine whether or not the employer securities should be rolled over into an IRA or whether they should be retained in the name of the participant, with the tax on the NUA deferred until the stock is sold. For any given client, the best solution may involve rolling over only a portion of the employer securities into the IRA, while retaining the remaining portion in the name of the participant. A mix-and-match approach is entirely acceptable. In this way, the participant can diversify a larger percentage of retirement assets, while still taking advantage of some of the benefits associated with retaining employer securities and not paying tax on the NUA until the stock is sold.

In performing this analysis, the advisor should be aware that, when the stock is sold, the IRS allows long-term capital gain treatment on the NUA amount, regardless of how much time has passed from the date on which the company stock had been distributed to the participant, until the date on which the stock is sold. However, any appreciation of the company stock after the distribution date will be taxed at either short-term capital gains rates or long-term capital gains rates, depending on how much time has elapsed from the distribution date until the date on which the stock is sold. The advisor should also be aware that the NUA amount is considered to be income in respect of the decedent (IRD) and, accordingly, is not afforded a step up in basis at the time of the participant's death. However, if the company stock appreciated in value subsequent to the date on which the stock was distributed to the participant, all post-distribution appreciation would be stepped up in value at the participant's death, should the participant continue to own the stock as of the date of his or her death.

The advisor should also be aware that the special income tax treatment afforded to the distribution of employer securities is available only in those instances in which the distribution was part of a qualifying lump-sum distribution from the plan (except that the rule requiring an individual to be a participant in the plan for five years before the year of the plan distribution is not applicable in this case). If the distribution from the plan does not qualify as a lump-sum distribution, no favorable tax treatment will be afforded to the distribution to the participant of employer securities. Finally, in doing this analysis, the advisor should also be aware that if the participant had received a distribution of employer securities before he or she attained age 59½, there may be a 10 percent premature distribution excise tax associated with the distribution, unless any one or more of the exceptions associated with the 10 percent excise tax is applicable. (See Chapter 12 for a fuller discussion of the 10 percent premature distribution excise tax and the 14 exceptions that may apply to limit the imposition of that tax.)

Tax-Free Recovery of PS-58 Costs

As discussed previously, there are numerous ways in which favorable tax treatment may be afforded to participants in a qualified plan. This includes favorable tax treatment with respect to the tax benefits associated with the accumulation and distribution phases of retirement planning, and especially the benefits associated with establishing a multigeneration IRA. On the accumulation phase, favorable tax treatment is afforded to the participants so that, upon retirement, the tax-sheltered benefits that have been accumulated can be used to provide yearly retirement income to the participants and, in many cases, to their spouses or other family members.

During the early days of qualified plans, benefits were provided only to plan participants, with all periodic pension payments ceasing once a participant died, even if the participant was survived by a spouse. In pre-ERISA days (before 1974), it was permissible for a participant's entire benefit in the plan to be forfeited upon the individual's death. The theory behind this forfeiture rule was that a pension plan was designed primarily to provide for retirement income for the participant, and not to provide any form of death benefit for the participant's heirs. The IRC rules, pre-ERISA, did permit qualified plans to maintain insurance coverage on the lives of participants, but only when the insurance benefits provided was merely "incidental" to the primary purpose of the plan, which was to provide yearly retirement income to the participants. Many of these pre-ERISA incidental benefit rules survived ERISA and, in fact, continue to this day.

One such rule limits the amount of insurance coverage that can be maintained on the lives of plan participants. Another rule taxes the participants currently on the economic benefit received each year when plan assets, or employer contributions made to the plan, are used to maintain insurance coverage on the participants' lives. The value of the benefits on which the participants are required to pay tax each year is equal to the annual renewable term premium cost, based on the amount of the insurance policy's death benefit. The theory behind this rule is that by having the plan maintain insurance coverage on their lives, the participants receive an economic benefit each year; this benefit can be quantified, even if the participants should survive for the entire year.

The value of the economic benefit attributable to those premiums can be computed using either the annual renewable term rates or the PS-58 rates. The PS-58 rates were derived from an IRS table used to determine the actual cost of the term component of a cash value policy. One methodology or the other is utilized each year in computing the taxable value of the economic benefit derived by the participant each year that premiums have been paid. However, for the sake of simplicity in this discussion, both methodologies will be referred to as the "PS-58 costs."

As the participant ages, the cost of pure term coverage in the policy, whatever type of policy it is, increases. Even if the policy has a feature that allows for dividends or policy earnings to pay premiums, and even if the employer no longer pays the premiums, the economic benefit derived from the policy's continued maintenance still applies.

PS-58 costs are passed on to the plan participants each year. The participants receive a Form 1099 statement or a letter from the insurance company, plan trustee, or plan administrator indicating the taxable portion of the insurance premiums paid by the plan that year on the insurance policies maintained on their lives or paid directly by the employer sponsoring the plan. The participants are then required to include the PS-58 cost amounts on their personal income tax returns each year. If this step has been followed each year, eventually each participant can accumulate a significant cost basis in the life insurance policy maintained by the plan. An example will explain how this procedure works.

> **Example:** Carol is a participant in a profit sharing plan that maintains an insurance policy on her life. Each year the plan administrator has provided Carol with a Form 1099 statement indicating the PS-58 costs associated with the maintenance of that policy for that year. Initially, the PS-58 costs for the first year in which Carol had been a plan participant were only $200. During this last year, the PS-58 costs had risen to $350. Carol terminates her employment with the company and is entitled to a distribution from the plan. Were she to add up all of the cumulative PS-58 costs that she had previously included on her personal income tax returns for each of the prior ten years, she would find that the cumulative PS-58 costs would equal $2,450. Because Carol had previously paid income tax on the $2,450 amount, when she receives her distribution from the plan that portion of her plan distribution representing her cumulative PS-58 costs should not be subject to income tax again. The method by which Carol avoids the payment of the income tax on the $2,450 amount again is known as "recovering the PS-58 costs." Had Carol not picked up the PS-58 costs on her personal income tax returns each year, she would not be entitled to recover that amount tax-free when she receives her distribution from the plan.

One would imagine that whenever a participant in a qualified plan has a cumulative PS-58 cost, and receives a distribution from the plan the cumulative PS-58 cost amount would automatically always be available to reduce the amount of the taxable income attributable to the plan distribution. However such is often not the case. In many instances, the participant is not told about the cumulative PS-58 costs and, accordingly, may actually pay tax a second time, on the same amounts on which the participant had already paid tax each year. Alternatively, if the distribution to the participant is not handled correctly, the cumulative PS-58 costs may be lost, causing the participant to pay tax a second time on the same amounts. This could occur where the insurance policy on the participant's life is cashed in by the plan, with the policy's net cash surrender value then being used to increase the value of the participant's plan benefit. The correct way to recover the cumulative PS-58 costs is to distribute the ownership of the insurance policy directly from the plan into the name of the participant as part of the plan distribution process. When the distribution is handled in this way, the cumulative PS-58 costs remain attached to the policy, and are then available as an offset to the amount of the taxable plan distribution.

However, there is one caveat when using this approach: the cash surrender value of the insurance policy can greatly exceed the cumulative PS-58 costs. In such a case, a participant would be required to pay current income tax on the difference between the cumulative PS-58 costs and the net cash surrender value of the policy, and would not be able to avoid the income tax on that amount by rolling over the difference into an IRA. This problem cannot be avoided by rolling over the insurance policy itself into an IRA, insofar as current law prohibits an IRA from owning an insurance policy. Fortunately, however, there is a way for the participant to avoid any current income tax liability when receiving ownership of the insurance. There is also a way in which, at the same time, the participant can recover the cumulative PS-58 cost amount on a tax-free basis. The solution to this problem requires the plan trustees to borrow out the excess net cash surrender value of the policy. An example illustrates this approach.

> **Example:** In the above example, Carol had accumulated a $2,450 cumulative PS-58 cost basis in the insurance policy maintained by the profit sharing plan on her life. Assume that at the time of her termination of em-

ployment, the insurance policy had a net cash surrender value of $10,000 and that, at that time, the value of Carol's other benefits in the plan amounted to $20,000. Therefore, between the value of the life insurance policy of $10,000 and the value of the side fund plan benefit of $20,000, Carol is entitled to a total distribution from the plan worth $30,000. Were Carol to receive a distribution of the actual life insurance policy in her name, in addition to receiving a cash distribution of $20,000 from the plan, Carol would have received a total benefit from the plan valued at $30,000. She could roll over the $20,000 cash distribution into an IRA, thereby avoiding any current income tax liability on the receipt of that amount. However, because the ownership of the life insurance policy cannot be transferred into an IRA, Carol would be required to pay current income tax on the value of the life insurance policy. Of the $10,000 net cash surrender value of the policy, $2,450 would be exempt from tax, as representing the return to Carol of her cumulative PS-58 costs. However, that would still leave Carol with current income tax liability on the remaining $7,550 amount ($10,000 – $2,450). Instead, Carol could have requested that the plan trustees borrow out the amount of the net cash surrender value of the policy leaving only the amount of the cumulative PS-58 costs in the policy. Were the trustees of the plan to follow that direction, the policy would be stripped of $7,550 of its value, with the $7,550 amount then immediately deposited into the plan, and then immediately used to increase the cash distribution to Carol from $20,000 to $27,550. Carol could then roll over the entire $27,550 cash distribution into an IRA, thereby avoiding any current income taxation on her higher cash distribution. The plan trustees would then transfer the ownership of the life insurance policy into Carol's name. Because $7,550 of the value of the policy had previously been borrowed out at the time that the ownership of the policy had been transferred to Carol, the policy would then be worth only $2,450, which amount coincides

> with Carol's cumulative PS-58 cost. In this way, Carol can increase her cash distribution from the plan (and her rollover amount), while at the same time recovering the full amount of her cumulative PS-58 costs on an entirely tax-free basis.

Once the ownership of the life insurance policy has been transferred to Carol's name, Carol would have the option of maintaining the policy each year or cashing it in. Should she decide to continue to maintain the policy, yearly premiums would be due. In addition, at the time of the transfer of ownership of the policy to Carol's name, the policy had been encumbered by a $7,550 policy loan. The policy loan will accrue interest at the rate specified in the insurance policy. Carol has several options in this regard: She may decide to (1) pay off the policy loan immediately, (2) pay off only portions of the policy loan each year, (3) pay only the current year's accrued interest on the policy loan each year, or (4) pay no portion of the policy loan each year or any portion of any yearly interest charges associated therewith. However, if the policy loan is large enough, in the future the premiums on the policy may not build up subsequent cash surrender value fast enough to maintain the policy in force. In other words, once the ownership of the insurance policy is transferred to Carol's name, she may have to pay not only the yearly premiums due on the policy, but also a portion of the policy loan (or at least the interest accrued thereon) in order to continue to maintain the policy in effect.

Alternatively, once the ownership of the insurance policy has been transferred into Carol's name, she could decide to cash it in immediately, receiving its net cash surrender value of $2,450. Because Carol recovered the $2,450 amount on a tax-free basis, she would have the full $2,450 amount available to her to spend for any purpose. Under these circumstances, the advisor may suggest that she use the cumulative PS-58 cost amount recovered to purchase a new insurance policy on her life. In this way, she can fund a new insurance policy on her life that she may regard as "found money."

There are several benefits associated with purchasing a new insurance policy on the participant's life. If the new policy had never been owned by the participant, but had instead been initially owned by his or her children or by an irrevocable life insurance trust, the proceeds from that policy would immediately be exempted from any estate tax in the participant's estate. Had the participant continued to maintain the insurance policy that had been owned by the plan, on the participant's death the proceeds from that policy would have been fully included in the participant's estate. Had the ownership of the plan insurance policy been previously transferred to the children's name or to an irrevocable life insurance trust, the proceeds from that policy would have been exempt from tax in the participant's estate, but only if the participant had survived at least three years from the date on which the ownership of the policy had been transferred. The new insurance policy can avoid the estate tax includability immediately, without having to wait the three-year period.

CHAPTER 16
REGULATORY DEVELOPMENTS

16 REGULATORY DEVELOPMENTS

On January 17, 2001, the IRS published in the Federal Register revised proposed regulations under IRC §§ 401(a)(9), 403(b), 408, and 4974 on the Required Minimum Distribution rules. In issuing the revised proposed regulations of January 17, 2001, the IRS created certain new rules and planning opportunities for individuals. (See the Introduction for a detailed discussion.) However, in changing some of the prior rules and in creating some of the new rules, the IRS inadvertently created certain new issues and potential problem areas which it will need to clarify or resolve in the future. It is hoped that those clarifications and resolutions will be made a part of the final regulations when they are issued in late 2001 or early 2002. In addition, several of the issues that had previously existed in this area have not been resolved by the revised proposed regulations of January 17, 2001, despite the IRS's attempt to simplify this area of the law, and despite the over 13 years that it has had to digest, reflect on, and synthesize its thinking in this area since it first issued the initial proposed regulations on July 27, 1987. It is hoped that these preexisting issues, too, will all be adequately addressed in the final regulations when they are issued by the IRS.

New Issues Created by and Prior Issues Left Unresolved by the Revised Proposed Regulations of January 17, 2001

Following are questions that have arisen concerning the many new issues created by the revised proposed regulation of January 17, 2001, as well as questions pertaining to many preexisting issues that were left unresolved after the issuance of the revised proposed regulations. The issues are arranged in subject matter order and represent those transition and effective-date issues which have been created as a result of the issuance of the revised proposed regulations, those issues which have been addressed in the revised proposed regulations but in a somewhat ambiguous way and which are thus capable of multiple interpretations, and those issues which have not been addressed at all in the revised proposed regulations.

Within the first six months of 2001, several representatives of the National Office of the IRS have voiced their opinions in numerous public forums on many of the issues discussed. However, even where the position of the IRS is probably known in a particular area, the question has remained on the list because all of those IRS speakers had prefaced their remarks with the caveat that they were speaking only for themselves and that their pronouncements in this area did not necessarily reflect the views of the IRS or of their superiors within the IRS. Therefore, until the following issues have been resolved by the final regulations or by some other written IRS announcement, they are still unresolved, from both an official and a practical point of view.

Life Expectancy Issues

Where an estate has been named as the IRA beneficiary, but the estate is closed by December 31 of the calendar year immediately following the calendar year of the IRA owner's death, transferring at that time to the estate beneficiaries (e.g., the four children of the IRA owner) all rights to all estate assets (including the IRA assets), can the life expectancies of the children of the IRA owner then be used for purposes of determining subsequent yearly Required Minimum Distribution amounts?

Where the spouse beneficiary survives the IRA owner, but dies without having established a spousal rollover IRA, and where subsequent Required Minimum Distributions are to be based on the remaining life expectancy of the surviving spouse, after determining the spouse's remaining life expectancy determined in the year of his or her death, does one first subtract 1 from that remaining life expectancy for the year *following* the year of the surviving spouse's date of death or does one first subtract 1 from that remaining life expectancy for the year *following* the year of the one-year anniversary of the surviving spouse's date of death?

When an IRA owner who has passed his or her Required Beginning Date marries an individual who is more than ten years his or her junior, is the couple permitted to use their actual remaining joint life expectancy each year thereafter while they are both alive for purposes of determining their Required Minimum Distributions? Is the answer the same if the individual had been married to the same spouse *prior* to his or her Required Beginning Date, but designated the spouse as beneficiary subsequent to that date?

In order to be able to use the actual joint life expectancy of the IRA owner and spouse who is more than ten years younger than the IRA owner, must the spouse be the sole beneficiary of the *entire* IRA benefit, or can the spouse be one of several beneficiaries of the IRA? If the spouse must be the beneficiary of the entire IRA benefit in order to be able to use the actual joint life expectancy of the IRA owner and spouse, does this rule apply *separately* to each IRA of the individual, or must all IRAs of the individual be aggregated for purposes of this rule?

Where an IRA owner has designated his or her spouse as the IRA beneficiary, and where the spouse is more than ten years younger than the IRA owner, if the spouse were to die *after* the IRA owner's Required Beginning Date, should subsequent Required Minimum Distribution amounts during the balance of the IRA owner's lifetime be made based on the continued use of the actual joint life expectancy table of the IRA owner and now-deceased spouse, or must subsequent Required Minimum Distribution amounts during the balance of the IRA owner's lifetime be based on the use of the Uniform Distribution Period Table? If subsequent Required Minimum Distribution amounts are to be based on the use of the Uniform Distribution Period Table, is the switch from the actual joint life expectancy table to the Uniform Distribution Period Table to occur in the year of the spouse's death or in the subsequent year? Would there be any difference in the application of this rule if the spouse had not died, but, instead, the IRA owner had divorced the spouse after his or her Required Beginning Date, retaining the now-former spouse as his or her IRA beneficiary?

Where a Q-TIP Trust that qualifies as a Designated Beneficiary has been named as the IRA beneficiary, and where the spouse is more than ten years younger than the IRA owner, is it permissible to use the actual joint life expectancy of the IRA owner and spouse, or is the IRA owner required to use the Uniform Distribution Period Table for purposes of computing yearly Required Minimum Distribution amounts while the IRA owner is alive?

Where an IRA owner has died after his or her Required Beginning Date with either no named Designated Beneficiary or with his or her estate named as the beneficiary, or where the IRA Custodial Agreement defaults to the individual's estate as the beneficiary, for the year following the year of the IRA owner's death and for each year thereafter (when Required Minimum Distributions are based on the remaining life expectancy of the IRA owner determined in the year of his or her death and by subtracting 1 for each year thereafter), which life expectancy table is to be used at that time, the Uniform Distribution Period Table or the single life expectancy table applicable to the deceased IRA owner?

Spousal Rollover Issues

Where there are multiple beneficiaries of an IRA, can a spouse beneficiary roll over his or her portion of the IRA amount into a spousal rollover IRA, or must the surviving spouse be the sole beneficiary of the entire IRA balance to be afforded this rollover right? If the surviving spouse must be the beneficiary of the *entire* IRA balance to be afforded this right, are all IRAs of the same IRA Custodian or all IRAs of the deceased spouse (regardless of the number of different IRA Custodians which are being used) aggregated for purposes of this rule? Where the spouse must be the beneficiary of the entire IRA balance to be afforded this rollover right, can a separate share for the benefit of the surviving spouse be created by December 31 of the calendar year immediately following the calendar year of the IRA owner's death and, in so doing, thereby enable the surviving spouse to establish the spousal rollover IRA with his or her separate share?

Do the revised proposed regulations of January 17, 2001 make any distinction in the application of the spousal rollover rules between those cases in which a spousal rollover IRA has been physically created following the death of the IRA owner (either by retitling the IRA owner's account or by physically moving the IRA assets to another IRA account in the name of the surviving spouse) and those cases in which a "deemed" spousal rollover has been established (where, following the IRA owner's death, the IRA has *not* been retitled and has *not* been physically moved to another IRA account in the name of the surviving spouse)?

Where an IRA owner has died, and the spouse beneficiary begins to receive payments from the Inherited IRA before the spouse has attained age $59^1/_2$ without any 10 percent premature distribution excise tax being paid, is the spouse later permitted to establish a spousal rollover IRA, and, if so, what is the outside date on which that spousal rollover IRA can be established, with the life expectancies of the beneficiaries of that spousal rollover IRA then being used for Required Minimum Distribution purposes following the death of the surviving spouse?

Where the surviving spouse of an IRA owner dies prior to December 31 of the calendar year immediately following the calendar year of the IRA owner's death, will all subsequent Required Minimum Distribution amounts for the IRA beneficiaries be computed assuming that the IRA is still in the name of the IRA owner, or will they be computed assuming that a deemed spousal rollover IRA had been established?

Over the years, the IRS, in many Private Letter Rulings, has developed exceptions to the general rule denying a surviving spouse the right to roll over inherited IRA benefits, where the spouse had not been named as the direct beneficiary of those assets, but where instead a trust established for the benefit of the spouse had been named as beneficiary. In each instance, the exceptions turned on the degree of spousal control over the trust. Is each of these previously developed exceptions to the spousal rollover rules still applicable under the revised proposed regulations?

The surviving spouse is the sole primary beneficiary of the IRA owner's first IRA and is also the sole income beneficiary of a Q-TIP Trust established by the IRA owner, (which trust is the beneficiary of the IRA owner's second IRA). Can the surviving spouse aggregate distributions from both IRAs and take distributions disproportionately from one or both of the two IRAs, while still satisfying the Required Minimum Distribution rules?

Spousal Deferral Rule

Where the surviving spouse is the primary beneficiary of a trust that was named as the IRA beneficiary, under what circumstances can the surviving spouse avail himself or herself of the Spousal Deferral

Rule? Must the trust be a strict Conduit Trust or Power of Appointment trust for the Spousal Deferral Rule to be permissible?

The Five-Year Rule/Life Expectancy Rule

Where the IRA owner had died in 2000 prior to his or her Required Beginning Date and where the beneficiary has failed to take the first year's Required Minimum Distribution amount by December 31, 2001, can the beneficiary still use the Life Expectancy Rule for purposes of computing the Required Minimum Distribution amounts due for 2002 and for each year thereafter, or must the beneficiary adhere to the Five-Year Rule for each year going forward? Assume that the IRA Custodial document had *not* required the use of the Five-Year Rule, nor had the IRA owner elected into the application of the Five-Year Rule. Assume further that the beneficiary will pay the 50 percent excise tax in 2002 on the failure to have timely taken the Required Minimum Distribution amount for 2001.

An IRA owner who has designated his son as his IRA beneficiary has provided for no contingent beneficiary. The IRA owner dies prior to his Required Beginning Date and is survived by his son, who, in turn, dies prior to December 31 of the calendar year immediately following the calendar year of the IRA owner's death. The IRA Custodial Agreement then defaults to the IRA owner's estate as the IRA beneficiary. Will the beneficiaries of the estate, who are the IRA owner's other children, be required to take distributions from the IRA under the Five-Year Rule, or can they base subsequent Required Minimum Distributions on the life expectancy of the deceased son? What would be the result if the IRA owner had died after his Required Beginning Date?

How does the beneficiary of an Inherited IRA elect to have his or her IRA benefits payable pursuant to the Five-Year Rule, where the IRA owner has died prior to his or her Required Beginning Date? Must this election be made in writing, or is it sufficient for the beneficiary to pay out all of the assets in the Inherited IRA by December 31 of the calendar year containing the fifth anniversary of the IRA owner's death? If such election must be in writing, when must this election be made? In addition, how can this election be made if the IRA Custodian is unwilling to provide the necessary election forms and may even be unwilling to accept an election document prepared by either the IRA owner prior to his or her death or by the beneficiary of the Inherited IRA following the IRA owner's death? Where the IRA Custodian will not accept any such election documents, will it be sufficient if the election document is sent instead directly to the IRS?

Distributions in the Year of the IRA Owner's Death

Where an IRA owner has died and the surviving spouse establishes a rollover IRA in the year of the IRA owner's death, is the surviving spouse required to receive two Required Minimum Distributions in that year?

Beneficiary Issues

Aside from the death or disclaimer of a primary beneficiary following the death of the IRA owner but prior to December 31 of the calendar year immediately following the calendar year of the IRA owner's death, are there any other ways or circumstances in which a beneficiary can be determined for the balance of the IRA account following the IRA owner's death but prior to December 31 of the calendar year immediately following the calendar year of the IRA owner's death, other than by the IRA owner or by the primary beneficiary under those circumstances having previously designated a contingent beneficiary for those benefits? For instance, can the Executor, Administrator, or Personal Representative of the IRA owner's estate select the next beneficiary? If a new beneficiary can be so determined, or can be determined in any other way, will the life expectancy of that new beneficiary be allowed to be used for purposes of determining subsequent Required Minimum Distribution amounts?

Where the Trustee of a trust that has been named as the IRA beneficiary has discretionary authority to allocate the IRA proceeds into either the A Sub-Trust (the Credit Shelter Trust portion) or the B Sub-Trust (the Q-TIP Trust portion), does this discretionary authority on the part of the Trustee prevent both sub-trusts from qualifying as Designated Beneficiaries and, accordingly, from having life expectancies? Is this problem solved in those cases in which the allocation of the IRA proceeds as between the two Sub-Trusts is determined pursuant to a set formula clause contained in the beneficiary documents? What is the result if the Trustee of the trust retains this discretionary authority, but has completed the exercise of this authority *prior* to December 31 of the calendar year immediately following the calendar year of the IRA owner's death?

Must the right of the beneficiary to select the next taker following the IRA owner's death (should the beneficiary survive the IRA owner but die while there are still assets remaining in the IRA) be a right specified in the IRA Custodial document in order to be valid?

Trusts as Designated Beneficiaries

Will a direction contained in a trust which has been named as IRA beneficiary to pay estate taxes, funeral expenses, and other estate administration expenses prevent the trust from qualifying as a Designated Beneficiary and, accordingly, from having a life expectancy? Is this problem solved if each of those expense items is paid in full by the trust prior to December 31 of the calendar year immediately following the calendar year of the IRA owner's death? Is this problem solved if the trust document is silent on this issue? Is this problem solved if the trust document precludes the payment of each of those expense items, even though, by law, those expense items may have to be paid with those trust assets if the other assets in the estate are insufficient to pay those amounts? Is this problem solved if the trust document were to preclude the payment of each of those expense items "unless required to do so under applicable Federal or State law"? What about the case of a Q-TIP Trust that has been designated as the IRA beneficiary? Typically, under those types of trusts, estate taxes in the estate of the surviving spouse are payable proportionately from the assets in the Q-TIP Trust.

Where a trust has been named as the IRA beneficiary, and where the three children of the IRA owner and a charity are the trust beneficiaries, if the charity is paid out in full by the trust by December 31 of the calendar year immediately following the calendar year of the IRA owner's death, can subsequent Required Minimum Distribution amounts be based on the life expectancy of the oldest of the three children (assuming that the trust otherwise meets each of the other rules for qualifying as a "Designated Beneficiary")? Is the answer the same if the charity is *not* paid out in full by December 31 of the calendar year immediately following the calendar year of the IRA owner's death, but if by that date the entire remaining share for the charity is segregated into a separate sub-trust share or account within the trust as a whole?

When must a copy of the trust document be provided to the IRA Custodian in a case in which an IRA owner, who has passed his or her Required Beginning Date, first designate a trust as the IRA beneficiary and where the spouse who is the income beneficiary of that trust is more than ten years younger than the IRA owner?

Separate Shares

Must separate shares for the benefit of each IRA beneficiary be established by the Required Beginning Date in order to be permitted to base Required Minimum Distribution amounts on the life expectancies of each IRA beneficiary, or is it sufficient if the separate shares are established by no later than December 31 of the calendar year immediately following the calendar year of the IRA owner's death, even in those cases in which the IRA owner had died *after* his or her Required Beginning Date?

In order for the Separate Share Rule to be applicable, must the division of the IRA into separate shares following the death of the IRA owner be made pursuant to a requirement to establish the separate shares, as set forth in either the IRA Custodial document or in the beneficiary forms and election documents executed by the IRA owner prior to his or her death? Can the beneficiaries of the IRA establish the separate shares themselves on an ad hoc basis, absent any prior direction to do so in either the IRA Custodial Agreement or in the beneficiary forms and election documents executed by the IRA owner prior to his or her death, where the IRA Custodial Agreement is silent on this issue? Are the answers to these questions the same regardless of whether the IRA owner had died before or after his or her Required Beginning Date?

Assume that the amounts payable from an IRA are to go to several beneficiaries and that one of the shares for one beneficiary is in a set dollar amount that will *not* participate in any increase in the value of the IRA following the IRA owner's death (if the IRA has been divided into separate IRAs for each beneficiary after the IRA owner's death but prior to December 31 of the calendar year immediately following the calendar year of the IRA owner's death). In such a case, can the life expectancy of the IRA beneficiary whose IRA share was a set dollar amount use his or her life expectancy in his or her separate Inherited IRA for Required Minimum Distribution purposes? Can the other IRA beneficiaries, whose shares were adjusted for any post-date-of-death increase in the value of the IRA before its division into separate IRAs, use their own life expectancies for Required Minimum Distribution purposes for their separate IRAs, even though one of the shares did not participate in any portion of the post-death increase in the value of the IRA prior to its division?

Marital Deduction and Other Income and Estate Tax Issues

Where a clause in an IRA beneficiary designation form allows the Executor of the Will the discretionary authority to establish a Q-TIP Trust, which had been named as the beneficiary of the IRA assets, in either a specific pecuniary amount or on a fractional basis, will this discretionary authority on the part of the Executor render the Q-TIP Trust ineligible for the Federal estate tax marital deduction?

Where a Q-TIP Trust has been named as the primary beneficiary of an IRA, with the IRA owner's children named as the contingent beneficiaries, will marital deduction be allowed in the estate of the IRA owner for the value of the IRA, if the spouse of the IRA owner were to survive the IRA owner but then die prior to December 31 of the calendar year immediately following the calendar year of the IRA owner's death?

Where an IRA owner has designated his grandchildren collectively to be the beneficiary of $1 million in IRA benefits, with his son, *per stirpes*, designated as the beneficiary for a second $1 million in IRA benefits, where the son survives the IRA owner but then dies prior to December 31 of the calendar year immediately following the calendar year of the IRA owner's death, will the IRA owner be deemed to have provided the grandchildren collectively with $2 million in IRA benefits for purposes of the generation-skipping transfer tax rules?

Where separate shares have been established for an individual's IRA benefits by December 31 of the calendar year immediately following the calendar year of the IRA owner's death, can the income in respect of the decedent (IRD) deduction be allocated pro rata to each of the separate shares established for each different IRA beneficiary? If it is acceptable to allocate the IRD deduction in this way, are the beneficiaries then free to recover their allocable portion of the IRD deduction in any way legally permissible, even if each of the beneficiaries has selected different recovery methods for the IRD amount?

Annuity Rules

To what extent are the annuity rules on Required Minimum Distributions which were set forth in the original July 27, 1987 proposed regulations (and which were not changed by the revised proposed regulations of January 17, 2001) mandatory, in the case where it is possible for the IRA annuitant to partially accelerate yearly annuity distributions. Under those circumstances, is the IRA annuitant (and the beneficiary of the IRA annuity, following the IRA annuitant's death) free to adopt the individual account rules applicable to Required Minimum Distributions, even though there may still be certain substantial restrictions on the ability of the IRA annuitant (or of the beneficiary) to make larger yearly withdrawals from the IRA annuity contract?

Transition Rules and Effective Dates

How can IRA owners and the beneficiaries of Inherited IRAs "choose" in 2001 to be covered under the revised proposed regulations of January 17, 2001? Is there any requirement that this decision be made in writing, that it be signed by the IRA owner or by the beneficiaries of Inherited IRAs, and/or that it be filed with either the IRA Custodian or with the IRS?

For 2001, must an IRA owner choose to be covered under the rules set forth in the revised proposed regulations of January 17, 2001 or under the rules in effect prior to the issuance of those revised proposed regulations for *all* IRAs similarly, or can the IRA owner for 2001 elect to be covered under the revised rules for some IRAs, while choosing to be covered under the prior rules for other IRAs? If all IRAs of the individual must be treated the same in 2001 with respect to the two sets of rules, does this requirement apply only to all IRAs of the individual with the same IRA Custodian, or does it apply to *all* IRAs of the individual, regardless of the number of different IRA Custodians being used? If all IRAs must be treated the same for 2001 with respect to the application of these two sets of rules, does this requirement apply only to all of the individual's own IRAs, or does it also apply to all Inherited IRAs for which the individual had been named as beneficiary?

Can the beneficiaries of an IRA owner who had died in 2000 choose to be covered under the revised proposed regulations of January 17, 2001 for purposes of computing their Required Minimum Distribution amounts due for 2001 and for subsequent years? What if the IRA owner had died in 1999, 1998, 1997, or in 1996?

Where a trust had been named as the IRA beneficiary and the IRA owner had died in 2000 with the trust paying the estate taxes and estate administration expenses in full prior to December 31, 2001, can the beneficiaries for 2001 and beyond base their Required Minimum Distribution amounts on their own life expectancies, assuming that, at the IRA owner's death, the Five-Year Rule was not required to apply to the payment of benefits from the IRA?

Where, at an IRA owner's Required Beginning Date, he or she had elected a Recalculation/Recalculation Method for his or her IRA benefits, with the IRA owner's spouse named as the Designated Beneficiary (where the spouse had died in 1999 and where the IRA owner died in 2000 at age 82), will the children, who are the contingent beneficiaries, be able to base subsequent Required Minimum Distributions on their remaining life expectancies under the revised proposed regulations of January 17, 2001 for 2001 and beyond?

Assume that the IRA owner died in 1998, before his Required Beginning Date. The beneficiaries of the Inherited IRA had initially intended to take their distributions from the IRA pursuant to the Five-Year Rule. Accordingly, no Required Minimum Distribution amounts had been taken for the years 1999 and 2000. Can the beneficiaries now elect to have the remaining amounts in the Inherited IRA paid out to them pursuant to the Life Expectancy Rule, by paying the 50 percent excise tax attributable to the Required Minimum Distributions amounts that had not been taken in 1999 and 2000?

How can a participant in a 403(b) plan take advantage in 2001 of the new Required Minimum Distribution rules under the revised proposed regulations of January 17, 2001, when there is often no formal document setting forth the rules of the 403(b) plan?

Is it too late in the 2001 plan year for a plan sponsor of a qualified plan to adopt the Model Amendment set forth in the revised proposed regulations of January 17, 2001, effective as of January 1, 2001, without avoiding an operational defect with respect to those plan distributions which may have been made earlier in the year 2001 under the prior set of proposed regulations?

Where an individual who has a TEFRA Section 242(b)(2) election in effect breaks that election in 2001, are the prior Required Minimum Distribution amounts, which are required to be made up for all years prior to 2001, to be based on the rules in effect prior to the issuance of the revised proposed regulations of January 17, 2001 or on the revised rules? Is the decision to use one or the other of those two sets of rules a matter that can be determined by the individual in his or her sole discretion? Would the answers be different if the TEFRA Section 242(b)(2) election had been broken in 2002? What if the TEFRA Section 242(b)(2) election had been broken in 2000, but the individual had waited until 2001 to take any prior make-up Required Minimum Distribution amounts?

Do the revised proposed regulations of January 17, 2001 apply to distributions from Roth IRAs following the death of the Roth IRA owner and/or the deaths of the Roth IRA owner and spouse? Will the reporting requirements of the yearly Required Minimum Distribution amounts to be imposed on IRA Custodians also require IRA Custodians to report those yearly amounts from Roth IRAs following the death of the Roth IRA owner and/or the deaths of the Roth IRA owner and spouse?

When will the rules become effective requiring IRA Custodians to report the yearly Required Minimum Distributions amounts, as set forth in the revised proposed regulations of January 17, 2001, and will those effective dates be different with respect to the reporting of those amounts to the IRS, when compared to the reporting of those amounts to IRA owners and to the beneficiaries of Inherited IRAs?

Section 634 of EGTRRA contains a requirement that the IRS update all of the life expectancy tables which are used to compute yearly Required Minimum Distribution amounts "to reflect current life expectancy." Will the IRS materially change many of the proposed rules contained in the revised proposed regulations of January 17, 2001 when issuing the final regulations in this area, so that plan participants, IRA owners, and the beneficiaries of Inherited IRAs will not then be permitted to avail themselves of both the liberalized rules as set forth in the revised proposed regulations of January 17, 2001, and the liberalized and updated life expectancy tables as mandated by Congress in EGTRRA? If the IRS is considering taking this approach, will it publish the revised life expectancy tables and any amendments to the revised proposed regulations, and then reschedule the comment period and hearings on the revised and then amended proposed regulations, before those revised and then amended proposed regulations are finalized?

APPENDIX

CONTENTS

Specimen Engagement Letter

Mr. & Mrs. Client
Address

Dear Mr. & Mrs. Client,

(Firm Name) will assist you in evaluating and monitoring the important decisions relative to your retirement distribution strategy. The services we will provided are limited to those listed below. Please allow this letter to serve as a summary of the estate and retirement distribution services we propose to render to you.

We shall:

Develop a retirement income schedule that reflects your projected retirement income needs based on the assumptions you provided.

Identify all sources of taxable (non-investment) income and create an income projection to identify the estimated future income tax rates. This includes earned income, social security income, as well as any non-investment income. We will analyze these results, along with the prior two years' personal income tax returns. The primary objective of this tax analysis is to identify an optimal level of retirement plan distributions for a given year, based on that year's applicable tax rates. In conducting this analysis, we will seek the input and advice of your other advisors as necessary.

Integrate your projected retirement income needs with your investment income generated from personal assets.

Identify the actual annual return on investment of retirement plan and personal investments based on the contributions and distributions made during the year, as well as beginning and year-end balances.

On a year by year basis, monitor actual contributions, distributions, effective tax rates and return on investment as compared to the original distribution projection. We will evaluate the need for annual adjustments including a change in distribution amounts, contribution amounts, type and structure of retirement/investment accounts, etc.

Review and monitor all beneficiary designations for retirement plan assets including IRAs, Pension Plans, Profit-Sharing Plans, Keogh Plans, 401(k) Plans, 403(b) Plans and Tax-Deferred Annuity Plans. We must receive copies of current beneficiary designation forms and we will generate a tracking report to include primary and contingent beneficiary elections. This tracking report will also include beneficiary designation elections for current trusts and in-force life insurance policies.

As you approach age $70^1/_2$, we will educate and assist you with regard to the mandatory elections and important beneficiary decisions on which the minimum distribution calculations will be based. This includes illustrating various distribution amounts based on the client's life expectancy and beneficiary options. We will evaluate alternatives such as single vs. joint life expectancy, term certain vs. the recalculation methods and the minimum distribution incidental benefit (MDIB) rules.

We will annually calculate the current and projected estate and income taxes on retirement plan assets due upon death, assuming current plan balances and current methods of distributions. At your discretion, we will also calculate the estate tax on other assets.

We will provide you with a life insurance company financial ratings summary for all in-force life insurance policies. This allows you to annually monitor the financial strength and claims paying ability of your carriers.

Where applicable, we will generate the IRS required "crummy letters" to be sent periodically by the trustee of a life insurance trust to the trust beneficiaries. This procedure allows the annual gift for premium payments to qualify for the $10,000 annual gift exclusion.

We will monitor all the tax law changes which are relevant to your distribution strategy to identify potential positive or negative impacts to your plan.

We will make an active effort to integrate our analysis and monitoring service with your financial advisors including your accountant, attorney, pension consultant investment advisor and life insurance agent.

Our fee for providing the above referenced services is _______ per year. The fee is payable upon the execution of this letter of understanding and on each subsequent anniversary of this agreement. Our liability is limited to the performance of such services only, or the return of up to a maximum amount equal to the fee paid.

Agreed to and accepted by:

_________________________________ _______________

Client Signature Date

_________________________________ _______________

Spouse Signature Date

NOTICE TO TRUST BENEFICIARY OF WITHDRAWAL RIGHT

Dated:

TO: Beneficiary or Beneficiary's Legal Representative
Address

FROM: Trustee Name, as Trustee under Trust Agreement made Date
by Grantor Name, as Grantor

SUBJECT: Addition to Trust Fund

This is to advise you that a gift of $_________ was made on (date) to the (Grantor's) Trust dated _________.

Pursuant to Article _________ Paragraph_________ of such Trust, you as a beneficiary may have the right to demand a withdrawal of a portion of the principal from the Trust under the terms and conditions thereof.

To exercise your right of withdrawal, please respond in writing to the undersigned Trustee, at the address below within 30 days of the date of this notice. Any questions you have about this right of withdrawal or its exercise should be directed to the undersigned Trustee.

Your truly,

____
Trustee

Trustee _________________________
Attention _________________________
Address _________________________
____

Confidential Retirement Distribution Questionnaire

Advisor Name: ________________ Phone __________Date:_____

Personal Information:

Client: ____________________________ DOB: ___/___/___ M / F

Spouse: ___________________________ DOB: ___/___/___ M / F

Address:____

City: _______________________________State: ___Zip:______

Phone: __________Fax: __________ e-mail: ________________

Planning Assumptions:

Projected Retirement Age: ___________________
Projected Distribution Age: __________________
Have you begun taking plan distributions?: Yes / No - $____ per year
Have you made your age $70^1/_2$ elections?: Yes / No
Where was election made? ___________________
Are you interested in creating a Multi-Generation IRA?: Yes / No
Will you consider trusts for Children?: (Yes / No)
Grandchildren?: (Yes / No)
Annual Gifting Amount: $__________ # of Yrs: _____

Estate Tax Rate: _____ Income Tax Rate: _____
Unified Credit Available: Participant $________ Spouse $________
GSTT Exemption Available: Participant $______ Spouse $______

Estate Values

Other Assets: $______________________ as of (date) ___/___/___
Life Insurance Death Benefit Inside the Estate: $________________
Life Insurance Death Benefit Outside the Estate: $________________
(Note: See following life insurance inventory.)

Retirement Account Information:

(Circle Appropriate Plan Types)

Client's Accounts:

Total Retirement Assets: $______________ as of (date) ___/___/___ Return ___%

Pension / Keogh $______ as of (date) __/__/__ Add'l Contrib.$______ for __yrs.

Primary Beneficiary: ______________ DOB ___/___/___ Relationship _______

Contingent Beneficiary: ____________ DOB ___/___/___ Relationship _______

Existing Custodian: ____

Profit-Sharing/401(k) $____ as of (date) __/__/__ Add'l Contrib. $_____for __yrs.

Primary Beneficiary: ______________ DOB ___/___/___ Relationship _______

Contingent Beneficiary: ____________ DOB ___/___/___ Relationship _______

Existing Custodian: ____

IRA $___________ as of (date) ___/___/___ Add'l Contrib. $_______for ___yrs.

Primary Beneficiary: ______________ DOB ___/___/___ Relationship _______

Contingent Beneficiary: ____________ DOB ___/___/___ Relationship ______

Existing Custodian: ____

IRA $__________ as of (date) ___/___/___ Add'l Contrib. $_______for ___yrs.

Primary Beneficiary: ______________ DOB ___/___/___ Relationship _______

Contingent Beneficiary: ____________ DOB ___/___/___ Relationship _______

Existing Custodian: ____

Spouse's Accounts:

Total Retirement Assets: $_______________ as of (date) ___/___/___ Return ____%

Pension / Keogh $______ as of (date) ___/___/___ Add'l Contrib.$_____ for __yrs.

Primary Beneficiary: ______________ DOB ___/___/___ Relationship _______

Contingent Beneficiary: ___________ DOB ___/___/___ Relationship _______

Existing Custodian: ____

Profit-Sharing/401(k) $____ as of (date) __/__/__ Add'l Contrib. $_____for __yrs.

Primary Beneficiary: ______________ DOB ___/___/___ Relationship _______

Contingent Beneficiary: ___________ DOB ___/___/___ Relationship _______

Existing Custodian: ____

IRA $__________ as of (date) ___/___/___ Add'l Contrib. $________for ____yrs.

Primary Beneficiary: ______________ DOB ___/___/___ Relationship _______

Contingent Beneficiary: ___________ DOB ___/___/___ Relationship _______

Existing Custodian: ____

(Note: Please submit all beneficiary and plan documents for review of custodial accounts.)

Retirement Distribution Goals: (Number in the order of priority; 1 to 7)

________ Minimize the required distribution to the lowest possible amount

________ Minimize the tax erosion on retirement assets

________ Protect retirement assets from creditors

________ Control the distribution of retirement assets to grandchildren

________ Control the distribution of retirement assets to children

________ Leave retirement assets to charity

________ Provide for an equitable distribution of retirement assets among spouses and/or children from a prior marriage

________ Other: ________________________________

Beneficiary Information:

Beneficiary Percentage (%)		Participant Account	Spouse Account
Spouse: ________________	DOB: __/__/__	___%	
Child: (1)________________	DOB: __/__/__	___%	___%
Grandchild: (1)____________	DOB: __/__/__	___%	___%
Grandchild: (2)____________	DOB: __/__/__	___%	___%
Grandchild: (3)____________	DOB: __/__/__	___%	___%
Grandchild: (4)____________	DOB: __/__/__	___%	___%
Child: (2)________________	DOB: __/__/__	___%	___%
Grandchild: (1)____________	DOB: __/__/__	___%	___%
Grandchild: (2)____________	DOB: __/__/__	___%	___%
Grandchild: (3)____________	DOB: __/__/__	___%	___%
Grandchild: (4)____________	DOB: __/__/__	___%	___%
Child: (3)________________	DOB: __/__/__	___%	___%
Grandchild: (1)____________	DOB: __/__/__	___%	___%
Grandchild: (2)____________	DOB: __/__/__	___%	___%

Grandchild: (3)________________ DOB: ___/___/___ ____% ____%

Grandchild: (4)________________ DOB: ___/___/___ ____% ____%

Child: (4)____________________ DOB: ___/___/___ ____% ____%

Grandchild: (1)________________ DOB: ___/___/___ ____% ____%

Grandchild: (2)________________ DOB: ___/___/___ ____% ____%

Grandchild: (3)________________ DOB: ___/___/___ ____% ____%

Grandchild: (4)________________ DOB: ___/___/___ ____% ____%

Financial and Personal Decisions:

What do you want to do during your retirement?

____

____

____

When do you plan to begin taking distributions from retirement assets?

____

____

____

What level of income do you need from your retirement assets?

____

____

____

Does your spouse need your IRA assets upon your death?

____

____

____

How do you feel about paying up to 80% in taxes on your retirement assets?

____

____

____

What are your wealth transfer philosophies?

____

____

____

What are your asset protection issues?

____

____

____

What are your investment philosophies?

____

____

____

Inventory Of Assets:

	Client	Spouse	Joint	Total
Residence	________	________	________	________
Cash Equivalents	________	________	________	________
Stocks & Funds	________	________	________	________
Bonds & Funds	________	________	________	________
Life Insurance C.V.	________	________	________	________
Annuities	________	________	________	________
IRA Accounts	________	________	________	________
Retirement Plans	________	________	________	________
Property/ Real Estate	________	________	________	________
Art/Collectibles	________	________	________	________
Other	________	________	________	________

Other	________	________	________	________
Total Assets	________	________	________	________
Total Liabilities	________	________	________	________
Total Net Worth	________	________	________	________

Life Insurance

Insured	Face Amount	Insurance Company	Policy Type	Date	Issues	Owner	Beneficiary
______	______	______	______	______	______	______	______

Purpose of Policy:

____

______	______	______	______	______	______	______	______

Purpose of Policy:

____

______	______	______	______	______	______	______	______

Purpose of Policy:

____

______	______	______	______	______	______	______	______

Purpose of Policy:

____

(Please list additional policies on a separate sheet of paper)

Retirement Income Needs Analysis:

Income:

Monthly Income	Client	Spouse	Total
Salary	________	________	________
Bonus	________	________	________
Interest/Dividends	________	________	________
Capital Gains	________	________	________
Rental	________	________	________
Retirement Distributions	________	________	________
Total Monthly Income	________	________	________
Total Annual Income	________	________	________

Expenses:

Mortgage/Rent		________
Property Taxes		________
Utilities/Housing Maint.		________
Food		________
Clothing		________
Insurance:	Life	________
	Medical	________
	Disability	________
	Property	________
Car Payment/Insurance		________
Car Maint/Gas		________
Alimony/Child Support		________
Vacations/Entertainment		________
Charitable Contribution		________
Other ________		________
Other ________		________
Other ________		________
TOTAL		________

Beneficiary Designation Tracking Report
For Dr. & Mrs. Smith
(As Of May 1998)

Qualified Retirement Plans

	Owner	*Plan Name*	*Account #*	*Primary Beneficiary*	*Contingent Beneficiary*
1	Dr. Smith	Hospital Pension Plan	123-abc-0021	Mrs. Smith	None Listed
2	Dr. Smith	Hospital Profit Sharing Plan	456-def-0021	Mrs. Smith	None Listed
3	Dr. Smith	401k	001900129	Mrs. Smith	None Listed

IRA's

	Owner	*Plan Name*	*Account #*	*Primary Beneficiary*	*Contingent Beneficiary*
1	Dr. Smith	Fidelity Investments	00192838	Mrs. Smith	Trustees Under Will
2	Dr. Smith	Smith Barney	A-4145100	Mrs. Smith	Children Equally
3	Mrs. Smith	Fidelity Investments	001987741	Dr. Smith	Children Equally
4	Mrs. Smith	Chase Bank	23145787	Dr. Smith	Children Equally

Life Insurance Policies

	Insured	*Owner*	*Policy Number*	*Company & Type*	*Death Benefit*	*Primary Beneficiary*	*Contingent Beneficiary*
1	Dr. Smith	Pension Plan	L001254	Allmerica UL	$423,546	Pension Plan	None
2	Dr. Smith	Irrevocable Trust	N212121	Hancock Surv. WL	$2,500,000	Irrevocable Trust	None
3	Dr. Smith	Dr. Smith	WS002145	William Penn Tern	$500,000	Mrs. Smith	None
4	Mrs. Smith	Irrevocable Trust	N212121	Hancock Surv. WL	See Policy 2	Irrevocable Trust	None
5	Mrs. Smith	Mrs. Smith	L0094039	William Penn Term	$500,000	Dr. Smith	None

Trust

	Name	*Grantor*	*Primary Trustee*	*Contingent Trustee*	*Income Beneficiary*	*Principal Beneficiary*
1	Irrevocable Life Insur. Trust	Dr. Smith	Jim Baker Bill Smith	Lori Smith	Spouse	Spouse & Children

Retirement Distribution Planning Checklists

Documents Checklist:

Do you and your spouse have the following checklists?

	Client	Spouse
Will	______	______
Power of Attorney	______	______
Revocable Trusts	______	______
Irrevocable Trusts	______	______
Retirement Plan Documents	______	______
Retirement Plan Beneficiary Designations	______	______
IRA Beneficiary Designations	______	______
Current Statements for Retirement Assets	______	______
Life Insurance Policies, Ledgers and Summary	______	______
Family Limited Partnerships	______	______
Other: ________________	______	______

Advisor Checklist:

Which advisors will play a role in the retirement distributions planning process?

Accountant	(Yes / No)	Name: ________________ Telephone; ______________
Attorney	(Yes / No)	Name; ________________ Telephone: ______________
Pension Consultant	(Yes / No)	Name: ________________ Telephone: ______________

Insurance Agent (Yes / No) Name: ________________
Telephone: ______________

Investment Advisor (Yes / No) Name: ________________
Telephone: ______________

Family Member Checklist:

Which family members will play a role in the retirement distribution planning process?

Spouse (Yes / No) Name: ________________
Comments: _____________

Children (Yes / No) Name: ________________
Comments: _____________

Grandchildren (Yes / No) Name: ________________
Comments: _____________

Other (Yes / No) Name: ________________
Comments: _____________

Letter Ruling Summaries

A summary of significant official source material—Private Letter Rulings, Technical Advice Memoranda, IRS Notices, Revenue Rulings, and the Goldblatt decision—follows. You will find the full text of these materials on the included CD-ROM.

NOTE: These materials are included as a convenience to the user. They are not exhaustive, and new authority is released frequently. Accordingly, the user is cautioned to research a particular area before taking any action.

Letter Ruling 8038101

Beneficiary selection, life expectancy table selection and life expectancy calculation method choices are generally not final for minimum distribution purposes until the Required Beginning Date has passed.

Letter Ruling 8527083 (4/12/85)

In the event a working spouse dies, the IRS ruled that a contribution may be made to a spousal IRA by the nonworking surviving spouse, if a joint income tax return is filed for the year for which the contribution was made.

Letter Ruling 8622051 (3/06/86)

IRS allowed a contribution to an IRA with a cash advance drawn by April 15th on the IRA owner's bank credit card.

Letter Ruling 8708041 (11/25/86)

There is no requirement that a rollover from a qualified plan be made to a single IRA. As long as these rollovers are made within the required 60 day time frame from receipt by the employee, the lump-sum (or other) distribution may be divided up and rolled over into more than one IRA.

Letter Ruling 8742062 (7/23/87)

The IRS ruled that when an IRA is left in the decedent's name, withdrawals to the surviving spouse are required to begin by the time the decedent would have attained age 70½. The surviving spouse was not allowed to defer the first year's distribution until April 1st of the following calendar year, even though the decedent would have been allowed to do so, had he survived.

Letter Ruling 8927070 (4/13/89)
A qualified plan distribution that is rolled over tax-free to an IRA will not be treated as a recovery of the grandfather amount under Code §4980A.

Letter Ruling 9004042 (11/06/89)
Payments from an IRA due to the death of the IRA owner, are not subject to a 10% excise tax under Code §72(t) for early distributions, even where they are payable to a trust as Designated Beneficiary, which trust in turn distributes the payment to a named trust beneficiary.

Letter Ruling 9010007 (12/14/89)
An IRA distribution that is redeposited into the same IRA or into another IRA within 60 days of its receipt will be treated as a rollover contribution, and not be subject to income tax, the 10% additional excise tax on early distributions or the 6% excise tax on excess contributions. However, only one such distribution and repayment may be made in any one calendar year.

Letter Ruling 9011031 (12/19/89)
After a Participant's Required Beginning Date, a QDRO divided his IRA, awarding one-half to his wife. Participant sought to have his Required Minimum Distribution amount for that year based on his reduced IRA balance. The IRS held that his Required Minimum Distribution amount for that year was required to be computed based on the unreduced value of the IRA as of the prior December 31st.

Letter Ruling 9012009 (11/06/89)
Same ruling as 9004042.

Letter Ruling 9037048 (6/20/90)
A testamentary trust that has been named as a contingent beneficiary under an IRA can continue the original distribution schedule

elected by the IRA owner at his Required Beginning Date, where the primary beneficiary had timely executed a qualified disclaimer under Code §2518. The IRS ruled that because the disclaimer met all the requirements of Code §2518, the decedent's IRA passed to and was taxed to the contingent beneficiary. The IRS ruled that because an executed copy of the Trust was found to have been in the decedent's possession at the time of death, the requirement that the trust instrument be provided to the Plan before the Required Beginning Date, was satisfied.

Letter Ruling 9043063 (8/02/90)

An individual who had suffered a heart attack, rolled over his qualified plan distributions into an IRA, pursuant to disability provisions contained in the two qualified plans in which he had participated. The IRS held that the exception to the 10% excise tax for early distributions under Code §72(t) for disability payments, would be applicable to the payments from the IRA, if as it develops, the Participant's disability meets the standards set forth for disability payments in Code §72(m)(7).

Letter Ruling 9045050 (8/15/90)

Decedent named an inter vivos trust as his IRA beneficiary. Spouse, as trustee and beneficiary of that trust, filed a qualified disclaimer of the benefits, with the results being that all of the benefits passed outright to the spouse rather than to the trust. This enabled the spouse to establish a spousal rollover with the benefits.

Letter Ruling 9132021 (5/02/91)

Beneficiaries who cashed out an IRA to pay estate taxes will be subject to income taxes on the payments from the IRA that were paid to the estate and used to pay the estate taxes.

Letter Ruling 9202003 (10/09/91)

A farmer transferred hogs to his wife, who was a bona fide employee, as compensation for her services to his farming business. The IRS ruled that the value of the hogs constituted compensation that could be used as the basis for the wife making deductible contributions to her IRA.

Letter Ruling 9211059 (12/20/91)

A surviving spouse may not roll over that portion of the decedent's IRA which is attributable to Required Minimum Distribution amounts that the decedent had not taken in the year of his death, or which had not been taken in the year following the year of his death.

Letter Ruling 9226058 (3/31/92)

Participant had designated his spouse as primary beneficiary of his IRA benefits, with his two children as contingent beneficiaries. Upon his death before his Required Beginning Date, his spouse timely filed a renunciation of the IRA benefits. The IRS ruled that the two children thereby became the beneficiaries of the IRA benefits.

Letter Ruling 9237020 (6/12/92)

The IRS permitted a charitable remainder unitrust to be designated as beneficiary of the IRA benefits, and to receive the benefits after the death of the IRA owner. The terms of the charitable remainder unitrust provided that the trust beneficiary (the son) would receive a lifetime payout based on a specified percentage of the trust assets each year. The IRS held that as a tax-exempt entity, the trust would not be taxed on the benefits received from the IRA.

Letter Ruling 9237038 (6/16/92)

Spouse died within two years of the IRA Participant, and before she could establish a spousal rollover IRA. IRS stated that the only beneficiary who could elect to treat the entire interest in an IRA as the beneficiary's own account is the individual's surviving spouse. The IRS ruled that the exercise of the spouse's right to elect to treat the IRA as her own could not be made by the Executor of the spouse's estate. The IRS held that on her death, the remaining interest in the IRA passed to the contingent beneficiary, and accordingly her estate had no further interest in the IRA.

Letter Ruling 9253052 (10/07/92)

If there is more than one beneficiary of a trust designated as beneficiary of an IRA, the beneficiary with the shortest life expectancy must be used as the measuring life for calculating Required Minimum Distribution amounts. In this case, a copy of the trust had been provided to the Trustee of the IRA.

Letter Ruling 9253054 (10/08/92)

Designating a trust as the beneficiary of an IRA is an acceptable approach. Such a designation does not by itself constitute a distribution.

Letter Ruling 9305025 (11/12/92)

The death distribution pattern may be specified with IRA documents, or the IRA plan may state that either the IRA owner or the beneficiary is to make the choice. If the choice is to be made by the beneficiary, it should generally be made no later than December 31st following the year of death. IRS allowed the division of an IRA into six separate but equal IRAs for the six children after the death of the parents provided that annual distributions continued to be made from all six of the accounts based on the life expectancy of the oldest of the six children.

Letter Ruling 9311037 (12/22/92)

A surviving spouse may assert ownership after a surviving spouse's own required beginning date has been reached by rollover or by transferring ownership but not by making new contributions.

Letter Ruling 9317025 (1/27/93)

IRS held the trust corpus and IRA would qualify for the estate tax marital deduction as qualified terminable interest property when under the terms of the IRA, incorporating a specific provision of the irrevocable trust, the IRA complied with all of the requirements under the Code establishing qualified terminable interest property.

Letter Ruling 9330042 (5/07/93)

The actual life expectancy of the surviving nonspouse beneficiary may be used if the IRA owner dies before his or her required beginning date. However, if the IRA owner has passed his or her required beginning date, the distributions to a nonspouse beneficiary after the death of the IRA owner are based on the actual life expectancy of the IRA owner and the nonspouse beneficiary at the required beginning date, less the number of years the IRA owner survived beyond the required beginning date.

Letter Ruling 9331055 (5/13/93)

A sale of assets held in an individual's IRA is not a distribution to the individual when the sale proceeds are retained by the IRA Custodian.

Letter Ruling 9345044 (8/16/93)

The commencement of benefit payments attributable to a Participant's December 31, 1986 account balance in a tax sheltered annuity can be deferred until the time when the Participant attains age 75, regardless of employment status. For post-December 31, 1986 earnings and accruals, a tax sheltered annuity can permit the commencement of benefit payments until the earlier of the Participant's attainment of age 75 or the April 1st following the year of retirement.

Letter Ruling 9351041 (9/30/93)

A direct trustee to trustee transfer of a decedent's interest in a qualified plan to an IRA owned by the decedent's surviving spouse is a direct rollover.

Letter Ruling 9401039 (10/18/93)

If the marital trust is the beneficiary, rollover treatment will be foreclosed unless the spouse has the right to revoke the trust or a lifetime power to withdraw assets from the trust.

Letter Ruling 9416016 (1/13/94)

The IRS held that an IRA qualified as QTIP where the IRA paid all of its income (or the required minimum distribution if greater) annually to the marital trust which, in turn, treated the IRA income as income for trust accounting purposes and paid all of its income annually to the spouse.

Letter Ruling 9416037 (1/25/94)

An individual who is the owner or beneficiary of more than one IRA must calculate the required minimum distribution with respect to each IRA. However, the amounts required to be distributed may then be aggregated and the distribution taken from any one or more of the IRAs.

Letter Ruling 9422060 (3/14/94)

IRS ruled that when an individual and his spouse entered into a private separation agreement providing for a division of the individual's IRA, the transfer to the spouse was taxable to the individual because the agreement was not incident to a decree of divorce or legal separation.

Letter Ruling 9439020 (7/07/94)

A married couple's agreement to divide the husband's IRA, a community property asset, into separate shares that could be disposed of separately by each spouse did not constitute a distribution or transfer of amounts from the IRA for income tax purposes so that no amount was includible in either individual's gross income because the reclassification of community property into separate property did not constitute an actual distribution or payment from the IRA.

Letter Ruling 9442032 (7/27/94)

Plan Participant named his spouse as primary beneficiary and his living trust as contingent beneficiary. To enable the estate to fully utilize the available unified credit, the spouse disclaimed her interest in the IRA and then as beneficiary of the marital trust, disclaimed her general powers over the marital trust. Then as Executor she made a fractional QTIP election for the IRA and the Trust. Thus the non-elected portion of the IRA and marital trust became in effect the credit shelter trust.

Letter Ruling 9450040 (9/22/94)

IRA distributions based on joint life expectancy of husband and wife recalculated annually with distribution already begun. Wife files a qualified disclaimer. IRS ruled that the children are the new beneficiaries and that since the children have a life expectancy that is longer than their mother's life expectancy, the children must use their mother's life expectancy recalculated to determine the remaining IRA distribution period. The IRS specifically refused to treat a qualified disclaimer as a "death" for purposes of determining the designated beneficiary under the minimum distribution rules.

Letter Ruling 9450041 (9/22/94)

Benefits were payable to a marital trust and upon spouse's death, the marital trust must pass to a family trust for the children and grandchildren. Spouse disclaimed all interest in the marital trust and the benefits passed to the family trust. Every beneficiary of family trust disclaimed their interest causing the benefits to pass by intestacy to the spouse who rolled them over into her own IRA.

Letter Ruling 9450042 (9/23/94)

A surviving spouse who is over age $70^1/_2$ may still implement a generation-skipping strategy when a spousal IRA rollover is performed under Code section 402(c)(9).

Letter Ruling 9501044 (10/14/94)

Although an estate is making distributions to the trust beneficiaries through the estate, the right to base distributions on the life or life expectancy of the trust beneficiaries had not been established because an estate may not be "looked through" to enable the beneficiaries of an estate to be treated as the designated beneficiary of an IRA. IRS ruled that the proposed regulations do not provide that an estate be looked through for section 401(a)(9) purposes and therefore decedent is treated as having no designated beneficiary for his IRA when he named his estate as beneficiary.

Letter Ruling 9504045 (11/02/94)

IRS concluded that a trustee to trustee transfer of an IRA from one financial institution to another institution is permissible under section 408 and will not alter the tax deferred status of the IRA or the immediate taxable distribution to the child.

Letter Ruling 9505023 (11/09/94)

An IRA owner who previously rolled over a distribution from a qualified retirement plan into a conduit IRA was not precluded from rolling over amounts from the conduit IRA into the plan that made the initial distribution, as long as the IRA owner had not commingled these assets with other assets.

Letter Ruling 9524020 (3/21/95)

Spouse claimed a statutory share of the estate. Spouse exercised this right by directing the trustee of the decedent's qualified retirement plan, which was payable to the estate, to transfer assets of the plan directly into an IRA in spouse's own name. This was held to be a valid direct rollover, as the IRS ruled the proceeds came from the decedent and not from the estate.

Letter Ruling 9534027 (6/01/95)

The deadline for a distribution attributable to a rollover IRA after the individual has attained age 70½ is the December 31st of the year following the year of rollover. IRS ruled that there is no requirement that a surviving spouse not have reached the required beginning date in order for such individual to claim an IRA as his or her own.

Letter Ruling 9537005 (6/13/95)

The problem of assignment of IRD does not exist when IRD assets are divided up to fulfill fractional benefits.

Letter Ruling 9545010 (8/14/95)

Spouse was not the sole beneficiary but was the residuary beneficiary and also the Executrix. As Executrix, she distributed the right to receive the decedent's retirement benefits, which were payable to the estate, to herself in partial fulfillment of the residuary bequest, and the IRS then allowed her to then roll the benefits over in a trustee to trustee transaction.

Letter Ruling 9547047 (9/01/95)

Distributions required to satisfy the minimum distribution rules under which payments must begin in specified minimum amounts after age 70½ are not eligible for rollovers.

Letter Ruling 9548031 (9/05/95)

Decedent had nine IRAs, naming wife as beneficiary of five and daughter of four and utilizing the joint life expectancy of the beneficiaries to determine minimum distributions. After starting minimum distributions, decedent changed beneficiaries to his estate, but after realizing his mistake sought to undue the election and continue to use joint life expectancy instead of single life expectancy for minimum distributions, IRS ruled that there is no provision under IRC section 401(a)(9) to retroactively correct such an error. The IRS ruled that if a participant changes the beneficiary after the required beginning date, the distribution period may be shortened, but it can never be lengthened.

Letter Ruling 9604028 (11/01/95)

IRS will not allow rolled over assets from one qualified plan to go to another qualified plan, when the qualified plan assets are commingled with non-rollover IRA assets, even when the commingling had been inadvertently done.

Letter Ruling 9604029 (11/02/95)

IRS ruled that a distribution made and received in 1995 from a qualified plan following a lawsuit was an eligible rollover distribution, even though it was received eight years after the participant separated from service.

Letter Ruling 9608042 (12/01/95)

IRS ruled that a spouse when withdrawing any benefits from the decedent's IRA penalty free before age $70^1/_2$ would be making an "irrevocable election" not to treat the decedent's entire IRA as her own IRA.

Letter Ruling 9638040 (6/27/96)

IRS ruled that an otherwise valid TEFRA §242(b) election was invalid because it failed to name the account's beneficiary in the event of the taxpayer's death prior to full distribution of the account. The omission was not cured by the plan provision providing that a participant's surviving spouse would be the beneficiary of a death benefit, in the event that no beneficiary designation had been supplied in writing by the participant.

Letter Ruling 9641031 (7/16/96)

Ruled that if an IRS owner has more than one designated beneficiary as of the applicable date for determining the designated beneficiary, the designated beneficiary with the shortest life expectancy will be the designated beneficiary for purposes of determining the distribution. In addition, the decision to transfer the IRA into subaccounts remaining in the name of the decedent did not affect the tax deferred status of the IRA and did not constitute a distribution.

Letter Ruling 9651040 (9/26/96)

IRA owner has IRA with multiple beneficiaries including surviving wife, and had begun minimum distributions prior to death. Prior to required beginning date, IRA owner made a written election under IRA to receive minimum distribution based on single life expectancy and recalculation method. Default provision for IRA owner and/or the spouse is the one year reduction method. IRS ruled that nonspouse beneficiary may use the one year reduction method based on surviving spouse's life expectancy as basis for minimum distributions based on nonspouse beneficiaries contention that pursuant to the IRA document, recalculation may be, not must be, used to determine applicable life expectancies, and because IRA owner could have, but did not elect recalculation as the method to determine the life expectancy of the surviving spouse, the oldest of the beneficiaries, that the life of the surviving spouse must be determined pursuant to the IRA plan document by the one year reduction method.

Letter Ruling 9710028 (12/09/96)

Surviving spouse may defer minimum distributions until such time as the IRA owner would have been required to take required minimum distribution.

Letter Ruling 9712032 (12/23/96)

The estate of a deceased owner of an IRA that had no designated beneficiary was not required to receive a distribution of the entire account balance because the IRA owner had not provided instructions for distributions to the IRA custodian, and pursuant to the default provisions of the IRA Agreement, distributions would be made over the life expectancy of the owner using the term certain method. Thus post-death distributions from the IRA based on the term certain method satisfied the minimum distribution requirements.

Letter Ruling 9739044 (9/26/97)

A transfer of an individual's interest in an IRA to the individual's spouse or former spouse under a divorce decree or a written instrument incident to the divorce is not a taxable distribution or transfer, and the transferred interest is treated as the IRA of the transferee spouse or former spouse.

Letter Ruling 9802046 (10/16/97)

The conservator of the beneficiary of an inherited IRA can have the IRA funds transferred directly to a new IRA if the new IRA is maintained in the name of the decedent. This type of transfer is not a rollover and does not result in a taxable distribution to the beneficiary.

Letter Ruling 9807029 (11/19/97)

IRS has ruled that a surviving spouse who was designated as beneficiary of her deceased husband's IRA was considered to have made the election to treat the IRA as her own, even though she did not affirmatively make the election prior to her death. The surviving spouse died before her required beginning date and had not received any distributions. The election was deemed to have been made since no required distributions to her deceased husband had been made in the year of his death.

Letter Ruling 9809059 (12/04/97)

Part of decedent's IRA was payable to trust "K." In ruling that trust K was entitled to use the "life expectancy method" for the IRA benefits payable to it, the IRS noted that trust K does not provide that trust assets shall be used to pay funeral costs, probate expenses or estate taxes.

Letter Ruling 9810031 (12/10/97)

Surviving spouse rolled over husband's IRA benefits, naming her three children as beneficiaries and utilized the life expectancy of the oldest child to calculate minimum required distributions. The three children were allowed to divide the IRA into three subaccounts remaining in the name of the deceased IRA owner and to distribute assets based on the eldest child's life expectancy.

Letter Ruling 9810032 (12/10/97)

Distributions to a beneficiary that are made after the death of the IRA owner are exempt from the 10 percent penalty for pre-59$^{1}/_{2}$ withdrawals under Code section 72(t)(2)(A)(ii)

Letter Ruling 9810033 (12/10/97)

A deceased widow's three sons were permitted to create three subaccounts after their mother's death and transfer each such subaccount to a new IRA at a different financial institution, provided the IRA remained in the mother's name as owner. IRS ruled that the ten percent premature distribution penalty does not apply if an early distribution is made because of the IRA owner's death or disability.

Letter Ruling 9812034 (12/22/97)

If a beneficiary of an IRA is not timely notified of his or her status, the IRA document will control the distribution option.

Letter Ruling 9816028 (1/21/98)

The application of a 3 percent cost of living factor to each distribution would not violate the requirements that the distributions be substantially equal periodic payments.

Letter Ruling 9818009 (1/08/98)

IRA distributions made upon an individual's death to a charitable organization or to a charitable beneficiary is exempt from tax.

Letter Ruling 9818055 (2/02/98)

Ceasing to make IRA distributions prior to the later of age $59^1/_2$ or 5 years from commencing distributions would constitute an impermissible modification and would result in a 10 percent early distribution penalty.

Letter Ruling 9820010 (2/06/98)

IRS ruled that if the primary beneficiaries of an IRA were to execute written disclaimers of their interests in the IRA, the IRA would pass to the contingent beneficiary. Because the contingent beneficiary of the IRA was the surviving spouse, the IRS permitted such spouse to transfer the IRA assets to a spousal rollover IRA.

Letter Ruling 9820020 (2/18/98)

IRA owner's surviving spouse was the sole Trustee of a revocable trust named as the IRA beneficiary, and the IRS permitted the spouse to allocate the IRA proceeds to a subtrust of which the spouse was beneficiary, and then exercise a power of appointment to withdraw the funds and roll over to a spousal IRA within 60 days of distribution. The IRS allowed the surviving spouse to roll over the amount to a spousal IRA, but only because the trust allowed an immediate and full nondiscretionary transfer to the surviving spouse.

Letter Ruling 9820021 (2/18/98)

A QTIP marital trust was named as beneficiary, with the QTIP trust providing the surviving spouse with income and principal limited to an ascertainable standard and a limited power of appointment. Three charities were named to share in any portion of the trust that did not pass by exercise of the limited power of appointment. The IRS ruled that the three charities are included as designated beneficiaries, even though their benefit is contingent on a number of events, because contingencies based on events other than the participant's death are ignored. Therefore the IRS ruled the IRA owner would be treated as having no designated beneficiary, where a trust for his spouse was established for payments of IRA income during her lifetime, but that payments of IRA principal would be retained in the trust for the benefit of the charity after the death of the spouse.

Letter Ruling 9821056 (2/24/98)

If the effect of the interruption of substantial equal periodic payments is to make a distribution that is not consistent with the established calculation pattern, the 10 percent penalty will be applied not just to that distribution, but to the whole series of distributions for which the Section 72 exemption was being claimed, to the extent the distributions were made before age $59^1/_2$. A change in the calculation methodology to account for greater than expected investment returns would constitute an impermissible modification and will result in the application of an additional 10 percent tax on early distributions.

Letter Ruling 9822059 (3/06/98)

If a surviving spouse fails to elect to roll over her deceased spouse's IRA into her own prior to her death, the surviving spouse's estate cannot make the election.

Letter Ruling 9826036 (3/30/98)

IRA funds withdrawn by an IRA owner must be rolled back into a qualified plan (or to an IRA) within 60 days of receipt of the distribution in order to avoid inclusion in income.

Letter Ruling 9846034 (8/18/98)

IRS acknowledged that the more remote beneficiaries, namely the intestate heirs who take only if all of the contingent beneficiaries have predeceased, are not to be considered as designated beneficiaries, provided that the contingent beneficiaries have not actually died as of the time of participant's required beginning date.

Letter Ruling 9901023

Charitable Remainder Trust (CRT) is the beneficiary of retirement plan assets. IRS ruled that distributions from the retirement plan to the CRT are "first tier" ordinary income and the annuity payments from the CRT to the individual beneficiaries "carry out" this income first. The IRS ruled that IRD deduction does not come out with the first tier income.

IRS Notice 88-38

The individual IRA owner can aggregate all IRAs and can take Required Minimum Distribution amount for any one or more IRAs. No Required Minimum Distributions are required to be actually taken from each.

TAM 9220007 (1/30/91)

IRS held that the value of an IRA payable to a QTIP trust was not eligible for QTIP treatment, because none of the authorized distribution options at the date of the decedent's death gave the surviving spouse a qualified income interest for life.

Goldblatt v. FDIC, No. 95-56426 (9th Cir. 1997)

An individual's interest in an IRA must be nonforfeitable. The nonforfeitable status of an IRA, however, did not provide the IRA owner with a preference over other depositors in the distribution of an insolvent bank's assets, where the individual had lost his IRA asset as a result of the bank's failure.

Rev. Ruls.

Rev. Rul. 79-265

A qualifying rollover distribution can be established in multiple rollover IRAs, without subjecting the distribution to immediate income taxation.

Rev. Rul. 89-87

A qualified plan is not considered to be terminated where all assets are not distributed as soon as is administratively feasible after the stated termination date. If the distribution of all Plan assets is not completed within one year following the date of Plan termination, it will be presumed to have not been made as soon as administratively feasible.

Rev. Rul. 89-89

IRS held that the decedent's Executor can elect under section 2056(b)(7) of the Code to treat a decedent's IRA as QTIP property if (a) the decedent elected an IRA distribution option requiring the principal balance to be distributed in annual installments to a testamentary QTIP trust and the income earned on the undistributed balance of the IRA is to be paid annually to the trust, and (b) the trust requires that both the income earned on the undistributed portion of the IRA which it receives from the IRA and the income from the assets already in the QTIP trust be paid currently to the decedent's spouse for life.

Rev. Rul. 92-47

Sets the rules for calculating the amount of IRD with respect to amounts payable to a nonspouse beneficiary of a decedent's IRA.

INDEX